Cognitive Perspectives on Children's Social and Behavioral Development

The Minnesota Symposia on Child Psychology

Volume 18

edited by
MARION PERLMUTTER
The University of Michigan

LEA LAWRENCE ERLBAUM ASSOCIATES, PUBLISHERS
1986   Hillsdale, New Jersey   London

Lawrence Erlbaum Associates, Inc., Publishers
365 Broadway
Hillsdale, New Jersey 07642

Library of Congress Cataloging-in-Publication Data

Cognitive perspectives on children's social and
  behavioral development.

  Papers presented at the 18th Minnesota Symposium on
Child Psychology, held Oct. 27–29, 1983, at the
University of Minnesota and sponsored by the Institute
of Child Development.
  ''The Minnesota Symposia on Child Psychology,
volume 18.''
  Includes bibliographies and indexes.
  1. Child psychology—Congresses. 2. Child
development—Congresses. 3. Cognition—Congresses.
I. Perlmutter, Marion. II. University of Minnesota.
Institute of Child Development. III. Minnesota
Symposium on Child Psychology (18th : 1983 : University
of Minnesota) [DNLM: 1. Child Development—congresses.
2. Cognition—congresses. W3 MI607 v.18 /
WS 105 C675 1983]
BF721.C564 1986   155.4'13   86-2097
ISBN 0-89859-546-0

Printed in the United States of America
10 9 8 7 6 5 4 3 2 1

Contents

iii

Preface

This volume contains the papers presented at the eighteenth Minnesota Symposia on Child Psychology, held October 27–29, 1983, at the University of Minnesota, Minneapolis. As has been the tradition for this annual series, the faculty of the Institute of Child Development invited internationally eminent researchers to present their research and to consider problems of mutual concern to scientists studying development.

The theme of the eighteenth symposium, and the present volume was cognitive perspectives on social and behavior development. Ken Rubin, Ken Dodge, Kurt Fischer, Tom Berndt, John Weisz, and Jackie Goodnow presented informative papers on a broad range of issues. Phil Kendall, Kim Dolgin, Len Breslaw, Ellen Berscheid, Linda Heath, and David Olson provided helpful integrative commentaries.

I wish to thank all the presenters and discussants for their stimulating contributions. In addition, I would like to thank the many members of the Minnesota community who helped with the symposium, especially

Margarita Azmitia
Sue Bergman
Andy and Carolyn Collins
Virginia Eaton
Rosemary and Bill Hartup
Debby Jacobwitz
Kathy Kolb
Ardis Ronnie

Finally, I would like to acknowledge the financial support provided by William Maddux.

Marion Perlmutter
The University of Michigan

1 Social-Cognitive and Social Behavioral Perspectives on Problem Solving

Kenneth H. Rubin
University of Waterloo

Linda Rose Krasnor
Brock University

I. INTRODUCTION

Experimenter: "Now let's see; can we pretend that a new kid has come into town and that you would like to be friends with her/him? What could you do or say so that s/he will become friends with you?

Child A's Response: (A normal 5-year-old female): "You wanna be my friend? I'll let you sleep in my bed."

Child B's Response: (A withdrawn and socially rejected 8-year-old boy): "Can you teach me how to be your friend?"

Child C's Response: (A normal 8-year-old girl): "That's a neat pair of jeans. How'd you like to come over and play at my house? I've got lots of Barbie dolls.

(Two children in the Rubin backyard, Summer 1983)

Joshua: (A 3-year-old male): "Hey Cara; you wanna be my friend?"
Cara (A 4-year-old female): "No!"
Joshua: "Yes?"
Cara: "No!"
Joshua: "Yes!"
Cara: "No!"
Joshua: "Yes, you're gonna be my friend!"
Cara: "No!"
Joshua: (Runs towards Cara's mother) "Hey, Marianne, Cara won't be my . . ."
Cara: "I'm your friend; I'll be your friend!"

In the examples presented above, we provide the reader with a sample of the data and methodologies used commonly to study children's abilities to think about and manage their interpersonal problems. We also illustrate the variability in the ways that children of different ages and sociability status solve their social problems. These examples, thus, set the stage for the remainder of this chapter, which as the reader may have guessed, concerns children's social problem solving skills.

The social problems that children face with regularity include initiating friendship, acquiring objects, seeking and offering help, seeking attention or information, and stopping others from acting in some way or another. It would seem commonplace to predict that children who cannot achieve these social goals effectively and consistently will experience difficulties with normal adjustment and development. Inadequate social problem solvers, regardless of age, have long been held to be "at risk" for psychological adjustment problems (Goldfried & D'Zurilla, 1969; Jahoda, 1953, 1958; Muus, 1960). Yet, until recent years, there has been a dearth of research and theory concerning the development of social problem solving in childhood. Instead, our knowledge concerning problem solving has derived mainly from those who have focused theoretically and empirically on the abilities of people to deal strategically with syllogisms, puzzles, and other impersonal general-reasoning tasks (e.g., Newell & Simon, 1971).

The acceleration of efforts to examine social problem solving in childhood draws heavily from three sources. First, in the late 1960s and early 1970s, the study of social-cognition in children began to blossom. Quite simply, the examination of how children cognized about their social worlds was a research topic whose time had come. Social psychologists had been investigating person perception and attribution theory for many years prior to the 1970s (e.g., Heider, 1958) but paid little attention to its developmental course. In the early 1960s, influential North American developmental psychologists began calling for a convergence between the social and cognitive developmental approaches (e.g., Bronfenbrenner, 1963). Shortly thereafter Flavell, Botkin, Fry, Wright, and Jarvis (1968) and Kohlberg (1964) were instrumental in bringing our attention to and extending the early work of Piaget (1926, 1965) on perspective-taking and moral development. Thus, the study of how children think about solving interpersonal dilemmas meshed well within the Zeitgeist.

Second, George Spivack and Myrna Shure, two psychologists at the Hahnemann Community Mental Health Cener in Philadelphia, suggested that the well broadcast problem solving deficiencies of lower class children were evident not only in the impersonal domain (e.g., Sigel & McBane, 1967) but also in the interpersonal domain. Spivack and Shure's early research (Shure & Spivack, 1970, 1972; Spivack & Shure, 1974) dove-tailed nicely with statements by central figures in the Head Start movement that the focus of compensatory education should be broadened. Throughout the late 1960s and the early 1970s compensatory early education efforts were aimed at preventing future or ame-liorating present cognitive developmental deficits. As a reaction, in part, to the lack of breadth in intervention programming, Ed Zigler (1973), who was then Director of the Office of Child Development, noted that Head Start programmers should attempt "to bring about greater social competence in disadvantaged chil-dren." His suggestions were echoed by Anderson and Messick (1974), two leaders of the early Head Start program. Thus, the call for more broadly focused compensatory education brought increased visibility to the research of Spivack and Shure.

Finally, the third source responsible for the proliferation of social problem solving research emanates from current concerns about the causes and conse-quences of abnormal peer relationships and social skills in childhood. In the past decade, researchers have discovered that those who experience poor peer rela-tions in the middle years of childhood are "at risk" for a variety of social, psychological, and educational ills when they reach adolescence and early adulthood (e.g., Cowen, Pederon, Izzo, Babigian, & Trost, 1973; Roff, Sells, & Golden, 1972). It has been further assumed that some peer relations problems (e.g., social withdrawal) are mediated, in part, by social problem solving dificits (Shure & Spivack, 1972; Shure, Spivack, & Jaeger, 1971).

Given the rapid accumulation of published research concerning social prob-lem solving in the past few years, and given the potential of its impact for educators and for applied developmental and clinical child psychologists, it would seem appropriate, at this time, to pause and reflect on the conceptualiza-tion of the construct and on the research findings. We have several goals in writing this chapter. First, it is our intention to provide a brief review of the issues that have guided extant social problem solving research efforts. Second, we introduce a model of interpersonal cognitive problem solving skills. Despite a decade of social problem solving research, it is surprising to note that the field is largely devoid of attempts at model building and/or testing; we attempt to reme-dy this deficiency. Moreover, in describing our model, we provide the reader with a summary of some of our own current research efforts to assess compo-nents of this model. We further delineate those areas that remain barren of data in an attempt to stimulate further research in what we believe to be a complex and rich area of study.

II. HISTORICAL OVERVIEW OF SOCIAL PROBLEM SOLVING RESEARCH

One of the initial conceptualizations of social problem solving was articulated by Goldfried and D'Zurilla (1969; D'Zurilla & Goldfried, 1971). They defined *social competence* as "the effectiveness or adequacy with which an individual is capable of responding to various problematic situations which confront him" (p.

161). They stated further that ineffective problem solving can be labeled "abnormal behavior," and that any individual who repeatedly experiences an inability to resolve interpersonal dilemmas is at risk for a variety of psychological problems (D'Zurilla & Goldfried, 1971).

The model of problem solving developed by D'Zurilla and Goldfried (1971) was not unlike many that had been proposed earlier by those working in the impersonal problem solving domain. Briefly, D'Zurilla and Goldfried sketched a multi-step process of problem solving that included:

1. the identification of a situation as problematic;
2. the generation of possible alternatives to solve the problem;
3. the decision of choosing the appropriate alternative for the situation; and
4. strategy implementation.

One major limitation of D'Zurilla and Goldfried's model was the lack of focus on developmental issues. For example, there was no consideration given to how and when the components of the social problem solving process developed. Perhaps because the authors did not deal specifically with social problem solving development in childhood, the major burden of introducing social problem solving to developmental psychologists fell to Spivack and Shure (1974). These psychologists, in their long-standing programmatic research efforts, have attempted to demonstrate that social problem solving skills are necessary elements for the development of normal mental health. As such, their research has always been guided by applied concerns.

Spivack and Shure (1974) have indicated that social problem solving or interpersonal cognitive problem solving skills consist of a number of interrelated elements. These elements include: (a) sensitivity to or the recognition of interpersonal problems; (b) the ability to generate alternative solutions to solve these problems; (c) the ability to consider step-by-step means to reach social goals ("means-ends thinking"); (d) the ability to articulate consequences of social acts ("causal thinking"); and (e) the ability to identify and understand the motives and behaviors of others.

To a very limited extent, these elements were cast into a developmental framework. Spivack and his colleagues (Spivack & Shure, 1974; Spivack, Platt, & Shure, 1976) suggested that the ability to produce alternative solutions to alleviate social problems is a developmental precursor to "means-ends" and "consequential thinking" and to sensitivity to social dilemmas. The last three elements listed above are presumed to require perspective-taking skills and the appreciation of consequences, which, according to Spivack et al., are virtually non-existent in early childhood.

In support of their developmental perspective, Shure and Spivack cite data from a number of correlational and experimental studies. For preschoolers, measures of casual thinking, means-ends thinking, and sensitivity to interpersonal problems do not add significantly to the variance accounted for by alternative thinking performance when predicting teacher ratings of behavioral adjustment (Shure & Spivack, 1973). As predicted, the relation between the ability to produce alternative strategies to hypothetical social problems and ratings of behavioral adjustment declines in the middle years of childhood. Instead, the theoretically more "advanced" interpersonal cognitive problem solving skills appear to be better predictors of adjustment (Spivack et al., 1976).

Despite some evidence to support their developmental propositions (e.g., Shure & Spivack, 1973, 1974), Spivack and Shure's attempts at theorizing fell short on a variety of conceptual and empirical grounds. For one, the development of each of the problem solving skills is likely not an "all-or-none" process; rather, children show evidence of each of these abilities to varying degrees throughout childhood. Given that this is the case, it may well be that the developmental sequence of problem solving skills is not as readily fixed as originally suggested. Thus, sensitivity to some interpersonal problems may appear long before children can *articulate* alternative strategies. For example, Zahn-Waxler, Iannotti, and Chapman (1982) indicated that 2-year-olds are sensitive to needs for help-giving and help-seeking and are able to deal strategically with these problems before they could possibly generate verbal solutions to hypothetical versions of dilemmas. As such, it would appear as if the concept of sensitivity predates rather than postdates the production of alternative solutions in actual interpersonal situations.

These conceptual weaknesses aside, it behooves us to provide the reader with a brief review of Spivack and his colleagues' empirical contributions to the social problem solving literature. Basically, Spivack and Shure wanted to develop procedures to identify children with social problem solving deficits. They then set out to design programs to alleviate these deficits. In an effort to meet their applied goals, Spivack and Shure developed a set of hypothetical-reflective tests to measure a variety of social problem solving abilities. We label their procedures as "hypothetical-reflective" because hypothetical problem situations are presented to the children in an attempt to measure their abilities to "reflect" on a response.

In studies employing hypothetical-reflective techniques, the social goals are presented to the child by the experimenter. These goals have included object acquisition (Spivack and Shure, 1974), providing help to someone in need (Ladd & Oden, 1979), and initiating friendship (Asher & Renshaw, 1981). The interviewer attempts to elicit from the child relevant strategies to meet these selected social goals. Spivack and Shure's work with children has relied heavily on the use of four particular tests in which basically only two social goals are presented. In the Preschool Interpersonal Problem-Solving (PIPS) test, children are asked to generate alternative strategies to deal with (1) a peer oriented dilemma in which a child seeks to obtain a toy that is in the possession of another child and (2) an adult-oriented dilemma in which a child seeks to avoid his mother's anger after damaging property. The child is provided with a number of stories, each of which has the same theme; the test is scored by totaling the number of different relevant solutions suggested by the child. The PIPS test thus measures one element of interpersonal problem solving, namely the production of alternative solutions.

For older, elementary school-aged children, Spivack et al. (1976) have developed the Means-Ends Problem-Solving (MEPS) test; a measure that purportedly assesses the ability to plan goal-directed strategies in step-by-step fashion and to consider alternative actions and potential obstacles. The test consists of six stories, each of which includes only the beginning and end of the tale. As with the PIPS, the primary focus is on the *number of alternatives* suggested for how the given end could have been achieved. Other hypothetical-reflective tests designed by Spivack et al. (1976) for older children include the What Happens Next Game (WHNG), in which consequential thinking is measured, and the Sensitivity to Interpersonal Problems test (SIP). Details for administration and scoring of these four hypothetical reflective measures may be found in Spivack and Shure (1974), Spivack et al. (1976), and Shure and Spivack (1974).

In their research, the Hahnemann group found that lower-class children were less able to provide quantitatively as many solutions to the various hypothetical measures than their middle-class age-mates. Moreover, children rated by their teachers as maladjusted or ''aberrant'' (i.e., withdrawn or impulsive/aggressive) seemed to produce fewer alternative solutions on various subsets of the Spivack and Shure hypothetical-reflective battery of social problem solving tests.

In an effort to assess the hypothesis that social cognition mediates behavior, a series of training studies was carried out by Spivack and his colleagues in the early 1970s. The training curricula (Shure & Spivack, 1978; Spivack et al., 1976; Spivack & Shure, 1974) usually involved teaching small groups of children emotion recognition, perspective-taking, and social problem solving skills (alternative thinking, consequential thinking, etc.) over a number of weeks. As an outcome of this curriculum, trained groups of children appeared to have improved their social adjustment scores (as rated by teachers) and their social problem solving reasoning skills to a greater extent than control groups of children who did not receive the tutorial sessions (see Shure & Spivack, 1980 and Spivack et al., 1976 and Urbain & Kendall, 1980 for discussions of the training research findings). These findings, reported mainly at regional conferences, in unpublished documents, and in two books (Spivack et al., 1976; Spivack & Shure, 1974) were instrumental in eliciting a flurry of similar studies concerning the assessment and training of social problem solving skills during the early and mid 1970s.

For the most part, the research emanating from Spivack and Shure's work did not provide substantive variation from the original efforts. The assessment of social problem solving in the 1970s remained primarily hypothetical-reflective in nature (e.g., Elardo & Cooper, 1977). One important advance was the recognition that hypothetical-reflective tests must be psychometrically strong and ecologically valid; concerns for such issues seemed by-passed in the early rush to aid children ''at risk'' for social competence deficits. In response to the concerns for ecological validity, Larcen and his colleagues (Allen, Chinsky, Larcen, Lochman, & Selinger, 1976; McClure, Chinsky, & Larcen, 1978) developed a ''consultant'' measurement technique. An adult confederate, in apparent ''real'' need of assistance, elicited alternate solutions from a child subject who was cast in the role of consultant. In one variation the confederate asked the ''consultant'' for advice concerning three problems that her ''own'' child faced on entering school (making friends, getting lost on a bus, having a teacher-related academic problem). The child's strategies were scored for quantity, persistence in the face of obstacles, and problem-sensitivity.

Another methodological advance was the development of the ''analogue situation'' technique. McClure et al. (1978), provided small groups of elementary school children (''Friendship Clubs'') with a set of relatively structured social dilemmas. For example, in one situation the children were not given enough chairs for all of its members nor were there sufficient numbers of ''club offices'' for each child. The group's task was to provide solutions to these dilemmas. The solutions were scored for quantity, persistence, and sensitivity.

The other major focus of social problem solving work in this period concerned attempts to train children to become more socially competent. In general, there was a shift from targeting disadvantaged preschoolers to targeting elementary school-aged and middle-class children for intervention. The training programs, many of which have been described in a recent review by Urbain and Kendall (1980), allowed further examination of the hypothesis that social problem solving skills mediate social behavioral competence. The findings were decidedly mixed.

In general, training effects during this period showed less consistently positive results than the studies conducted by Spivack and his colleagues. Elardo and Cooper (1977), for example, reported no significant effects of social problem solving training in role-taking, hypothetical-reflective social problem solving skills, or teacher ratings. Only short term improvements were found by Allen (Allen et al., 1976) on a number of hypothetical-reflective social problem solving variables, and no significant treatment effects for a variety of other relevant measures. A similar lack of consistency in treatment effects was reported by McClure (McClure et al. 1978).

In a conclusion which foreshadowed current concerns, McClure et al. observed that increasing the variety of strategies available to a child would not necessarily imply that the strategies would be *used* in a given situation. The extant models of social problem solving offered little explanation for this failure of hypothetical-reflective skills to ''materialize'' in actual performance.

III. THE SECOND WAVE: NEW PRIORITIES IN SOCIAL
PROBLEM SOLVING RESEARCH

In the years following the first wave of research efforts to study social problem solving, a number of critical issues emerged. For one, it had been assumed by practitioners who provided children with skills training, that social problem solving could be framed as a developmental variable; young children were thought to be less competent than older children at producing multitudinous and varied social problem solving strategies.

Given this assumption, and the assumption that SES disadvantaged youngsters more closely resembled their younger middle-class counterparts than their same-age or older middle-class counterparts in social problem solving skill, amelioration programs were provided for the former group. Unfortunately, however, the initial wave of research provided little information concerning the developmental course of hypothetical-reflective social problem solving reasoning. As such, there was little information concerning the veracity of the first assumption upon which the training programs were based.

Second, the measures sampled a very narrow range of problems (e.g., object acquisition, friendship initiation, avoiding adult anger); little, if any information was provided concerning the significance of these problems to children and the degree to which these problems actually occurred in naturalistic social encounters.

Third, despite some data concerning the test-retest reliability and internal consistency of various hypothetical-reflective social problem solving measures (e.g., Platt & Spivack, 1975; Shure & Spivack, 1974), there was virtually no information about the ecological validity of the extant test batteries. Thus, the extent to which children's naturalistic social problem solving strategies could be predicted from their responses to hypothetical dilemmas was unknown. Such an examination would have had to entail a qualitative assessment of social problem solving strategies; yet, as aforementioned, most of the early instruments were scored by profiling children's abilities to produce quantitatively numerous strategies to the neglect of their content.

Finally, the external validity of the early social problem solving measures remained somewhat of a mystery. Despite Spivack et al.'s (1976) claim that children who behaved in "aberrant" fashions evidenced social problem solving deficits, data supportive of this notion were never clearly produced. For one, the teacher rating scales that Spivack and his colleagues have used as outcome measures following social problem solving training (the Devereux Child Behavior Rating Scale, Spivack & Spotts, 1966 and the Hahnemann Preschool Behavior Rating Scale, Shure, Newman, & Silver, 1973) have unknown *published* psychometric strength. In more recent research efforts in which hypothetical-reflective reasoning has been linked to peer or teacher ratings of children's social competence, the results have been mixed (e.g., Asher & Renshaw, 1981; Butler,

1978; Ladd & Oden, 1979; Sharp, 1978). Interestingly, when significant relations have been found they tend to exist between qualitative (type of strategies) rather than quantitative (number of strategies) aspects of hypothetical-reflective social problem solving ability.

Given the problems noted above as well as those indicated in an earlier critical review by Krasnor and Rubin (1981), we began a series of programmatic studies concerning the development of social problem solving skills in the early and middle years of childhood.

The Waterloo Training Study

Our original efforts to study social problem solving in children derived from applied concerns. In 1974 The University of Waterloo Early Childhood Education Center was founded by Ken Rubin; one of the original teachers was Linda Krasnor. When the Center first opened, a Piagetian cognitively-oriented curriculum was developed and directed to a group of predominantly middle-class children. The development of this curriculum took us approximately $2\frac{1}{2}$ years, after which we were faced with a dilemma. Our preschoolers were becoming competent classifiers and seriators; however, we knew little about their social competencies.

It was at this point that we became aware of Spivack & Shure's (1974) applied research. Although their curriculum had considerable intuitive appeal and some, albeit questionable, empirical support, we had several major concerns. First, Spivack and Shure's program scripts were developed for use with language and cognition deficient children. Our receptive audience was a group of white, middle-class Canadian 4-year-olds. Despite our northern climate and our deprivation of many American television programs, we anticipated that these children would not be suffering from the more severe behavioral adjustment problems and language skills deficiencies faced by Spivack and Shure's lower SES group. Thus, in our first study we examined the relative strength of two different programs designed to improve the social problem solving skills of young children. The first program was taken directly from the scripted lessons and dialogue described by Spivack and Shure (1974). The second program consisted of dialogues between children and teachers concerning social problems as they occurred in the classroom. A thorough description of the latter program may be found in Krasnor (1977).

Second, as aforementioned, we had reservations about the psychometric strength of the hypothetical-reflective measures of social problem solving skill. Thus, in the first Waterloo study we decided to examine the relation between children's strategies used to solve hypothetical and matching naturalistically occurring social problems. This analysis was not carried out simply to satisfy our curiosity about the validity of social-cognitive measures. Rather, we were very concerned that applied developmental psychologists would replace observations

of behavior change with laboratory assessments of social thinking as the outcomes of ameliorative efforts to *change behavior!* Thus, it was imperative to
examine the thought-behavior relationship.

To reach our goals we designed a new hypothetical-reflective test of social
problem solving, the Alternative Solutions Test (AST). Three different types of
social problems were presented to the children: (a) an object acquisition problem;
(b) a problem in which a child attempted to gain adult aid to obtain an object; and
(c) a problem in which a child attempted to comfort a peer in distress. Instead of
presenting a different story to elicit a series of single strategies as in the commonly used PIPS, we read a single story for each problem type; the child was
asked repeatedly what she or he would do or say if the strategy suggested
originally did not work. This alteration better approximated actual interaction in
which a child's first social problem solving attempt to solve a problem is unsuccessful; yet the problem itself remains and requires further strategies for solution.

In an effort to examine qualitative differences in strategy production, social
problem solving alternatives were coded as threat/bribe, cry/whine, call, ask,
use of politeness markers ("please"), tell or explain, appeal to authority, command, and laugh. The nonverbal strategies elicited from the children were coded
as force on object, force on person, gesture, comfort, escape, distract, wait,
share, punish, and obtain from alternate source.

An observational system was developed to correspond with the strategy coding system used for the AST. We employed an event sampling procedure to
record the children's strategies for solving problems. In addition, strategies were
coded for observed outcome.

Our findings indicated that neither didactic program was especially effective
in improving hypothetical-reflective reasoning skills. It was our anecdotal impression that the children in the Spivack and Shure scripted program became
increasingly bored and impatient with the social problems presented during training; moreover, these problems were strikingly similar to those used in the AST
and the PIPS. This led to our suspicion that some earlier reported treatment
success was due to "training to task" rather than to generalized problem solving
effectiveness.

In retrospect, our most interesting finding concerned what we had labeled
initially as "the problem of ecological validity." Basically, the specific strategies observed during children's naturalistic problematic encounters could not be
predicted from the strategies they generated in the test situation. The discrepancy
between the hypothetical-reflective and naturalistic measures of strategy selection varied with the particular problem; it was greater for the "peer toy" situation than for the "adult" problem. The comforting problem occurred too infre-
quently in the natural setting to allow data analysis.

The probability that a child would display behaviorally a strategy if she or he
had offered the same alternatives on the AST was .42 for the adult situation
and .26 for the toy situation. We also attempted to predict test performance from

observed behavior and even lower probabilities emerged (.22 and .18 for the adult and toy situations respectively). The predictability varied by strategy. For example, politeness markers ("say please") were suggested often to solve the hypothetical toy acquisition problem; this same strategy was *never* observed in parallel naturalistic social encounters.

Another interesting and surprising finding was that the number of alternatives generated on the AST was uncorrelated with children's observed success at managing their social dilemmas. This brought into serious question the theoretical assumption upon which Spivack and Shure's training program was based; that is, that increasing the child's ability to produce numerous alternative solutions should improve social skills.

Taken together, our analyses indicated that strategies generated to solve hypothetical social problems varied significantly in quantity and quality from those observed in natural settings. Furthermore, the number of alternatives generated did not predict observed social problem solving effectiveness. Although these findings did surprise us to some degree, they nevertheless meshed well with those reported by others in the late 1970s and early 1980s (e.g., Butler, 1978; Enright & Sutterfield, 1980; McClure et al., 1978; Sharp, 1981). In these latter reports the data revealed that hypothetical-reflective measures of social problem solving skills did not correlate significantly with behavioral ratings of social competence and that changes in social problem solving reasoning were not directly associated with changes in behavior. Moreover, these data paralleled those found generally in the literature concerning relations between social cognition and social action. For example, although researchers had long speculated that perspective-taking should be linked positively to observations of altruistic behavior and negatively to aggression, the extant data were not clearly supportive of these hypotheses (see Shantz, 1983 for a relevant review). Collectively, these data were sufficiently puzzling to us that we decided to track possible reasons for the lack of a correlational link between social thought and social behavior.

Explaining the Relation Between Cognition and Behavior

In retrospect, the non-match between social problem solving cognition and behavior makes much sense. Yet, in the throes of Spivack and Shure's (1974) exciting training findings, it seemed natural to expect a social problem solving cognition-behavior relation. These psychologists set out to change behavior by changing thought; moreover, Spivack and Shure reported consistently that children whose social behavior and social problem solving scores changed the most following training (as assessed by teacher ratings) were those who had the greatest social problem solving deficits to begin with. How then, were we to explain our own findings as well as those of others emerging in the late 1970s?

One possibility concerned the psychometric strength of hypothetical-reflective measures of social cognition. Several psychologists have questioned the reliability of various measures of social reasoning (e.g., Ford, 1979; Rubin, 1978). But certainly not all measures of social cognition are psychometrically weak. Thus, other suitable explanations for the low-to-moderate thought-behavior relation had to be found.

We bumped into one answer in a separate project involving an analysis of children's play and games (Rubin & Pepler, 1980). For our analysis, we examined the levels of perspective-taking ability described by Selman (1980). Selman has proposed a multi-leveled model of perspective-taking and, until recently, his primary method of assessment has involved the presentation of hypothetical dilemmas and the careful probing of responses to these dilemmas. In our analysis we were able to infer those different levels of perspective-taking that were required for competent participation in commonly occurring children's games. For example, one form of play typical of 6- to 8-year-olds is the simple, competitive game with rules. As Sutton-Smith (1971) has noted, in the competitive games of this age group, the sides or roles chosen are transitory and winning is episodic. The games do not have ultimate or fixed winners. The games of dodge ball and frozen tag are examples and they require an understanding of reciprocity and role-reversibility, both of which are criteria for Selman's (1980) Stage 2, self-reflective perspective-taking skills. During this stage, children need not simultaneously consider points of view from a third-person perspective; one need only keep in mind that "When you are it, I have to flee," and "When I am it, you have to flee." Furthermore, in this stage there is little skill at speculating about strategies based on recursive thought processes. The lack of necessity for "third person" thinking and recursive thought is exemplary of the simple game-with-rules. According to Selman, the stage of self-reflective role-taking occurs between 8 to 10 years; the behavioral manifestations of such skills are evident between 6 and 8 years.

Given this analysis, it became quite clear to us that children were displaying, behaviorally, levels of social-cognitive thought at *younger* ages than would be expected given children's responses to hypothetical-reflective assessments of their social cognitions. This finding was in keeping with the Piagetian perspective that knowledge is first constructed through action and only later emerges in hypothetical-reflective thought.

Play and games by definition, however, are voluntary situations that involve maximal levels of pleasure and minimal levels of negative anxiety. The real-life solution of social dilemmas may evoke negative affect and, consequently, in some cases behavior may lag behind thought. Take, for example, the proposition of Cooney and Selman (1978) that there are three domains of social-cognitive reasoning: (1) initial interpersonal orientation (the first response to a hypothetical dilemma); (2) reflective reasoning (the thoughtful, probed responses to the dilemma); and (3) reasoning in action (responses to the dilemma in a natural setting).

Cooney and Selman suggest that a child's reflective reasoning is most likely to demonstrate the highest social-cognitive developmental level. The initial response is thought to reflect more closely the child's recognition of the "need" to use reasoning in the test situation. These psychologists hypothesized that reflective reasoning would fall at the same level as, or at a higher developmental level than, that indicated by behavior. This would be the case because time pressures, affect (e.g., anxiety, anger), and self-interest, among other factors, could mediate against higher levels of "practical knowledge" (Damon, 1977). Alternately, the level of initial orientation responses (or "knee jerk" verbal reactions) to hypothetical dilemmas were hypothesized to fall somewhere in between reflective reasoning and reasoning in action.

These theoretical propositions seem reasonable and, for the most part, remain virtually unexplored empirically. Yet they provided us with some explanation for the lack of strong thought-behavior relations beyond the usual vilification of social-cognition measures.

Another explanation came from the then emerging literature on social scripts (Langer, 1978; Schank & Abelson, 1977). It has been suggested that some routines of social behavior involve little, if any, thought. In contrast, there are other social situations that call for more reflective cognitive processing. For example, the process of metacognition (Flavell, 1981) may be relevant in novel or significant social situations. Assessment procedures that probe a child's understanding of social action in hypothetical dilemmas "pull for" thinking, whereas everyday behavior in situations parallel to those discussed in the lab may reflect automaticity and a lack of thinking. Thus, differences *would* be expected in comparisons between "thinking" versus "scripted" responses to the same social dilemmas.

Another explanation for the lack of correspondence between social thought and behaviors emanates from our own analysis of the ethological approach to the study of human interaction. Ethologists view behavior as interactive and flowing; they do not examine units of behavior in isolation (Cairns, 1979). Functional aspects of behavior as well as structural components are emphasized and chains or sequences of behavior are tracked and analyzed. Probabilities that given behaviors lead to given outcomes are computed. From this perspective, social problem solving sequences and strategy effectiveness can be explored.

The ethological approach may thus provide the researcher with a different viewpoint concerning social problem solving than the hypothetical-reflective method. In the case of hypothetical-reflective measurement, a child may be able to produce only one or two *verbal* strategies to a variety of social problems; consequently that child may be identified as socially unskilled and as an appropriate subject for social problem solving training. Yet, it may well be that *observations* of this child indicate that her or his limited repertoire is both very effective and acceptable to his social community of parents, teachers, and peers. As such, adults might view the child as competent, she or he may be popular among peers even though her/his hypothetical-reflective social problem solving scores may be low. Once again a viable explanation for the social thought-behavior discrepancy can be identified; in this case the reliance on quantitative dimensions of alternative thinking sheds no light on the actual effectiveness of particular strategies in natural settings.

In summary, we believe that cognition-behavior discrepancies may exist because (a) in some cases thought lags behind behavior; (b) in some cases behavior lags behind thought; and (c) in some cases no correspondence should be expected. We have provided examples of these cases herein. Our newfound discoveries concerning cognitive scripts, affect, and behavior sequences led us to realize that what the social problem solving literature really needed was a thorough concentration on the *processes* involved in thinking about social problems. This realization turned us to the information processing literature.

IV. AN INFORMATION PROCESSING MODEL OF SOCIAL PROBLEM SOLVING

The relevant models that guided our own formulations of social information processing were drawn heavily from Newell and Simon (1972), Schank and Abelson (1977), and Flavell (1981). From Newell and Simon we borrowed the model of problem solving information flow. This model is presented briefly as follows:

(a) The problem and relevant associated material (e.g., environmental factors) is encoded. During this initial encoding phase the "problem space" or set of solution possibilities is defined. This problem space is somewhat analogous to the "strategy repertoire" referred to in the social problem solving literature (Krasnor & Rubin, 1981);

(b) a specific problem solving method is selected;

(c) the method is applied;

(d) dependent on outcome, one of three options is followed: another strategy is attempted; the goal is reformulated; or the solution is abandoned;

(e) the method produces a new (perhaps easier) problem or sub-goal which may be attempted or set aside.

Strongly related to the information processing approach was the development of the "script" as a construct used to explain automaticity in problem solving. Schank and Abelson (1977) defined a script as a general event representation consisting of an ordered sequence of actions tied to a specific type of event (e.g., going grocery shopping). Specific action sequences, thus, were stored awaiting evocation by specific features that could be either internal (e.g., feeling hungry) or external (e.g., an empty refrigerator).

Although scripts were introduced primarily as cognitive structures for representing knowledge and interpreting routine social sequences, increasing attention was directed toward scripts as guides to social *actions* and as frameworks which facilitated communication and interaction between individuals (e.g., Nelson, 1981). Abelson (1982) suggested that three conditions were necessary for scripted social behavior: (a) a stable cognitive representation of the script; (b) a context which contained elements evoking the script; and (c) entrance into the script by the individual.

The existence of a script means that the individual has an accessible routine sequence of actions corresponding to a familiar social situation. If the script can be successfully implemented, there is little "problem" in the classical sense. Scripts may be blocked, however, when appropriate eliciting conditions are not present or when an obstacle prevents an action from being completed. In addition, without appropriate context and individual engagement little correspondence would be expected between the existence of a script and actual behavior. Once an individual enters a script, the scripted behaviors unfold in a relatively automatic fashion.

Finally, from Flavell we borrowed speculations concerning those conditions under which *active* social cognition is likely to occur. These conditions include situations which demand conscious processing (e.g., a hypothetical-reflective interview) and situations that are novel, significant, or violate expectations or have had unsuccessful resolutions in the past. It is important to note that these conditions preclude the possibility of activating social scripts.

Given the integration of material from Newell and Simon's work on problem solving, Schank and Abelson's research on scripts, and Flavell's speculations on metacognition, we formulated the social problem solving model described below.

The Social Problem Solving Model

In order to illustrate the model, the following examples are used.

Matthew and Sean are third-grade children who worked together on a block construction problem. At one point in their interaction we observed the following:

Matthew: "Where'd you put the head?"
Sean: (no apparent contingent response)
Matthew: ?"Huh? Where'd you put the head?"
Sean: (no response)
Matthew: ?"Aw, c'mon. With the eyes and stuff?"

Sean: (grabs block from Matthew)
Matthew: ?''Where is it? Where'd you put the head?''

In this sequence Matthew's apparent goal was to get information about a block from Sean. When his original strategy failed (i.e., Sean did not comply with the request for information) Matthew persistently pursued a rather inflexible approach to problem solution.

In another dyad, Sarah and Lisa attempted to solve the same block construction problem. We observed the following:

Sarah: "Hey (reaches over). We can make it wider. Here, wanna do it?"
Lisa: (no response)
Sarah: "Don't you think it should be a bit wider?"
Lisa: (no response)
Sarah: "Yeah, let's make it wider."
Lisa: (makes construction wider).

Sarah has demonstrated persistence similar to Matthew. Yet she is more flexible in her pursuit of her goal following initial failure.

Our model of problem solving begins with the identification of a *goal*. In the examples described above, Matthew's social goal is to obtain information and Sarah's is to elicit action on the part of Lisa. We also are able to note the initial *strategies* employed by the children to meet their goals. No doubt these strategies were chosen because of particular *environmental factors* such as relative familiarity of partner and social context and because of previous experiences using different strategies with varying success rates in similar situations. Again, as in many contemporary models of problem solving, we can record the *outcome* (response by target in context of the goal) of the particular strategies actually employed. Given initial failure we examine whether follow-up strategies are attempted and, if so, what those strategies are.

A description of our social problem solving information processing model is presented in Figure 1. The central features of the model involve (a) the selection of a social goal; (b) consideration of the social environment; (c) accession and selection of strategies given consideration of features (a) and (b); (d) strategy production; (e) strategy outcome; and (f) strategy sequencing following an initial social problem solving failure. A discussion of the individual components of the model and means for assessing these components follows.

Selecting the Social Goal

Children have a complex range of social needs and face, with regularity, a wide variety of social obstacles. Some of their goals include (1) eliciting action from another; (2) object acquisition; (3) gaining attention or acknowledgement; (4)

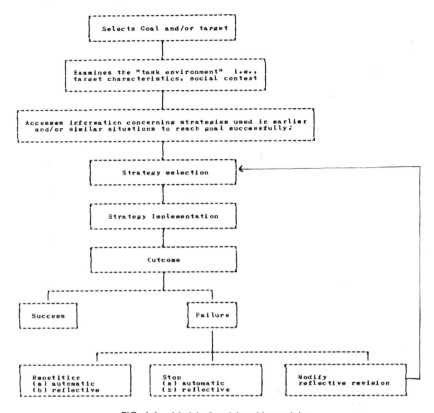

FIG. 1.1.   Model of social problem solving.

information acquisition; (5) giving and/or seeking help; (6) soliciting permission to act; (7) defense; (8) avoiding anger and/or ''loss of face''; and (9) initiating social play. Certainly these represent but a subset of children's social goals. In setting a goal, the individual establishes the criteria by which she or he will judge the success or failure of social problem solving attempts. The goal, by definition, is a representation of the end state of the problem solving process. A goal may be broken down into subgoals, or a goal may be changed during the social problem solving process, but the goal ''in force'' at a particular time provides the basis for outcome feedback.

The study of social problem solving and, perhaps more generally, the study of social competence involves analyzing how well children achieve their social goals. Until recently, however, an examination of goals has not garnered much attention. This has undoubtedly been the result of acknowledged dangers in attempting to infer children's goals from adultomorphic perspectives. In this section, however, we argue that social goals can be examined, not only in the lab, but also in natural and semi-natural settings.

The solution of specific social goals is investigated most commonly through the use of hypothetical-reflective procedures. Through this method the goals are set for the child by the interviewer. Some of the goals studied using interview methods include object acquisition (e.g., Spivack & Shure, 1974), friendship initiation (Renshaw & Asher, 1982); help giving (Ladd & Oden, 1979), help seeking (Nelson-LeGall, 1981); eliciting action (Clark & Delia, 1976); and avoiding anger (Spivack & Shure, 1974). These adult posed problems, however, do not guarantee that the child's personal task-related goals mirror those of the interviewer. Naturally, a psychologist would hope that the responses gleaned from setting these hypothetical problems would provide information about how children actually go about solving their interactive dilemmas. The child, however, may not be sufficiently motivated to provide verbal responses to these problems; the outcome is probably not as salient or significant when compared to the outcome following a behavioral response to a real social dilemma. Moreover, the child's goal may be to provide the adult listener with a culturally acceptable response rather than a response that reflects actual behavior. In short, the adult's experimental goal and the child's social goals may be quite different.

Researchers are only now beginning to realize that the hypothetical situation does not, in itself, define the goal for children, and appropriate methodologies are being developed to deal with the problem (Renshaw & Asher, 1982). For example, Renshaw (1981) has asked "What are you trying to do by doing (or saying) those things?" Although this refinement does not deal with motivation problems or the fact that an adult interviewer (often a stranger) is probing the child to discover what may be considered private information, it nevertheless does provide a reasonable methodological addition to the hypothetical-reflective examination of social goals.

In keeping with a social interactive perspective of problem solving it is interesting to note that researchers have begun recently to examine children's interpretations of others' social goals (e.g., Dodge, Murphy, & Buchsbaum, 1983). No doubt interpretation of others' intentions may have some impact on a child's own social goals and behaviors.

Analogue situations also allow the researcher to examine specific social goals. For example, Putallaz (1983) and Dodge, Schlundt, Schocken, and Delugach (1983) have primed target children to try to enter a social situation in which others are already interacting. The goal is to gain access to the ongoing play situation. Damon (1977) has demonstrated the utility of the simulated situation technique in his research concerning distributive justice. In one of Damon's paradigms children are asked to decide how a pizza pie should be divided given that some group members have contributed more than others to the task that led to the reward. The goal, in this case, is to make a just decision. Other researchers who have employed simulated or analogue situations include McClure et al. (1978) who had groups of children face a series of preset social problems such as assigning roles in a Friendship Club.

The analogue method can provide opportunities for researchers to observe how children go about achieving set goals in relatively naturalistic situations. The method does not have many of the testing constraints of the hypothetical-reflective procedure. Nevertheless, the goals are set by the investigator and, as such, it is not clear how significant they are to the children participating in the study. Moreover, the "set goals" and the children's goals may very well differ. For example, in the entry situations examined by Putallaz (1983) and Dodge et al. (1983), the goal of some children may be to avoid potential prospects of losing face or being the target of others' assertive behaviors. Despite this potential problem, the analogue situation technique certainly deserves further attention and refinement in future work on social problem solving.

In light of the possibility that the use of hypothetical-reflective and analogue situations to assess children's goals is based on a potentially erroneous assumption that children's goals are the same as those set by the experimenter, we suggest an alternative methodological strategy: inferring goals from observations of naturally occurring behavior. In our observational research we have considered problems to be "social" when the means or strategies employed by the child involve another individual, either in an active (e.g., helping) or passive (e.g., allowing object to be taken) sense. Naturalistic observations of social goals necessitate the examination of sequences of strategic behaviors that define an "episode." The episode itself defines the social goal. For example, in the situation described earlier involving Sarah and Lisa, a series of strategies was observed in a single social problem solving episode, the goal of which was to elicit action from a peer. Similarly, in the sequence of behaviors described at the outset of the chapter, Joshua's goal was to solicit agreement or affirmation from Cara.

We recognize that judgments of intention which are based on observed behavior pose complex philosophical and psychological dilemmas concerning whether the actor or observer should be considered the best (or only) judge of "real" intention (Beck, 1978). From a subjective or phenomenological approach, one would stress the necessity of relying on the actor's perspective to make a valid judgment of intent (Klinger, Barta, & Maxinera, 1982). However, the elevation of the actor to the position of primary judge of his or her own intention has been challenged on both philosophical (Beck, 1978) and empirical grounds (Bem, 1972; Nisbett & Wilson, 1977). The debate concerning who should be the "true" judge of intention may, in fact, be unresolvable. Pike's (1967) distinction of *etic* and *emic* approaches to the study of behavior may help to put this issue in perspective. According to Pike, an emic viewpoint reflects that of the actor. Within this approach, behavioral descriptions are based on distinctions that are meaningful to the actor using criteria selected from within his or her own systems. In contrast, an etic viewpoint represents that of an observer external to the behavioral system. The behavioral categories used to describe the system are created a priori by the observer and can be used as starting points for analyzing systems by providing access to the actor's viewpoint. Both the emic and etic approaches are equally valid means to study human behavior (Harris, 1979). The adequacy of etic descriptions should be judged on the basis of both reliability considerations and the generation of scientifically productive theories.

Within the etic approach it is possible, therefore, for an observer to specify, a priori, the criteria for identifying social problem solving attempts; criteria based on conventional interpretation of specific overt acts. Social goals, for example, can be judged on the basis of the surface or conventional meaning of the act (Harris, 1979). The goal of Matthew's social problem solving attempt would be judged to be one of information acquisition.

In summary, there appear to be three ways to study children's social goals; hypothetical-reflective interviews, analogue situations, and naturalistic observations. Although each technique has certain benefits and drawbacks, we express a positive bias for the observational technique. We recognize that etic judgments may vary from emic, "subjective" judgments of social goals; however, we nevertheless believe that cataloguing *reliably* observed social problem solving goals represents a valid starting point for analyzing purposeful and directive social behavior.

Examining the "Task Environment"

It seems reasonable to expect that children survey situational features before choosing strategies to achieve specific goals. Support for this contention derives from research that shows even 2 and 3-year-olds vary social behaviors in response to environmental cues.

For the most part, researchers have studied children's sensitivity to "personal" or animate task features. The social strategies employed to meet given goals have been examined in relation to the sex (Jacklin & Maccoby, 1978), age (Whiting & Whiting, 1975), peer status (Putallaz & Gottman, 1981) and familiarity (Doyle, 1982) of the protagonist and target. In much of the extant literature, the focus of study has been the covariation of strategy and target given particular goals of interest to the researcher. However, it may well be that the goals chosen by children covary with situational features. For example, children view older peers as sources for gaining information and tutorial aid; they view age-mates and younger children as sources for goals of friendship initiation and help giving (e.g., French, 1984; Lewis & Feiring, 1979).

There are, of course, "impersonal" or inanimate task features that have some impact on the social problem solving process; however, for the most part, these features have remained unexplored. These task environmental variables include general value (home vs. school vs. playground), population density, and visibility (public vs. private encounters). The assessment of the significance of task environmental properties in the social problem solving process can be derived in three ways. In hypothetical dilemmas, researchers can provide children with a series of problems, all with the same goal (e.g., object acquisition). The sole variant could be the characteristics of the protagonist and target (e.g., a younger child attempting to gain an object from an older child).

In analogue situations, children who vary with regard to selected features could be brought together in a social problem solving setting. For example, one might examine whether children's social entry goals (e.g., Putallaz, 1983) are accomplished differently when the targets are familiar versus infamiliar, of the same versus opposite-sex, perceived status superiors versus inferiors, and so forth. In the natural setting, any number of different goals and strategies can be investigated in relation to specific task environmental features. We shall provide examples of these covariations in a later section of this chapter.

Accessing and Selecting Strategies

There are several ways by which strategies may become available for use in achieving social goals. First, the child may have a set of strategies stored in long-term memory. The child retrieves one or more of these strategies and brings them into a "working space" or short-term memory for consideration or implementation.

The sequence of strategy retrieval may depend on variables such as (a) an access rule that is guided by assessment of the task environment (e.g., knowledge of target, familiarity of setting), (b) the ease with which a strategy may be implemented, and/or (c) a random process.

Strategy retrieval may be relatively automatic or scripted. Alternately, retrieval may be conscious and deliberate. The one common element among variations in the retrieval methods described above is that the strategies must exist already in the individual's repertoire. In addition, *new* strategies may be *constructed* by the individual through the cognitive transformation of available strategies. Strategy repertoires may vary in size, complexity, and perceived acceptability and effectiveness.

The *selection* process involves an evaluation of the strategy or strategies produced in the preceding phase. Several methods of evaluation are possible. If a script is available to guide behavior, strategy selection is relatively automatic. In these instances, evaluation focuses on whether the setting conditions for action are met. If so the strategy is implemented and the script proceeds in the usual manner. If the conditions are not met, there may be a shift to more conscious processing.

"Generate and test" is another strategy selection procedure. In this case each strategy, as it becomes accessible, is compared to preset criteria of acceptability, "performability" (can it be performed?), and potential effectiveness. If a strategy does not meet these criteria, another strategy is retrieved or constructed. The first strategy to match the criteria is implemented.

A strategy may be evaluated not only as a solution in itself but also as a *step* toward solution. A partial solution can be defined as a strategy which moves the situation "closer" to the goal state, or one which increases the likelihood of achieving a goal. In order to assess the utility of a strategy as a partial solution in the former sense, it is necessary to "map out" a series of steps toward a goal. For example, a gradient toward the goal of getting another to agree to a request might be the set of responses (a) "no," (b) "I'll think about it," (c) "maybe," (d) "yes." Steps in establishing friendship may be mapped as follows: (a) respond to conversational initiative; (b) initiate conversation; (c) respond to play invitation; (d) initiate play; (e) invite home; (f) confide in; and (g) make the friendship bond public (e.g., give a friendship pin).

One example of the second definition of partial solution is to make achievement of a goal more likely through affect manipulation. For example, a subgoal of making a person happy may increase the likelihood that she or he will agree to a subsequent request for joint play. Other ways of increasing the probability of future compliance may be to introduce external motivation for the target or to make necessary resources more accessible.

When more than a single strategy is accessed, the selection phase will involve a comparison between them. One or more of the evaluation processes described above may be employed; however, in this case, the "best" of the accessible strategies is selected.

The assessment of strategy accessibility and selection is not an easy matter. At this phase of the processing model, it would appear as if the hypothetical-reflective interview has advantages over analogue and naturalistic settings. An interviewer can present a problem (e.g., object acquisition) and request that the child produce as many relevant solutions as possible. A count of all strategies may be considered the response repertoire. The experimenter can also vary task environmental features (e.g., sex, age of problem solver, and target); the response repertoire may then be shown to covary with these experimentally manipulated environmental variables. Finally, the interviewer can ask the child to justify her or his response(s) to the hypothetical dilemma(s). Alternatively, the interviewer can present a problem, provide a number of possible solutions, and then ask the child to choose the "best" one. The child could then be asked to explain why the choice of the particular strategy was made. These verbal justifications may provide insights into the workings of the strategy selection process itself.

The use of scripts in strategy selection may be assessed by using a measure of response latency to the given problems. The process of strategy production requires finite periods of processing time. We expect, therefore, that an individual who produces a scripted strategy would be able to respond faster to requests for problem solutions than an individual who must recall or construct a strategy. This time difference should become increasingly apparent as the length of the scripted behavioral sequence increases.

From our perspective, neither the analogue situation nor the natural setting seems to be appropriate for the study of strategy accessibility and selection. One might ask a child to "think aloud" during an analogue social problem solving situation; however, the information gleaned from such procedures would detract from the "naturalism" of the setting and, as such, data interpretation would be extremely difficult. These methods would "pull for" conscious and reflective processing, thus making the study of automatic social responding very difficult.

Strategy Implementation

Once a strategy has been selected the next step is to produce it in the relevant context. In our conceptualization of the social problem solving process we assume that the strategy of choice is one which the problem solver is capable of performing. Consideration of performance factors is part of the strategy selection process. If factors which were not anticipated arise suddenly, the original strategy choice may be abandoned and the social problem solving process begins again.

Strategy implementation can be assessed through the use of all three methodologies described above. In an interview, the child can be asked what *she or he* would do in a given social situation. The strategy indicated by the child might not necessarily correspond with actual implementation for reasons discussed in previous sections.

The assessment of strategy implementation is better done via observations in natural situations. The strategies produced can be coded quantitatively (the number of strategies used to solve a problem) and qualitatively (as above). Examples of coding frames used to quantify and qualify strategy implementation in hypothetical-reflective interview and observational settings are described in Section V.

It seems important to note that there have been relatively few attempts to measure performance ability per se, independent of environmental constraints and motivational variations. Failure to observe a strategy, therefore, may not mean that the child lacks implementation ability. Feldman (1983) has attempted to separate performance skills from other social problem solving components by requiring children to "act out" specific strategies. In this way the child's spontaneous production can be separated from performance ability, albeit with the reduction of ecological validity.

Strategy Outcome

In order to assess outcome, the problem solver must take a "reading" of the environment after the strategy is implemented. Information gathered at this stage is compared to the pre-established criteria for success to examine whether the goal has been partially or fully achieved. In this way, the problem solver can judge a strategy as a success, failure, or partial success.

The success of a strategy in achieving a goal may be examined via all three methods. The effectiveness of an observed strategy in the natural or analogue setting may be judged by the overt responses of others. These judgments are made from a "spectator" perspective in a context relevant to the child. Actor and observed judgments of success may differ, since each judges an outome from his or her own view of the goal. If perceived goals differ, then judgment of the effectiveness of a strategy may also differ. Cues to whether observer and actor outcome judgments agree may emerge in observation of the problem solver's affect or by an analysis of strategy reattempts. Negative affect following target response or a reattempt of the same strategy would indicate failure. The *absence* of negative affect or reattempts, however, cannot be interpreted unambiguously as indices of success since the child may perceive failure but choose to "give up." The child may also not react negatively if the goal was relatively unimportant. In addition, a researcher could interview a child regarding the goals and perceived effectiveness of prior strategies; this procedure, however, would be reactive. Young children may not be able to articulate this information. Even among adults it is clear that individuals are often unaware of their own motivations in specific situations and may, themselves, be unreliable self observers.

In hypothetical-reflective interviews, success of a strategy must be judged in the "abstract." Adult or child judges must be relied upon to formulate opinions concerning a strategy's potential for success/failure in situations involving specific goals and targets. The validity of such judgments has yet to be established in the research literature.

The judgment of success or failure outcome by the actor represents a clear branching point in the social problem solving process. If the strategy is judged to be successful, the social problem solving process ends. Presumably, information about the success of the strategy is, thereafter, retained. This information may affect the storage position of the strategy (e.g., it may rise in the hierarchy and be evoked sooner or faster in subsequent situations). If a strategy is judged as a partial success, the individual may accept the outcome as successful "enough" and proceed as if the outcome was a success; alternatively, the individual may decide to reattempt the goal, as if the outcome were a failure.

If an attempted strategy is judged to have failed, three general options are apparent:

1. The problem solver may stop making attempts, thus leaving the goal unfulfilled. In this case, information about the relative ineffectiveness of the strategy is stored for future access; a new or modified goal may be chosen and the process re-started.
2. The problem solver may repeat the same strategy.

3. The problem solver may modify the previous strategy while maintaining the same goal; modifications may be relatively minor or substantial. In the model, this option may be represented by a return to the "encode task information" or "strategy selection" stages.

The individual's responses to failure may progress either reflectively or automatically. Thus, an individual may repeat a failed strategy after conscious consideration, or simply persist in an unthinking manner. Similarly, a social problem solver may decide reflectively to stop a social problem solving attempt or to reattempt the goal with a change in strategy. The abandonment of a goal or modification of a strategy may also proceed automatically, but only in those instances in which the individual has had opportunities to build a scripted sequence of response to failure (e.g., if asking fails, then cry). In these familiar cases, a *change* in behavior may occur without thinking. In most situations, however, we would expect that behavioral changes following failure would be accompanied by reflective cognitive processing.

We may hypothesize about the conditions which might make the choice of each of these options more likely. The decision to continue to pursue a failed goal or to stop may depend heavily on the importance of the goal to the individual (values, attitudes) as well as on the "cost" of the strategy (and of persistence itself) in relation to the benefits of the goal. Another important factor in the decision to continue pursuing a social goal is the nature of the feedback from the target. Wilcox and Webster (1980), for example, found that children were more likely to reattempt the same strategy if the target responded with a query (e.g., "What?") than if a refusal was made. Refusals tended to be followed by explanation or other modifications of the prior strategy. The probability of a repetition or modification may also be a function of the individual's strategy repertoire. A child who has relatively few available or accessible strategies may be more likely to repeat an earlier strategy than one who has more potential strategies from which to select.

In addition, an individual's causal attributions for the social failure may affect her or his response to negative outcomes. Researchers in more *cognitively*-oriented domains (e.g., Dweck, Davidson, Nelson, & Enna, 1978; Weiner, 1982) have found that children with stable, internal or uncontrollable attributions for unsuccessful outcomes tend to demonstrate nonproductive responses to failure. Initial investigations in the *social* domain (e.g., Goetz & Dweck, 1980) show similar results. Thus, individuals who attribute their social failure to relatively permanent, personal causes would tend to either perseverate or to give up more often than those who attribute failure to external unstable and/or controllable reasons.

Failure may also be accompanied by strong negative affect, particularly if the goal was heavily valued, if the target was important to the problem solver, or if the failure was highly visible. Anger, for example, may interfere with strategy selection processes after failure; high levels of anger may make it more likely for an individual to repeat than to change a prior strategy, since the latter option may require more processing complexity. In contrast, the anxious individual may be more likely to give up rather than reattempt a failed goal, since this "stop" option would allow her/him to terminate an unpleasant emotional state.

Individual responses to failure may be measured using each of the three general methods. Observation of failure responses during naturalistic interaction would have the most ecological validity but would require the most inference. It would be necessary to follow an individual for extended periods in order to detect sequences which may occur over indefinite time periods. The researcher must also await for failure to occur "naturally."

An alternative to the rather costly naturalistic approach is to experimentally introduce failure in analogue situations and to observe an individual's responses (e.g., to instruct a target to deny requests for joint play). Obstacles to goal achievement could be introduced similarly in hypothetical-reflective methods (e.g., by telling the child that the story character failed to achieve the set goal). By introducing failure, either behaviorally or hypothetically, the researcher can measure the individual's tendency to "give up, repeat, or modify" after failure. The child's responses, however, would not necessarily be representative of responses in more naturalistic settings.

V. DEVELOPMENTAL ISSUES

What are the goals of childhood? How are they accomplished? It seems to us that infants, toddlers, young, and older children may all have different social priorities. In infancy, proximity seeking and attention getting may be two of the more significant goals; in older children friendship initiation and information gathering might rank high in the list of social priorities. This change in priorities does not mean that the goals that are important to infants are not of significance to 10-year-olds. Most certainly, older children seek proximity and attention; but the primary targets of proximity and attention seeking are likely to change with age. We expect that older children would focus these goals on peers rather than on adult targets. We might ask further whether less active thinking is involved in achieving these well practiced goals in later childhood than in infancy. We might ask also whether less active thinking is involved for situations involving adults versus children. There is some theoretical justification for hypothesizing, for example, that peers are less predictable than adults (Lee, 1975).

The social problem solving processes and outcomes described above *can* be cast into a developmental framework. The questions posed in the preceding paragraph can only whet the appetite of developmental psychologists interested in the emergence of social competence and social problem solving in childhood. Unfortunately, at this time, we can produce far more questions than answers.

Admittedly, over the years some relevant research has appeared in the literature. For example, the observational study of social goals has a relatively long history (e.g., Jersild & Markey, 1935 re: object acquisition; Murphy, 1937 re: help giving). Considerable information is available concerning goals of proximity seeking, interaction initiation and affiliation, help giving and seeking, information seeking, and object acquisition throughout the years of childhood (see Rubin & Ross, 1982 for relevant reviews). Yet, with few exceptions (Whiting & Whiting, 1975), the study of these goals has not been examined developmentally. Thus it is unclear (a) whether social goals emerge in some predictable sequence during infancy and childhood and (b) whether some goals are perceived as being more or less important at different points in childhood.

The same may be said of the relations between goals, task environmental factors, strategy production, and goal outcomes. The extant relevant research has a decidedly non-developmental and non-theoretical orientation. Thus, there have been observational studies relating strategy production to task environmental features in infancy and toddlerhood (e.g., Eckerman & Stein, 1982; Hay, Pederson, & Nash, 1982; Lee, 1975), in early childhood (Doyle, 1982; Shatz & Gelman, 1973), and in middle and late childhood (Putallaz & Gottman, 1981). Unfortunately, in this corpus of research, investigators have not examined how children of varying ages go about meeting the *same* goals. Instead goals that appear salient to the age groups of concern in the studies are identified; the behaviors and, for older children, the thoughts directed toward meeting these goals are investigated.

The bottom line is that developmental data concerning social problem solving processes, production, and outcome are scarce. As such, developmental *norms* for thinking about, producing, and implementing social problem solving strategies are generally unavailable. Without such normative data the more applied issues that guided the original work of Spivack and Shure (1974) may seem well-meaning but misplaced. How *can* one identify children with social problem solving deficits if normative data are unavailable?

In the research that we describe below we show how different contact points in the model proposed above can be related. In some cases, our data are developmental; in others we present individual differences data within specified age groups. From those data we are able to examine children's perceptions and productions of acceptable and effective means to meet clearly specified social goals.

VI. A PROGRAM OF SOCIAL PROBLEM SOLVING RESEARCH

Our research has been guided by a concern to fill in the pieces of the social problem solving information processing model. We have examined five points in the model: (1) goal selection, (2) strategy selection, (3) utilization of task environmental information, (4) outcome, and (5) strategy sequencing following failure. In our research we have employed both hypothetical-reflective and observational methodologies; some studies have focused on developmental differences, others have concerned individual differences.

Hypothetical-Reflective Reasoning

A first step in examining components of the social problem solving model involved the development of a new test of hypothetical-reflective thinking. The Social Problem Solving Test (SPST) consisted of five pictured problem situations in which the central story character wants to play with a toy or use some material that another child possesses. The child was asked what the protagonist could do or say to gain access to the toy or activity. Thus, the goal in all SPST stories may be considered "object acquisition."

The characters in the stories varied systematically with regard to either sex or age. In one case, both characters were of the same age and sex as the subject. In the two *age related* stories, the protagonist (a child of the same age and sex as the subject) was desirous of a toy or an activity possessed or dominated by either a younger (by 2 years) or older (by 2 years) same-sex child. In the *sex related* stories, the sex of the characters was varied and age was held constant. The two stories were: (a) a female wanted a toy or access to an activity in the possession of a same-aged male, and (b) a male wanted a toy or access to an activity dominated by a same-age female. These variations were included to tap the influence of task environmental features on strategy production.

After the child's first response, the interviewer was instructed to say: "If that didn't work, what else could X do or say so that she or he could have Y?" This probe allowed us to examine strategy sequencing following social problem solving failure.

The children's responses were scored for the number of relevant categories (i.e., whether or not it was a feasible solution) produced per story and for flexibility of strategy sequencing. Flexibility was computed by giving a score of *0* if the child failed to offer a response to the interviewer's probe following the initial answer; a *1* was accorded if the second response involved only the same category/categories as the first response; and a *2* was scored if the second response was a modification of the original answer or if it was a completely novel answer.

In addition, each response was coded as to its quality. The number of responses falling into each of the following categories was computed.

1. *Prosocial*—includes ask; politeness; wait; command accompanied by a politeness marker; share or take turns; loan (e.g., "Can I have the ball please?").

2. *Agonistic*—includes direct imperatives; force/grab; physical attack on person; damage to property (e.g., "I would push him off the swing.").
3. *Authority intervention*—(e.g., "Tell his mom to get the book for him.").
4. *Bribe, trade, or finagle*—(e.g., "Say that she will give the boy a balloon if he lets her read the book.").
5. *Manipulate affect*—(e.g., "If you gimme that ball I'll be real happy.").

The number of responses falling within each category was calculated for each story separately.

The initial studies using the SPST concerned the provision of developmental norms. Thus, Rubin and Krasnor (1983) administered the SPST to preschool and kindergarten children. The children did not differ from each other on the number of relevant solutions produced on the test; however, kindergarten children were more flexible than preschoolers when providing follow-up solutions following initial failure. These data support the naturalistic observations of Levin and Rubin (1983) who reported increased flexibility in social problem solving with age following receipt of noncompliance to requests. Thus, it appears as if strategy sequencing and not strategy production is a differentiating developmental factor in early childhood, at least insofar as the goal of object acquisition is concerned. Response flexibility may be advantageous in solving problems since perseveration and rigidity would imply a lack of adaptive response to outcome feedback. These results have since been replicated in a recent unpublished study using the SPST with kindergarteners versus first-grade children.

Children were more likely to suggest the use of prosocial strategies to solve the object acquisition problems than any other strategies. Agonistic strategies were emitted more often than the adult intervention, trade-bribe, and manipulate affect categories. In short, these data are suggestive of a hierarchical ordering of strategies to solve object acquisition problems in early childhood. We should note again that these results have been replicated in a sample of first-grade children.

The age and sex of target manipulation produced strategy differentiation in *both* age groups. For the most part, the differentiating categories were the prosocial and agonistic strategies. In data drawn from preschoolers, kindergarteners, and first-grade children, the suggested use of prosocial strategies increased with age of the target. Alternately, the suggestion of agonistic strategies decreased with increasing target age. Prosocial strategies were also produced more often when a female protagonist tried to solve the social problem with a male target. These data corroborate observational research in which the use of less assertive and aggressive strategies has been demonstrated towards targets of higher status or dominance (Hold, 1976; Whiting & Whiting, 1975) and nurturant or prosocial activities are more commonly directed toward younger targets (Whiting & Whiting, 1975). In summary, these data support earlier reports that young children do consider task environmental factors when interacting or when thinking about interacting with others. From this first developmental study using the SPST we turned to a concern for individual differences in hypothetical-reflective social reasoning.

Individual differences in hypothetical-reflective reasoning.   The theoretical bases for our work on individual differences in hypothetical-reflective reasoning stemmed from Piaget and Sullivan. From a Piagetian perspective, it was noted that the cooperation and mutuality engendered in early peer relationships allowed children to gain broader viewpoints concerning their social worlds. Piaget (1926) considered young children to be neither willing nor able to take into account the perceptions, questions, or intentions of their social partners. Egocentrism in childhood wained, however, with increasing opportunities to interact with peers, and to experience conflicts and negotiations emanating from a world of multiple perspectives. These conflicts and negotiations centered around the acquisition of objects or around differing opinions or conceptions of the social world. Piaget believed that peer conflict and negotiation carried with them the power of eliciting compromise, reciprocity, and a more sociocentered view of the child's world. In years following the original publications of Piaget concerning the rise and fall of egocentrism, numerous writers have posited that children who play with their peers eventually begin to realize that positive and productive interaction is marked by compromise and by socialized thinking. Sullivan (1953) suggested that friendship relations in middle childhood were responsible for the development of mutual respect, interpersonal sensitivity, and cooperation.

These classical theoretical statements have received some empirical support in the peer relationships literature. Experimentally manipulated peer communication, conflict, and role-playing experiences have been shown to produce improvements in perspective taking and prosocial behaviors and to decrease aggressive behaviors (e.g., Chandler, 1973; Iannotti, 1978). Moreover, similar experimental manipulations have promoted short-term advances in the acquisition of knowledge concerning the impersonal world (Botvin & Murray, 1975). Children also gain knowledge about their social worlds through direct peer instruction and vicarious learning (see Hartup, 1983 for a review).

Given these theoretical and empirical perspectives it is possible to infer that children who lack sufficient or positive peer interactive experiences will be "at risk" for social and social-cognitive developmental problems. As supportive evidence for this contention there is the oft-cited work of Kohn and Clausen (1955), Roff et al. (1972), and Cowen et al. (1973). These researchers reported that social difficulties during the early elementary school years are predictive of school drop-out, anti-social behavior, delinquency, sexual disorder, and psychopathology in adolescence and in the early years of childhood. More recent corroborative data stem from a study by Coie and Dodge (1983) which demonstrated that peer ratings of rejection in middle childhood remained stable over a 5-year period.

These data perked our interest in studying possible connections between peer relationships and social problem solving skill. Does observed lack of interaction with peers correlate concurrently and predictively with social problem solving deficits? Do children who are disliked by their peers evidence hypothetical-reflective reasoning patterns that differentiate them from their better liked age-mates?

In a series of recent cross-sectional and longitudinal studies we have attempted to discover whether differences in social-cognition account, to any significant degree, for differences in observed and peer rated indices of social adjustment. The results of these studies are presented below.

Social problem solving thinking and social isolation in early and middle childhood.   The theoretically based suggestions that social withdrawal (or lack of peer interaction) may lead to social cognitive deficits and that peer interaction may lead to social cognitive advantages are being examined in a longitudinal research program currently in progress. In recent reports concerning initial data, we have described the social problem solving correlates of isolate and sociable behavior (e.g., Rubin, 1982a; Rubin, 1982b; Rubin, Daniels-Beirness, & Bream, 1984). In general, these correlational studies have indicated that children who display high frequencies of isolate behavior during free play time in pre-school and kindergarten produce fewer relevant solutions and less flexible solutions than their more sociable counterparts. Moreover, we have found consistently that withdrawn children are more likely to suggest that adults intervene on the part of the hypothetical protagonist. It is important to note, however, that the correlations, although significant, have all been in the low to moderate range. Furthermore, isolate behavior in the early years of childhood is hardly a stable phenomenon. For example, in Rubin et al. (1984), 72 children were observed during free-play in kindergarten and first grade. Although the correlation between isolate play in both grades was significant, $r=.39$, $p<.001$, the phenomenon could not be viewed as highly stable.

What happens when one controls for stability of sociability? It seems logical to assume that the best "acid" test for the peer interaction-social cognition relation is to find children who are experiencing *continuously* high, moderate, or low frequencies of peer interaction throughout the early years of childhood. A comparison can then be made between these different groups of children concerning quantitative and qualitative dimensions of social problem solving thinking.

A method for identifying severely withdrawn and highly sociable children has been developed recently by Rubin (1982a). Briefly, children are observed during free play for six 10-second time intervals each day over a period of about 6 weeks. Relevant behaviors coded for purposes of this presentation include isolate and sociable play. Isolate play consists of the sum of unoccupied + onlooker +

solitary activity. Sociable play consists of the sum of group behavior + peer conversations.

The children are then targeted into one of three categories. *Isolates* are those children whose nonsocial behavior is 1 standard deviation above the mean for their entire age group and 10% above their particular classroom means for nonsocial behavior. Moreover, isolates produce social behavior that is 1 standard deviation below the entire age group and 10% below their classroom means.

Sociable children are those whose social behavior is 1 standard deviation above the entire age group mean and 10% above their class means. Moreover, sociable children produce nonsocial behavior that is 1 standard deviation below the entire age group mean and 10% below their class means. The two extreme groups of children represent collectively no more than 30% of the sample in any given year. All other children are considered *Average*. It is important to note that the isolate children do represent an extreme group that does not often interact with their peers. In kindergarten and first grade, isolates interacted with peers only 13% of the time.

In an effort to examine possible social problem solving differences between children who experience *continuously* high, moderate, or low rates of peer interaction, we identified those children who were targeted as either isolate, average, or sociable in both kindergarten and first grade. Out of a total sample of 72 children, 8 were identified as isolates, 30 as average, and 10 as sociables in each of the 2 years. Social problem solving data were available in both kindergarten and first grade for all but one of the isolate and 11 of the average children. An initial analysis of variance indicated nonsignificant differences between groups on a measure of verbal intelligence (PPVT).

An analysis of the number of SPST alternatives produced by each child revealed nonsignificant differences between groups for the number of relevant solutions to the social problems. However, a significant interaction was discovered, and post-hoc comparisons revealed that in kindergarten sociable children generated significantly more alternatives ($M=15.10$) than either the average ($M=12.68$) or isolate ($M=12.43$) children. In first grade, there were no significant differences between groups. In addition, only the isolate ($M=14.87$) and normal ($M=15.00$) children's strategy repertoires increased significantly from kindergarten to first grade. The sociable children's repertoire actually declined somewhat ($M=13.30$), but the change was nonsignificant.

A similar analysis was computed for flexibility scores. Once again grade and group main effects were nonsignificant. However, a target group $\times$ grade interaction was found. In kindergarten, sociable children were more flexible ($M=16.00$) than their isolate ($M=12.14$) and average ($M=11.53$) counterparts. In first grade, nonsignificant differences exist between groups. Only the isolate ($M=15.86$) and average ($M=16.95$) children evidenced significant change from kindergarten to first grade.

Finally, an analysis was performed on the proportion of SPST alternatives that fell into each of the five categories. Nonsignificant group, grade, and category effects and interactions were found.

In summary, highly sociable children seem to have a head-start in both strategy breadth (number of relevant solutions) and strategy sequencing (flexibility) when in kindergarten. By first grade, however, all differences are washed out. As reported in the section of age differences, asymptote may have been reached on breadth of strategy for object acquisition problems by most children in first grade. It may well be that the sociable children reached ceiling by kindergarten; the other two groups may have done so by first grade. Thus, for highly sociable children there may be little room for improvement; the slight declines in strategy repertoire and flexibility may well reflect their conceptualization of what the most appropriate strategies are in object conflict situations. Once the appropriate strategies are discovered, then verbally *expressed* response breadth and flexibility may remain the same or it may wain. That is, once children discover what "works," or once they meet some personal cognitive criteria of sufficiency, there is little need to produce further responses. One interpretation of these results is that social-cognitive scores can be predicted reliably from observed sociability in kindergarten but that the relation is no longer significant in first grade. The lack of significant main effects for breadth of strategy repertoire and for response flexibility support this conclusion, as do the "catch up" interaction results.

Given the concern for response ceiling being reached by first grade, another hypothetical social problem was introduced into our longitudinal project. Friendship initiation was thought to be more appropriate and perhaps more challenging than object acquisition for second grade children. Briefly, children were asked how central characters in a series of stories should go about making friends with a same-sex child. As with the SPST, the age of the target child was varied. In addition to coding the number of relevant alternatives and response flexibility as on the SPST, specific strategies generated fell into one of the following categories: (1) *invitation* to join in play ("Would you like to come over to my house?"); (2) *prosocial* and complementary means to initiate friendship (e.g., being nice to the other; making the target feel good about him/herself); (3) *adult intervention;* (4) *conversation openers* (e.g., "Hi, how're ya doin'?"); (5) *nonassertive,* nondirective friendship seeking acts (proximity seeking; making suggestions or "hinting" at desire for joint play); (6) *assertive,* directive friendship seeking acts ("Be my friend"; "I'm gonna be your friend").

These friendship problems were administered individually to 85 second-graders whose behaviors were observed during 48 minutes of free play (12 minutes for each of four sessions in which the child was in a playroom with three same-sex age-mates. The three playmates differed for each session). Observed isolate behavior correlated significantly and negatively with the proportions of invitations and prosocial suggestions for initiating friendship. A positive correlation was evinced between isolate behavior and non-assertive friendship bids. The frequency of observed sociable play correlated positively with the number of relevant categories and the proportions of invitations and prosocial bids.

As with the SPST correlations (Rubin et al., 1984), these results portray the child who displays a high frequency of isolate behavior as a somewhat passive, nonassertive problem solver. Yet, once again, the significant correlations could best be described as in the low to moderate range (range = .22 to .35). Thus, to test the relation between social problem solving competence and the *cumulative* impact of sociability, children were targeted into one of four groups. First, there were children who were targeted as isolates in 2 of their 3 years in the study, one of those years being second grade. Eight children met these criteria, six of whom had been targeted as isolates in all 3 years.

A second group was comprised of all children identified as isolates in kindergarten and/or first grade, but not in second grade. There were 11 children in this group. The third group consisted of those children whose sociability scores were "average" for all 3 years. Fourteen children met these criteria. Finally, the fourth group was comprised of second-grade sociable children who were targeted as either sociable or average in the previous years ($n=10$). Four of these children had been targeted as sociable in all 3 years.

The friendship initiation data were analysed in terms of the number of solutions produced by each child. The analyses indicated neither main effects nor an interaction for group or category. A subsequent analysis was computed for the flexibility scores. The results indicated nonsignificant groups differences. As an aside, similar analyses were computed with the SPST stories. Neither significant main effects nor interactions were found for any SPST variables.

In summary, the analyses presented above indicate quite clearly that children who are extremely withdrawn *throughout* the early years of childhood (kindergarten through second grade) do not suffer from social-cognitive deficits when in second grade. Although kindergarten isolates perform more poorly than their more sociable age-mates on the SPST, by second grade the cumulative impact on social problem solving thinking is practically nil. These data do not support the contention that a high frequency of peer interaction is a necessary ingredient in facilitating developing knowledge concerning social problem solving. It may be that a relatively low level of peer interaction is sufficient for stimulating social problem solving development, or that children may gain knowledge of social strategies by observing others in action or through conversations with adults. We can generalize this statement also to another area of social cognition, that is, perspective-taking. Employing the same four-way target classification scheme as described above, we have found that continued isolate status into second grade does not predict role-taking deficits as assessed by Flavell et al.'s (1968) 7-4 picture story. Whether social isolation in early childhood affects other areas of social-cognition remains unknown.

These results have a number of important implications. First, for years psychologists have been concerned with the possibility that social withdrawal during the *early* years places children "at risk" for a variety of problems (see Strain, Kerr, & Ragland, 1981 for a relevant review). This hypothesis may, in fact, turn out to be true; however it is clear from our data that social cognitive development is not part and parcel of the risk factors. In terms of our model, the strategies produced by young isolate children are alike in numerosity and, for the most part, in quality to those of more sociable children. Given these data we would beg to differ from Spivack and Shure (1974) and others (e.g., Conger & Keane, 1981) who argue that the effort, time, and finance required to provide social problem solving cognitive training to *young* withdrawn children is well-worthwhile. Instead, we would like to suggest the following.

First, we believe that many psychologists have misinterpreted or misrepresented the theories that have guided research concerning social withdrawal in early childhood. If one reads Piaget's (1962) and Sullivan's (1953) work carefully, one would not expect a lack of peer interaction to have an impact on social-cognitive development until the concrete operational period or until the middle years of childhood. Both of these theorists would have suggested that mutual respect for the opinions and values of peers and the conviction that compromise with peers is necessary for the development of normal and trusting friendship relations is not evident until *at least* 8 to 10 years of age. Perhaps, then, social withdrawal does have an impact on social-cognitive development, but not until the middle or late childhood years. We await the collection of relevant data to examine this suggestion.

Second, young isolate children may, in fact, demonstrate deficits in other domains relevant to social problem solving. For example, they may evidence social-behavioral difficulties. These difficulties might emanate from affective factors (e.g., anxiety, feelings of low self-efficacy) that mediate between competent social cognizing and the actual production of social behaviors. We examine this possibility in another section.

Social problem solving thinking and peer status in early childhood. As mentioned, another group of children considered to be "at risk" for later psychological and educational problems are those who are rejected by their peers. It may well be that a particular constellation of behaviors is responsible for peer acceptance and rejection in childhood. Recent research has indicated that aggressive behaviors (Coie & Kupersmidt, 1983; Dodge, 1983; Rubin & Clark, 1983; Rubin & Daniels-Beirness, 1983), immature or inappropriate solitary play (Coie & Kupersmidt, 1983; Rubin, 1982b), and hovering, whining, and calling undo attention to the self (Putallaz, 1983; Putallaz & Gottman, 1981) are all predictive of peer rejection in childhood. Popularity, on the other hand, is associated with the display of prosocial and cooperative behavior (e.g., Dodge, 1983; Rubin & Daniels-Beirness, 1983).

In recent years several psychologists have suggested that the display of aggressive and prosocial behaviors in early childhood is mediated by social cognition (see Shantz, 1983 for a relevant review). Thus, the abilities to take the perspectives of others or to think about solutions to social problems have been postulated to correlate negatively with those behaviors associated with peer rejection and positively with behaviors related to peer popularity. However, the direct link between sociometric status and hypothetical-reflective social problem solving has not been subject to much scrutiny over the years.

Most research concerning the relations between social problem solving and peer status has focussed on the mid-to-late years of childhood. Thus, for example, popular second through fifth-graders have been found to display more knowledge, and more relevant solutions to hypothetical object conflict and friendship initiation dilemmas than their less popular peers (e.g., Gottman, Gonso, & Rasmussen, 1975; Richard & Dodge, 1982). Rejected children produce a greater number of inappropriate or unique strategies on dilemmas concerning the provision of aid to someone in need of help (Ladd & Oden, 1979). In one of the few studies of young children, Asher and Renshaw (1981) found that unpopular kindergarteners suggested more inappropriately negative and aggressive strategies and fewer relationship enhancing strategies for dilammas concerning friendship initiation and maintenance, and object conflicts.

In our research program we have found that sociometric status correlates significantly with SPST performance in kindergarten (Rubin & Daniels-Beirness, 1983; Rubin, Daniels-Beirness, & Hayvren, 1982). Thus, popular kindergarteners produce significantly more relevant and prosocial strategies and fewer agonistic strategies than their less popular age-mates. Interestingly, of 32 observational, teacher rating, perspective-taking, and social problem solving variables employed in a multiple regression analysis, only three significantly predicted sociometric status in kindergarten. Two of these variables were the number of agonistic SPST strategies (a negative contribution) and the number of relevant alternatives (a positive contribution). The third contributing variable was the number of observed prosocial peer interchanges. In our first-grade data base, however, the only significant social problem solving correlate of peer popularity was the proportion of prosocial strategies produced on the SPST.

The hypothesis that social-cognitive development may be directly or indirectly responsible for peer popularity and rejection has also been examined in our corpus of data. Briefly, we have found that the number of relevant SPST solutions produced in kindergarten predicts popularity in first grade; alternately the proportion of agonistic and manipulation of affect strategies offered in kindergarten predicts peer rejection in first grade (Rubin & Daniels-Beirness, 1983). In a more recent analysis of our longitudinal data set we have discovered that the number of SPST categories and the proportion of prosocial strategies produced in kindergarten predict peer popularity in *second* grade ($n=40$), $rs=.35$ and $.38$

respectively. These concurrent and predictive correlational data are thus very much supportive of those reported by other researchers who have studied older children. Moreover, our data provide a small hint concerning the possible causes of peer rejection; unpopular children appear to have a higher percentage of aggressive means in their strategy repertoires, whereas popular children's repertoires contain a higher percentage of prosocial means. These variations in repertoire composition may reflect differences in the availability of aggressive and prosocial strategies during the strategy selection phase of the social problem solving process. The increased availability of specific types of strategies may make these strategies more likely to be acted upon than other, less salient behaviors.

We should note that sociometric status, like observed social withdrawal in early childhood is not an extremely stable phenomenon (Hymel, 1983). Employing a peer-rating scale (Asher, Singleton, Tinsley, & Hymel, 1979) we have found that the correlation between kindergarten and first grade status is .48, $p<.001$ $(n=72)$. As with behavioral isolation, it seems to us that the children at greatest risk for social and educational problems are those who evidence peer rejection over a long period of time. In order to examine this hypothesis we identified children as rejected, average, and popular in both kindergarten and first grade. Rejected children were those whose same-sex sociometric rating scores (after standardization) fell into the bottom third for their grade; popular children's scores fell into the top third for their grade. All other children were considered "average."

Of the 19 rejected kindergarteners for whom sociometric data were available in first grade, 12 maintained their status. Fifteen of the 28 popular kindergarteners maintained their status, whereas only 7 of 25 kindergarteners remained "average." Social problem solving data were available in both grades for 8 rejected children, 13 popular children, and 6 average children. An analysis of variance was computed for the number of alternatives that fell within each category. A non-significant group main effect was found; thus the number of relevant categories did not vary with sociometric status. However, a significant three-way interaction between group, grade, and category was discovered and indicated that in kindergarten, the rejected children produced fewer prosocial strategies $(M=8.14)$ than the average $(M=13.00)$ and popular children $(M=14.78)$. This finding was replicated in first grade (Rejected $M=7.14$; Average $M=16.37$; Popular $M=13.33$). Although the number of agonistic strategies did not vary significantly between groups in both grades, it is important to note that the rejected children were as likely to suggest an agonistic as prosocial strategy in kindergarten $(M=5.29)$ and first grade $(M=6.57)$. For average and popular children, however, the numbers of agonistic strategies produced in both grades were significantly fewer than the number of prosocial strategies ("Average" kindergarten $M=1.62$, first grade $M=1.12$; "Popular" kindergarten

$M = 1.89$; first grade $M = 3.78$). Thus, it would appear as if aggressive strategies represent a more significant option in the repertoire hierarchy for rejected children than for their more peer favored age-mates. An analysis of flexibility scores did not reveal any significant results.

Briefly, we administered the SPST and the peer sociometric ratings to children in second grade. Despite problems of restricted range on the SPST we discovered that second grade popularity correlated positively and significantly with the number of relevant categories and the proportion of suggested prosocial strategies. Popularity correlated negatively with the proportion of agonistic strategies. These data are entirely consistent with the kindergarten and first grade findings. For the friendship initiation problems, however, *none* of the correlations with sociometric status were significant.

Taken together, our data suggest that rejected children do think about solving some social problems differently than their more popular age-mates. For the object acquisition or activity manipulation problems presented in the SPST, rejected children are as likely to suggest the use of an agonistic strategy as a prosocial strategy. Average and popular children appear to have a more well-defined strategy hierarchy in which prosocial strategies outnumber agonistic ones by a substantive margin.

It would be somewhat of a conceptual leap to suggest that these differences in thinking about solutions to social goals are responsible, in part, for the consistent finding that rejected children are viewed by their peers and teachers, and are observed to be, more aggressive than their more popular counterparts. Nevertheless, the possibility that this situation might be the case is intriguing and should be explored in future research.

Insofar as friendship initiation problems are concerned, we did not find evidence for problems of strategy breadth and strategy selection in rejected second-grade children. Thus it would seem that situations involving peer confrontation are more problematic than situations involving social initiations for rejected children to think about. It may be, however, that rejected children differ from other children when they actually attempt to initiate friendship in everyday situations. Moreover, it could be that problems concerning initiation strategies become more evident for rejected young children at older ages than those considered herein.

Given our data, as well as those of others, we thus conclude that there is some basis for social-cognitive intervention among rejected children. It appears as if there is some real need to train young rejected children to think about the consequences of agonistic strategy production during peer confrontation situations. The fact that aggressive behaviors can be harmful and that negative reputations are more likely strengthened by such acts should be brought to the attention of young rejected children who evince non-normative social problem solving thinking.

Naturalistic social problem solving

During the late 1970s, research concerning pragmatics in children began to blossom (e.g., Ervin-Tripp & Mitchell-Kernan, 1977). In some respects this work served as a reaction to the extensive referential communication literature in which young children were described as psychologically egocentric and communicatively unsophisticated (see Glucksberg, Krauss, & Higgins, 1975 for a relevant review of this early work on referential communication). The more recent naturalistic approach taken by those psychologists studying pragmatics presented a picture of preschoolers being extremely competent, non-egocentric communicators (e.g., Dore 1978; Garvey, 1975). Yet these discourse analyses were generally non-developmental in nature (preschoolers seemed uniformly to comprise the subject group of interest) and the data analyses themselves were, for the most part, merely descriptive (see Gottman & Parkhurst, 1978 and Levin & Rubin, 1983 for relevant reviews). Given this context, Levin and Rubin (1983) conducted a developmental study of how children attempted verbally to get others to do what they wanted them to do; as such, the study could be construed as one of the first attempts to study social problem solving in the natural setting.

The primary unit of analysis in the Levin and Rubin study was the verbal request for action. The request for action was defined as any verbal utterance in which the "intended meaning effect" (Grice, 1969) was that the listener carry out a specified action (e.g., "Come over here."; "Look at me."; "Can you give me that crayon?").

One purpose of the study was to examine the frequencies with which children of various ages attempted to direct the activities of their peers. Thus, the requests of preschool and first-and third-grade children were observed during unstructured dyadic interaction. The proportion of requests to the total number of utterances did not change with age. To some extent then, preschoolers were observed to be as socially directive as their older counterparts, a result that might be taken as evidence contradicting the assumption that early childhood represents a stage of egocentric communication.

The second research question addressed the issue of repertoire breadth. In the literature on child discourse there appear to be two request categories that can be used to achieve the broad goal of "changing another's behavior." These categories include the *direct* request which is issued in the imperative ("Gimme dat Ernie doll.") and the *indirect* request in which the intended meaning is imbedded in an interrogative (e.g., "How 'bout lending me your scissors?"), a declarative (e.g., "You could gimme that crayon."), or an inferred request (e.g., "Those dolls should be on the house."). The latter, indirect request forms, because of their non-literal meanings, are more cognitively complex than the imperative. Nevertheless, preschoolers produced proportionally as many indirect requests as did their older counterparts.

The third major question in the Levin and Rubin study focussed on strategy/request outcome. In these analyses, developmental differences were found for percentage success in requestive acts. Children in first and third grades were more successful in obtaining compliance to requests than the preschoolers.

Finally, Levin and Rubin went beyond previous research by examining sequences of requests. Older children were expected to demonstrate greater strategy flexibility and less rigidity following failure than younger children. This prediction was based primarily on findings taken from the referential communication literature that the responses of young children to the question "Can you tell me anything more about this drawing?" (i.e., can the child provide more information concerning a particular referential stimulus) were more likely to be repetitive of the original, whereas those of older children were more likely to contain modifications or rephrasings (e.g., Glucksberg & Krauss, 1967; Rubin, 1973). Consistent with the prediction, and consistent with the developmental data concerning flexibility on hypothetical-reflective social problem solving measures (Rubin & Krasnor, 1983), Levin and Rubin found that the percentage of rigid re-request strategies decreased with age (31.3%, 18.4%, and 8.6% for preschool, first grade and third grade respectively), and flexibility of requests after failure increased (17.2%, 22.4%, and 29.0% respectively).

The examination of developmental differences in request forms and outcomes, and the flexibility analysis presented in this study made novel contributions to the social problem solving literature. Most important, the data were relevant to the strategy, outcome, and sequencing components of our social problem solving model. Insofar as the use of requests is concerned, developmental differences were not found for differential employment of direct and indirect requests. However, social problem solving outcome became more successful and the use of flexible alternatives following initial strategy failure increased with age.

From a social problem solving perspective, the study's limitations were readily apparent. The data did not include information on the specific content of the requests. Moreover, the range of strategies studied was relatively narrow, and there was no analysis of the effect of specific task features or environmental variables.

The Levin and Rubin (1983) communication study was conducted at approximately the same time as the Krasnor and Rubin (1978) social problem solving training and validation study described earlier. On the basis of the results of both of these studies, it was clear that a more thorough observational procedure was needed for the study of naturalistic social problem solving. Drawing from our first attempt at outlining a theoretical framework (Krasnor & Rubin, 1981), we decided to focus on four points of social problem solving assessment: (a) the influence of situational variables; (b) the repertoire of strategies; (c) the linkage between strategy and situational variables, judged on the basis of effectiveness and/or acceptability; and (d) the sequence of strategies and utilization of feedback after failure. It was also necessary to develop a taxonomy of goals and strategies that had a wider scope than those used in previous studies. The methodology chosen for use had to meet several criteria. First, the setting had to be unstructured, so that the child was free to interact with a variety of targets and to pursue self-chosen goals. The setting also had to allow extended periods of observation, so that sequences of social problem solving behavior could be followed to their conclusion. The methodological procedure had to provide sufficient contextual detail so that goals could be judged and strategic outcomes could be determined.

The observational taxonomy was developed for a study (Krasnor, 1981; Krasnor, 1982; Krasnor & Rubin, 1983) in which the major purposes were (a) to determine the frequency distribution of social problem solving goals, strategies, and outcomes; (b) to test the relative importance of goals, strategies, and individual variables in predicting social problem solving success; and (c) to assess the interdependencies between targets, strategies, and goals. The ability to "match" strategies and goals to the target was considered an index of social competence.

Fifteen preschoolers were each observed for 10 one-half hour sessions using a focal individual sampling method. Data were collected using narrative audio recordings. Social problem solving attempts were identified as those behaviors which were judged as socially-oriented, directive in nature, and initiated by the focal child. Once an individual social problem solving attempt was identified, its target, strategy, goal, and outcome were coded. Categories and their definitions are presented in Table 1.1. Attempts judged to be directed at the same goal were grouped into "episodes." Flexibility and persistence after failure were scored within these series of related social problem solving strategies.

A total of 6,338 social problem solving attempts were identified. The most frequently observed goal was "other action" followed by attempts to obtain information, elicit attention, and to make non-specific initiations. Stopping the action of another, object acquisition, affection seeking, and attempting to obtain permission for self action were observed to occur less frequently. There were no sex differences in the distribution of goals. The frequency with which goals were observed may be taken tentatively as an index of preschoolers' social priorities. The one surprise to us was the relatively low frequency of object acquisition goals; this is the most commonly presented goal in hypothetical-reflective measures of social problem solving. Yet, out of the eight broadly defined goals we examined, object acquisition fell seventh in terms of relative frequency.

Children's strategy *repertoires* can also be inferred from our observations. Again sex differences were not found for strategy distribution. Directives, descriptions, orienting acts, and questions, were the most commonly observed social problem solving strategies. The least common strategies included all agonistic acts, claims, and playnoises.

The ability of preschoolers to match their social problem solving goals and

TABLE 1.1
Categorization of Social Problem-Solving Attempts

STRATEGY

Directives	Personal need statements, direct imperatives, imbedded imperatives, permission directives, bribes/threats
Suggestions	Propositions, want questions
Statements	Descriptions of objects, persons, events, etc.
Claims	Assertive statements which claim ownership
Interrogatives	Direct questions, rhetorical questions, titles or greetings
Play noise	Nonword or playful vocalizations during play
Unintelligible	Inaudible vocalizations
Orienting acts	Actions which direct attention to an object, event, or person (e.g., showing, pointing)
Object agonistic	Use of force or threatened force directed at object
Person agonistic	Use of force or threatened force directed at person
Affiliative	Positive, nonforceful contact with another (e.g., hugging, holding hands, giving object)

GOAL

Stop action	Attempts to prevent or stop the action or intended action of another
Self-action	Attempts to obtain permission or to perform an action made by the focal child (e.g., to join ongoing play)
Other action	Attempts to elicit an active response from another not otherwise coded
Object acquisition	Attempts to gain sole possession or access to an obect or activity
Attention/ Acknowledgment	Attempts to direct another's attention to a concrete object, event, or person
Affection/ Comfort	Attempts to elicit or give positive, prosocial, physical or verbal affection
Information	Attempts to elicit information, clarification, or agreement not otherwise coded
Nonspecific initiations	Attempts to initiate interaction (no interaction with target within the full 10-sec interval preceding the attempt) not otherwise coded

OUTCOME

Success	Action specified in the attempt is performed by the target within the 10-sec interval following the interval following the interval in which the attempt occurred and prior to the next related attempt; when an object is taken from the target without a contingent response, the outcome is judged successful if the focal child retains the object for 10 seconds; similarly, if the goal is stop action, the specified action must be stopped for a full 10-sec interval
Partial success	Target specifically indicates a need for clarification or performs part of the specified act within 10 seconds of the focal child's attempt and before the next related attempt
Failure	Focal child performs the act himself; nontarget other performs the act; target performs act after the 10-sec period; all other noncompliance circumstances
Uncertain	Either the goal is unknown or the target response is not observed or is unintelligible

(From Krasnor, 1982)

TABLE 1.2
Goal by Target Distribution of Social Problem Solving Attempts

Goal	Target				
	Boys	Girls	Teacher	Multiple	Total Frequency
Other-Action	586 [1] (40.3) [2] (24.7)	522 (35.9) (28.3)	276 (19.0) (15.2)	71 (4.9) (28.6)	1,455 (23.2)
Stop-Action	466 (65.8) (19.6)	196 (27.7) (10.6)	26 (3.7) (1.4)	20 (2.8) (2.9)	708 (11.3)
Object Acquisition	171 (40.4) (7.2)	160 (37.8) (8.7)	83 (19.6) (4.6)	9 (2.1) (3.6)	423 (6.7)
Self-Action	125 (29.3) (5.3)	108 (25.3) (5.9)	177 (41.4) (9.8)	17 (4.0) (6.9)	427 (6.8)
Attention	318 (31.1) (13.4)	181 (17.7) (9.8)	485 (47.5) (26.7)	37 (3.6) (14.9)	1,021 (16.2)
Affection	7 (17.1) (0.3)	22 (53.7) (1.1)	12 (29.3) (0.7)	0 (0.0) (0.0)	41 (0.1)
Information	305 (31.9) (12.8)	377 (39.4) (20.4)	243 (25.4) (13.4)	31 (3.2) (12.5)	965 (15.2)
Initiation	396 (31.7) (16.7)	279 (22.3) (15.1)	513 (41.0) (28.3)	63 (5.0) (25.4)	1,251 (20.0)
Total	2,374 (37.8)	1,845 (29.4)	1,815 (28.9)	248 (3.9)	6,282

[1] Row percentages.
[2] Column percentages.
(From Krasnor, 1982)

strategies to situational variables (in this case, the target of the social problem solving attempt) was then examined (Krasnor, 1982). The distributions of specific goals and strategies over different target groups (males, females, teachers) are presented in Tables 1.2 and 1.3. Our data analyses revealed that *goals* were clearly distributed differently among the target groups. Boys received a relatively high percentage of stop action goals and a low percentage of affection goals, compared to baseline levels. Teachers were frequently targets of attempts to seek attention, nonspecific conversational initiatives, and permission for self-action, but received relatively few other-action, object acquisition and stop-action goals. Girl targets received relatively more affection goals than expected by chance and relatively fewer attention goals. As shown in Table 1.2, not all goals were equally differentiated. It may be that some goals are appropriate for all target groups (e.g., initiating conversation), whereas others (e.g., stop action) are

TABLE 1.3
Strategy by Target Distribution of Social Problem-Solving Attempts

			Target		
Goal	Boys	Girls	Teacher	Multiple	Total Frequency
Directives	860 [1] (39.2) [2] (24.9)	682 (31.1) (24.8)	565 (25.8) (22.6)	84 (3.8) (23.0)	2,191 (24.2)
Suggestions	165 (38.9) (4.8)	187 (44.1) (6.8)	53 (12.5) (2.1)	19 (4.5) (5.2)	424 (4.7)
Descriptions	828 (36.0) (24.0)	645 (28.0) (23.4)	719 (31.2) (28.8)	110 (4.8) (30.1)	2,302 (25.5)
Claims	91 (61.5) (2.6)	44 (29.7) (1.6)	8 (5.4) (0.3)	5 (3.4) (1.4)	148 (1.6)
Questions	386 (31.4) (11.2)	468 (38.1) (17.0)	325 (26.5) (13.0)	49 (4.0) (13.4)	1,228 (13.5)
Callings	110 (33.2) (3.2)	75 (22.7) (2.7)	136 (41.1) (5.4)	10 (3.0) (2.7)	331 (3.6)
Play Noises	77 (61.6) (2.2)	15 (12.0) (0.5)	20 (16.0) (0.8)	13 (10.4) (3.5)	125 (1.4)
Object Agonistic	215 (63.2) (6.2)	105 (30.9) (3.8)	16 (4.7) (0.6)	4 (1.2) (1.1)	340 (3.8)
Person Agonistic	70 (61.4) (2.0)	41 (36.0) (1.5)	2 (1.8) (0.1)	1 (0.9) (0.3)	114 (1.3)
Orienting	438 (31.8) (12.7)	393 (24.1) (14.3)	545 (39.5) (21.8)	53 (4.6) (16.8)	1,379 (15.2)
Affiliative	212 (43.8) (6.1)	158 (32.6) (5.7)	107 (22.1) (4.3)	7 (1.4) (1.9)	484 (5.3)
Total	3,452 (38.1)	2,753 (30.4)	2,496 (27.5)	365 (4.0)	9,066

[1] Row percentages.
[2] Column percentages.
(From Krasnor, 1982)

inappropriate for specific groups (e.g., teachers). Similarly, it may be that some goals (e.g., affection seeking) are best predicted by the identity of particular individuals rather than by a general target group category.

Social *strategies* were likewise found to be differentiated by target group. Boys, for example, received a relatively high percentage of object-agonistic acts, whereas girls received approximately as many of these strategies as expected and teachers received significantly fewer than expected. Strategies showed varying levels of differentiation by target group. Unlike the sharp distinctions demonstrated for agonistic acts, questions showed close to baseline probabilities across target groups. Interestingly, the greatest differentiation of strategies was found for teacher targets. This finding might indicate that children monitor their strategy selection and deployment more closely for adult (non-parent) targets than for peer targets. It may be also that strategy deployment varies with regard to other individual differences between peers. For example, as described in a following section, we examined whether children who evidenced low sociability status received more assertive strategies than higher status age-mates.

In addition to goal and strategy selection, a third component of our social problem solving model, *outcome,* was examined. Outcome was defined as percentage success, partial success, or failure. In general, the children were successful in 56.7% of their social problem solving attempts. Successes were significantly more common than failure (39.2%) or partial success (4.1%). Yet, failure in naturalistic social problem solving was relatively common. Partial success was relatively rare, indicating that compliance, when it did occur, was either "all or nothing." It was also apparent that if compliance was to occur, it occurred relatively quickly (within 10 seconds) after the social problem solving attempt.

One of our major concerns was the identification of task and individual factors associated with social problem solving effectiveness. We assumed that the social problem solving goal would be a significant predictor of outcome. Some goals (e.g., attention seeking) may be less costly than others (e.g., other action) in terms of effort required by the target. As such, from one perspective, the goal of the social problem solving attempt may be the most important predictor of the outcome of that attempt. Some goals (e.g., attention seeking) may have consistently successful outcomes, while others (e.g., other action) may be expected to result in failure at relatively high levels of probability. In general, we hypothesized that goals which required relatively little interruption of the target's activity or involved little "cost" to the target would tend to be successful.

A second potential outcome predictor of social problem solving was *type of strategy* employed. Some strategies may be particularly successful in social problem solving interactions (e.g., bribing), while others may be predictably ineffective (e.g., just waiting). Knowledge of the specific strategy employed in social problem solving attempts may thus be used to predict outcome.

In addition to goal and strategy dimensions, *target identity* can be used as an outcome predictor. Some targets ("pushovers") may be more consistently compliant than others (see discussion concerning socially withdrawn children below). Target variables that have been found to relate to outcome in earlier studies include sex and age (Whiting & Whiting, 1975), relative peer popularity (Putallaz & Gottman, 1981), and dominance (Strayer, 1981).

A fourth potential predictor of outcome may be the *problem solver's identity.* Particular individuals may be consistently successful, independent of the specific strategy, target, or goal used in the social problem solving attempt. Intelligence (Charlesworth, 1976), flexibility (Spivack & Shure, 1974), or social status (Putallaz & Gottman, 1981) may be some of the personal attributes associated with individual differences in success.

In an effort to discover whether social problem solving outcome could be predicted reliably from knowledge of the goals, strategies, target groups, and the problem solver's identity, a series of reduction of uncertainty (Steinberg, 1977) analyses was computed. Although none of these four variables accounted for a high percentage of variance, knowledge of the goal (7.5%) and of the individual problem solver's identity (7.5%) showed the greatest reduction of uncertainty in predicting outcome, over knowledge of baseline probabilities alone. The specific strategies used and identity of the target group predicted little outcome variance (respectively, 3.3% and 0.9% reductions of uncertainty).

Analyses of the outcome data also revealed the relative effectiveness of *specific* goals, strategies, and targets, as well as the differential effectiveness of specific strategies for each goal. The goals of eliciting attention (71.5% success), nonspecific initiations (62.6%), and information-seeking (61.1%) were the most successful. Least successful were social problem solving attempts with object-acquisition (48.7%) and other action goals (46.2%). The results are consistent with our hypothesis that "low cost" social goals would be more successful than "high cost" goals.

Analyses of the relation between the identity of the target group and social problem solving success yielded only a trend level of significance. Multiple targets showed somewhat less compliance (47.4%) than other target groups. Interestingly, teachers (61.0%) showed approximately the same proportion of compliance as girl targets (58.5%) and slightly greater compliance than boy targets (53.0%).

As indicated above, strategies explained only a negligible percentage of the variation in outcome. Although we will not discuss the details of this analysis (see Krasnor & Rubin, 1983), we will briefly summarize the results of the strategy × goal analysis in which we examined the relative effectiveness of specific strategies for each goal. The two major questions in this analysis were: (a) Given a specific goal, are there variations in the relative effectiveness of different strategies? (b) Are specific strategies effective for some goals but not others? In other action goals, for example, social problem solving attempts which included descriptions, callings, questions, or affiliative acts were more successful than expected on the basis of baseline probabilities; suggestions, playnoises, and agonistic acts used for these goals were less successful than expected. Although agonistic acts were relatively ineffective for eliciting action on the part of another, they tended to be among the more effective strategies for the goals of gaining attention, self-action, and object acquisition. No single strategy emerged as generally successful across all goals, indicating, perhaps, that a broad repertoire of strategies may be necessary for overall social effectiveness.

Knowledge of the problem solver's identity also led to a reduction of uncertainty in predicting social problem solving outcome. Several individual difference variables were examined in an attempt to understand this relationship. Intelligence, as measured by PPVT scores, was significantly and positively correlated with success (Krasnor, 1981). Individual differences in flexibility of strategy sequencing after failure were unrelated to overall success. This finding was surprising, given the theoretical assumptions of our social problem solving model. It may be that flexibility is not a *generally* adaptive strategy, but its success may be dependent on situational variables such as the target's identity or the specific type of response received from the target following the initial attempt.

Individual differences in the degree of differentiation of social problem solving behavior on the basis of situational variables was also expected to relate to social problem solving effectiveness. Basically we wanted to ascertain whether knowledge concerning the degree to which a child's strategies and goals were differentiated by target could predict social problem solving outcome. This differentiation was reflected in the percentage reduction of uncertainty in predicting the strategy or goal of a social problem solving attempt given knowledge of target group, over predictions made on baseline probabilities alone. Two indices were thus calculated for each child. One index was based on the child's own strategy × target matrix and the second index was calculated from his or her goal × target matrix. These indices were correlated with individual success percentages. Thus, significant positive correlations would indicate that situation-related differentiation was associated with social effectiveness. For both indices, with the effects of IQ partialled, the correlations between differentiation and success were positive and significant.

In summary, then, characteristics of individual problem solvers which seemed to be most strongly related to success were intelligence (as measured by PPVT), and observed differentiation of social problem solving goals and strategies by targets. Other social problem solving components examined were the persistence and flexibility in strategy sequencing after failure (Krasnor, 1981). Persistence was clearly demonstrated by the preschoolers; over half of all failed social problem solving attempts were reattempted. The probability of success once a previous failure had occurred, however, was significantly less than the baseline success probability. Given a prior failure, the children tended to modify their strategies. Such flexibility, however, did not significantly increase the probability of success over a simple rigid repetition of the prior unsuccessful strategy.

Social isolation and social problem solving in the natural setting.   In an earlier section we considered whether socially withdrawn children differed from their more sociable peers when thinking about social problems. The data indicated few differences in social-cognitive reasoning for second-grade children who had stable histories of sociability status. We now consider whether there are individual differences in the ways in which children go about solving their real-life personal problems.

The research described below stemmed directly from Rubin's earlier work on children's requests (Levin & Rubin, 1983). The particular questions asked in this study by Rubin and Borwick (1984) included: (a) Do isolate children produce fewer requests directed at their peers during dyadic free play then their more sociable age-mates? If there is any generalization of isolate status across social situations, then one would expect that withdrawn children (targeted during classroom free-play) would produce fewer requests than their more sociable age-mates during dyadic interaction. (b) Do children who vary with regard to sociability attempt to achieve different goals when issuing requests? (c) Do withdrawn children produce strategies (requests) that are qualitatively different from those of their more sociable counterparts? For example, isolate children may be less assertive than sociable children; consequently, they may be less likely to use imperatives than indirect request forms. (d) Does social problem solving outcome vary with sociability status? Are withdrawn children more likely to have their requests meet with failure? (e) Given social problem solving failure, what is the sequence of children's behavior? Are withdrawn children more likely to give up or to repeatedly use the original request strategies? Are they more likely to attempt to ''save face'' or defer to their partner by changing the topic of conversation or by following the partner's change of subject? In short, through an analysis of children's conversations during dyadic play we (Rubin & Borwick, 1984) attempted to examine individual differences concerning different aspects of the social problem solving model.

The sample was comprised of 10 isolate and 10 sociable preschoolers and kindergarteners who were paired with same-age, same-sex ''average'' children for two 15-minute free play sessions. The targeting procedure was taken directly from Rubin (1982a) as described in a preceding section. Each session was videotaped and subsequently transcribed.

Data were coded as in Levin and Rubin (1983). Thus, the numbers of direct and indirect requests, strategy consequences, and strategies used following failure were coded. In addition the speaker's intention was coded from a viewing of the videotapes and a reading of the transcripts. Request goals included (a) *elicit action:* requests that the partner do something; (b) *stop action;* (c) *acquire object;* (d) *gain attention;* and (e) *joint action:* requests for the partner to join the self in some activity.

The distribution of goal, strategy, and outcome variables was examined in a series of planned comparisons. First, the social problem solving goals and behaviors of isolate children was compared with those of their ''average'' play partners. Second, the goals and behaviors of sociable children were compared with those of their ''average'' play partners. Finally, the communicative data for the average children paired with isolates versus average children paired with sociables were compared. Taken together, these analyses painted pictures not only of the production of social problem solving strategies and outcomes but also of the reception of social problem solving goals and strategies by the protagonist's play partners.

The data indicated that the distribution of children's goals, the means by which they attempt to meet these goals, and the success rates of these means varied in accord with their sociability. Concerning goals, isolate children were more likely to attempt to draw the attention of their peers and were less likely to attempt to acquire objects or elicit action than their "average" playmates. Attention seeking comprised 51% of the social goals of isolate children (as opposed to 26% of the goals of their "average" playmates). These goals required only that the listener glance momentarily at the "speaker" in order for "success" to be coded. The latter two goals were more "costly" in that they required active compliance, often involving the cessation of ongoing activity and movement across the playroom. Thus, isolate children's goals appeared "safer" in that they involved less "cost" to the play partner.

Given the high proportion of low cost goals, one might expect that isolate children's requests would be *more* successful than those of their "average" playmates; they were not. Success rates for isolate and their average playmates were 54% and 65% respectively.

Overall, the isolate children were less socially directive towards their peers than were sociable and average peers. They produced fewer utterances and directives and total numbers of requests than their more sociable age-mates. The number of indirect requests did not differ between groups. These data on frequency of social speech suggest that there is some continuity between sociability as observed in the classroom and in the dyad. The data also indicate that the isolate children employ request strategies at different rates than do more sociable children; they are less inclined to use assertive (direct request) strategies.

Isolate children were also *more* likely than their average playmates to modify their direct requests following failure; thus, when they used assertive strategies, they often met with failure and then resorted to less assertive bids. In short, isolate youngsters seemed able to monitor their strategies and proved quite resilient following failure.

In actuality, the entire corpus of data portrays children as sensitive monitors of their social environments. In many respects the isolates paired with average children resembled average children paired with sociables. The average children paired with sociables were less assertive and less successful than both average children paired with isolates, and sociable children. Following failure, average children paired with sociables were more inclined than sociable children to modify their original requests. It thus appears as if a high sociability status brings with it deference on the part of play partners. The data may well reflect perceived dominance as well as sociability status. At the bottom of the dominance hierarchy are children who (a) may have less confidence in themselves and thus generate low cost, non-assertive attention getting requests, and (b) who give in, or comply, with the requests of their more assertive play partners. These children are, of course, the "isolates." The most dominant children appear to be the sociable, confident children who (a) generate high-cost requests and (b) do not feel compelled to comply with the social problem solving strategies of their lower status partners.

Admittedly, these conclusions are highly inferential. Data concerning dominance status and feelings of self-efficacy are only now being gathered in our studies. Nevertheless, the conclusions are implicitly sound.

In summary, our data concerning the relations between observed sociability and social problem solving thinking and behavior are most informative. We have discovered that *young* isolate children do *not* evince social problem solving cognitive deficits. This is in sharp contrast with the perspective of Spivack and Shure (1974) who believed that children targeted by teachers as withdrawn were "at risk" for social problem solving problems. We have discovered also that extremely withdrawn children are "sensitive" to social situational factors during naturalistic interaction. Their social goals and strategies are less assertive, less "costly," and less successful than those of their more sociable age-mates. These latter data suggest that the isolate child is not at risk for social-cognitive problems; rather their problems may concern self-perceptions and self-efficacy. If, as we believe, young isolate children are more socially anxious than their average and highly sociable counterparts, it might be appropriate to provide them with confidence-boosting peer experiences. From earlier studies (e.g., Rubin, 1982a) we know that isolate children are somewhat less mature cognitively and in their play patterns than more sociable children. Thus, an appropriate intervention technique might be to provide withdrawn children with opportunities to interact with playmates who are on a social and cognitive plane similar to their own; that is, younger children. Furman, Rahe, and Hartup (1979) have actually carried out such an intervention study and found that the procedure was more effective in increasing social interaction than was the pairing of isolate children with age-mates. Whether the same intervention strategy would change the social goals, strategies, and social problem solving outcomes for young isolate children is as yet unknown.

Peer reputation and social problem solving in the natural setting.   Our corpus of data has indicated that rejected children *think* about solving social dilemmas in ways different from their better liked peers. Are there data to suggest that negative peer reputations are drawn, in part, from their social problem solving behaviors?

In a recent study of kindergarteners, 38 children were video-taped during free play with a same-sex age-mate. The communicative data were transcribed in much the same way as described in the preceding section. Same-sex sociometric data were gathered by administering the rating scale developed by Asher et al. (1979). Analyses revealed that the sociometric status correlated negatively and significantly with (a) the issuance of imperatives (direct requests), (b) the employment of "rigid" repetitions of the original strategy following its failure, and (c) the proportion of goals aimed at gaining the partner's attention. Sociometric status correlated positively and significantly with the proportion of initial strategies that failed and were followed by the requestor's change in the topic of conversation, and with the proportion of elicit action goals.

In general, popular children were less forceful in their delivery of requests, and they were more resilient when their original requests failed. These data indicate differences between popular and unpopular children in their social goals, the strategies employed to meet these goals, and in the flexibility of strategy production following a negative outcome.

Interestingly, sociometric data for all children were available in first grade. Thus, we were able to consider whether kindergarten social problem solving behaviors could predict sociometric status one year hence. We found that first grade peer status was correlated positively and significantly with the proportion of social problem solving goals that had a successful outcome, and with those failed attempts that were followed by a modification of the original strategy. First grade status correlated negatively and significantly with the proportion of unsuccessful social problem solving attempts, and the proportion of rigid, inflexible attempts employed following initial failure.

The longitudinal findings reinforce the concurrent correlational results described above. Although specific kindergarten goals did not predict first grade popularity, flexibility in strategy development did. Moreover, socially successful kindergarteners were more popular in first grade than their less successful counterparts.

In summary, our social-cognitive and behavioral data indicate that young rejected children have difficulties in thinking about and in actually solving their social problems appropriately and successfully. Their suggested and actual strategy deployment often consists of assertive acts. Furthermore, the lack of behavioral flexibility following failure may indicate a breakdown in the social problem solving thought process. It may be that when the rejected child's initial social problem solving strategy fails, there is no available default option. Instead, the original strategy is produced automatically or the child gives up. This lack of reflection may be indicative of an impulsive cognitive style on the parts of rejected children. Indeed, in several recent studies, significant correlations have been found between ratings of impulsivity and peer rejection or negative peer status (e.g., Olson, Johnson, Parks, Barrett, & Belleau, 1983; Rubin & Clark, 1983). Furthermore, in a recent study, Krasnor (1983a) found that peer nominations for negative (aggressive) roles in a class play (Masten & Morison, 1981) were negatively related to a naturalistic index of social problem solving persistence following failure. That is, third- and fourth-grade children rated highly on the negative, aggressive Class Play factor were observed to be less likely to pursue a goal following initial failure.

Taken together, these results suggest that rejected children might do well to be involved in cognitive-behavioral social problem solving training programs (e.g., Meichenbaum, 1977; Spivack & Shure, 1974) in efforts to broaden the social problem solving response repertoire, to encourage cognitive and behavioral flexibility, and to "slow down" the cognitive processes involved in strategy selection and persistence.

Social-Cognitive Correlates of the Social Problem Solving Model: Causal Attributions and Social Problem Solving Failure.

Some children continue to pursue their social goals when their original attempts to meet them have failed; others are more likely to give up, to change the subject of conversation, or to follow the countersuggestions of their "targets." What factors contribute to these differences in persistence and response flexibility following social problem solving failure?

There seems to be some evidence that causal attributions for success and failure influence persistence and flexibility in the more impersonal cognitively-oriented domains (e.g., Dweck & Reppucci, 1973; Weiner, 1982). Whether or not these attributions play a role in mediating responses to social problem solving failure is, as yet, unknown.

Basically, causal attributions have been characterized into two major dimensions: stability and locus of origin. For example, a specific cause, such as luck, may be classified as relatively unstable and as having an external locus of origin. Ability, on the other hand, is generally viewed as a relatively stable and internal cause. Evidence from the achievement literature (e.g., Weiner, Kun, & Benesh-Weiner, 1980) has suggested that children with an overall internal locus of control and those who make internal-stable attributions for success and external-unstable attributions for failure tend to show adaptive responses after failure. At present there is scant, but encouraging, evidence that similar attributional processes mediate responses to social failure (Goetz & Dweck, 1980). In the research described below, the relations between social causal attributions and social problem solving was explored in a sample of 40 third-and fourth-grade children (Krasnor, 1983a). This research was designed to examine our social problem solving model-based assumption that an individual's causal attributions for social failure might affect his or her response to negative social problem solving outcomes.

Social attributions were assessed by a group-administered test consisting of a set of common social situations (e.g., attempting to get a peer to play; trying to borrow something from a classmate), expressed in the first person. Each of eight situations was presented twice, once with a successful outcome and once with an unsuccessful outcome. Four causal options followed each situation, representing external-stable, external-unstable, internal-stable, and internal-unstable choices. The children circled the causal alternative which they judged "most likely to be true" from among the four options.

The attributional data were related to indices of both hypothetical-reflective and naturalistic social problem solving skills. Social problem solving cognitions were measured by asking children what a story character could "do or say" to solve each of four peer relations problems (getting a turn on a bike, avoiding a peer's anger, getting peers to stop teasing, and getting to take the class gerbil home when a classmate also wanted it). After the first response, the child was asked what the character could do or say if the original strategy failed. These probes continued until the child failed to generate additional strategies.

The total number of strategies generated by the child was scored as a measure of strategy repertoire and persistence. Three measures of flexibility were also derived: (a) the total number of different strategy categories for all stories combined; (b) the average number of different types of strategies per story; and (c) the proportion of times the child changed his or her strategy category within pairs of successive responses.

The measures of social problem solving sequencing were expected to correlate positively with the two mastery-oriented attributions (internal-stable for social success and external-unstable for social failure). Partial correlations controlling for age and sex of subject revealed that persistence, as measured by the number of strategies generated, was non-significantly related to either attribution. Flexibility, as assessed by sequential changes in strategies following failure (index "c" above) was likewise non-significantly correlated with the attribution measures. A second measure of flexibility (index "a") was also unrelated to the two attribution scores; however, the measure was correlated significantly with a *general* orientation toward internal attributions summed across outcome and stability variables.

The third flexibility measure, average number of different types of strategy per story, was significantly correlated with internal-stable attributions for success, but not to external-unstable attributions for failure. Both of the relations can be explained largely by a positive correlation between this measure of flexibility and the general measure of internality.

Persistence and flexibility in social problem solving behaviors were assessed in 10-minute semi-structured dyadic interactions. Children were paired randomly with same-age, same-sex peers (20 dyads) and were asked to construct one animal from a set of blocks. The interactions were recorded on videotape; the tapes were then coded for social problem solving strategies, goals, and outcomes. The likelihood that a failed goal would be re-attempted, and the probability that a failed strategy would be changed, given that a re-attempt was made, constituted measures of observed persistence and flexibility respectively. Details of the coding system can be found in Krasnor and Rubin (1983). Correlations were controlled for sex and age, and scores from one randomly selected member of each dyad were used.

Although the frequency of internal-stable attributions for social success was non-significantly related to observed persistence after failure, the use of external-unstable attributions for failure was significantly and negatively related to persistence. This relation was relatively specific to this type of attribution, since the correlation between persistence and external-stable attributions for failure was much weaker as was the relation between general externality and persistence.

These results contradicted our expectations based on previous attribution research conducted in the cognitive domain. In this study, children who tended to attribute their failure to external sources were *less* likely to try to solve the social problems following initial failure. This finding suggests that social problems may not be comparable to impersonal problems; in the case of social problems, re-attempts at a failed social goal may not be adaptive if failure is blamed on external factors. For example, "mastery-oriented" children may alter their goal or try to "save face," since the probability of success after previous social problem solving failure may be relatively low (Krasnor & Rubin, 1983). A second interpretation of these results is that the use of internal attributions for failure may be more facilitative of sustained action than an external orientation since control of the social outcomes is perceived to rest in the actor.

The probability that a child would change a strategy after failure (flexibility) was also analyzed in relation to the social attribution measures. Only the measure of overall internality was significantly correlated with observed response flexibility.

In summary, social causal attributions did show some predictable relation with the sequencing components of social problem solving cognitions and behavior. Flexibility in social problem solving thinking and behaviors seems to be related to a *general* preference for internal attributions (or lack of preference for external attributions) rather than to a more differentiated attribution process based on stability and outcome. Contrary to expectation, observed persistence was negatively related to a specific preference for external-unstable attributions. Any interpretation of these findings should be made in the context of methodological problems common to attributional research. These limitations include the use of adult-derived, fixed choice alternatives for the attribution measure, and the aggregation of attributions across a variety of social situations. Nevertheless a connection does seem to exist between the ways that children interpret success and failure and their thoughts and deeds concerning the outcomes of interactive episodes. Perhaps a stronger match between children's casual attributions and their social problem solving skills will emerge when the methodologies used to assess the two variables are derived in the same social context. For example, a child's attributions concerning success or failure in gaining the attention of a peer might be related to her or his responses to failure in parallel attention getting situations. This perspective would enable a more focused examination of the link between children's thoughts about social causes and their responses to their own social problem solving successes and failures.

VII. APPLIED CONCERNS: CASE STUDY APPROACHES TO STUDYING SOCIAL PROBLEM SOLVING

For the past 15 years, researchers have examined the social problem solving process and its correlates in preschool and elementary school-aged children. To this time, almost all of the data in the area have been presented as group-averaged information; thus, an ideographic perspective has been virtually non-existent. Little is known about how individuals organize their social problem solving goals, strategies and outcomes, or about the structure of particular social problem solving strengths and weaknesses.

An individual analysis of social problem solving is particularly important for the development of treatment programs for children who are socially "at risk." In general, the extant social problem solving training research has been characterized by the use of demographic indices of risk or by teacher ratings of aggression and/or withdrawal (e.g., Spivack & Shure, 1974). Treatment groups have typically received a full range of social problem solving training, without regard to specific individual problems and skills. In the following paragraphs we will describe two approaches to an ideographic study of social problem solving in children "at risk" for social problems. In the first approach, the social problem solving behaviors and cognitions of two children who were targeted by a combination of observed sociability and rated sociometric status are described. In the second approach, the child was targeted on the basis of his high social problem solving failure rate during observed interaction with peers and teachers.

Alex is a 5-year-old boy who was observed to be an isolate using the criteria described above and in Rubin (1982a). His sociometric rating scores fell in the bottom third for his age cohort. In short, Alex can be described as an isolated-rejected child. Is it possible that Alex demonstrates social problem solving deficits that may be responsible for his peer status?

First, we turn to the age group norms for the hypothetical-reflective social problem solving skills. A glance at Table 1.4 reveals that on the SPST, Alex deviated from his age-group by one standard deviation on each of the following measures: number of relevant categories, flexibility, and proportions of prosocial, agonistic, and adult intervention strategies. For the first three variables, Alex's performance fell one *SD* below his age group mean; on the latter two variables, this performance fell one *SD* above the mean.

In *second grade*, Alex was still targeted as an isolated-rejected child. He was administered both the SPST and the friendship initiation problems. Although he was able to produce as many relevant and flexible solutions as his age-mates on both sets of problems, the quality of his responses deviated from the norm. For example, on the SPST the age group means (*SD*s) for the proportion of prosocial and agonistic responses were .81 (.18) and .05 (.09) respectively. Alex's relevant scores were .70 and .20 respectively. On the friendship problem the age group means (*SD*s) for the proportion of direct friendship bids ("Be my friend")

TABLE 1.4
Case Study Means and Standard Deviations for
Social Problem-Solving Variables

Variable	Kindergarten[1]		Alex	Tanny
	M	SD		
SPST:				
Categories	13.31	2.42	8.00	15.00
Flexibility	13.12	4.93	8.00	8.00
Proportion prosocial	.73	.25	.18	.56
Proportion agonistic	.16	.21	.64	.00
Proportion adult	.06	.12	.18	.44
Proportion trade	.03	.07	.00	.00
Proportion affect	.02	.05	.00	.00
Behaviors[2]				
Direct requests	7.66	4.75		2.00
Indirect requests	13.85	7.49		6.00
Total requests	21.51	6.12		8.00
Direct requests:				
success	.585	.199		.375
fail	.382	.199		.625
Direct requests:				
follow partner	.079	.13		.500
Indirect requests:				
rigid follow-up	.086	.09		.250
Total requests:				
success	.602	.152		.500
fail	.370	.149		.500
rigid follow-up	.085	.069		.125
modify follow-up	.394	.174		.208
follow partner	.100	.114		.250
Goals:				
Direct stop action	.254	.166		.000
Direct gain attention	.338	.280		.750
Indirect stop action	.087	.087		.000
Total stop action	.170	.104		.000
Total gain attention	.400	.209		.660

[1] SPST n = 77; behavior n = 52
[2] Average number/proportion of units per session

and "indirect" friendship bids ("I'd go stand beside him") were .21 (.19) and .17 (.20) respectively. Alex's relevant scores were .50 in each case. Alex did not suggest the use of prosocial overtures, invitations, or conversation openers as did his age-mates, means = .14 (.18), .14 (.18), .31 (.20) respectively.

These data indicate that Alex has a good deal of difficulty in producing strategies for the goals of object acquisition or activity manipulation as well as for friendship initiation in hypothetical-reflective tasks. His response repertoire seems "out-of-sync" with those of his age-mates. As such, it might prove beneficial for Alex to participate in a social skills training program in which social-cognitive, role-taking, or role-playing experiences are provided (e.g., Spivack & Shure, 1974).

Tanny is another kindergartener who was identified as both isolated and rejected. Reference to Table 1.4 reveals that Tanny deviated from group norms on her ability to modify her original responses upon being informed that the strategy might not work. Moreover, almost one-half of the suggested strategies involved reliance on adult intervention; a technique suggested only 6% of the time by her age cohort.

Unfortunately we did not have second grade data for Tanny. However, she was one of the children for whom we had video-taped communication data. As aforementioned, children were video-taped on two separate 15 minute occasions with a same-sex "average" (sociometrically and observationally rated) peer. Table 1.4 indicates that Tanny's behavior in the dyad was significantly less socially assertive than that of her same-age counterparts. Tanny produced fewer requests than her peers. Moreover, her direct requests, despite being aimed primarily at satisfying "low cost," attention-getting goals, were more likely to be unsuccessful. When Tanny's initial strategies failed she was less likely to modify it; instead she either repeated the original strategy or, in the case of failed direct requests, she followed her partner's lead or countersuggestions.

In summary, Tanny deviates from the norms of her age group in both social problem solving thoughts and deeds. Our social problem solving data suggest that Tanny is an unassertive, perhaps adult-dependent child for whom social interactive goals often fail. Tanny demonstrates a lack of flexibility in thinking about alternative solutions to social dilemmas. This flexibility or resilience deficit is reflected also in Tanny's social problem solving behavior. Taken together these factors may mediate against Tanny's gaining popularity amongst her peers. From the perspective of an applied psychologist, Tanny might do well to be placed in a social problem solving training program like that outlined by Spivack and Shure (1974); moreover, confidence building peer experiences like those suggested by Furman et al. (1979) for young, withdrawn children might be in order.

Although both Alex and Tanny were selected by the same criteria (isolated-rejected) they showed divergent patterns of cognition. Alex was more likely to suggest aggressive or assertive means to solve social problems; Tanny was more likely to suggest third party (adult) intervention. *Neither* child evidenced a normal pattern of flexible social problem solving thinking. Tanny's observational profile was generally consistent with the hypothetical-reflective flexibility index. She demonstrated somewhat more failure than her peers in the use of direct requests, although her overall failure rate was close to the "norm." In contrast, the subject of our third ideographic analysis was chosen specifically for his high social failure rate in observed interactions. High failure rates may reflect the inability of the child to meet his or her needs in a social environment; consistent lack of success may prevent a child from achieving a sense of mastery and competence.

To demonstrate the potential of observational methods for individual social problem solving assessment, a sample profile analysis of Jason was undertaken (Krasnor, 1983b). The frequency and outcome of Jason's observed social problem solving behaviors were compared to the average for his same-sex peers in order to determine areas of relative strength and weakness. Examples of the frequency and success profiles constructed for Jason are presented in Figures 1.2 and 1.3 respectively for observed social goals. In general, Jason's profiles re-

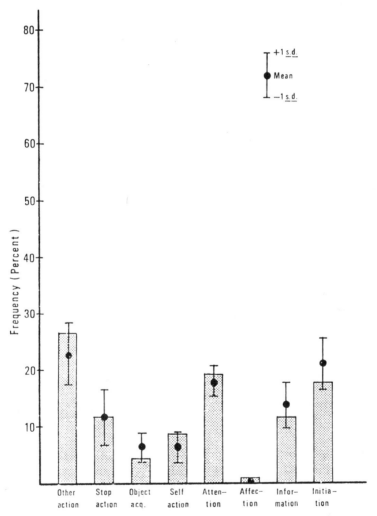

FIG. 1.2.   Individual frequency of goals compared to mean for boys (from Krasnor, 1983b).

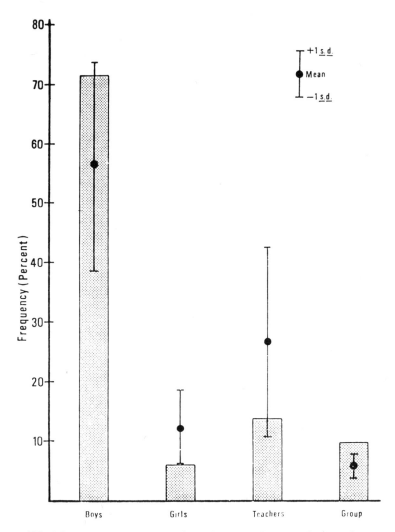

FIG. 1.3.   Individual success rate for goals compared to mean for boys (from Krasnor, 1983b).

vealed that the relative distribution of his social problem solving goals, strategies, and targets were within one standard deviation of his peers, but his success levels were consistently depressed. In comparison to peers, he had particularly low success with boy targets, in achieving stop-action and object acquisition goals, and with object agonistic strategies. Using this *intra-individual* analysis, Jason appeared to be most successful with teachers and most effective when using orienting strategies. Suggestions were relatively ineffective. These profiles of his relative abilities and deficits indicate the aspects of his social problem solving skills which do not meet normative or absolute criteria. These areas could be used as focal points for an individualized intervention program. On the basis of the observational data, he might be encouraged to build on his successes (e.g., to include orienting strategies in his social problem solving attempts more frequently) and thus increase his mastery experiences. A final point regarding Jason should be made in this context. Although Jason had the lowest success percentage in the sample and was rated relatively low in social competence by his teachers, he showed average popularity (as measured by "play with," "work with," and "do anything with" peer nominations).

This finding suggests, as does Tanny's social problem solving profile, that peer popularity, teacher perception of competence, and social effectiveness may have a complex interrelationship. There has, as yet, been little evidence of any attempts to adapt social problem solving training programs to the specific characteristics of children's cognitions and behaviors. Success in developing more effective means of treating children who are socially "at risk" may depend on the type of ideographic analyses that we have described herein.

CONCLUSIONS

In this chapter we have attempted to describe a model of social problem solving processing that has provided a framework for our research concerns for the last 5 years. Various components of the model have been examined substantively through the use of hypothetical-reflective interviews and observations of naturally occurring social behaviors. The social problem solving skills of children who vary in age, observed sociability, and peer popularity have been investigated. The results of our research efforts to date can be summarized briefly as follows:

1. Children as young as 4 years of age consider "task environmental" features such as the age or sex of their social targets when selecting social goals and the means to meet these goals (Krasnor, 1982; Rubin & Krasnor, 1983).

2. The ability to produce alternative means to solve some social problems that have met with initial failure appears to increase with age (Levin & Rubin, 1983; Rubin & Krasnor, in press).

3. There appear to be individual differences in the ways that children think about and go about solving their social dilemmas. For the most part, socially withdrawn children do not evince social cognition deficits. There is a tendency for withdrawn children to suggest third party (adult) intervention to solve problems involving social confrontation (Rubin, 1982a; Rubin, Daniels-Beirness, & Bream, 1984). The problem solving behaviors of withdrawn children, however, are suggestive of a lack of social confidence during peer interaction. They are

less assertive than, and deferent to, their more sociable age-mates (Rubin & Borwick, 1984).

Socially rejected children appear to differ from their more popular counterparts in the ways they think about and actually attempt to solve their social problems. Agonistic and assertive strategies seem to hold a place of strong standing in the social problem solving strategy repertoire. Moreover, in the face of social problem solving failure, rejected children have problems thinking about or employing alternative, flexible means to achieve their social goals (Rubin, et al., 1982; Rubin & Daniels-Beirness, 1983). To some extent, their social problem solving behaviors following failure are indicative of impulsivity. Rejected children are less flexible and persistent in comparison to their more popular age-mates (Krasnor, 1983a).

4. Cognitive variables such as social attributions appear to be implicated in the social problem solving process. Children's thoughtful reactions to hypothetical social features are related to the production of flexible and persistent means to deal with actual social problem solving failure (Krasnor, 1983b). Children who attribute social failure to external sources appear *less* likely to attempt to resolve a social dilemma following initial failure. It may be that such attributions lead to the assumption that persistence in the face of social failure may be maladaptive, causing "loss of face" or subsequent conflict. However, when children who do not attribute social failures to external factors *do* attempt to solve their initially unsuccessful problems, they are more likely than "externalizers" to use flexible follow-up social strategies. Thus, those who attribute hypothetical *social* failures to internal factors appear to produce more adaptive strategies in the face of actual social failure.

One problem with initiating a large-scale research program is that when the data start arriving in analyzed form, inevitably the researchers end up with more unanswered questions than they started with. Such is the case with our social problem solving research program.

In the near future we shall begin our quest to discover whether children's observed social goals and the means by which they achieve those goals varies with development. We shall also begin to examine whether (a) social goals, (b) the strategies employed to meet those goals, (c) the strategy outcome, and (d) the responses to outcome failure vary when children interact with friends, acquaintances, and strangers, or with age-mates versus younger or older children or at home versus at school. At this time we do not have a good "feel" for the generalizability of the social problem solving process across social domains.

Another area that requires attention concerns the possibility that socially isolated and/or peer rejected children may be less sensitive to the relations between goals, strategies, and targets than their more sociable or popular age-mates. For example, are rejected children as likely to suggest or produce aggressive means to solve social dilemmas when their targets are younger versus older? Relative insensitivity to task environmental features may explain why it is that some children are rejected by their peers.

The role of affect in the social problem solving process is still a mystery. If children are unsure of themselves in their social millieus do they evidence social problem solving problems? Are their goals, strategies, and responses to social failure different from their more self-confident age-mates?

Finally, we know little, if anything, about the socialization correlates and precursors of social problem solving competence. Several psychologists (e.g., Baumrind, 1971) have argued that child-rearing patterns may influence the development of social competence. Maccoby and Martin (1983), in their recent review of socialization in the context of the family, reported that children of "authoritarian" or power-assertive parents are less socially competent and more withdrawn than children whose parents are "authoritative." It may well be that those behavioral patterns definitive of authoritative child-rearing (e.g., expectation for mature behavior; encouragement of independence; open communication between parent and child) are more conducive to the development of flexible and successful social problem solving behavior than those patterns definitive of authoritarian child-rearing (e.g., controlling child behavior in accord with an absolute set of values; discouraging verbal give-and-take between parent and child).

Parental responsivity or sensitivity to children's needs, emotions, and behaviors (Ainsworth, Blehar, Waters, & Wall, 1978) and parental involvement or commitment to fostering "optimal child development" (Maccoby & Martin, 1983) has been found to predict ratings of sociability and social competence (Pulkinnen, 1982; Sroufe, 1983). The extent to which such child-rearing factors are implicated in the development of social problem solving is currently unknown.

The bottom line is that we have a considerable amount of homework to do in an effort to answer the plethora of questions concerning the development of social problem solving in childhood. We are quite certain that the questions posed directly above and those that were raised in the body of this paper are sufficient in number to keep many researchers busy for years to come; we welcome those who wish to join us in our quest for a better understanding of the social problem solving process in childhood.

ACKNOWLEDGMENTS

The research reported in this chapter was supported by grants to the first author from The Ontario Ministry of Community and Social Services and from Health and Welfare Canada. We would like to extend our appreciation to Anne Emptage for her assistance in collecting and analyzing the data and to Susan Sherry and Shelley Hymel for their helpful editorial comments during the preparation of this chapter.

REFERENCES

Abelson, R. D. (1982). Three modes of attitude-behavior consistency. In M. Zanna, E. T. Higgins, & C. P. Herman (Eds.), *Consistency in social behavior.* Hillsdale, NJ: Lawrence Erlbaum Associates.

Ainsworth, M. S., Blehar, M., Waters, E., & Wall, S. (1978). *Patterns of attachment.* Hillsdale, NJ: Lawrence Erlbaum Associates.

Allen, G., Chinsky, J., Larcen, S., Lochman, J. E., & Selinger, H. (1976). *Community psychology and the schools. A behaviorally oriented multilevel preventive approach.* Hillsdale, NJ: Lawrence Erlbaum Associates.

Anderson, S., & Messick, S. (1974). Social competency in young children. *Developmental Psychology, 10,* 282–293.

Asher, S. R., & Renshaw, P. (1981). Children without friends: Social knowledge and social skill. In S. R. Asher & J. M. Gottman (Eds.), *The development of children's friendships.* New York: Cambridge.

Asher, S. R., Singleton, L., Tinsley, B., & Hymel, S. (1979). A reliable sociometric measure for children. *Developmental Psychology, 15,* 443–444.

Baumrind, D. (1971). Current patterns of parental authority. *Developmental Psychology Monograph, 4(1).*

Beck, L. W. (1978). *The actor and the spectator.* New Haven: Yale University Press.

Bem, D. (1972). Self-perception theory. In L. Berkowitz (Ed.), *Advances in experimental social psychology* (Vol. 6). New York: Academic Press.

Botvin, G., & Murray, F. B. (1975). The efficacy of peer modeling and social conflict in the acquisition of conversation. *Child Development, 46,* 796–799.

Bronfenbrenner, U. (1963). Developmental theory in transition. In H. W. Stevenson (Ed.), *Sixty-second yearbook of the National Society for Studies in Education.* Chicago: University of Chicago Press.

Butler, L. (1978, June). The relationship between interpersonal problem-solving skills and peer relations and behavior. Paper presented at the annual meeting of the Canadian Psychological Association, Ottawa.

Cairns, R. (1979). *Social development.* San Francisco: W. H. Freeman.

Chandler, M. (1973). Egocentrism and anti-social behavior: The assessment and training of social perspective-taking skills. *Developmental Psychology, 9,* 326–332.

Charlesworth, W. (1976). Human intelligence as adaptation: An ethological approach. In L. Resnick (Ed.), *The nature of intelligence.* Hillsdale, NJ: Lawrence Erlbaum Associates.

Clark, R. A., & Delia, J. G. (1976). The development of functional persuasive skills in childhood and early adolescence. *Child Development, 47,* 1008–1014.

Coie, J. D, & Dodge, K. A. (1983). Continuities and changes in children's social status: A five-year longitudinal study. *Merrill-Palmer Quarterly, 29,* 261–282.

Coie, J. D., & Kupersmidt, J. B. (1983). A behavioral analysis of emerging social status in boys groups. *Child Development, 54,* 1400–1416.

Conger, J. C. & Keane, A. P. (1981). Social skills intervention in the treatment of isolated or withdrawn children. *Psychological Bulletin, 90,* 478–495.

Cooney, E., & Selman, R. (1978). Children's use of social conceptions: Towards a dynamic model of social cognition. In W. Damon (Ed.), *Social cognition.* San Francisco: Jossey-Bass.

Cowen, E., Pederson, A., Babigian, H., Izzo, L., & Trost, M. (1973). Long-term follow-up of early detected vulnerable children. *Journal of Consulting Clinical Psychology, 41,* 438–446.

Damon, W. (1977). *The social world of the child.* San Francisco: Jossey-Bass.

Dodge, K. A. (1983). Behavioral antecedents of peer social status. *Child Development, 54,* 1386–1399.

Dodge, K., Murphy, R., & Buchsbaum, D. (1984). The assessment of intention-cue detection skills in children: Implications for developmental psychopathology. *Child Development, 55*, 163–173.

Dodge, K., Schlundt, D., Schoken, I., & Delugach, J. (1983). Social competence and children's sociometric status: The role of peer group entry strategies. *Merrill-Palmer Quarterly, 29*, 390–336.

Dore, J. (1978). Holophrases, speech acts and language universals. *Journal of Child Language, 2*, 21–40.

Doyle, A. B. (1982). Friends, acquaintances, and strangers: The influence of familiarity and eth-nolinguistic background on social interaction. In K. H. Rubin & H. S. Ross (Eds.), *Peer relations and social skills in childhood*. New York: Springer-Verlag.

Dweck, C., Davidson, W., Nelson, S., & Enna, B. (1978). Sex differences in learned helplessness: II. The contingencies of evaluative feedback in the classroom. III. An experimental analysis. *Developmental Psychology, 14*, 268–276.

Dweck, C. & Reppucci, N. (1973). Learned helplessness and reinforcement responsibility in children. *Journal of Personality and Social Psychology, 25*, 109–116.

D'Zurilla, T. J., & Goldfried, M. R. (1971). Problem-solving and behavior modification. *Journal of Abnormal Psychology, 78*, 107–126.

Eckerman, C. O., & Stein, M. R. (1982). The toddler's emerging interactive skills. In K. H. Rubin & H. S. Ross (Eds.), *Peer relations and social skills in childhood*. New York: Springer-Verlag.

Elardo, P., & Cooper, M. (1977). *Project AWARE: A handbook for teachers*. Reading, MA: Addison-Wesley.

Enright, R., & Sutterfield, S. (1980). An ecological validation of social cognitive development. *Child Development, 51*, 93–100.

Ervin-Tripp, S., & Mitchell-Kernan, C. (Eds.) (1977). *Child discourse*. New York: Academic Press.

Feldman, E. (1983, April). Cognition and social adjustment in children. Paper presented at the biennial meeting of the Society for Research in Child Development, Detroit.

Flavell, J., Botkin, P., Fry, C., Wright, J., & Jarvis, P. (1968). *The development of role-taking and communication skills in children*. New York: Wiley.

Flavell, J. H. (1981). Monitoring social cognitive enterprises: Something else that may develop in the area of social cognition. In J. H. Flavell & L. Ross (Eds.), *Social cognitive development*. New York: Cambridge University Press.

Ford, M. (1979). The construct validity of egocentrism. *Psychological Bulletin, 86*, 1169–1188.

French, D. (1984). Children's knowledge of the social function of younger, older and same-age peers. *Child Development, 55*, 1429–1433.

Furman, W., Rahe, D., & Hartup, W. (1979). Rehabilitation of socially withdrawn preschool children through mixed-age and same-age socialization. *Child Development, 50*, 915–922.

Garvey, D. (1975). Requests and responses in children's speech. *Journal of Child Language, 2*, 915–922.

Glucksberg, S., & Krauss, (1967). What do people say after they have learned how to talk? Studies of the development of referential communication. *Merrill-Palmer Quarterly, 13*, 309–316.

Glucksberg, S., Krauss, R., & Higgins, E. T. (1975). The development of referential communication skills. In F. D. Horowitz (Ed.), *Review of child development research*. Vol. 4, Chicago: University of Chicago Press.

Goetz, T., & Dweck, C. (1980). Learned helplessness in social situations. *Journal of Personality and Social Psychology, 39*, 246–255.

Goldfried & D'Zurilla (1969). A behavioral-analytic model for assessing competence. In C. D. Spielberger (Ed.), *Current topics in clinical and community psychology*. New York: Academic Press.

Gottman, J., Gonso, J., & Rasmussen, B. (1975). Social interaction, social competence, and friendship in children. *Child Development, 46*, 709–718.

Gottman, J. & Parkhurst, J. (1980). A developmental theory of friendship and acquaintanceship processes. In W. Collins (Ed.), *Minnesota Symposium in Child Development, Vol. 13.* Hillsdale, NJ: Lawrence Erlbaum Associates.

Grice, P. (1969). Utterer's meaning and intentions. *Philosophical Review, 78,* 147–177.

Harris, M. (1979). *Cultural materalism: The struggle for a science of culture.* New York: Vantage Books.

Hartup, W. W. (1983). The peer system. In E. M. Hetherington (Ed.), *Handbook of child psychology: Socialization, personality and social development.* New York: Wiley.

Hay, D., Pederson, J., & Nash, A. (1982). Dyadic interaction in the first year of life. In K. H. Rubin & H. S. Ross (Eds.), *Peer relations and social skills in childhood.* New York: Springer-Verlag.

Heider, F. (1958). *The psychology of interpersonal relations.* New York: Wiley.

Hold, B. (1976). Attention structure and rank specific behavior in preschool children. In M. Chance & R. Larsen (Eds.), *The social structure of attention.* London: Wiley.

Hymel, S. (1983). Preschool children's peer relations: Issues in sociometric assessment. *Merrill-Palmer Quarterly, 29,* 237–260.

Iannotti, R. (1978). Effects of role-taking experiences on role-taking, empathy, altruism, and aggression. *Developmental Psychology, 14,* 119–124.

Jacklin, C., & Maccoby, E. (1978). Social behavior at thirty-three months in same-sex and mixed sex dyads. *Child Development, 49,* 557–569.

Jahoda, M. (1953). The meaning of psychological health. *Social Casework, 34,* 349–354.

Jahoda, M. (1958). *Current concepts of positive mental health.* New York: Basic Books.

Jersild, A. T., & Markey, F. V. (1935). Conflicts between preschool children. *Child Development Monographs,* No. 21.

Klinger, E., Barta, S. G., & Maxinera, M. (1982). Current concerns: Assessing therapeutically relevant motivation. In P. Kendall & S. Hollon (Eds.), *Cognitive-behavioral interventions: Assessment.* New York: Academic Press.

Kohlberg, L. (1964). Development of moral character and moral ideology. In M. L. Hoffman & L. W. Hoffman (Eds.), *Review of child development research.* New York: Russell Sage Foundation.

Kohn, M., & Clausen, J. (1955). Social isolation and schizophrenia. *American Sociological Review, 20,* 265–273.

Krasnor, L. R. (1977). Alternate social problem-solving: A training and validation study. Unpublished Masters Thesis, University of Waterloo.

Krasnor, L. R. (1981). An observational study of social problem solving in preschoolers. Unpublished doctoral dissertation, University of Waterloo.

Krasnor, L. R. (1982). An observational study of social problem solving in young children. In K. H. Rubin & H. S. Ross (Eds.), *Peer relations and social skills in childhood.* New York: Springer-Verlag.

Krasnor, L. R. (1983a, April). Social attribution and social problem-solving. Paper presented at the Biennial Meeting of the Society for Research in Child Development, Detroit.

Krasnor, L. R. (1983b). An observational case study of failure in social problem solving. *Journal of Applied Developmental Psychology, 4,* 81–98.

Krasnor, L., & Rubin, K. (1978, June). Preschoolers' verbal and behavioral solutions to social problems. Paper presented at the annual meeting of the Canadian Psychological Association, Ottawa.

Krasnor, L., & Rubin, K. (1981). Assessment of social problem-solving in young children. In T. Merluzzi, C. Glass, & M. Genest (Eds.), *Cognitive assessment.* New York: Guilford.

Krasnor, L. R., & Rubin, K. H. (1983). Preschool social problem solving: Attempts and outcomes in naturalistic interaction. *Child Development, 54,* 1545–1558.

Ladd, G., & Oden, S. (1979). The relationship between peer acceptance and children's ideas about helpfulness. *Child Development, 40,* 402–408.

Langer, E. (1978). Rethinking the role of thought in social interactions. In J. Harvey, W. Ickes, &

R. Kidd (Eds.), *New directions in attribution research,* (Vol. 2). Hillsdale, NJ: Lawrence Erlbaum Associates.

Lee, L. (1975). Toward a cognitive theory of interpersonal development: Importance of peers. In M. Lewis & L. Rosenblum (Eds.), *Friendship and peer relations.* New York: Wiley.

Levin, E., & Rubin, K. H. (1983). Getting others to do what you want them to do: The development of children's requestive strategies. In K. Nelson (Ed.), *Children's Language,* (Vol. 4). Hillsdale, NJ: Lawrence Erlbaum Associates.

Lewis, M., & Feiring, C. (1979). Child's social network: Social object, social functions and their relationship. In M. Lewis & L. Rosenblum (Eds.), *The child and its family.* New York: Plenum.

Maccoby, E. E., & Martin, J. (1983). Socialization in the context of the family: Parent-child interaction. In E. M. Hetherington (Ed.), *Handbook of child psychology: Socialization personality, and social development.* New York: Wiley.

Masten, A., & Morison, P. (1981, April). The Minnesota revision of the class play: Psychometric properties of a peer assessment instrument. Paper presented at the biennial meeting of the Society for Research in Child Development, Boston.

McClure, L. F., Chinsky, J. M., & Larcen, S. W. (1978). Enhancing social problem solving performance in an elementary school setting. *Journal of Educational Psychology, 70,* 504–513.

Meichenbaum, D. (1977). *Cognitive behavior modification: An integrative approach.* New York: Plenum.

Murphy, L. (1937). *Social behavior and child personality.* New York: Columbia University Press.

Muus, R. (1960). Mental health implications of a preventative psychiatry program in light of research findings. *Marriage and Family Living, 22,* 150–156.

Nelson, K. (1981). Social cognition in a script framework. In J. H. Flavell & L. Ross (Eds.), *Social cognitive development.* New York: Cambridge University Press.

Nelson-LeGall, S. (1981). Help-seeking: An understudied problem solving skill in children. *Developmental Review, 1,* 224–246.

Newell, H., & Simon, H. (1972). *Human problem solving.* Englewood Cliffs, NJ: Prentice-Hall.

Nisbett, R. E., & Wilson, T. D. (1977). Telling more than we can know: Verbal reports on mental processes. *Psychological Review, 84,* 231–259.

Olson, S. L., Johnson, J., Parks, J., Barrett, E., & Belleau, K. (1983, April). Behavior problems of preschool children: Dimensions and social and cognitive correlates. Paper presented at the Biennial Meeting of the Society for Research in Child Development, Detroit.

Piaget, J. (1926). *The language and thought of the child.* New York: Harcourt, Brace & Co.

Piaget, J. (1965). *The moral judgment of the child.* New York: Free Press.

Platt, G., & Spivack, G. (1975). *Manual for the Means-Ends Problem-Solving Procedure.* Unpublished manuscript, Hahnemann community Mental Health Center.

Pulkinnen, L. (1982). Self Control and continuity from childhood to adolescence. In P. B. Baltes & O. G. Brim (Eds.), *Life-span development and behavior,* (Vol. 4). New York: Academic Press.

Putallaz, M. (1983). Predicting children's sociometric status from their behavior. *Child Development, 54,* 1417–1426.

Putallaz, M., & Gottman, J. (1981). An interactional model of children's entry into peer groups. *Child Development, 52,* 986–994.

Renshaw, P. (1981). Social knowledge and sociometric status: Children's goals and strategies for peer interaction. Unpublished doctoral dissertation, University of Illinois.

Renshaw, P., & Asher, S. (1982). Social competence and peer status: The distinction between goals and strategies. In K. H. Rubin & H. Ross (Eds.), *Peer relationships and social skills in childhood.* New York: Springer-Verlag.

Richard, B., & Dodge, K. (1982). Social maladjustment and problem solving in school-aged children. *Journal of Consulting and Clinical Psychology, 50,* 226–233.

Roff, M., Sells, S., & Golden, M. (1972). *Social adjustment and personality development in children.* Minneapolis: University of Minnesota Press.

Rubin, K. H. (1973). Egocentrism in childhood: A unitary construct? *Child Development, 44,* 102–110.

Rubin, K. H. (1978). Role-taking in childhood: Some methodological considerations. *Child Development, 49,* 428–433.

Rubin, K. H. (1982a). Social skill and social-cognitive correlates of observed isolation behavior in preschoolers. In K. H. Rubin & H. S. Ross (Eds.), *Peer relations and social skills in childhood.* New York: Springer-Verlag.

Rubin, K. H. (1982b). Non-social play in preschoolers: Necessarily evil? *Child Development, 53,* 651–667.

Rubin, K. H., & Borwick, D. (1984). Communication skills and sociability. In H. Sypher & J. Applegate (Eds.), *Communication by children and adults: Social cognitive and strategic processes.* Beverly Hills: Sage.

Rubin, K. H., & Clark, L. (1983). Preschool teachers' ratings of behavioral problems: *Journal of Abnormal Child Psychology, 11,* 273–285.

Rubin, K. H., & Daniels-Beirness, T. (1983). Concurrent and predictive correlates of sociometric status in kindergarten and grade one children. *Merrill-Palmer Quarterly, 29,* 337–352.

Rubin, K. H., Daniels-Beirness, T., & Bream, L. (1984). Social isolation and social problem-solving: A longitudinal study. *Journal of Consulting and Clinical Psychology, 52,* 17–25.

Rubin, K. H., Daniels-Beirness, T., & Hayvren, M. (1982). Social and social-cognitive correlates of sociometric status in preschool and kindergarten children. *Canadian Journal of Behavioral Science, 14,* 338–348.

Rubin, K. H., & Krasnor, L. R. (1983). Age and gender differences in the development of representative social problem solving skill. *Journal of Applied Developmental Psychology, 4,* 463–475.

Rubin, K. H., & Pepler, D. J. (1980). The relationship of child's play to social-cognitive development. In H. Foot, T. Chapman, & J. Smith, (Eds.), *Friendship and childhood relationships.* London: Wiley.

Rubin, K. H., & Ross, H. S. (eds.). (1982). *Peer relationships and social skills in childhood.* New York: Springer-Verlag.

Schank, R., & Abelson, S. (1977). *Scripts, plans, goals, and understanding.* Hillsdale, NJ: Lawrence Erlbaum Associates.

Selman, R. *The growth of interpersonal understanding: Developmental and clinical analyses.* New York: Academic Press, 1980.

Shantz, C. U. (1983). Social cognition. In J. H. Flavell & E. Markman (Eds.), *Handbook of child psychology: Cognitive development.* New York: Wiley.

Sharp, K. (1978, August). Interpersonal problem-solving capacity and behavioral adjustment. Paper presented at the annual meeting of the American Psychological Association, Toronto.

Shatz, M., & Gelman, R. (1973). The development of communication skills: Modifications in the speech of young children as a function of the listener. *Monographs of the Society for Research in Child Development, 38(2),* 1–37.

Shure, M. B., Newman, S., & Silver, S. (1973, March). Problem solving thinking among adjusted, impulsive, and inhibited Head Start Children. Paper presented to the Eastern Psychological Association.

Shure, M. B., & Spivack, G. (1970, March). Problem-solving capacity, social class, and adjustment among nursery school children. Paper presented at the Eastern Psychological Association, Atlantic City, New Jersey.

Shure, M. B., & Spivack, G. (1972). Means-ends thinking, adjustment and social class among elementary school-aged children. *Journal of Consulting and Clinical Psychology, 39,* 348–353.

Shure, M. B., & Spivack, G. (1973, April). A preventive mental health program for four-year-old Head Start children. Paper presented at the Society for Research in Child Development, Philadelphia.

Shure, M. B., & Spivack, G. (1974). *Preschool interpersonal problem solving (PIPS) test: Manual.* Hahnemann Community Mental Health Center.

Shure, M. B., & Spivack, G. (1978). *Problem-solving techniques in child rearing.* San Francisco: Jossey-Bass.

Shure, M. B., & Spivack, G. (1980). Interpersonal problem-solving as a mediator of behavioral adjustment in preschool and kindergarten children. *Journal of Applied Developmental Psychology, 1,* 29–44.

Shure, M. B., Spivack, G., & Jaeger, M. (1971). Problem-solving thinking and adjustment among disadvantaged preschool children. *Child Development, 42,* 1791–1803.

Siegel, I., & McBane, S. (1967). Cognitive competence and level of symbolization among five-year-old children. In J. Hellmuth (Ed.), *Disadvantaged child.* New York: Brunner-Mazel.

Spivack, G., Platt, J., & Shure, M. (1976). *The problem-solving approach to adjustment.* San Francisco: Jossey-Bass.

Spivack, G., & Shure, M. (1974). *Social adjustment of young children.* San Francisco: Jossey-Bass.

Spivack, G., & Spotts, J. (1966). *Devereux child behavior rating scale manual.* Devon, PA: Devereux Foundation.

Sroufe, A. (1983). Infant-caregiver attachment and patterns of adaptation in preschool: The roots of maladaption and competence. In M. Perlmutter (Ed.), *Minnesota Symposia in child psychology* (Vol. 16). Hillsdale, NJ: Lawrence Erlbaum Associates.

Steinberg, J. (1977). Information theory as an ethological tool. In B. Hazlett, (Ed.), *Quantitative methods in the study of animal behavior.* New York: Academic Press.

Strain, P., Kerr, M. M., & Ragland, E. U. (1981). The use of peer social initiations in the treatment of social withdrawal. In P. S. Strain (Ed.), *The utlization of classroom peers as behavior change agents.* New York: Plenum.

Strayer, F. F. (1981). The organization and coordination of asymmetrical relations among young children: A biological view of social power. In M. Watts (Ed.), *Research methods in bio-paletics.* San Francisco: Jossey-Bass.

Sullivan, H. S. (1953). *The interpersonal theory of psychiatry.* New York: Norton.

Sutton-Smith, B. (1971). A syntax for play and games. In R. R. Herron & B. Sutton-Smith (Eds.), *Child's play.* New York: Wiley.

Urbain, E., & Kendall, P. (1980). Review of social-cognitive problem-solving interactions with children. *Psychological Bulletin, 83,* 109–143.

Weiner, B. (1982). An attributionally-based theory of motivation and emotion: Focus, range, and issues. In N. Fentler, (Ed.), *Expectations and actions,* Hillsdale, NJ: Lawrence Erlbaum Associates.

Weiner, B., Kun, A., & Benesh-Weiner, M. (1980). The development of mastery, emotions, and morality from an attributional perspective. In W. A. Collins (Ed.), *Minnesota symposia on child psychology,* (Vol. 13). Hillsdale, NJ: Lawrence Erlbaum Associates.

Whiting, B., & Whiting, J. (1975). *Children of six cultures: A psycho-cultural analysis.* Cambridge, Mass.: Harvard University Press.

Wilcox, M. J., & Webster, E. J.. (1980). Early discourse behavior: An analysis of children's responses to listener feedback. *Child Development, 51,* 1120–1125.

Zahn-Waxler, C., Iannotti, R., & Chapman, M. (1982). Peers and prosocial development. In K. H. Rubin & H. S. Ross (Eds.), *Peer relations and social skills in childhood.* New York: Springer-Verlag.

Zigler, E. (1973). Project Head Start: Success or failure? *Learning, 1,* 43–47.

2

Comments on Rubin and Krasnor: Solutions and Problems in Research on Problem Solving

Philip C. Kendall
Temple University

Having been a Professor at the University which serves as the host for this symposium, and being one who wishes to be cordial to both foreign visitors and scientists working in a research area of interest to me, I want to be cautious in my criticisms of the work just described. However, being among my colleagues of the Institute of Child Development and Department of Psychology, I must be aware of the disfavor that would be assigned to me if I were to be an *un*critical reader. Simply applauding Rubin and Krasnor's paper would leave me in local disrepute. Thus, while I want to be a critical and provocative discussant, I also wish to avoid the unseemly acrimony that I find so distasteful. I have a problem, a social problem. How am I going to solve it?

Solutions to problems such as this one do not materialize from thin air. Rather, successful problem solving often results from an involvement in the operation of cognitive strategies which allow the person to consider possible courses of action, reflect on potential outcomes, and make decisions about options. Several of my more creative, if bizarre, solutions, have been mentally edited and discarded already. The selected resolution was chosen from among several alternatives, after consideration of potential consequences of each. In the comments that follow, I outline some of the general positive features of the work reported by Rubin and Krasnor. Information from analyses of data gathered by myself and Gary Fischler are also included in order to corroborate some of the findings reported in the paper under discussion, while also underscoring the need for qualitative analysis, precise assessment of diverse child behavior disorders, and control of intellectual ability.

ADVANCING SOLUTIONS

I begin by outlining what seem to be some of the general strengths of the research program and theoretical analysis described by Rubin and Krasnor. First, it was a tremendous relief for me to see intentional emphasis on the ecological validity of the social problem-solving assessments. I would have been troubled had the conclusions been based on what has become the somewhat conventional paper-and-pencil measures of problem-solving. Instead, I find my methodological anxieties assuaged by the authors attention to ecologically valid assessments. Second, I was not only relieved but also impressed by the deployment of longitudinal designs. While I have elsewhere criticized the lack of effort toward a truly developmental analysis and urged additional developmental theory on the social cognitive problem solving process (Kendall, 1984), I mention the topic here in praise. The present logitudinal and process analyses add meaningfully to the overall contribution.

It should therefore not be surprising to learn that some data generated in my own lab are consistent with those presented by Rubin and Krasnor (this volume), and that we too are interested in ecological validity. Briefly, I would like to summarize this work as it relates to the Waterloo study, reported in the previous chapter. Our examination focused on the ecological validity of the standard (paper-and-pencil) ICPS tests (means-ends problem solving, alternatives thinking). We gathered test data and actual interpersonal problem-solving behavior in the laboratory situation (Kendall & Fischler, 1984).

One hundred and fifty families, with a son or daughter between the ages of 6 and 11, participated in the study. There were twenty five families with a son between 6 and 7 years old; between 8 and 9; and between 10 and 11. An equal number and distribution of families included a daughter. Fathers' mean age was 37.93, mothers' mean age was 36.09. Mean WAIS Full Scale IQs for fathers was 118.29 (SD = 10.29) and 114.82 (SD = 9.84) for mothers. Children's mean WISC-R Full Scale IQs were 113.18 (SD = 13.36) for 6- to 7-year-olds; 113.92 (SD = 13.28) for 8- to 9-year-olds; and 114.56 (SD = 14.6) for 10- to 11-year-olds. According to the Hollingshead 2 Factor Index of Socioeconomic Status, the families were middle class (M = 31.2). Ninety-seven percent of the families were white; and 3% were black. Three ICPS skills were measured (means-ends thinking, alternative solution thinking, and consequential thinking) yielding four scores (means-ends, obstacles, alternatives, and consequences) for each subject.

Problem-solving behaviors were assessed through an interactional problem-solving task in which the entire family participated. Specifically, the procedure was as follows: First, each member of the family was individually instructed: "Your family has been promised $50.00 for participating in this research. I would like you to think of 3 ways you would like to spend the money. Write each way you would like to spend the money on a separate index card. (For young children, the experimenter wrote them down). Do you have any questions?" The subjects kept their own cards. Next, the family members were regrouped and told, "Each of you has come up with 3 ways you would like to spend the $50.00. Here is a check for $50.00 [placed on the table in plain sight of the subjects]. Some of your suggestions may be similar for all or a couple of you, but some are probably different. We would like the three of you to discuss for the next 15 minutes how you are going to come to agreement about spending the money. If you decide on how to come to an agreement, then you should come to one, but you should spend the time discussing *how best to decide*. Any questions?" The experimenter then left the room. It should be emphasized that the family was not merely solving an *impersonal* problem (i.e., how to spend the money), but rather was solving an *interpersonal* one (i.e., how to come to an agreement), albeit one that is admittedly only an analogue of real-life interpersonal interactions. In order to aid comparisons, the problem-solving behavioral codes were designed to closely parallel written ICPS measures. That is, we wanted to compare, in as direct a manner as possible, interpersonal problem-solving abilities as assessed by the traditional written tasks, and those *same abilities* as they might be expected to be manifested in an analogue interpersonal problem-solving situation.

The results indicated limited ecological validity. Table 2.1 presents the relationship between written ICPS measures and problem-solving behaviors for the three separate age groups and boys and girls separately. For boys, there was a significant correlation between written ICPS and the corresponding behavior in only 2 of 12 instances. These 2 cases were for 6- to 7-year-old boys, where written ICPS alternatives and consequences were significantly related to alternative and consequence behaviors. These relationships did not hold for the older boys. In 3 of 12 cases, girls' ICPS written and problem-solving behaviors were significantly related. In particular, there was only a relationship between girls' written and behavioral alternatives at 6- to 7-years-of-age, and consequences at 8 to 9 and 10 to 11 years of age. Written alternatives for 6- to 7-year-old girls were significantly correlated with all problem-solving behavior. However, none of these relationships held for 8- to 9-year-olds, and only 2 were significant (i.e., obstacles, consequences) for 10- to 11-year-olds. In general, alternatives thinking and consequential thinking, and only in limited areas, showed significant correlations with actual problem-solving behavior. These data were scored as Spivack and Shure prescribe (a *quantitative* analysis where the greater number of solutions are seen as better), and the validity coefficients were limited. Moreover, relationships to ratings of adjustment were severely lacking. We employed mother, father, and teacher ratings using the Achenbach (1978) Child Behavior Checklist (CBCL) and the Self-Control Rating Scale (SCRS; Kendall & Wilcox, 1979). These scales were used to overcome what we perceived to be a weakness in earlier measurements of psychopathology where gross categories, such as "aberrant," were employed. The relationship of social problem-solving skills to adjustment, we feel, must be studied in terms of specific types of psychopathology. Our results demonstrated that *quantitatively* scored problem solving

TABLE 2.1
Intercorrelations of Children's Written ICPS Measures and Problem-Solving Behaviors for
Separate Age Groups with IQ Partialled Out

Age Groups	Measure	ICPs Written				Problem-Solving Behaviors			
		1	2	3	4	1	2	3	4
6-7	Written ICPS								
	1. Means-ends		.48*	.50*	.17	[-.28]	.00	.08	-.04
	2. Obstacles	.22		.14	-.17	.21	[-.15]	.11	-.11
	3. Alternatives	-.03	-.02		.57**	-.14	.08	[.39*]	.25
	4. Consequences	-.06	.17	.40*		.22	.00	.13	[.56**]
	Problem-Solving Behaviors								
	1. Means-ends	[-.02]	-.11	.62**	.03		.05	.09	-.14
	2. Obstacles	.03	[-.16]	.41*	-.13	.75**		.28	-.02
	3. Alternatives	.19	-.17	[.51*]	.06	.72**	.61**		.17
	4. Consequences	-.29	-.16	.40*	[.21]	.62**	.44**	.59**	
8-9	Written ICPS								
	1. Means-ends		.18	-.12	.00	[.27]	-.02	-.13	.16
	2. Obstacles	.01		-.07	.52**	-.23	[-.07]	-.13	-.13
	3. Alternatives	.28	.47*		.31	-.08	-.11	[-.16]	-.24
	4. Consequences	.23	-.17	.26		-.19	.12	-.02	[-.23]
	Problem-Solving Behaviors								
	1. Means-ends	[.01]	-.03	-.14	.28		.65**	.68**	.70**
	2. Obstacles	-.15	[.14]	-.16	.14	.58**		.51*	.54**
	3. Alternatives	-.12	-.01	[-.13]	.19	.90**	.51*		.51*
	4. Consequences	.09	.02	-.10	[.43*]	.62**	.26	.56**	
10-11	Written ICPS								
	1. Means-ends		.28	.39	.06	[-.07]	.00	.27	.09
	2. Obstacles	-.11		.06	-.06	-.14	[-.07]	.30	.14
	3. Alternatives	-.19	.39*		.47*	-.38*	-.24	[-.31]	-.01
	4. Consequences	-.16	.08	.77**		-.17	-.22	-.18	[-.03]
	Problem-Solving Behaviors								
	1. Means-ends	[.26]	.30	.26	.13		.11	.69**	.22
	2. Obstacles	.11	[.26]	.36*	.21	.76**		.42*	.45*
	3. Alternatives	-.04	.09	[.25]	.24	.82**	.83**		.56**
	4. Consequences	.14	.52*	.50*	[.40*]	.83**	.76**	.70**	

*p < .05, **p < .005
Note: Boys are above the diagonal, girls are below it. ICPS = Interpersonal Cognitive Problem-Solving. Boxed-in correlations represent convergent validity coefficients. Reprinted by permission from Kendal & Fischler, 1984. Behavioral and adjustment correlates of social problem-solving: Validational analyses of interpersonal cognitive problem-solving measures. *Child Development*, 1984, 55, in press.

was not related to these otherwise validated indices of adjustment. It is because of the limited ecological validity found for the paper-and-pencil ICPS measure that I was pleased to see the type of assessments employed by Rubin and Krasnor.

Another positive feature of the data presented by Rubin and Krasnor concerns the examination of the *quality* of social problem-solving responses. As was evident in the data set that I have briefly described, *quantity* was not particularly associated with behavioral problem solving. In addition, there was a marked absence of a relationship between quantitatively scored problem solving and adjustment. Thus, my pleasure in Rubin and Krasnor's application of qualitative scoring. Similarly, in a subsequent examination of the Kendall and Fischler data (Fischler & Kendall, 1985), qualitative, quantitative, and topological analyses were conducted. The quality of the social problem-solving responses were rated on the dimensions of effectiveness, appropriateness, aggressiveness, passivity, affective understanding, and interpersonal content. These specific ratings were analyzed and also converted into topological variables, such as maximum quality, consistency within situations, and consistency across situations. These analyses indicated that children whose solutions were more socially appropriate and consistent across situations were better adjusted (i.e., not socially withdrawn) than children whose solutions were less appropriate or more inconsistent. Where quantity showed no significant relationship to adjustment, 5 of 11 qualitative factors were related to adjustment ratings—even with intellectual ability controlled.

Apparently, as judged from the collective data sets, qualitative variability in problem solving is predictive of adjustment. However, I do not wish to take the shine off the Rubin and Krasnor paper by calling attention to our similar findings, and, therefore, I wish to take a few moments to mention some of the additional positive features of their work that we have not addressed. These features can be seen as important trends in the analysis of social problem solving, and I suspect that we will learn a great deal more about this area as the research data and theoretical ramifications are published and integrated. For purposes of efficiency and conservation of space I will mention each of these features only briefly.

Inclusion of the child's goals.   It is clearly the case that social problem-solving strategies that are effective in acquiring a toy from another child vary significantly from those that would effectively calm an angry peer who wanted to fight. The choice and deployment of a strategy is moderated by several contextual factors, and the goal of the action is an important one. The enthusiasm justifiably associated with goal assessments must, however, be tempered by the fact that an accurate determination of a child's goal(s) is not as straight forward as it may seem.[1]

Examination of the actual outcomes *of the social problem-solving behavior.*   The inclusion of outcomes is central since not all problem-solving efforts achieve success. Even those efforts which outsiders view as likely to be suc-

---

[1]I am not one to abhor nonbehavioral terminology. Indeed, while holding methodological behaviorism near, I entertain to examine the more illusive and intriguing psychological concepts, and I champion the role of self-talk in psychological adjustment. My resolve is unfalsifiable, but only data are truly compelling. Rubin and Krasnor propose the examination of the goals of children's behavior by inferring them from observations. True, children may not know enough about their own motivations to be able to self-report goals, but inference and/or projective methods are no more likely to be fruitful. Methodologically, the direct manipulation of the experimental situation to produce situations where certain goals obtain, and the subsequent analysis of their effects, appeals to this writer's research preferences.

cessful may, in actuality, be ineffective. Correspondingly, it is only after a problem solution has been attempted and found to fail that we can examine the child's subsequent problem-solving efforts. Recognizing an ineffective solution and changing the strategy suggests that the individual possesses a more adaptive and cooperative plan than simply repeating one approach in a persistent manner or giving up entirely.

The target of the social problem-to-be-solved is also likely to account for portions of the variance. Almost any response may work with obsequious peers or peers who have a long established history of "working things out" together. In contrast, resistant peers might render a high-probability-of-success response surprisingly ineffective.

The inclusions of goals, outcomes, and targets will, in my opinion, offer substantial richness, if not complexity, to the analysis of how children resolve the naturally complex process of social problem solving. Complex problems require complex solutions.

CONTINUING PROBLEMS

Let us turn now to some of the shortcomings that may be potentially detrimental to any attempt to draw definitive conclusions. The shortcomings identified here are by no means unique to Rubin and Krasnor. Rather, they are problems that have plagued a series of social problem-solving investigations.

First, more attention needs to be paid to the classification of children into types of psychopathology. Proper categorization is required before social problem-solving theory can be successfully integrated into clinical research in psychopathology. It is valuable to know that isolates and socially active children differ, and I would only want to take this further. Using additional and more diverse categories of child behavior problems would help to specify more exactly the role of cognitive problems in child psychopathology. On a related treatment note, the proper matching of treatments to disorders would be facilitated by the identification of specific childhood psychopathologies where problem-solving deficits are seen as crucial. Unless and until we know that a certain disorder has an associated deficit or distortion in problem solving, a problem-solving intervention (e.g., Baucom, 1982; Kendall & Braswell, 1985; Robin, 1981; Sarason & Sarason, 1981; Weissberg, Gesten, Rapkin, Cowen, Davidson, deApodaca, & McKim, 1981; see also Urbain & Kendall, 1980) may not be the treatment of choice. I should add, however, that Rubin and Krasnor's data do point to the need for social problem-solving training specifically for rejected children (not isolated children)—thus moving in the direction of prescriptive interventions for identified deficits and/or distortions.

Second, the role of intellectual abilities deserves methodologically rigorous assessment. If intelligence is in some way said to be intertwined within the social problem solving "faculty," then intelligence must be controlled or its effects otherwise taken into account. That intelligence is functionally involved in social behavior is typically acknowledged and researchers proceed by trying to remove the variability accounted for by intellectual ability. However, the measures of intellectual ability that are often employed are less than comprehensive. For instance, Rubin and Krasnor, as well as others such as Spivack and Shure, have used the Peabody Picture Vocabulary Test (PPVT, a measure of receptive vocabulary) to partial out the effects of intelligence. While it is true that vocabulary correlates highest with overall IQ, vocabulary alone does not account for all of intellectual functioning. In the Rubin and Krasnor data, for instance, PPVT IQ was significantly correlated with problem-solving success (see page 47 , this volume). Use of the age appropriate Wechsler scale would be a preferred intellectual assessment. If properly assessed, mental age, as an absolute marker of intellectual ability, may be a more appropriate covariate than the relative marker, IQ. Also, I clearly recognize the attendant difficulties (e.g., time consumption, need for trained examiners) associated with the recommendation to use more comprehensive measures of intelligence. Nevertheless, the variance accounted for by intellectual ability must be dealt with properly.

APPROACHING THEORY

Because children, as adults, are not gifted with premonitions, they do not know when a social problem is going to exist nor how to correct it until they first recognize the problem, inhibit routine or rash reactions, and engage in problem-solving thought and action. Correspondingly, I advance the position that a theory of social problem solving must address (a) social cues and (b) impulse control.

Skills in social problem solving are associated with the acquisition of cue recognition skills: a child with "social antennae" picks up the signal that a social problem requiring a solution is emerging, and does so much sooner than a child lacking recognition of social cues. Because social problem solving involves an interruption in routine interaction, the first step in social problem solving is impulse control: a child with impulse control will be able to refrain from rash action, entertain various potential problem solutions without prematurely selecting and acting out one, and control any action tendencies that may be triggered by the social problem but detrimental to its resolution. The ability to recognize the cues, inhibit initial reactions, and subsequently engage in problem solving involves social schemata. These social schemata, or guiding templates for interaction, develop as a child comes to gain more experience in social situations and simultaneously learns to make finer and finer discriminations. A system of cues develops where the child recognizes a great deal about the social situation from small amounts of information, and these cues trigger cognitive functioning and control behavior.

It should be recognized, however, that the development of a potent social schema requires much time and numerous interactions in the context in which the social problems typically emerge (e.g., with peers). In contrast to a schema about a physical object, social schemata require more experience since the child must evaluate the various features of each social encounter, and these social encounters are highly variable.

Before closing, I want to add one more note of praise. Drs. Rubin and Krasnor deserve credit for taking a difficult question and *settling in* to searching out the answers. Their's is not a flash-in-the-pan paper, nor is it a whimsical analysis. Drs. Rubin and Krasnor are going beyond being seminal pioneers— they are becoming valued settlers.

REFERENCES

Achenbach, T. M. (1978). The Child Behavior Profile, I: Boys aged 6–11. *Journal of Consulting and Clinical Psychology, 46,* 478–488.

Baucom, D. H. (1982). A comparison of behavioral contracting and problem-solving/communications training in behavioral marital therapy. *Behavior Therapy, 13,* 162–174.

Fischler, G. L., & Kendall, P. C. (1985). *Social cognitive problem solving skills and childhood adjustment: Qualitative and topological analyses.* Manuscript submitted for publication, Temple University.

Kendall, P. C. (1984). Social cognition and problem-solving: A developmental and child-clinical interface. In B. Gholson & T. Rosenthal (Eds.), *Applications of cognitive development theory.* New York: Academic Press.

Kendall, P. C., & Braswell, L. (1985). *Cognitive-behavioral therapy for impulsive children.* New York: Guilford.

Kendall, P. C., & Fischler, G. L. (1984). Behavioral and adjustment correlates of problem-solving: Validational analyses of interpersonal cognitive problem-solving measures. *Child Development, 55,* 879–892.

Kendall, P. C., & Wilcox, L. E. (1979). Self-control in children: The development of a rating scale. *Journal of Consulting and Clinical Psychology, 47,* 1020–1030.

Robin, A. L. (1981). A controlled evaluation of problem-solving communication training with parent-adolescent conflict. *Behavior Therapy, 12,* 593–609.

Sarason, I. G., & Sarason, B. R. (1981). Teaching cognitive and social skills to high school students. *Journal of Consulting and Clinical Psychology, 49,* 908–918.

Urbain, E. S., & Kendall, P. C. (1980). A review of social-cognitive problem solving interventions with children. *Psychological Bulletin, 88,* 109–143.

Weissberg, R. P., Gesten, E. L., Rapkin, B. D., Cowen, E. L., Davidson, E., de Apodaca, R. F., & McKim, B. J. (1981). Evaluation of a social-problem-solving training program for suburban and inner-city third-grade children. *Journal of Consulting and Clinical Psychology, 49,* 251–261.

3

A Social Information Processing Model of Social Competence in Children

Kenneth A. Dodge
Indiana University

History suggests that the most rapid and widespread advances in our knowledge of basic scientific processes often occur in pursuit of the solution to a practical and applied problem. The applied problem guiding the field of research to be described in this chapter is a simple one: How can aggressive children be taught to adopt nonaggressive behavioral patterns in their interactions with peers? In pursuing the solution to this problem I have frequently borrowed ideas from the theories of cognitive, social, and developmental psychology. At the same time, one outcome of this research program may well be a contribution to those theories. The interplay between the basic and the applied is an aspect of this research which seems to have a favorable impact on both theory and practice.

The conceptual framework guiding this research is the following: What is the nature of the relations among social cognition, antisocial behavior, and social maladjustment in children? There obviously exists a long history of studying children's social cognitive development (reviewed by Shantz, 1983), as well as a long history of studying children's prosocial and antisocial behaviors (cf. Parke & Slaby, 1983). There also exists an emerging literature on children's social maladjustment and the implications of unfavorable early peer relations for later psychiatric and social outcomes (cf. Asher & Hymel, 1981). Until recently, these fields of research have existed as separate entities, with little cross-fertilization of ideas about how cognition, behavior, and adjustment may relate to each other. Indeed, Flavell and Ross (1981) commented only several years ago that the study of the relation between social cognition and social behavior is "almost virgin terrain" (p. 314) for researchers. A goal of this chapter is to describe, conceptually and empirically, how these processes may be intertwined.

In this chapter, research efforts to relate social cognition to social behavior are reviewed selectively, with the intent of understanding factors involved in past failures. Three of the most striking factors are noted. These include the myth of the single factor solution, overgeneralizability across social situations, and the absence of a comprehensive theoretical model of the cognition-behavior relation. While some researchers have been interested in the relation between various environmental circumstances and patterns of social cognition in a single instance (such as Ferguson & Rule, 1980), the present chapter is concerned both with processing at one point in time and with enduring cognitive processes such as skills. A model of social competence, based on the social information processing principles put forth by Flavell (1974), Goldfried (Goldfried & d'Zurilla, 1969), McFall (1982), and Simon (Newell & Simon, 1972), is described in detail. Selected studies of social information processing are interpreted according to this model. A major hypothesis of this model is that a comprehensive assessment of the skills and sequential patterns involved in a child's processing of social information will yield powerful predictions about that child's social behavior and adjustment. Two novel empirical studies testing this hypothesis are described. These studies have implications for a theory of social information processing as well as for the assessment and treatment of children's social maladjustment.

PAST FAILURES AND SUCCESSES

In the search for explanations of children's deviant aggressive behavior, researchers in the past decade have begun to study the role of social cognitive processes, particularly skill deficits (Eron, 1980; Kendall & Finch, 1979). While this research has provided support for the hypothesis that cognitive skill deficits are related to deviant social behavior, refutations of this hypothesis also have been found frequently. Three cognitive skills have received the most attention from researchers studying aggression: role-taking, empathy, and problem-solving. Chandler (1973) and Selman (1976) have found in their studies that delinquent and institutionalized emotionally disturbed boys who displayed aggressive behavior were relatively deficient in the skills of role-taking and perspective-taking. More impressively, Chandler (Chandler, Greenspan, & Barenboim, 1974) has also demonstrated that training in these skills can lead to improvements in adolescents' behavior, as rated by counselors. Other studies, such as that by Kurdek (1978), have demonstrated that a *high* score on tests of perspective-taking abilities may be associated with frequent disruptions and fighting. The relation between role-taking ability and deviant aggressive behavior, then, remains uncertain.

Feshbach (1970) has hypothesized that both cognitive and affective components of the construct of empathy should lead children who are empathic to behave in prosocial ways and to refrain from aggression. According to Feshbach, the cognitive component enables a child to understand another's perspective during a conflict with a peer, thereby reducing the probability that the child will view the peer as deserving of aggressive retaliation. The affective component allows the child to experience vicariously the emotional distress of a victim during an aggressive interaction. This distress should lead to an instinctive withdrawal of aggression. Feshbach and Feshbach (1969) have found support for this hypothesis, as assessed by a negative correlation between scores on the Feshbach and Roe Affective Situation Test for Empathy and aggressive behavior. This support was limited to boys over 5 years of age and did not extend to girls, however. Mixed results have also been found by Eisenberg-Berg and Lennon (1980) and Rothenberg (1970).

The relation between problem-solving skills and antisocial behavior also has been studied extensively, particularly by Spivack and Shure (1974; Spivack, Platt, & Shure, 1976) and Krasnor and Rubin (1981). The essence of Spivack and Shure's position is that the more solutions a child can generate to a hypothetical social problem the more likely that child is to respond to the problem in prosocial ways when he or she actually encounters it. Their empirical work supports this position and has led to training programs for children of all ages. Krasnor and Rubin, however, argue that the ability to generate many solutions to problems is at best marginally related to social outcomes. Their empirical work elegantly demonstrates the importance of assessing the quality of children's social problem-solving attempts, both in hypothetical situations and in naturally occurring circumstances.

The contradictory findings in each of these areas of research lead us to conclude that the promising aspirations of social cognitive psychology remain just a promise. Meta-analyses of these literatures are likely to lead to conclusions that the relation between any broadly conceived cognitive skill and antisocial behavior and adjustment is empirically significant but weak in magnitude. In other words, most studies of broad cognitive processes seem to account for only small portions of the variance in antisocial behavior.

At least three factors may be responsible for the low correlations between cognition and behavior. The first may be called the myth of the single factor solution. Researchers have proceeded as if a single social cognitive factor (such as role-taking skill) should predict all of social behavior and adjustment. Certainly, children's behavioral responses in social situations are determined by more than one cognitive process, as suggested by the wide variety of cognitive activities that have been studied in this context. These processes range from the inhibition of premature responding (Camp, 1977; Dodge & Newman, 1981) to the accurate reading of social cues (Dodge, Murphy & Buchsbaum, 1984; Gottman, Gonso, & Rasmussen, 1975). Even when researchers are aware of the multiple processes involved in cognition, they have rarely conducted assessments of multiple processes in a single study. Clinicians are equally guilty of accepting this myth when they have devised interventions directed toward altering a single process or training a single skill.

A second reason for the low correlations is that researchers have failed to attend to the situation-specificity of social behavior. A reference to Mischel's (1968) eloquent treatise of this point is obligatory here. Children who are anti-social do not behave in antisocial ways in all situations, just as a child's level of social cognitive skill performance varies across task domains (Fisher, 1980; Ford, 1979). Still, researchers have sometimes treated their cognitive and behavioral constructs as encompassing many situations. The outcome is an aggregated assessment of divergent performance levels and, therefore, weak predictive power (McFall & McDonel, 1983). This point is not a simple deferral to a radical notion of *no* cross-situational continuity. In fact, the processes assessed by researchers may have some cross-domain consistency. Nevertheless, the strongest predictions of the relation between cognitive processes and social behavior should come from assessments of cognitive processes in one situation and behavior in the same kind of situation.

Researchers must also provide more differentiated predictions about the nature of the relation between cognitive processes and behavior within a given situation. It is not enough to believe that the only prediction necessary is that "good cognition predicts good behavior." In an effort to provide a more differentiated prediction, Richard and Dodge (1982) assessed both the quantity and the competence of children's responses to hypothetical problems about how to persuade a peer to do something and then related those measures to the children's behavioral performance during an actual persuasion task. They found that the quantity of solutions that a child generated to the hypothetical problem predicted the quantity of persuasion attempts that the child later displayed, whereas the rated competence of the solutions that the child generated predicted the success that the child had in actually persuading a peer. Such a specific finding should encourage researchers toward more differentiated constructs and predictions.

Finally, researchers have not adequately described a theory of how social cognition can lead to particular behavioral responses. According to Shantz (1983), "In short, there is not specific and detailed theory guiding the research on social-cognitive/behavioral relations" (p. 526). Such a theory must be neither so broad as to be untestable, nor so idiosyncratic as to lack utility (Popper, 1962). Rather, the theory should specify the requisite cognitive processes involved in responding to environmental stimuli. The theory should also lead directly to methods of assessing cognitive processes and intervening to alter those processes that lead to antisocial behavior.

MODELS OF SOCIAL COGNITION

The framework for a comprehensive model of social cognition can be found in the writing of theorists in several disciplines, including cognitive, developmental, and clinical psychology. Flavell and Ross' (1981) comment about virgin terrain applies more to empirical work, for theories have sprung up in many places over the past decade. The model that is formulated in this chapter is derived from Flavell's (1974) conceptions of the steps involved in making social inferences, Goldfried and d'Zurilla's (1969) problem-solving strategy training program, Simon's (Newell & Simon, 1972) and Hayes' (1981) information processing theories of cognitive problem solving, and McFall's (1982; McFall & Dodge, 1982) reformulation of social skills theory. Other theories are also plausible (e.g., Ford, 1984) but have not been the basis of this work. Brief summaries of these positions provide a background to the present conjectures.

Flavell (1974) described four steps, or sequential cognitive events, involved in making social inferences. First is the awareness of the *existence* of the internal events or cognitions of another individual. Second, he described the child's recognition of the *need* to make an inference about another person. Third, the child must make an actual *inference* about the other's cognitive activities, and finally, the child must use the inference, in *application,* in determining his or her own behavior. Flavell posited that these events take place sequentially during a single social interaction, and that each step is acquired in sequential order during development. Flavell's model, being based in cognitive developmental theory, necessarily emphasizes the inference-making aspects of the cognition-behavior relation, at the expense of the behavioral aspects.

Goldfried and d'Zurilla (1969), on the other hand, outlined the following set of cognitive operations constituting their social problem-solving training program. These operations are thought to be prerequisites in order for an individual to behave in a competent manner. First, the individual must come to a clear understanding of the problematic situation or context which is confronting him or her. Second, the person must make a search of "possible alternative solutions" or behavioral responses to this situation. Third, the person must engage in a decision-making process in which possible consequences of various alternatives are contemplated and an optimal response is chosen. Finally, the individual must act out the optimal response in skillful behavior. This perspective has been called a behavior-analytic model and has been the basis for several intervention programs, with both adults and children.

Simon (Newell & Simon, 1972) and Hayes (1981) have utilized the metaphor of the computer to note the paths an individual takes in processing information and solving cognitive problems. Hayes described the following sequence of actions. First, the individual must find the problem, that is, become aware of its existence. Next, he or she must mentally represent the problem in an efficient manner. This representation may be aided by analogies, schemas, and imagery. Once the problem is mentally represented, the individual must begin a search for possible solutions. Search may take place through trial and error, systematic means-ends analysis, or other search heuristics. Next, the individual must carry out the selected solution, which is referred to as a protocol. This protocol must then be evaluated by the individual in order to determine whether or not the intended goal has been reached. Finally, the individual must use a memory to "consolidate gains" so that the problem will be easier to solve the next time it is confronted. Hayes (1981) has described how skillful processing at each of these steps can lead to efficient and effective solutions to complex cognitive tasks.

McFall (1982) distinguishes between social competence, which is a judgment by peers about the effectiveness of a person's social behavior, and social skills, which are objectively determined components of the overall behavior. The major social skill processes outlined by McFall are similar to some of those described by other theorists. These include decoding (skills of reading the cues presented in a situation), response search (skills of selecting a response), and encoding (skills of enacting the chosen response and monitoring its effectiveness). According to McFall, if a person displays skills in these component processes, the probability is high that he or she will behave in a manner that is judged as competent.

While these theoretical positions vary in the specific processes described, they have in common several characteristics. Each assumes that stimulus cues in the environment may be conceptualized as a problem or task which confronts the individual. The individual's behavior is goal-directed, that is, directed toward responding to this task. Each theorist describes a set of cognitive operations which are thought to be necessary in order to complete the task or to perform in a competent manner. Each describes the process in its ideal form, implying that deficiencies occur in the form of deviations from the ideal. This ideal form consists of a set of processes which must occur in sequential temporal order. These processes seem to include encoding and interpreting environmental cues (McFall's decoding process), deriving a behavioral response (Simon's problem solving), and enacting the chosen response in behavior (McFall's encoding process).

The model described in this chapter integrates and extends these ideas in a logical manner. The goal of the model is to describe how children process social information in order to respond in social settings. A unique feature of the proposed model is that it describes a set of operations which are thought to occur during each behavioral interaction, but which also may be conceptualized as enduring skills and typical patterns. While the model describes competent performance (like other models), it also describes how cognitions operate to result in behavior that is not easily conceptualized simply as competent or incompetent (such as aggression). This model forms the basis for the empirical work to be reported here. While the model was formulated specifically as a way of understanding individual differences in children's aggressive behavior, it also describes basic social cognitive processes and provides clear directions for clinicians interested in the assessment and treatment of behavioral disorders. Finally, the model can serve to organize the seemingly divergent literatures on the relation between social cognition and social behavior, by noting conceptual similarities among studies. A similar function was served recently by Ladd and

Mize's (1983) organization of the social cognitive treatment literature according to component processes.

A PROPOSED MODEL

According to the proposed model (depicted in Figure 3.1), a child comes to a particular social situation or task with a biologically determined set of response capabilities (analogous to a computer's hardware) and a data base (his or her memory store of past experiences, which predisposes the child toward a particular goal or way of responding), and he or she receives as input from the environment a set of social cues. That child's behavioral response to those cues occurs as a function of the way that he or she processes the presented social information. We presume that this processing occurs in sequential stages, or steps. Each step is a necessary part of competent responding. The steps, however, are not necessarily acted on in a conscious manner. Awareness of processing occurs only during highly novel or complex tasks, or when a cue is given to call the process into awareness (such as when a researcher asks a child what he or she is thinking). If the child processes the information skillfully, efficiently, and accurately, the probability is great that he or she will behaviorally respond in a manner that is judged by others to be competent. Failure to respond skillfully at a step or responding in a biased manner increases the probability that the child will behave in a deviant, possibly aggressive, way. Idiosyncratic processing presumably leads to idiosyncratic behavior.

The first step of social information processing for the child is to encode the social cues in the environment. The child must receive cues through sensory processes and then perceive them. Because of the tremendous amount of information present in the social environment at a single moment, the child must learn skills of attending to appropriate cues, chunking information, and using rehearsal and mnemonic devices in order to store the information. The child must perform this task efficiently, for the encoding occurs in real time. Also, the child must perform in a manner that is free from debilitating biases. For example, in responding to a provocation by a peer (such as being shoved out of line at school), a child may focus on the cues of the peer who has instigated the provocation, his or her internally generated cues of being hurt, or the cues of peer observers of the event. Because the child cannot attend to all cues simultaneously, he or she must learn heuristics for efficiently encoding cues. It is hypothesized that inefficiency or inaccuracy at this step increases the probability that the child will eventually behave in a deviant, incompetent, or inappropriate manner.

Once cues have been encoded, the next step for the child is to engage in a mental representation and interpretation process. The child must integrate the cues with his or her memory of past experiences and come to a meaningful

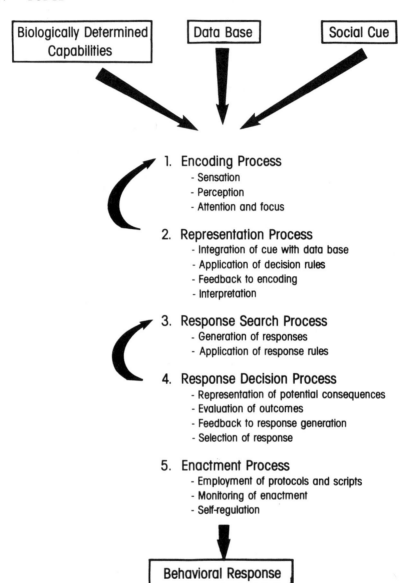

FIG. 3.1.   A social information processing model of competence

understanding of the cues. This step is often indistinguishable from the first, in that it is sometimes difficult to assess a child's encoding of cues without simultaneously assessing his or her representation of those cues. In fact, the representation step may have a feedback loop to the encoding step, if the child determines that not enough information has been encoded to interpret the gestalt of the stimulus or if contradictory interpretations are being made. The interpretation is presumed to be made by integrating the encoded cues with the existing data base through the application of heuristic programmed decision rules. These rules are either pre-programmed innately (such as recognition of threat) or are acquired in development, based on direct learning experiences or through the child's active construction of rules. For example, the child who is the recipient of a provocation by a peer must make an interpretation about the event. He or she may utilize cues about the severity of the outcome of the provocation to decide that the peer acted with hostile intent. Alternatively, he or she may utilize cues about the peer's surprised and sorrowful facial expression to decide that the peer acted benignly. A third possibility is that the child's representation of the event will be made in the absence of the utilization of presented cues. Such is the case when the child has failed to attend to the cues at all. At these first two steps of encoding and representation, it is obvious that both skill deficits (such as failing to interpret accurately the presented cues or failing to utilize these cues) and cognitive biases in processing (such as attending only to negative cues or overinterpreting hostile intentions) may lead to behavioral responses which are viewed by others as deviant.

The third step in processing social information is a response search. Once the child has represented the encoded information in a meaningful way, he or she can engage in a generative process of searching for possible behavioral responses. Since even young children have available in their repertoire a wide variety of responses, the individual learns to apply rule structures as a way of accessing reasonable responses to specific stimulus sets. For example, the child who has encoded information that he or she has been the victim of a provocation by a peer and has interpreted the peer's behavior as benign may apply the following response rule, acquired through socialization: If the peer acted without hostility, then I have available to me the option of forgiving the provocation. Piaget (1932/1965) pointed out that young children first acquire a different rule: If I have been hurt, then I can hit back. It is apparent that generative skills, acquired rule structures, past experiences, available response repertoires, and the sequence of processing up to that point (the encoding and representation of cues) all have an impact on the responses that are generated. It is the case that deviant responses may be generated either as a function of deviant processing up to that point (such as an aggressive response being generated as a function of an inaccurate interpretation that a peer has been hostile) or as a function of inadequate search skills or biased searching (such as when a child only generates or accesses a deviant response).

The next step of processing is a response decision step. Ideally, the child learns to evaluate the potential consequences of each generated response and to estimate the probability of favorable outcomes. In choosing a behavioral response, the child must take into account the environmental context and his or her own behavioral capabilities. One response may not be effective *in this situation,* whereas another response may not be effective because the child does not have the behavioral skills to carry it out (such as verbal skills in persuading a peer). Of course, the process of generating likelihood estimates of probable outcomes requires a kind of mental representational skill (Piaget, 1928) that is acquired in development. Young children may be unable to make accurate estimates because they cannot hold the necessary information in working memory for a sufficient period of time. A useful analogy here is the computer chess player. The computer responds to an opponent's move by generating countermoves and evaluating the consequences of each move. The move having the best consequences is selected for enactment. The size and sophistication of the computer's memory and the stored past experiences determine the computer's capability of determining probabilities of outcomes one, two, three, or more moves ahead. The more sophisticated the memory and operation of the computer, the more competent the chosen response will be.

Outcome estimates may also be biased, due to past experiences or to faulty processing at an earlier step. Such may be the case when a child has misinterpreted a peer's behavior as hostile; he or she may be likely to generate outcome estimates that are equally skewed. Even more obvious is the case when the computer has been fed inaccurate information about an opponent's prior move. The entire process of evaluating potential outcomes is also one that is acquired developmentally. A young child may respond deviantly because he or she has not engaged in an outcome evaluation process at all, and has simply enacted the first response that was assessed. Whalen, Henker, Collins, McAuliffe, and Vaux (1979) have proposed this possibility as an explanation of the impulsive behavior of hyperactive boys. The response decision process must have a direct feedback loop to the response search process, in the same way that the representation process loops with the encoding process. If the outcome evaluation leads to unsatisfactory outcome estimates for every response generated, the competent response would consist of returning to an earlier stage of processing, in order to generate more possible responses. The subprocesses involved in response decisions are obviously complex, and behavioral responding can be adversely affected by skill deficits, lags in development, and biased outcome estimates at this step of processing social information.

When an optimal response has been selected, the child then proceeds to act it out, in the fifth step of processing called enactment. Behavioral protocols (using Hayes', 1981, term) and scripts (using Abelson's, 1976, term), involving verbal and motoric skills, are important here. These skills are presumably acquired in development through rehearsal, feedback, and practice. Consider the child who has decided to respond to a peer's provocation with an inquiry of the peer as to why he may have committed the provocation. That child must possess verbal skills and be able to enact a behavioral script, in order to be successful with this behavioral strategy.

The model of social information processing outlined here is a transactional one (see Fig. 3.2). That is, it is presumed that the process does not terminate at the point of enactment because it involves another person. The child must monitor the effects of his or her behavior on the other persons involved in the social interaction. If the behavior is not leading to its desired effect, it must be altered accordingly. This is a self-regulatory process which is presumably mastered during development. The cues that a child would use to alter his or her behavior, however, constitute new input from the environment. This process is therefore a repetition of the five-step process already described. As shown in Fig. 3.2, a peer's behaviors, which are cues to the first child, are also enactments by the peer. It must be remembered that the peer is also engaged in social information processing. If a child responds in an inappropriately aggressive way to a social situation, the peer may be likely to process this information in a way which leads him or her to label the child as deviant and respond by rejecting the child. As a result, the child may acquire even further social difficulties. In this way, the cognitive operations of each child interact with each other's behavior in a transaction, as if in a chess match.

The proposed model is one of continual encoding of cues (input), operating on those cues (data crunching), and enacting the outcome of the operations (output). Each output is also an input for the next operation. The first, third, and fifth steps of the proposed process may be conceptualized as data-generating, or action, steps. The second and fourth steps and the regulatory process are data evaluating, or decision, steps. One limitation of the model as described here is its apparent static quality, as if each of these steps is independent of the others (J. Youniss, personal communication, 1982). Obviously, the steps exist in dynamic relation to each other. The encoding of cues influences how those cues are interpreted, but also the interpretation of cues influences how the cues are encoded. The response generation process sets the domain of response possibilities for the response decision process, but the decision process also has an impact on which responses get generated. Ford (1984) has presented a dynamic model of directive, regulatory, and control processes in interaction with each other. His model may have a richer flavor than the proposed model. The proposed model is rooted in the reality of time and logic, however. It is proposed that given a single stimulus, one step *must* precede the next. This aspect of the proposed model leads to testable hypotheses.

ASSUMPTIONS OF THE SOCIAL INFORMATION PROCESSING APPROACH

One assumption of the proposed model is that processing occurs at a very rapid rate. While the model has been described almost as if a controller sits inside the

A RECIPROCAL INFLUENCE MODEL OF AGGRESSION

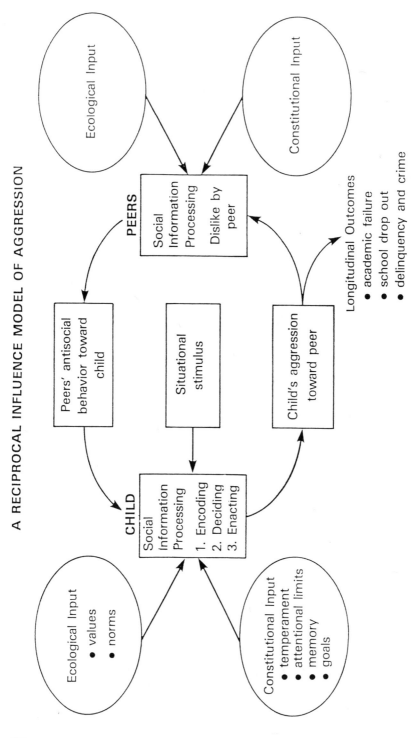

FIG. 3.2. A reciprocal influence model of aggression

88

child's head and meticulously weighs various options, it must be remembered that this description is a metaphor, in the same way that the "human computer" is a metaphor. The image of a thinking controller is obviously inaccurate, because it would preclude responding in real time.

It is further assumed that the processing of social information can occur at a nonconscious level. If not, it would preclude goal-directed social behavior in infants and persons who are not consciously aware of their cognitive and behavioral actions. In fact, this model relies on nonconscious processing to explain the occurrence of biases in processing and responding. Conscious processing is most likely to occur in highly problematic situations when a novel response is called for, or when there is a cue to bring the processing to the level of awareness. Nonconscious processing occurs either in children who have not yet learned principles of meta-cognition (Flavell, 1981) or in individuals who have over-learned responses to particular social stimuli and are acting in automatic (Shiffrin & Schneider, 1977) or mindless (Langer, Blank, & Chanowitz, 1978) processing modes. In the former case, rapid development in social competence may result from teaching the child that he or she can engage in a conscious process of operating on social stimuli. In the latter case, it is as if the individual is behaving in an "automatic-pilot" mode of guiding his or her own actions. In both cases, the proposed model assumes that the essential features and structures of social information processing are the same at conscious and nonconscious levels.

This last statement is highly speculative and must be considered carefully. If theory and research in social information processing continue to progress at the rate they have over the past 5 years, data may accumulate to evaluate this statement. Until then, it is an assumption. Even if the structures of social information processing are found to differ at conscious and nonconscious levels, the proposed model may still have utility in clinical applications. The steps proposed are logical units to be used in training individuals to become more skillful and efficient information processors. Meichenbaum (1977) has already made reference to Luria's (1961) theories of how usually nonconscious behavior sets can be segmented and taught in conscious fashion. Over time, the conscious process becomes automatic. It must be noted that mere consciousness of the proposed processes is not a necessary goal of all intervention efforts in this context. In fact, consciousness of the processing of social information may actually be debilitating, as in the example of a socially anxious adolescent who ruminates about the meaning of every cue from peers.

A final assumption of the proposed model is that the processes described at each step are separable. By separable, it is meant that they can be measured independently. They are also sequential, however, so an assessment of one step of processing is confounded by the effects of preceding steps. For example, assessing a child's response decision skills (step 4) will lead to measures that are confounded by the child's encoding (step 1), interpretation (step 2), and response search (step 3) skills. A deviant outcome may be a function of any step, or any combination of steps. A procedure for attaining independent measurements of each of these skills has been suggested by McFall and Dodge (1982) and consists of holding each preceding step constant. In order to measure only response decision skills as they are defined in step 4 of the proposed model, one must hold the preceding steps constant by standardizing them. For example, one could present various possible behavioral responses to a stimulus social cue and ask the subject to engage in a response decision process. This assumption provides the impetus for the empirical research to be described in this chapter and for a series of studies that have been conducted over the past several years. It also provides the conceptual basis for the potential clinical assessment of social information processing deficits in aggressive children.

SELECTED REVIEW OF SOCIAL INFORMATION PROCESSING RESEARCH

Even given a lack of theoretical grounding, as noted by Shantz (1983), the empirical literature on social information processing correlates of antisocial behavior in children has grown remarkably over the past decade. Even though many of these studies are not based explicitly on the theoretical structure provided in this chapter, just about all of the studies may be conceptualized as an assessment of one or more of the components of the proposed model. The following selected review demonstrates the utility of this model as an organizer of this literature. The bulk of this literature demonstrates that social information processing follows ontogenetic patterns and that measures of processing skills and styles are significantly, but moderately, correlated with measures of antisocial behavior and social adjustment. Particular emphasis is placed on the author's research, in order to provide a background for the studies to be described later. It is not implied that these studies have any greater significance than many studies not mentioned.

Assessments of social cues, goals, and past experiences. The proposed model postulates that the initial inputs into a social transaction involve a set of social cues from the environment and a set of goals and a memory store from the individual. The effect of characteristics of social cues on the probability that a child will respond aggressively is obvious (Feshbach, 1970). A provocation stimulus, such as being physically thwarted or injured by a peer, is a cue for an aggressive response, but only when the perpetrator of the stimulus acts with hostile and malicious intent (Berkowitz, 1977). When the perpetrator acts with benign intent, the individual is likely to refrain from aggression (Marshall & McCandless, 1957; Rule, Nesdale, & McAra, 1974). In spite of initial speculation that the effect of the perpetrator's intent on aggressive responding might emerge developmentally at the stage of cognitive decentration (Feshbach, 1970;

Piaget, 1965), the empirical literature has demonstrated that children even as young as five and six differentiate their behavior according to an intention cue (Darley, Klossen, & Zanna, 1978; Dodge, 1980). The magnitude of the effect of the intention cue does seem to grow with development, however (Shantz & Voydanoff, 1973).

There is also evidence that properties of the stimulus cue affect the accuracy of children's encoding and representation of the cue. For example, Dodge, Murphy, and Buchsbaum (1984) have found that hostile cues are more easily recognized by 5-year-old children than accidental or prosocial cues. More sophisticated and accurate representation of cues is known to occur when the stimulus person and the respondent are of the same gender (Deutsch, 1974; Feshbach & Roe, 1968), the same race (Klein, 1971), or the same age (Flapan, 1968). Other social cue variables associated with processing accuracy and anti-social behavior have been reviewed by Shantz (1983).

A major proposition of the present model is that social cues can be conceptualized as social tasks or problems. Whether these tasks are most usefully defined in broad terms (such as the task of adjusting to the beginning of school) or narrow terms (such as the task of responding to a greeting by a peer) is a matter of debate in the current clinical assessment literature (Goldfried & Linehan, 1977). Certainly the concept of tasks is not new, as it guided the developmental theories of Erickson (1950) and Freud (1969). The tasks discussed by those theorists were quite broadly defined, such as establishing a trusting relationship in infancy and discovering a sense of identity in adolescence. Argyle, Furnham, and Graham (1981) have conceptualized social tasks in a much more limited way, preferring to define tasks in terms of specific topographical properties of a stimulus at a given point in time. Because McFall and Lillesand (1971) and Schwartz and Gottman (1976) have found that assessments of responses to specific situations have stronger predictive power than do measures of global response patterns, the proposed model has been organized around the concept of the specific social task.

One feature of social tasks is that they specify a goal for a child. In fact, a child's competence in a particular social situation may be defined as the degree to which the child is successful at solving the relevant task and meeting a specified goal. While topographical chracteristics of the social stimulus help define the task and goal, past experiences and values of the child also help shape individual differences in how tasks are construed and how goals are prioritized. Renshaw & Asher (1982) have demonstrated, for example, that children have different social goals and that these varying goals are related to their sociometric status. Socially rejected children tend to place priority on avoidant or competitive goals, whereas popular children place priority on maintaining the social relationship.

The consideration of a child's social goals has received a great deal of attention from researchers recently (e.g., Ford, 1984; Krasnor, 1983). Locke, Shaw, Saari, and Latham (1981) have argued that goal setting itself has a major impact on task performance and must be considered an important part of information processing. One problem with the construct of goals is their measurement in a particular situation. While Renshaw & Asher (1982), Ford (1984), and Krasnor (1983) argue persuasively that goals act forcibly on processing and behavior, it is not clear that they can be measured separately from the steps of information processing in the proposed model. If goals have an effect on behavior in a single situation, this effect will emerge when the child's response search and response evaluation processes are assessed. If a child has avoidant goals, these will emerge as responses generated by the child. Krasnor (1983), for example, assessed children's strategies in response to social problems and inferred a set of social goals based on the quality of responses. Since goals may be transient and may be created as a function of the way information is processed, it may be more efficient simply to assess a child's processing of social information according to the proposed five steps and to relate these measures to behavior than to rely on an underlying construct of goals. Likewise, it may be difficult to intervene directly to change a child's goals. More effective behavioral change may occur by teaching a child to generate different behavioral responses. The child's goals would also change indirectly.

Assessment of the encoding process.   The first step of social information processing involves many substeps, beginning with the simple recognition that cues exist, as Flavell (1974) pointed out. Encoding patterns clearly evolve and become more sophisticated as children get older and learn to focus on certain cues. Livesley and Bromley (1973) have found that younger children tend to focus on concrete features of specific stimuli, whereas older children learn to attend to generalities and psychological aspects of stimuli, including traits, habits, and the beliefs of the stimulus person.

Recently, the author (Dodge & Newman, 1981) has developed a method for assessing children's encoding patterns. In one study, children were invited to listen to audiotaped social cues as long as they wanted until they were ready to make a decision about the intention of a peer represented in the cues. It was found that 6-year-olds listened to only two thirds as many cues as did 10-year-olds prior to making a decision. These findings suggest that as children get older their capacity and inclination for encoding many features of social cues increase.

Aspects of the encoding process have also been found to relate to antisocial behavior, as Mischel (1973) has hypothesized. Dodge and Newman (1981) found that nonaggressive boys searched for 40% more cues prior to making an attributional decision than did aggressive boys. Aggressive boys in this study were indentified on the joint bases of peer and teacher assessments of antisocial behavior. This selection procedure was adopted because longitudinal studies (e.g., Coie & Dodge, 1983) have shown that children so identified remain troublesome over long periods of time. Milich and Dodge (1984) found a similar difference in the encoding of cues between hyperactive, aggressive boys in psychiatric treatment and nonaggressive boys also in treatment. This difference may be interpreted as evidence that aggressive boys are "developmentally lagging" in the acquisition of adequate cue search skills since young children respond similarly; alternatively, it may be that they are "perceptually ready" to make attributional decisions about a peer's hostile intent, due to acquired expectancies based on past experiences. Perceptual readiness would lead to shorter cue search (Bruner, 1957). Of course, both explanations may have merit. Finch and Montgomery (1973) similarly found that impulsive, aggressive boys fail to recognize that they can "seek more information" prior to proceeding in a social response process that had nothing to do with attributions of hostile intent. The long-term significance of this cue search skill deficit is dramatically pointed out by recent findings by Mischel (1983) that a measure of a child's delay of gratification (or ability to inhibit premature responding in favor of cue search) in preschool predicted his or her level of social competence 10 years later in adolescence, as assessed by parent ratings.

In addition to the magnitude of the cue search undertaken by children, Dodge and Tomlin (1983) have studied the quality and focus of that cue search. They controlled the amount of cue search by presenting to children a series of eight verbal cues about a peer in a serial order, and asked the children to listen to them and make an attributional decision about the peer's intent in a single situation. They found that aggressive boys and girls (ages 11 to 14) were less likely than nonaggressive others to cite a specific presented cue when justifying their decisions. Instead, they were more likely to cite general expectancies about how peers usually intend to behave. This finding suggests, albeit indirectly, that aggressive children do not encode presented cues as thoroughly as do other children. The serial order of the presented cues also had a significant effect on the decisions by these children. In one experiment, half of the cues suggested that the peer was hostile (these were presented as either the first four cues or the last four cues) and the other half suggested that the peer was benign. The aggressive children displayed a bias toward basing their decisions primarily on the cues presented last, to the neglect of cues presented first (called a recency bias). It was hypothesized that when faced with a decision task, the cue-utilization strategies of aggressive children are deficient (i.e., neglectful of early presented information) and could lead to inaccurate decisions at a later step of information processing. As a test of this hypothesis, a second experiment was conducted. Again, cues were presented to aggressive and nonaggressive children. In this study, six of the eight cues presented to subjects supported one decision while two cues supported an alternate decision. The placements of the two discrepant cues varied systematically as the first two cues presented, the middle two cues, or the last two cues. When the discrepant cues were presented last (and only in this condition), the decisions made by aggressive children were significantly less accurate than the decisions made by other children. This study provides evidence for a specific kind of cue search and utilization deficit in aggressive children.

Assessment of the interpretation process.   The second step of information processing is to make sense of the encoded cues by mentally representing them and interpreting them. As noted earlier, this step is sometimes indistinguishable from the first step because it is not always possible to control experimentally what a child encodes in order to measure only the interpretation made of the encoded cues. Piaget's (1965) distinction between type I and type II processes in making moral judgments may be analogous to the distinction between the first two steps of the proposed model. Research on the processes involved in making inferences about social cues probably constitutes the largest category of social cognitive development research. It exists under a variety of names, including social cognition (Shantz, 1975, 1983), person perception (Livesley & Bromley, 1973), decision theory (White, 1969), decoding (McFall, 1982; Rosenthal, Hall, DiMateo, Rogers, & Archer, 1979), role-taking (Chandler, 1973; Selman, 1976), attributions (Jones & Davis, 1965), and representation of schemas (Miller, 1969) and scripts (Abelson, 1976; Nelson, 1981).

A large number of studies have demonstrated that skills in inference processes develop dramatically during childhood. For example, Camras (1980) has shown that skills in reading facial expressions develop with age. Kendler (1968) has noted that the mental representation necessary in order to make an accurate interpretation of another's intention is a complex cognitive operation which may be difficult for young children. This representation is a part of the construction of decision rule structures which are then applied to the encoded cues. How these rules are constructed and applied is a matter of debate (Flavell, 1977), but it is clear that skills in the use of rules develop ontogenetically (Ruble & Rholes, 1982). Specifically, children acquire in development the use of covariation information (DiVitto & McArthur, 1978; Kelly, 1967), discounting principles (Costanzo, Grumet, & Brehm, 1974), and multiple sufficient and multiple necessary causes (Smith, 1975). They also learn to dispel primitive rules, such as the immanent justice notion (Piaget, 1965).

Aggressive children have been shown in several studies to display distinct patterns in inference making, indicating both biases in interpretations and skill deficits. In a first study of inferences made by aggressive children, we (Dodge, 1980) presented a simple hypothetical ambiguous provocation stimulus to each subject in the form of a brief story (so simple that encoding differences are unlikely to account for the findings). Aggressive boys were 50% more likely than nonaggressive boys to decide that the peer perpetrator of the hypothetical provocation had acted with hostile intent rather than benign intent. Nasby, Hayden, and dePaulo (1979) found a similar attributional bias among institutionalized aggressive adolescent boys, using photographs as stimuli. The attributional bias phenomenon has since been replicated with psychiatrically referred hyperactive, aggressive boys (Milich & Dodge, 1984) and with aggressive girls (Dodge & Tomlin, 1983). Steinberg and Dodge (1983) found that this phenomenon also occurs in actual peer interactions. They subjected aggressive and nonaggressive adolescent boys and girls to an actual ambiguous provocation (having their building blocks knocked to the ground by a peer, which the subject viewed through a one-way mirror), and then asked them to interpret this event. The aggressive subjects were more likely than others to attribute a hostile intention to the peer, both when the peer was familiar to them and when the subject had never met the peer.

Dodge and Frame (1982) examined the limits of the attributional bias phenomenon by asking children to make interpretations of hypothetical events in which they were to imagine themselves as the object of a provocation and other events in which they were to imagine themselves as the observer of a provocation by one peer toward a second peer. If attributional biases were found for the latter situation, it would be concluded that aggressive children hold a generalized hostile world view. They found instead that aggressive boys demonstrated a hostile attributional bias only when they were the object of the provocation, indicating either that placing oneself into a social interaction (real or imagined) disrupts normal interpretation processes among aggressive children or that these children make quite specific, paranoid interpretations of ambiguous events.

In several studies, we have examined the relationship between encoding patterns and interpretive biases in aggressive children. The Dodge and Tomlin (1983) study has already been cited. Dodge and Frame (1982) found that a child's interpretation of a set of cues (including both hostile and benign cues) could be predicted from that child's recall of those cues. Those children who recalled a high proportion of hostile cues were more likely to make hostile interpretations of the stimulus person displaying the cues. Similar findings have been obtained by Dodge and Newman (1982) and Dodge and Tomlin (1983). Of course, recall is only an indirect measure of encoding. Dodge and Newman also found that those children who failed to attend to all possible social cues were the ones most likely to be biased in their interpretations of the cues. It is reasonable to infer that biases in attributions are more likely to occur when clearly encoded cues are not available. It is under these circumstances that a child may rely on pre-existing expectancies to make an attribution. Given that the encoding skills of aggressive children are relatively deficient, they are more likely than others to find themselves in a situation in which they have to rely on their expectations.

Dodge and Frame (1982) wondered whether the biases displayed by aggressive boys applied not only to their interpretations of the intentions of peers' past behavior but also to their expectations that the peer would be likely to continue to act in a hostile manner in the future. Berkowitz (1977) and Novaco (1978) have pointed out that the relation between the interpretation of a peer's actions and subsequent behavior toward the peer may be stronger for an interpretation of the peer's probable future behavior (whether or not the individual perceives a future threat from the peer) than for an interpretation of the peer's past behavior. If so, biased expectations about peers' future behavior would be particularly diagnostic of a child's probable behavioral responses. Dodge and

Frame asked their subjects to make probability estimates about peers' future behavior and found that, indeed, the aggressive children were biased in presuming continued hostility. Ford (1984) points out the distinction between interpretations of past events and interpretations of probable future events, by referring to the latter as *feedforward* (in contrast to feedback). Bandura's (1977) notion of self-efficacy expectations are another example of feedforward biases. Following a review of the evidence on inference-making biases, Nisbett and Ross (1980) concluded that an individual is less likely to utilize presented cue information in making inferences when feedforward is already readily accessible to the individual.

The consensus of these studies leads us to conclude that it is probable that the relation between encoding and interpretation is reciprocal; that is, encoding patterns have an impact on the individual's interpretation of presented cues, while the interpretation has an impact on the selective attention and search that an individual is likely to display the next time that cues must be encoded.

In addition to attributional biases, a number of studies have shown that aggressive children display deficient interpretation skills. Chandler's studies (1973; Chandler et al., 1974) have already been cited as evidence that aggressive children are deficient in role-taking and perspective-taking. Rosenthal et al. (1979) have found a correlation between antisocial adaptation and the ability to decode, or interpret, nonverbal cues from peers. Argyle (1981) found that aggressive juvenile delinquents are deficient in being able to recognize approval and annoyance in others.

In our own work (Dodge et al., 1984), we found that the intention-cue detection skills of rejected, aggressive children are deficient relative to other children, but that the deficiency is restricted to certain kinds of cues. Cues which were known to be hostile, benign, or accidental were presented to children on videotape. The children were asked to make interpretations of the cues. The deviant children were found to be as skilled as others in the accurate detection of hostile intentions in others, but they were deficient in detecting prosocial and benign (accidental) intentions. Consistent with the previously described biases in these children, their errors were most frequently ones of overattribution of hostile intent when the actual intent was prosocial or benign.

While deficiencies in cue-interpretation skills may be correlated with academic skill deficiencies and intelligence, it is not the case that general intelligence differences can account for the interpretation deficiencies observed in aggressive children. In the Dodge et al. (1984) study, for example, the deviant children were deficient even when skill at detecting nonsocial cues (geometric shapes) was taken into account through analyses of covariance. The deficiencies in social information processing among some children being described here appear to be domain-specific and not accountable by general intelligence factors.

Assessment of the response search process.   The third step of processing social information is to generate potential behavioral responses. A good deal of research on response search patterns and skills has been conducted by Spivack and Shure (1974; Spivack et al., 1976), Krasnor (1983), Rubin (1982), and others under the rubric of social problem solving. Typically, this process is assessed by holding the first two processing steps constant and asking a child to generate one or many possible behavioral solutions to hypothetical social problems. Developmental differences in response search skills have been found repeatedly (Pressley, 1979; Spivack et al., 1976), as long as the age differences among children in the studies have been several years or more. Typically, older children are able to generate more, more varied, and more competent responses to hypothetical social problems than younger children.

Differences between aggressive and nonaggressive children have been more complex. The essence of Spivack and Shure's position, for which they gathered a great deal of support, was that the more solutions a child could generate to social problems the more likely that child would be to select and enact a competent solution and be successful in social interactions. Indeed, in their studies, it appeared that socially deviant children generated fewer solutions than their well-adjusted peers. More recently, other researchers (e.g., Krasnor & Rubin, 1981) have argued that the quantity of solutions or responses generated by a child is not as critical as the quality of those solutions. Work in our laboratory has supported this notion. Richard and Dodge (1982), for example, found that the proportion of solutions that a child generated which were classified as incompetent by adult raters was higher for aggressive boys than for popular boys. While aggressive boys generated fewer responses than popular boys did overall, these differences were small (10%). Krasnor (1983), Ladd and Oden (1979), Rubin (1982), and Rubin and Daniels-Beirness (1983) have collectively found that aggressive and deviant children are more likely than others to generate agonistic responses, authority intervention responses, and statistically unique responses (such as bargaining) than are average and well-adjusted children. A reformulation of Spivack and Shure's position is obviously necessary. Generating many responses will not lead to positive behavioral outcomes, unless the responses generated tend to be competent ones. In fact, generating deviant responses makes it more likely that a deviant response will be enacted (presumably because it is more accessible). It also appears that the competent solution-generating capacities of aggressive children may be limited to a single response. In Richard and Dodge's (1982) study, aggressive children were able to generate a single competent response to a hypothetical problem situation, and then began to generate agonistic and ineffective responses, whereas popular children continued to generate competent responses. The sequencing of responses generated, therefore, may also have important consequences. Even with the contradictions in the literature on the response search process noted by Krasnor and Rubin (1981), Krasnor (1983) has found that of all the social behavioral variables that have been related to this process, aggression emerged as the one most strongly implicated.

Response search processes have also been studied by researchers in other areas under other names. Mischel and Patterson (1976; Mischel, 1983), for example, have studied the plans that children generate for responses in situations calling for self-control. Nelson (1981) has studied the scripts that children generate. Friedman, Rosenthal, Donahoe, Schlundt, and McFall (1978) have used a behavior-analytic technique to demonstrate that the responses generated by juvenile delinquents are less competent than those of others. All of these constitute aspects of problem solving and response search.

Another aspect of studying the responses children generate is to assess the relation between the interpretation of a cue made by a child (step 2 of the proposed model) and the response that he or she generates to the cue (step 3 of the model). Hoffman (1977) has noted that ineffective responding to some empathy-soliciting cues may occur either because the child has been unable to make an appropriate interpretation (called empathy) or because that child has been unable to use an empathic interpretation to generate an appropriate response (because of cognitive limitations). In several studies of aggressive children, it appears that both kinds of patterns may operate. In our work (Dodge, 1980), we have found that the interpretation made by a child about an ambiguous provocation cue had a profound impact on the response that he or she generated. When a child made a hostile interpretation, that child generated an aggressive response in 65% of the cases. When a child made a benign interpretation, that child generated an aggressive response only 26% of the time. Because aggressive children made more interpretations of hostility, they generated more aggressive responses. Dodge, Murphy, and Buchsbaum (1984) extended this work by presenting children with several kinds of provocations (hostile, benign, prosocial, and ambiguous) on videotape. They solicited children's interpretations of these stimuli and then asked them to generate their probable behavioral responses to the stimulus. They found that, indeed, responses varied directly as a function of the interpretation made by the child. When a hostile interpretation was made, an agonistic response was likely. In fact, the responses were generated more as a product of the child's interpretation of the stimulus than of the actual qualities of the stimulus. Differences in responses between normal and rejected, aggressive children arose from two independent sources: (1) their interpretations varied (which led to different responses); and (2) their responses varied, even when the same interpretations were made. A reasonable hypothesis to entertain as a result of this study is that the strongest prediction of aggressive behavior or status differences will come from a combined assessment of several steps of information processing, rather than just from an assessment of any single step.

Assessments of the response evaluation and decision process.   The fourth step in processing social information is to conduct utility evaluations of each behavioral response that has been accessed during the preceding response generation process. Obviously, this process is limited by the number and range of responses generated, so the link between these two steps is clear. As with the interpretation process, skillful performance at the response evaluation process requires complex cognitive representation and operation on mental structures. It is hypothesized that the response choice may be determined in a number of possible ways; the most efficient and complete way, as noted by Hayes (1981), would be to assign a probability for positive and desired outcomes by considering the next several moves in a social interaction. As noted by McFall and Dodge (1982), the individual might not be able to consider very many lags into the future, so he or she may develop heuristics, or "default rules," for response decisions. For example, in a social conversation, one default might be the stereotyped head nod to keep the other person talking. Even seemingly reasonable responses become ludicrous unless several lags in behavior are taken into account. Consider the man who tries to reach the moon by adopting a strategy of getting closer to the moon. That man will end up climbing mountains. Examples in the social sphere include the child who tries to purchase friendship with bribes or who coerces friendship with threats. The immediate outcome and the delayed outcome differ greatly.

Several theorists have described potential influences on the response decision process, including Mischel's (1973) behavior-outcome expectancies and Ford's (1984) feedforward notion. Kendall and Wilcox (1979) hypothesized that the impulsive aggressive child may bypass this process altogether. They suggest that this child merely enacts the first response generated, without engaging in an evaluation process. Few researchers have evaluated this process empirically, however. Some measures of the response decision process confound this process with the response research process by only asking the subject to evaluate responses that he or she has generated. Spivack and Shure (1974) have constructed the most widely researched measure of one component of this process, which they have called consequential thinking. They present a child with a potential response and ask the child to describe "what happens next." This measure has not had an impressive history of being related to aggression and social maladjustment (Krasnor & Rubin, 1981). For example, Richard and Dodge (1982) employed a similar method to that used by Spivack and Shure and found that aggressive boys were as accurate as popular boys in evaluating responses presented orally to them by an experimenter. Both groups correctly evaluated 85% to 90% of the responses. At least three explanations of these findings of nondifferences are plausible: (1) the task is typically too easy and suffers from a ceiling effect; (2) oral presentation of responses by the experimenter for evaluation by the subject involves subtle social pressures on the subject to respond in socially conforming ways, thereby obviating potential biased outcomes in expectancy effects; and (3) the non-difference accurately reflects the processing capabilities of aggressive children. If the last alternative proves to be the case, then a potential intervention for aggressive children might consist merely of helping the child to access competent alternative responses. Forty years ago, Chittendon (1942) had success with this approach by suggesting to aggressive children alternate ways of behaving. Zahavi and Asher (1978) experienced similar success. Still, adequate assessment of this process has rarely been achieved. It therefore became one goal of the research reported later in this chapter.

Assessment of the enactment and self-regulation processes.   The fifth step of social information processing is to enact the selected behavioral response in a skillful manner. Also included here are the processes of monitoring the effects of one's behavior on the environment and regulating that behavior accordingly. Verbal and motor skills, acquired over time through rehearsal, practice, and feedback, are necessary for competent performance, so the developmental advances in these processes are obvious. Developmental effects in monitoring and regulating behavior have also been demonstrated by Flavell, Speer, Green & August (1981).

Most assessments of the processes at this fifth step confound the enactment with previous steps of interpretation and response decision. A child may be given a situational cue and be asked to role play his or her response (McFall, 1977). The quality of the role play is a function of both decision skills and enactment skills. Still, clinical researchers have attempted to assess aspects of enactment such as speech duration and loudness (Bellack, Hersen, & Turner, 1976; Eisler, Miller, & Hersen, 1973) and behavioral skillfulness (Gottman et al., 1975). The relation between monitoring processes and social adjustment has received greater attention. Whalen et al. (1979) have hypothesized that a major deficit in hyperactive children is that they fail to alter their behavior according to environmental contingencies and they fail to use some sort of feedback loop when enacting responses. Meichenbaum and Goodman (1971) and Camp (1977) have demonstrated the importance of private speech as a method of self-regulation.

CONCLUSIONS ABOUT THE SOCIAL INFORMATION PROCESSING APPROACH

This selected review of research in this area leads to six tentative conclusions about the relation between social cognition and social behavior. First, the real time demands of processing social information attest to the incredible efficiency of the human organism, but these demands also suggest that breakdowns in behavior may be related to processing overloads. A child may "tune out" of a social interaction because of an inability to process and respond continuously. Inappropriate behavior, due to a loss of attention, may result. The efficiency of human information processing and the demands on the human information processor must be appreciated.

Second, each of the proposed steps appears to be a necessary part of competent performance, but, by itself, is insufficient as an explanation of competent or incompetent behavior. This hypothesis is drawn from logic as well as from the observation that measures of any single step are empirically related to behavioral and adjustment outcomes, but account for only small portions of the variance in those outcomes.

The third conclusion is that the steps of social information processing appear to take place in a temporal sequence. Again, logic supports this notion, but also relevant are the findings indicating that predictions about performance at one step can be made from information about processing at the preceding step. The predictions suggest that one step influences, but does not entirely determine, the next step. A corollary of this conclusion is that the most direct effects on behavioral outcomes occur as a function of the later steps of processing. These later steps are influenced by earlier steps, which are, in turn, influenced by the cues themselves and a memory store of previous experiences.

A fourth conclusion is that a breakdown or deviation in processing at any step can occur in any of three forms. First, the child may fail completely to act at a particular processing step. The child, for example, might respond without awareness of any social cues or without evaluating his or her response at all. This failure to process is a current hypothesis about the cause of impulsive behavior in hyperactive children (Whalen et al., 1979). Second, the child may display a skill deficit in processing, such as inaccurately interpreting a social cue or inaccurately estimating the probability of a successful outcome of a potential response. Of course, failing to process is a form of a skill deficit. Finally, the child may display a deviant bias in processing. The child may assume a social cue has qualities it does not have or may readily access a particular interpretation or response possibility simply because it is highly available. In many ways, deviant biases form another subcategory of skill deficits, in that by definition a deviant bias is inadequate processing. The notion of biases is an important concept to retain, however, because it may explain idiosyncrasies in behaviors which are not readily classifiable as competent or incompetent. For example, one child may consistently respond to a stranger's smile by averting his or her gaze while another child may respond with a return of the smile (see Babad, Alexander, & Babad, 1983). One may wish to refrain from judging either of these reponses as competent or incompetent (and the processing as skillful or unskillful). Biases in the processing of social information, rather than skills and skill deficits, may be able to explain and predict responses in such situations. Biases also highlight the role of affect and emotion in information processing. Biases are particularly useful constructs in assessing responding to unclear, ambiguous, or incomplete social cues. Given that a high proportion of children's aggressive behavior occurs following ambiguous social cues (Dodge, in press), the notion of processing biases may have direct relevance to understanding the evolution of an aggressive response.

A fifth conclusion, more a hypothesis at this point, is that a highly powerful prediction about behavior in a given situation, or overall social adjustment, can be made from a comprehensive assessment of processing at each of the steps of the model. If each step yields useful but insufficient information about potential responding, the aggregated information about processing from all the steps should yield a much stronger prediction. Very few tests of this hypothesis have been conducted. The goal of the first study to be reported later in this chapter is a test of this hypothesis.

A sixth conclusion, also more of a hypothesis, is that behavior in one domain or situation should be predicted more strongly from processing measures in that domain than from measures of processing in other domains. Again, very few tests of this assertion have been conducted. The goal of the second study reported here is a test of this hypothesis.

One final note at this point is a recognition of the fact that the proposed model itself is not being tested by these studies. The model is a heuristic which is not testable. Hypotheses growing out of the model are testable, however. The model can be evaluated by its predictive power and by its utility in leading to clinical assessments and interventions with aggressive children.

A STUDY OF PEER GROUP ENTRY PROCESSING AND BEHAVIOR

The hypotheses described above led to the design of a study in which the goal was to assess the aggregated power of assessments of each social information processing step in predicting children's behavioral responses to an important social task and to their general performance at this task as measured by peer and teacher ratings. The data collected consisted of measurements of information processing steps, measurements of competence and success in an actual behavioral interaction, and peer and teacher ratings of children's general response patterns.

The task selected for this study was that of initiating play with a group of peers who are already engaged in play. Peer group entry is often a necessary first step in the establishment of friendships (Corsaro, 1981) and may have importance for children's overall social development. It is a context that has been studied by researchers of several disciplines (e.g., Brain, 1977; Cicourel, 1974; Fine, 1981; Hess, 1972). Feldman's (1984) survey of teachers and Dodge, McClaskey, and Feldman's (1985) taxonomy of children's social situations reveal that teachers consider this task to be important in differentiating successful from deviant children. Corsaro's (1981) observational study revealed that entry is often a difficult task, resulting in resistance by peers at least half of the time. Since entry attempts are often precursors of aggressive behaviors (Corsaro, 1981), it is possible that children's processing of information about group entry may be an important mediator of aggressive behavior in this context. Putallaz and Gottman (1981) have demonstrated that the group entry context can be studied validly in the laboratory through naturalistic observation in a controlled setting. They found that behavior in this context is related to sociometric status in the classroom, and Putallaz (1983) has found that it predicts sociometric status acquired at a later point in time. Those researchers also conceived of group entry behavior as involving bids and strategies, terms suggestive of behavioral correlates of cognitive processes. In our own work, we (Dodge, Schlundt, Schocken, & Delugach, 1983) have found that the group entry task presents particular difficulties for aggressive children, both in the laboratory and in naturalistic peer group settings. The fact that hypothetical group entry problems often have been used in research on children's social information processing (e.g., Spivack & Shure, 1974) makes this context an ideal one for the study of social cognition-social behavior relations.

Method

This study was conducted in three waves, corresponding to the three types of data, and at three separate points in time. First, boys and girls in kindergarten and first and second grades were administered sociometric assessments of children's competence at peer group entry (similar to Asher, Singleton, Tinsley, & Hymel, 1979). Teachers also made these assessments. Second, 40 subjects participated in a private session designed to assess their processing of information about peer group entry. This assessment was conducted through the use of prepared videorecorded stimulus materials. Finally, each subject participated in an actual group entry task, in which he or she was asked to initiate play with two peers who were already at play. This behavior was videorecorded for later coding and analysis.

Two videorecorded stimulus tapes were prepared with paid child actors for use in assessing children's stepwise processing of group entry information. Because this assessment procedure is novel, it will be described in detail. In the first 20-sec segment of the narrated tape, two children of the same gender and approximately the same age as the subject could be viewed seated at a table together, playing a game. At the end of the segment, the back of a new child's head appears in the foreground of the scene, as if this child is watching the other two children. The scene then stops with the freeze of the last frame, and the narrator asks the subject to imagine that he or she is the child in the foreground of the scene. The narrator asks the following questions, in order (see Table 3.1 for a summary of the derived measures):

1. (Step 2) How much would the first child like you to join them and play with them? How about the second child? (Responses are each scored as 1 [not much], 2 [some], or 3 [very much] with the aid of pictorial scales and then combined to yield a mean score for positive interpretation of peers' behavior.)

TABLE 3.1

Summary of Social Information Processing Measures in the Group Entry Situation

Variable Number	Processing Step	Measure Label	Item Content
G1	1	Cue utilization	Does the child utilize presented cues in making an interpretation? (scored 0 or 1, with 1 yes)
G2	2	Interpretation	How much does the child expect that peers will want him to play with them? (scored 1 to 3, with 3 highest)
G3	3	Number of solutions	How many responses does the child generate spontaneously as potential solutions to the group entry task? (scored 0 and higher)
G4	3	Proportion of competent solutions	How many competent responses does the child generate?
G5	3	Proportion of aggressive solutions	How many aggressive solutions does the child generate?
G6	3	Proportion of self-centered solutions	How many self-centered solutions does the child generate?
G7	3	Proportion of passive solutions	How many passive solutions does the child generate?
G8	3	Proportion of authority intervention solutions	How many authority intervention solutions does the child generate?
G9	4	Accuracy of response evaluation	How well does this child evaluate the potential outcomes of all presented responses? (aggregated score of 0 to 32, with 32 most accurate)

G10	4	Endorsement of aggressive responses	How positively does this child evaluate the potential outcomes of aggressive responses? (scale of 0 to 9, 9 maximum endorsement)
G11	4	Endorsement of self-centered responses	How positively does this child evaluate the potential outcomes of self-centered responses?
G12	4	Endorsement of passive responses	How positively does this child evaluate the potential outcomes of passive responses?
G13	4	Endorsement of authority-intervention responses	How positively does this child evaluate the potential outcomes of authority intervention responses?
G14	4	Endorsement of competent responses	How positively does this child evaluate the potential outcomes of competent responses?
G15	5	Enactment	How skillfully does this child enact a given response?
G16	5	Self-description of behavior	How well does this child articulate the behavioral strategies that he or she employed?
G17		Teacher rating	Teacher's assessment of child's skill at group entry (mean of two items, 1 to 5 scale)
G18		Peer rating	Peers' assessment of child's social competence (mean of all peers, 1 to 5 scale)
G19		Behavioral competence	Rating of competence in group entry situation
G20		Behavioral success	Rating of success in the group entry situation
G21		Hosts' evaluation	Hosts' rating of entry child's skill at group entry (0 to 2, with 2 highest)
G22		Self-rating	Subject's rating of entry behavior (1 to 4, with 4 highest)

2. (Step 1) How do you know this? Why do you say that the first child would (or would not) play with you? How about the second child? (Responses are scored as 1 [using internally generated cues or inappropriate, irrelevant cues] or 2 [citing specific cues present on the videotapes stimulus] and are combined to yield a score for cue-utilization.)

3. (Step 3) Let's pretend that they want you to play and that you want to play with them. What could you do to get them to let you play? What else? What else? (Responses are categorized as competent, aggressive, self-centered, passive, or authority intervention. Scores are computed for the frequency of each type of response, as well as a total frequency score.)

4. (Step 4) Now you will see what one child did to try to get the others to play with him. (One of the five response types is enacted on the videotape. The tape is stopped just before the peers can respond. The response types included competent, aggressive, self-centered, passive and authority intervention responses.) Do you think that the children will let him (her) play now? (scored as 1 [yes], 2 [won't care], or 3 [no]). How good a job did that child do in trying to get the others to let him (her) play with them? (scored on a 1 to 4 scale with 4 as very good) (This script is repeated five times, once with each of the five response types.) Now that you have seen many ways to try to get others to play, which of these ways would you choose? Which way is the best way?

5. (Step 5) One of the ways that you could get the others to play with you is to ask them. Let's pretend that I am seated at the table and you would like to play with me. Could you show me how you would ask me if you could play with me? (scored for enactment skill on a 1 to 3 scale, 3 being most effective).

The questions above are paraphrases of the narrative. The experimenter clarified the questions for the child and made sure that the child gave interpretable responses. A second videotape was presented to the child, with new actors and a repetition of all questions, to increase the reliability of the measures. All stimulus materials were first presented to college students and normal kindergarten children in order to make sure that adults could correctly identify and evaluate all response segments and to make sure that children could understand the procedure.

At a later date, with the guidance of a new experimenter, each subject participated in a group entry session. Two same-gender, same-age peers (called hosts) were placed in a room and were asked to make a tall structure out of building blocks. Ten minutes later, the experimenter asked the subject to enter the room on his or her own and to begin playing with the children in the room. The subject's behavior inside the room was videorecorded for later analysis.

Two trained coders viewed each videorecorded segment and rated the child's performance on two scales, one assessing the success that the child experienced in gaining group entry and the second assessing the child's competence in making entry attempts (without regard to outcome). The intercoder agreement for each measure was quite high (coefficient alphas = .92 and .93, respectively).

Results and Discussion

Each of the behavioral ratings of children's performance in the group entry task (variables G19, G20, G21) was significantly correlated with each other (r's ranged from .58 to .89) and was moderately correlated with the teacher and peer ratings of social competence (r's ranged from .24 to .45). This pattern provides modest support for the validity of the group entry task as an index of social adjustment in the classroom.

As shown in Table 3.2, the correlations between the information processing variables and the behavioral variables were generally in the predictable low to moderate range. Seven of the 15 information processing measures were significantly correlated with at least one of the behavioral measures, even when effects of grade were partialed out. These measures came from steps 2, 3, 4, and 5 of the model. Hierarchical multiple regression analyses were conducted using grade as the first variable entered in order to assess the predictability of the behavioral variables from these seven information processing variables. The analysis for the competence outcome measure is found in Table 3.3. Variables from steps 1 (G1), 3 (G5), and 4 (G11 and G12) of the proposed model were found to provide significant incremental value in predicting competence (Multiple R = .58). The analyses for the other outcome measures yielded similar results, with multiple correlations using all seven information processing variables being .67 for behavioral competence, .65 for behavioral success, .64 for the hosts' evaluation, .58 for the teacher's rating, and .57 for the peers' rating.

The utility of the seven information processing variables in predicting which children performed in a competent versus incompetent manner at the group entry task was further demonstrated through discriminant function analyses. Children were classified as behaviorally competent or incompetent based on a median split of this measure, and the seven processing variables were then used to predict competency status. These measures correctly classified 74% of the competent children and 77% of the incompetent children. A similar median split (of variable G21) classified children as well received or poorly received by the hosts in the group entry situation. The seven processing variables correctly classified 96% of the poorly received children and 68% of the well-received children.

These analyses provide moderate support for the hypothesis that significant increments in the prediction of social behavior can be gained from assessments of theoretically derived information processing variables. While the predictive power from any single variable was small, the predictive power of a combination of variables was substantially higher. The multiple correlations and discriminant functions between cognitive variables and social behavior in this study were of the magnitude that begins to demonstrate clinical utility.

TABLE 3.2
Partial Correlations Between Information Processing Variables and
Behavioral Variables, Controlling for Grade Level of Subject

Information Processing Measure	Competence at Group Entry	Success at Group Entry	Hosts' Evaluation	Teacher's Rating of Group Entry Competence	Peer's Rating of Social Competence
Cue utilization (G1)	.31**	.21	.26*	.02	.21
Interpretation (G2)	.05	-.06	.04	-.09	.07
Number of solutions (G3)	-.08	-.03	-.01	-.19	-.23
Number of competent solutions (G4)	.01	.05	.07	-.21	-.20
Number of aggressive solutions (G5)	-.28*	-.38**	-.38**	-.13	-.15
Number of self-centered solutions (G6)	.05	-.01	.01	.14	-.02
Number of passive solutions (G7)	.01	.01	.02	.05	.04
Number of authority intervention solutions (G8)	-.03	.05	.06	-.05	-.01
Accuracy of response evaluation (G9)	.34**	.18	.16	.37**	.04
Endorsement of aggressive responses (G10)	-.32**	-.24	-.34**	.19	-.08
Endorsement of self-centered responses (G11)	-.33**	-.20	-.16	-.19	-.07
Endorsement of passive responses (G12)	-.29*	-.28*	-.30**	-.28*	-.10
Endorsement of authority intervention responses (G13)	-.13	-.11	-.08	-.16	-.10
Enactment (G15)	-.14	-.22	-.22	.25	-.14
Self-description (G16)	-.10	-.13	-.22	-.15	.35**

*Significance at the .10 level.
**Significance at the .05 level.

TABLE 3.3
Multiple Regression Analysis Predicting Behavioral Competence from Information Processing Variables

Step Number	Variable Entered	F Value of Increment	df	Increment in R^2	P Level of Increment	Multiple R
1	Grade	< 1	1,39	--	n.s.	.00
2	Endorsement of self-centered responses (G11)	4.39	1,38	.11	.04	.33
3	Number of aggressive solutions Generated (G5)	3.21	1,37	.07	.08	.42
4.	Cue utilization (G1)	4.39	1,36	.09	.04	.52
5.	Endorsement of passive responses (G12)	3.60	1,35	.07	.07	.58

A STUDY OF DOMAIN SPECIFICITY IN THE
INFORMATION PROCESSING-BEHAVIOR RELATION

While the study just described seemed to provide support for the predictability of behavioral outcomes in the group entry context from assessments of information processing in that context, replication was needed. The high number of variables relative to the low number of subjects renders the study suspect in terms of the robustness of the findings. A goal of a second study was replication of the findings of the first study with a population of clinically referred aggressive children. A second goal was to test the hypothesis that behavior in one domain is more predictable from information processing variables in the same domain than from variables in another context. In order to test this hypothesis, assessments of social behavior and information processing were conducted in a second context as well as the group entry context. The second context chosen was that of a provocation by a peer. There were several reasons for selecting this context, including the findings by Dodge (1983) that peer provocations are a major stimulus for the aggressive behavior of deviant children. Dodge, McClaskey, and Feldman (1985) also found that peer provocations are cited by teachers as a major difficulty of aggressive children. Finally, since the research program of the author that was reviewed earlier in this chapter has consisted primarily of assessments of children's processing about peer provocations, the selection of this context seemed ideal.

Method

As with the first study, this study was conducted in three waves. First, subjects were selected for participation on the basis of teachers' referrals to a treatment program for severely deviant, aggressive children. Next, the social information processing patterns of these subjects and a group of matched controls were assessed in the two domains of group entry and responses to provocations. Finally, in a third session, behavioral performance was assessed by having each subject participate in a group entry task and by exposure to a provocation by a peer.

From the 2400 children in the second, third, and fourth grades of 12 public elementary schools in Bloomington, Indiana, 48 (2%) children were targeted by their teachers as "severely aggressive and socially rejected" and in need of clinical intervention for behavior problems and/or emotional handicaps. These children also met criteria on the Achenbach Child Behavior Checklist–Teacher's Form (aggression scale T-scores of greater than 60) and peer sociometric assessments. A group of 18 children were also selected as normal controls for this study.

During a private session, each child was administered the same videotaped protocol used in study 1 to assess information processing in group entry situations. As well, each child was administered a second protocol designed to assess processing of information about a provocation by a peer. Nine videotaped stimuli were prepared in which one child ambiguously provokes a second child such as by knocking over his or her building blocks. The intention of the provacateur in the stimuli varied as hostile, prosocial, benign, or ambiguous. In each case, a narrator asks the subject to imagine being the child who was the object of the provocation. The narrator then asks the subject a series of questions, similar to those asked in the first study. These questions were designed to assess the processing of information at each of the steps of the model (see Table 3.4 for a summary of these measures).

TABLE 3.4
Summary of Social Information Processing Measures in the Provocation Situation

Variable Number	Processing Step	Measure Label	Item Content
P1	1	Cue utilization	Does the child utilize presented cues in making an interpretation? (0 is no, 1 is yes)
P2	2	Interpretation	How does the child interpret an ambiguous provocation? (0 is hostile, 1 is benign)
P3	2	Number of hostile misinterpretations	How many times does the child err in presuming hostility? (0-6)
P4	2	Number of accurate hostile interpretations	How many correct interpretations of hostility does the child make? (0-2)
P5	2	Number of accurate prosocial interpretations	How many correct judgments of prosocial intention does the child make? (0-2)
P6	3	Number of responses	How many responses does the child generate? (first segment only)
P7	3	Proportion of aggressive responses	What proportion of subject's responses (all stimuli) are aggressive?
P8	3	Proportion of competent responses	What proportion of subject's responses (all stimuli) are competent?
P9	4	Accuracy of response evaluation	How well does this child evaluate the potential outcomes of all presented responses? (1 to 6, high better)
P10	4	Endorsement of assertive responses	How positively does this child evaluate the potential outcomes of assertive responses?
P11	4	Endorsement of aggressive responses	How positively does this child evaluate the potential outcomes of aggressive responses?
P12	4	Endorsement of passive responses	How positively does this child evaluate the potential outcomes of passive responses?
P13	5	Enactment	How skillfully does this child enact a given response?
P14		Teacher rating	Teacher's assessment of child's skill at responding to classroom provocations
P15		Behavioral response to provocation	Rating of child's response to a laboratory provocation (1, negative; 2, neutral; 3, positive)

In a third session, each child participated in a group entry task similar to that in study 1. The hosts for this task were same-age, same-gender peers from a different school than the subject and who were not familiar with the subject. Following the group entry sequence, an actual provocation was contrived. One of the two hosts (who had been previously coached by the experimenter) knocked over the subject's toy building in as ambiguous a manner as possible. The subject's response to this provocation was scored as 1 if hostile, 2 if neutral, and 3 if benign or positive. Agreement on coding of this reponse was quite high (Percent Perfect Agreement = 85%).

Results and Discussion

Three kinds of data analyses were conducted. First, the differences between subject groups on each of the information processing and behavioral variables were assessed. Second, multiple regression analyses were conducted in which the behavioral variables were predicted from the processing variables. Finally, discriminant function analyses were conducted in which status was predicted from the processing variables.

The status group means for the measures of processing and behavior in group entry and provocation situations are found in Table 3.5, along with a summary of the significant status and grade effects in a series of 2 (status groups) × 2 (grade level) analyses of variance. There were few grade level effects. In the group entry situation, older children expected that the peers would be less receptive than did younger children. The older children gave more detailed descriptions of their group entry behavior than did younger children, and they were rated as more competent in the group entry task. In spite of this result, the older children assigned poorer ratings to their own performance following the group entry task than did younger children. In the provocation situation, older children demonstrated more skill than younger children by more accurately detecting prosocial intentions, by making fewer errors of presumed hostility, and by more often selecting competent responses to the provocation.

A number of status effects were found which supported the hypotheses under study. In the group entry situation, these effects occurred at processing steps 2 and 4 and in behavioral performance. The aggressive children were more likely than the others to expect that the peer hosts would not want to play with them. They were more likely to endorse passive and self-centered solutions to this task than nonaggressive children, and they were less likely to endorse competent solutions. Given the controversy in the literature concerning the generative problem-solving skills of these children, it is interesting to note that the aggressive children generated as many solutions to this situation as the others did, but they displayed a slight (nonsignificant) tendency to generate a higher proportion of incompetent solutions. When they participated in the group entry task, the aggressive children were rated as less competent and less successful in their behav-

TABLE 3.5

Status Group Means and Standard Deviations for Information Processing and Behavioral Variables (Study Two)

Variable	Processing Step	Subject Group Aggressive	Subject Group Control	Effects Grade F	p	Effects Status F	p
Group Entry Processing							
Cue utilization (G1)	1	0.90 (0.27)	0.97 (0.12)				
Interpretation (G2)	2	1.88 (0.76)	2.35 (0.61)	7.66	(.01)	4.97	(.03)
No. of solutions (G3)	3	1.41 (1.39)	1.38 (0.50)				
Proportion of competent solutions (G4)	3	0.88 (0.24)	0.96 (0.17)				
Proportion of aggressive solutions (G5)	3	0.03 (0.11)	0.00 (0.00)				
Proportion of passive solutions (G7)	3	0.09 (0.29)	0.04 (0.25)				
Accuracy of response evaluation (G9)	4	12.78 (8.35)	15.47 (9.41)				
Endorsement of aggressive responses (G10)	4	1.29 (1.68)	1.29 (1.86)				
Endorsement of self-centered responses (G11)	4	2.15 (1.96)	1.94 (1.43)				
Endorsement of passive responses (G12)	4	5.36 (2.39)	4.06 (2.26)			4.25	(.04)
Endorsement of authority-intervention responses (G13)	4	4.60 (2.94)	4.68 (2.29)				
Endorsement of competent responses (G14)	4	6.57 (1.86)	6.82 (1.76)				
Enactment (G15)	5	20.22 (5.34)	20.64 (6.71)				
Self-description of behavior (G16)	5	1.84 (0.90)	2.28 (0.91)	5.44	(.03)		
Provocation Processing							
Cue utilization (F1)	1	0.80 (0.41)	1.00 (0.00)				
Interpretation (F2)	2	0.13 (0.34)	0.05 (0.24)				
No. of hostile misinterpretations (P3)	2	4.38 (2.10)	3.74 (1.87)	15.09	(.001)	3.16	(.08)
Proportion of accurate hostile interpretations (P4)	2	1.00 (0.00)	0.86 (0.47)			4.39	(.04)
Proportion of accurate prosocial interpretations (P5)	2	0.41 (0.33)	0.58 (0.39)	11.51	(.001)	4.84	(.03)
No. of responses (P6)	3	3.01 (1.66)	2.31 (0.95)				
Proportion of aggressive responses (P7)	3	0.48 (0.29)	0.24 (0.16)			10.18	(.002)
Proportion of competent responses (P8)	3	0.22 (0.26)	0.30 (0.24)				
Accuracy of response evaluation (P9)	4	2.86 (1.03)	3.06 (0.93)	6.44	(.02)		
Endorsement of assertive responses (P10)	4	5.33 (2.23)	6.31 (2.55)			3.08	(.09)
Endorsement of aggressive responses (P11)	4	4.51 (1.65)	4.00 (1.07)				
Endorsement of passive responses (P12)	4	3.18 (2.08)	2.50 (2.34)			3.39	(.07)
Enactment (P13)	5	12.11 (5.67)	14.42 (6.33)			4.42	(.04)
Behavior Variables							
Teacher rating of group entry (G17)		1.61 (0.90)	3.05 (0.90)			60.94	(.001)
Teacher rating of provocation responses (P14)		1.62 (0.96)	2.89 (0.70)			46.95	(.001)
Behavioral competence at group entry (G19)		4.34 (1.25)	5.13 (0.68)			5.57	(.03)
Behavioral success at group entry (G20)		3.62 (1.22)	4.13 (0.64)			3.50	(.07)
Hosts' evaluation (G21)		1.16 (0.96)	1.53 (0.83)				
Self-rating of entry competence (G22)		3.08 (0.85)	2.57 (0.71)			3.91	(.06)
Behavioral response to provocation (P15)		1.84 (0.80)	2.70 (0.83)				

ior than the nonaggressive children. In spite of their ineptitude, they rated their own performance at this task more highly than the others did. It is clear that aggressive children process information about group entry situations in ways that are deviant compared to nonaggressive children. Further, this deviant processing makes it difficult for them to comprehend, understand, and ameliorate their failures in this domain.

In the provocation situation, the differences between status groups were even more striking. Processing differences occurred at all five steps of the proposed model. Aggressive children made statements about utilizing cues 80% of the time, compared to 100% of the time for the nonaggressive children. They were less skilled than the others at making accurate interpretations of prosocial intentions, and they made more errors in a direction of presumed hostility. It is important to note that the aggressive children were actually more accurate than others at interpreting hostile intentions, indicating that their deviant processing is not merely a function of a lack of a broad interpretive skill. Rather, it probably reflects a strong sensitivity to hostile portions of stimuli. As with the group entry situation, the aggressive children generated as many (nonsignificantly more) responses to the provocation stimulus as did other children. They were twice as likely to generate aggressive responses, however. When asked to evaluate responses which were presented to them, the aggressive children were less likely than the others to endorse assertive (nonaggressive) responses, but they were more likely to endorse passive responses and aggressive responses (nonsignificantly for the latter). When asked to enact a competent response suggested by the interviewer, they were less skilled in their responses. Finally, when they were confronted with an actual provocation by a peer, the aggressive children were 55% more likely to respond with some form of retaliatory aggression than were nonaggressive children. As with the group entry situation, the processing biases and deficits in the aggressive children are quite pronounced in the provocation situation. In fact, they pervaded all steps of information processing and behavioral responding that were assessed.

The second set of analyses consisted of predictions of behavior from the social information processing variables. The partial correlations between information processing variables in both domains and behavioral variables in those domains (controlling for grade level) are listed in Table 3.6. As shown there, processing variables from each step were significantly related to behavioral outcomes in each domain, usually at low to moderate levels of significance.

In order to examine the predictability of the behavioral outcomes from the processing variables, four series of multiple regression analyses were performed, in which group entry behavior and behavioral responses to a provocation were predicted from processing in group entry and provocation situations. In all analyses, grade level was entered as the first predictor variable. For the first series, three behavioral variables in the group entry task were each predicted from the set of group entry processing variables. The set of group entry processing vari-

TABLE 3.6

Partial Correlations of Information Processing Variables with Group Entry and Provocation Behavior, Controlling for Grade Level (Study Two)

Processing Variable	Outcome Variable			
	Entry Competence	Entry Success	Hosts' Evaluation	Response to Provocation
Group Entry Domain				
Cue utilization (G1)	.12	.16	-.02	.29
Interpretation (G2)	.44***	.42***	.14	.26
No. of solutions (G3)	-.03	-.10	-.19	.04
Proportion of competent solutions (G4)	.18	.26*	-.06	.21
Accuracy of response evaluation (G9)	.39***	.37***	-.02	.09
Endorsement of aggressive responses (G10)	-.23	-.28*	-.16	-.11
Endorsement of self-centered responses (G11)	-.19	-.28*	-.28*	-.05
Endorsement of passive responses (G12)	-.19	-.32**	-.19	-.02
Endorsement of authority-intervention responses (G13)	-.18	-.24	-.32***	-.06
Endorsement of competent responses (G14)	.00	.07	.08	-.04
Enactment (G15)	.05	.14	.13	.06
Self-description of behavior (G16)	.61***	.68***	.55***	.18
Provocation Processing				
Cue utilization (P1)	.24	.26	.19	.06
Interpretation (P2)	.25	.18	.17	-.26*
No. of hostile misinterpretations (P3)	-.31**	-.14	-.14	-.26*
Proportion of accurate hostile interpretations (P4)	-.03	-.15	.16	-.02
Porportion of accurate prosocial interpretations (P5)	.11	-.07	.07	.01
No. of responses (P6)	.08	-.07	.06	.06
Proportion of aggressive responses (P7)	.04	.11	.12	-.25*
Proportion of competent responses (P8)	.12	-.01	-.01	.28*
Accuracy of response evaluation (P9)	.02	-.03	.09	.32***
Endorsement of assertive responses (P10)	.09	-.01	.06	.17
Endorsement of aggressive responses (P11)	-.29*	-.27*	-.13	-.27*
Endorsement of passive responses (P12)	-.14	.02	-.05	-.11
Enactment (P13)	.29*	.32**	.27*	.02

*p < .10
**p < .05
***p < .01

ables was found to be highly predictive ($p<.001$) of ratings of group entry competence, Multiple $R = .72$, ratings of success at group entry, Multiple $R = .82$, and hosts' evaluations of the entry child's behavior, Multiple $R = .74$. Significant incremental prediction of one or more of the three behavioral variables resulted from variables at processing steps 1 (G1), 2 (G2), 3 (G4), 4 (G11, G12), and 5 (G15, G16).

The processing variables in the provocation domain did not significantly predict competence ratings, Multiple $R = .48$, success ratings, Multiple $R = .51$, or hosts' evaluations, Multiple $R = .60$. The set of group entry processing variables, therefore, was a better predictor of group entry performance than was the set of provocation processing variables.

The behavioral response to provocation was next predicted from each set of processing variables. The provocation processing set was found to be highly predictive of the behavioral response, Multiple $R = .75$. Singificant incremental prediction resulted from variables at steps 2 (P2, P3) and 4 (P9).

The set of group entry processing variables did not significantly predict the response to provocation, Multiple $R = .53$. These four series of multiple regression analyses provide key support for the hypothesis that the most powerful predictions of social behavior in a particular domain will occur as a function of measures of the processing of information about that domain.

The final set of analyses consisted of discriminant functions of status groups. In order to assess the utility of the information processing variables in predicting which kind of behavioral problem a child is likely to have, the subjects were next divided into three groups. Based on teachers' assessments of the extent to which a child experienced difficulty in group entry situations and in responding to provocations, the aggressive group of subjects was divided into two subgroups: those whose teachers rated them as having more difficulty in the group entry domain than in the provocation domain and those whose teachers rated them the reverse. The third group was the nonaggressive control group, whose teachers rated them as having significantly less difficulty than the other groups in each domain (see Table 3.5). The processing variables from each domain were then used to predict status classification in a discriminant function analysis. This analysis demonstrated that 6 group entry processing variables (#'s G2, G3, G4, G12, G14, and G15) and 6 provocation processing variables (#'s P1, P4, P5, P6, P7, and P12), when combined, could yield a significant prediction of the status classification, Wilks lambda $= .29$, X^2 (22) $= 57.24$, for the first function, and Wilks lambda $= .59$, X^2 (10) $= 24.08$, for the second function. These 12 variables resulted in the correct classification of 16 of 21 (76%) children as aggressive with group entry problems, 13 of 21 (62%) children as aggressive with provocation problems, and 13 of 17 (77%) children as nonaggressive controls. The distinction between the aggressive provocation problem children and the aggressive group entry problem children was significant. Also significant were the distinctions between the provocation problem children and the control children, and the group entry problem children and the control children. While this analysis is a strong indication of the diagnostic power of the information processing assessments, the results must be viewed with caution and in need of replication since more variables were assessed than were finally included in the discriminant functions.

The findings of this study support the hypothesis that social behavior in a given domain can be predicted from the way that a child processes information about that domain. This hypothesis held true for both the group entry domain and the provocation domain. Further, the predictive relation was found to be stronger within a domain than across domains. That is, processing about group entry situations more strongly predicted group entry behavior than did processing about provocation situations. Likewise, processing about provocation situations more strongly predicted behavioral responses to provocations than did processing about group entry situations. This finding is one that is not confounded by the intelligence of the children under study, since the same children responded about both domains. However, the moderate cross-domain predictability (i.e., correlations, though not significant, were still large) suggests either that: (1) the domains are not entirely independent; (2) general processing patterns may be present; or (3) deviance in one domain may over time lead to deviance in other domains and a general processing style.

The magnitudes of the predictive relations between processing and behavior in this study were extremely high. Multiple correlations were higher than in the first study and approached their upper limits. While these findings support the hypotheses under study, there are several reasons to be cautious about the magnitude of the results found. Because of the use of extreme subject groups and the high ratio of the number of variables to the number of subjects, the multiple correlations reported are probably an inflated estimate of the true magnitude of the relation between processing and behavior in a normal population. These findings must be replicated with a larger, representative sample in order to be more sure of the conclusions being made. On the other hand, one might expect that the relation may be even stronger if the measures used had higher reliability. Establishing more reliable processing and outcome measures may be a priority of future research. In the meantime, conservative optimism about the relation between social information processing patterns and social behavior is warranted.

IMPLICATIONS FOR CLINICAL ASSESSMENT AND INTERVENTION

This chapter concludes with a brief discussion of the implications of the social information processing approach for the assessment and treatment of children who display aggressive behavior and social deviance. The empirical findings reported in this chapter suggest that aggressive children are deficient and biased in their processing of information about two critical social situations: peer group entry and responding to provocations. It is reasonable to hypothesize that training in social information processing skills and "de-biasing" of deviant processing patterns may lead to reduced aggressive behavior and more favorable social adaptation in deviant children. Caution must be expressed about this hypothesis because the links between processing and behavior found in these studies have been correlational and not necessarily causal. It is plausible, even likely, that deviant social status and interpersonal behavior may lead a child to process social information in deviant ways. This possibility is depicted in the circular pattern of Fig. 3.2. The degree to which processing patterns have a direct causal effect on behavior is still open to speculation. However, the best method of testing this hypothesis is experimental manipulation of processing patterns in order to observe their effect on behavioral outcomes. Such manipulation is precisely what is proposed in experimental clinical intervention.

How this intervention should be implemented is not a simple matter. The theory and findings in this chapter suggest that the administration of the same clinical intervention to all aggressive children is likely to lead to marginal success, at best. Not all aggressive children experience difficulty in all social situations and not all aggressive children display deciant processing at all steps of the proposed process. Specific steps of processing seem to be the most critical to success in the group entry domain, namely the generation and selection of competent strategies for entry (steps 3 and 4). Different steps seem to play an important role in determining a response to a provocation, namely the accurate and benign interpretation of information about the provocateur (step 2). It is likely that because task demands vary across social domains, different processing steps will prove critical in differentiating positive and negative outcomes across these domains.

Dodge and Murphy (1983) and McFall and Dodge (1982) have proposed a multi-stage plan for the assessment and trestment of socially deviant behavior in adults and adolescents. This plan is a logical extension of the proposed model and can be applied to aggressive children. It consists of several steps.

Once an aggressive child has been identified, the clinician must survey the relevant social domains in which the child is displaying deviant aggressive behavior. Two possible domains are the ones studied in this chapter, peer group entry and peer provocations. There are many other potential domains, but they rarely have been studied systematically. Friedman et al. (1978) point out the need for "basic taxonomic research" on this problem. Feldman (1984) has recently surveyed teachers to develop a list of common situations which lead to deviant outcomes for aggressive children. This list may be a guide, but the clinician must also conduct detailed clinical interviews with the child, parents, and teachers, and observe firsthand the child's social interactions to determine the domains in which a particular child has the most difficulty. The situational list is likely to be idiosyncratic.

The next step is to conduct systematic assessments of the child's processing of social information in the situation identified as problematic for the child. The procedures employed in the studies reported in this chapter represent one approach to this assessment task. It is also reasonable to interview the child informally to determine whether the child is deficient in processing skills, such as response generation and response evaluation, or is biased in his or her style of processing in a direction which will lead to deviant outcomes. These processing assessments must be specific to each identified problematic domain because the cross-domain generalization may be weak.

At this point, the clinician will have a detailed profile in two dimensions of the child's processing strengths and weaknesses within a number of situations. Using this profile, the clinician must next design appropriate interventions for altering the manner in which a child processes social information. One method proposed for training social skills (Goldstein, Sprafkin, Gershaw, & Klein, 1980) may be adapted for the present circumstances. This method consists of the sequential tasks of didactic instruction, modeling, role playing, feedback, and reinforcement. The deviant processing patterns in aggressive children, however, may be so affectively bound and so self-reinforcing that they are resistant to instructional alteration. Indeed, the long term stability of aggressive behavior and the difficulty in treating aggressive children may be functions of this resistance. In this case, creative interventions involving repeated direct experience with stimuli that are incompatible with deviant processing may be most appropriate. For example, the clinician may design a social environment which is antithetical to the child's perception that others are hostile toward him or her. The child's deviant processing will often lead to a self-fulfilling prophecy (i.e., others eventually may become hostile toward the child as a result of the child's deviant processing and aggressive behavior), so this structured environment must be resistant to the child's coercion.

Finally, of course, the clinician must review the effectiveness of the intervention. One method for accomplishing this task is to work backward through the plan just described. The clinician must evaluate whether the intervention is carried out as planned; whether it reaches the desired proximal goal of altering the child's patterns of social information processing; whether it alters the child's typical behavior in specific situations, and finally, whether the referring agent is satisfied that the child is no longer deviant. If the evaluation indicates a failure at any of these steps, either the plan must be re-administered more carefully or an alternate conceptualization of the problem must be considered.

Closing Comment

This chapter provides a description of the ways in which a child's processing of social information may be related to his or her social behavior. The description is really just a crude framework, however, for integrating the many problems under study in the field called social cognition. This chapter provides a ''molar'' analysis of social information processing but falls short of providing understanding at ''molecular'' levels. The empirical research reported here demonstrates the predictive power of this approach, but it has many deficiencies, already expressed, which lead even the author to be somewhat skeptical about its merits.

With these reservations, it is hoped that the theory and data described here will push researchers in two seemingly divergent directions. First, it is hoped that the metaphor of a human computer which processes social information in sequential steps will be given further consideration and carried to its limits. Second, it is hoped that researchers studying social cognition will give further consideration to the role of affect in the processing of social information. The proposed model provides a scheme for studying affect under the concept of bias, without neglecting the role of processing skills as well. In fact, this approach integrates the concepts of affective bias and social cognitive skills in one framework.

ACKNOWLEDGMENTS

This chapter was written through the support of grants from the Foundations for Child Development and the National Institute of Mental Health (No. MH37062). The author acknowledges the cooperation of the Monroe County Community Schools Corporation. Many individuals have been helpful in the conduct of this work, particularly Cynthia McClaskey, Robin Murphy, Gregory Pettit, and Janice Sabet-Sharghi. Jack Bates, Teresa Blicharski, and Marion Perlmutter provided helpful editorial comments.

REFERENCES

Abelson, R. P. (1976). Script processing in attitude formation and decision making. In J. S. Carroll & J. W. Payne (Eds.), *Cognition and social behavior*. Hillsdale, NJ: Lawrence Erlbaum Associates.

Argyle, M. (1981). The contribution of social interaction research to social skills training. In J. D. Wine & M. D. Smye (Eds.), *Social competence*. New York: Guilford.

Argyle, M., Furnham A., & Graham, J. A. (1981). *Social situations*. Cambridge: Cambridge University Press.

Asher, S. R., & Hymel, S. (1981). Children's social competence in peer relations: Sociometric and behavioral assessment. In J. D. Wine & M. D. Smye (Eds.), *Social competence*. New York: Guilford.

Asher, S. R., Singleton, L. C., Tinsley, B. R., & Hymel, S. (1979). A reliable sociometric measure for preschool children. *Developmental Psychology, 15*, 443–444.

Babad, Y. E., Alexander, I. E., & Babad, E. Y. (1983). Returning the smile of a stranger: Developmental patterns and socialization factors. *Monographs of the Society for Research in Child Development, 48*, (5, Serial No. 203).

Bandura, A. (1977). Self-efficacy: Toward a unifying theory of behavior change. *Psychological Review, 84*, 191–215.

Bellack, A. S., Hersen, M., & Turner, S. M. (1976). Generalization effects of social skills training in chronic schizophrenics: An experimental analysis. *Behavioral Research and Therapy, 14*, 391–398.

Berkowitz, L. (1977). Situational and personal conditions governing reactions to aggressive cues. In D. Magnussen & N. S. Endler (Eds.), Personality at the crossroads: Current issues in interactional psychology. Hillsdale, NJ: Lawrence Erlbaum Associates.

Brain, R. (1977). Friends and lovers. New York: Pocket Books.

Bruner, J. S. (1957). On perceptual readiness. Psychological Review, 64, 123–152.

Camp, B. (1977). Verbal mediation in young aggressive boys. Journal of Abnormal Psychology, 86, 145–153.

Camras, L. A. (1980). Children's understanding of facial expressions used during conflict encounters. Child Development, 51, 879–885.

Chandler, M. J. (1973). Egocentrism and antisocial behavior: The assessment and training of social perspective-taking skills. Developmental Psychology, 9, 326–337.

Chandler, M. J., Greenspan, S., & Barenboim, C. (1974). Assessment and training of role-taking and referential communication skills in institutionalized emotionally disturbed children. Developmental Psychology, 10, 546–553.

Chittendon, G. E. (1942). An experimental study in measuring and modifying assertive behavior in young children. Monographs of the Society for Research in Child Development, VII, No. 1 (Serial No. 31).

Cicourel, A. (1974). Cognitive sociology. New York: Free Press.

Coie, J. D., & Dodge, K. A. (1983). Continuity of children's social status: A five year longitudinal study. Merrill-Palmer Quarterly, 29, 261–282.

Corsaro, W. A. (1981). Friendship in the nursery school: Social organization in a peer environment. In S. Asher & J. M. Gottman (Eds.), The development of friendship: Description and intervention. New York: Cambridge University Press.

Costanzo, P. R., Grumet, J. F., & Brehm, S. S. (1974). The effects of choice and source of constraint in children's attributions of preference. Journal of Experimental Social Psychology, 10, 352–364.

Darley, J., Klossen, E. C., & Zanna, M. P. (1978). Intentions and their contexts in the moral judgments of children and adults. Child Development, 49, 66–74.

Deutsch, F. (1974). Observational and sociometric measures of peer popularity and their relationship to egocentric communication in female preschoolers. Developmental Psychology, 10, 745–747.

DiVitto, B., & McArthur, L. Z. (1978). Developmental differences in the use of distinctiveness, consensus, and consistency information for making causal attributions. Developmental Psychology, 14, 474–482.

Dodge, K. A. (1980). Social cognition and children's aggressive behavior. Child Development, 51, 162–170.

Dodge, K. A. (1983). Behavioral antecedents of peer social status. Child Development, 54, 1386–1399.

Dodge, K. A. (in press). Social information processing variables in the development of aggression and altruism in children. In C. Zahn-Waxler, E. Cummings, & R. Ionnatti (Eds.), Social and biological origins of altruism and aggression. New York: Cambridge University Press.

Dodge, K. A., & Frame, C. M. (1982). Social cognitive biases and deficits in aggressive boys. Child Development, 53, 620–635.

Dodge, K. A., McClaskey, C. M., & Feldman, E. (1985). A situational approach to the assessment of social competence in children. Journal of Consulting and Clinical Psychology, 33, 344–353.

Dodge, K. A., & Murphy, R. R. (1983). The assessment of social competence in adolescents. In P. Karoly & J. J. Steffen (Eds.), Adolescent behavior disorders. Vol. 4 of Advances in child behavioral analysis and therapy. Lexington, MA: Lexington Books.

Dodge, K. A., Murphy, R. M., & Buchsbaum, K. (1984). The assessment of intention-cue discrimination cues in children: Implications for developmental psychopathology. Child Development, 55, 163–173.

Dodge, K. A., & Newman, J. P. (1981). Biased decision making processes in aggressive boys. Journal of Abnormal Psychology, 90, 375–379.

Dodge, K. A., Schlundt, D. G., Schocken, I., & Delugach, J. D. (1983). Social competence and children's sociometric status: The role of peer group entry strategies. *Merrill-Palmer Quarterly, 29*, 309–336.

Dodge, K. A., & Tomlin, A. (1983). *The role of cue-utilization in attributional biases among aggressive children.* Unpublished paper, Indiana University.

Eisenberg-Berg, N. & Lennon, R. (1980). Altruism and the assessment of empathy in the preschool years. *Child Development, 51*, 552–557.

Eisler, R. M., Miller, P. M., & Hersen, M. (1973). Components of assertive behavior. *Journal of Clinical Psychology, 29*, 295–299.

Erickson, E. H. (1950). *Childhood and society.* New York: Norton.

Eron, L. D. (1980). Prescription for reduction of aggression. *American Psychologist, 36*, 224–252.

Feldman, E. H. (1984). *Social-cognitive skills in rejected and neglected girls and boys.* Unpublished doctoral dissertation, Indiana University.

Ferguson, T. J., & Rule, B. G. (1980). Effects of inferential set, outcome severity, and basis of responsibility on children's evaluations of aggressive acts. *Developmental Psychology, 16*, 141–146.

Feshbach, N. D., & Feshbach, S. (1969). The relationship between empathy and aggression in two age groups. *Developmental Psychology, 1*, 102–107.

Feshbach, N. D., & Roe, K. (1968). Empathy in six and seven year olds. *Child Development, 39*, 133–145.

Feshbach, S. (1970). Aggression. In P. Mussen (Ed.),*Carmichael's manual of child psychology.* New York: Wiley.

Finch, A. J., Jr., & Montgomery, L. E. (1973). Reflection-impulsivity and information seeking in emotionally disturbed children. *Journal of Abnormal Child Psychology, 1*, 358–362.

Fine, G. A. (1981). Impression management and preadolescent behavior: Friends as socializers. In S. Asher & J. M. Gottman (Eds.), *The development of friendships: Description and intervention.* New York: Cambridge University Press.

Fisher, K. W. (1980). A theory of cognitive development: The control and construction of hierarchies of skills. *Psychological Review, 87*, 447–531.

Flapan, D. (1968). *Children's understanding of social interaction.* New York: Teachers College Press.

Flavell, J. H. (1974). The development of inferences about others. In T. Mischel (Ed.), *Understanding other persons.* Totowa, NJ: Rowman & Littlefield.

Flavell, J. H. (1977). *Cognitive development.* Englewood Cliffs, NJ: Prentice-Hall.

Flavell, J. H. (1981). Monitoring social cognitive enterprises: Something else that may develop in the area of social cognition. In J. H. Flavell & L. Ross (Eds.), *Social cognitive development: Frontiers and possible futures.* New York: Cambridge University Press.

Flavell, J. H., & Ross, L. (Eds.). (1981). *Social cognitive development: Frontiers and possible futures.* Cambridge: Cambridge University Press.

Flavell, J. H., Speer, J. R., Green, F. L., & August, D. L. (1981). The development of comprehension monitoring and knowledge about communication. *Monographs of the Society for Research in Child Development, 46* (5, Serial No. 192).

Ford, M. E. (1979). The construct validity of egocentrism. *Psychological Bulletin, 86*, 1169–1188.

Ford, M. E. (1984). Linking social-cognitive processes with effective social behavior: A living-systems approach. In P. C. Kendall (Ed.), *Advances in cognitive-behavioral research and therapy.* New York: Academic Press.

Friedman, B. J., Rosenthal, L., Donahoe, C. P., Jr., Schlundt, D. G., & McFall, R. M. (1978). A social-behavioral analysis of skill deficits in delinquent and non-delinquent adolescent boys. *Journal of Consulting and Clinical Psychology, 46*, 1448–1462.

Freud, A. (1969). Adolescence as a developmental disturbance. In G. Caplan & S. Laborici (Eds.), *Adolescence: Psychosocial perspectives.* New York: Basic Books.

Goldfried, M. R., & Linehan, M. M. (1977). Basic issues in behavioral assessment. In A. R. Ciminero, K. S. Calhoun, & H. E. Adams (Eds.), *Handbook of behavioral assessment*. New York: Wiley.

Goldfried, M. R. & d'Zurilla, T. J. (1969). A behavioral-analytic model for assessing competence. In C. D. Spielberger (Ed.), *Current topics in clinical and community psychology* (Vol. 1). New York: Academic Press.

Goldstein, A. P., Sprafkin, R. P., Gershaw, N. J., & Klein, P. (1980). *Skill-streaming the adolescent*. Champaign, IL: Research Press.

Gottman, J. M., Gonso, J., & Rasmussen, B. (1975). Social interaction, social competence and friendship in children. *Child Development, 46,* 709–718.

Hayes, J. R. (1981). *The complete problem solver*. Philadelphia: The Franklin Institute Press.

Hess, B. (1972). Friendship. In M. Riley, M. Johnson, & A. Fonner (Eds.), *Aging and society: A sociology of age stratification*. New York: Russell Sage Foundation.

Hoffman, M. L. (1977). Empathy, its development and prosocial implications. In C. B. Keasey (Ed.), *Nebraska Symposium on Motivation*, (Vol. 25). Lincoln: University of Nebraska Press.

Jones, E. E., & Davis, K. E. (1965). From acts to dispositions: The attribution process in person perception. In L. Berkowitz (Ed.), *Advances in experimental social psychology*, (Vol. 2). New York: Academic Press.

Kelly, H. H. (1967). Attribution theory in social psychology. In D. Levine (Ed.), *Nebraska Symposium on Motivation*, (Vol. 13). Lincoln: University of Nebraska Press.

Kendall, P. G., & Finch, A. J., Jr. (1979). Developing nonimpulsive behavior in children: Cognitive-behavioral strategies for self-control. In P. C. Kendall & S. D. Hollon (Eds.), *Cognitive-behavioral interventions: Theory, research and procedures*. New York: Academic Press.

Kendall, P. C., & Wilcox, L. E. (1979). Self-control in children: Development of a rating scale. *Journal of Consulting and Clinical Psychology, 47,* 1020–1029.

Kendler, T. S. (1968). Development of mediating responses in children. In J. C. Wright & J. Kagan (Eds.), Basic cognitive processes in children. *Monographs of the Society for Research in Child Development, 28,* 33–51.

Klein, R. (1971). *Some factors influencing empathy in six and seven year olds varying in ethnic background*. Unpublished doctoral dissertation, University of California, Los Angeles.

Krasnor, L. R. (1983). *Peer status differences in social problem solving*. Paper presented at the Biennial Meeting of the Society for Research in Child Development, Detroit.

Krasnor, L., & Rubin, K. (1981). The assessment of social problem-solving skills in young children. In T. Merluzzi, C. Glass, & M. Genest (Eds.), *Cognitive assessment*. New York: Guilford.

Kurdek, L. (1978). Relationship between cognitive perspective-taking and teachers' ratings of children's classroom behavior in grades one through four. *Journal of Genetic Psychology, 132,* 21–27.

Ladd, G. W., & Mize, J. (1983). A cognitive-social learning classification of social skill training methodology. *Psychological Review,* 127–157.

Ladd, G. W., & Oden, S. (1979). The relationship between peer acceptance and children's ideas about helpfulness. *Child Development, 50,* 402–408.

Langer, E., Blank, A., & Chanowitz, B. (1978). The mindlessness of ostensibly thoughtful action: The role of "placebic" information in interpersonal interaction. *Journal of Personality and Social Psychology, 36,* 635–642.

Livesley, W. J., & Bromley, D. B. (1973). *Person perception in childhood and adolescence*. London: Wiley.

Locke, E. A., Shaw, K. N., Saari, L. M., & Latham, C. P. (1981). Goal setting and task performance: 1969-1980. *Psychological Bulletin, 90,* 125–152.

Luria, A. (1961). *The role of speech in the regulation of normal and abnormal behaviors*. New York: Liveright.

Marshall, H. R., & McCandless, B. R. (1957). A study in prediction of social behavior of preschool children. *Child Development, 28,* 149–159.

McFall, R. M. (1977). Analogue methods in behavioral assessment: Issues and prospects. In J. D. Cone & R. P. Hawkins (Eds.), *Behavioral assessment: New directions in clinical psychology.* New York: Bruner Mazel.

McFall, R. M. (1982). A review and reformulation of the concept of social skills. *Behavioral Assessment, 4,* 1–35.

McFall, R. M., & Dodge, K. A. (1982). Self-management and interpersonal skills learning. In P. Karoly & F. H. Kanfer (Eds.), *Self-management and behavior change: From theory to practice.* New York: Pergamon Press.

McFall, R., & Lillesand, D. (1971). Behavioral rehearsal with modeling and coaching in assertive training. *Journal of Abnormal Psychology, 77,* 313–323.

McFall, R. M., & McDonel, E. (1983). The continuing search for units of analysis in psychology: Beyond persons, situations, and their interactions. In R. O. Nelson & S. C. Hayes (Eds.), *Conceptual foundations of behavioral assessment.* New York: Guilford.

Meichenbaum, D. (1977). *Cognitive behavior modification.* New York: Plenum.

Meichenbaum, D. H., & Goodman, J. (1971). Training impulsive children to talk to themselves: A means of developing self-control. *Journal of Abnormal Psychology, 77,* 115–126.

Milich, R., & Dodge, K. A. (1984). Social information processing patterns in child psychiatric populations. *Journal of Abnormal Child Psychology, 12,* 471–490.

Miller, G. A. (1969). The organization of lexical memory: Are word associations sufficient? In G. A. Talland & N. C. Waugh (Eds.), *The pathology of memory.* New York: Academic Press.

Mischel, W. (1968). *Personality and assessment.* New York: Wiley.

Mischel, W. (1973). Toward a cognitive social learning reconceptualization of personality. *Psychological Review, 80,* 252–283.

Mischel, W. (1983). Delay of gratification as process and as person variable in development. In D. Magnussen & V. P. Allen (Eds.), *Human development: An interactional perspective.* New York: Academic Press.

Mischel, W., & Patterson, C. J. (1976). Substantive and structural elements of effective plans for self-control. *Journal of Personality and Social Psychology, 34,* 942–950.

Nasby, W., Hayden, B., & dePaulo, B. M. (1979). Attributional bias among aggressive boys to interpret unambiguous social stimuli as displays of hostility. *Journal of Abnormal Psychology, 89,* 459–468.

Nelson, K. (1981). Social cognition in a script framework. In J. H. Flavell & R. D. Ross (Eds.), *Social cognitive development: Frontiers and possible futures.* New York: Cambridge University Press.

Newell, A., & Simon, H. (1972). *Human problem solving.* Englewood Cliffs, NJ: Prentice-Hall.

Nisbett, R. E., & Ross, L. (1980). *Human inference: Strategies and shortcomings of social judgment.* Englewood Cliffs, NJ: Prentice-Hall.

Novaco, R. W. (1978). Anger and coping with stress: Cognitive-behavioral intervention. In J. P. Foreyt & D. P. Rathjen (Eds.), *Cognitive behavioral therapy: Research and application.* New York: Plenum Press.

Parke, R. D., & Slaby, R. G. (1983). The development of aggression. In P. H. Mussen (Ed.), *Handbook of child psychology,* (4th ed.) (Vol. 4) *Socialization and personality processes,* volume editor, E. M. Hetherington. New York: Wiley.

Piaget, J. (1928). *Judgment and reasoning in the child.* New York: Harcourt, Brace.

Piaget, J. (1965). *The moral judgment of the child.* Glencoe, IL: Free Press. (originally published, 1932)

Popper, K. R. (1962). *Conjectures and refutations.* New York: Basic Books.

Pressley, G. M. (1979). Increasing children's self-control through cognitive interventions. *Review of Educational Research, 49,* 319–370.

Putallaz, M. (1983). Predicting children's sociometric status from their behavior. *Child Development, 54,* 1417–1426.

Putallaz, M., & Gottman, J. M. (1981). Social skills and group acceptance. In S. Asher & J. M. Gottman (Eds.), *The development of friendship: Description and intervention.* New York: Cambridge University Press.

Renshaw, P. D., & Asher, S. R. (1982). Social competence and peer status: The distinction between goals and strategies. In K. H. Rubin & H. S. Ross (Eds.), *Peer relationships and social skills in childhood.* New York: Springer-Verlag.

Richard, B. A., & Dodge, K. A. (1982). *Children's competence at persuasion: The relation between cognitive skills and social behavior.* Paper presented at the annual meeting of the Association for the Advancement of Behavior Therapy, Los Angeles, November.

Rosenthal, R., Hall, J. A., Mateo, M. R., Rogers, P. L., & Archer, D. (1979). *Sensitivity to nonverbal communication: The PONS Test.* Baltimore: Johns Hopkins University Press.

Rothenberg, B. B. (1970). Children's social sensitivity and the relationship to interpersonal competence, intrapersonal comfort, and intellectual level. *Developmental Psychology, 2,* 335–350.

Rubin, K. H. (1982). Nonsocial play in preschoolers: Necessarily evil? *Child Development, 53,* 651–657.

Rubin, K. H., & Daniels-Beirness, T. (1983). Concurrent and predictive correlates of sociometric status in kindergarten and grade one children. *Merrill-Palmer Quarterly, 29,* 337–352.

Ruble, D. N., & Rholes, W. S. (1982). The development of children's perceptions and attributions about their social world. In J. H. Harvey, W. Ickes, & R. F. Kidd (Eds.), *New directions in attribution research,* (Vol. 3). Hillsdale, NJ: Lawrence Erlbaum Associates.

Rule, B. G., Nesdale, A. R., & McAra, M. H. (1974). Children's reactions to information about the intentions underlying an aggressive act. *Child Development, 45,* 794–798.

Schwartz, R., & Gottman, J. M. (1976). Toward a task analysis of assertive behavior. *Journal of Consulting and Clinical Psychology, 44,* 910–920.

Selman, R. L. (1976). Toward a structural analysis of developing interpersonal relations concepts: Research with normal and disturbed preadolescent boys. In A. Pick (Ed.), *Minnesota Symposium on Child Psychology,* (Vol. 10). Minneapolis: University of Minnesota Press.

Shantz, C. U. (1975). The development of social cognition. In E. M. Hetherington (Ed.), *Review of child development research,* (Vol. 5). Chicago: University of Chicago Press.

Shantz, C. U. (1983). Social cognition. In P. H. Mussen (Ed.), *Handbook of child psychology* (4th Ed.), Vol. 3, *Cognitive development,* volume editors, J. H. Flavell & E. M. Markman (pp. 495–555). New York: Wiley.

Shantz, D. W., & Voydanoff, D. A. (1973). Situational effects on retaliatory aggression at three age levels. *Child Development, 44,* 149–153.

Shiffrin, R. M., & Schneider, W. (1977). Controlled and automatic information process: II. Perceptual learning, automatic attending, and a general theroy. *Psychological Review, 84,* 127–188.

Smith, M. C. (1975). Children's use of the multiple sufficient cause schema in social perception. *Journal of Personality and Social Psychology, 32,* 737–747.

Spivack, G., Platt, J. J., & Shure, M. B. (1976). *The problem-solving approach to adjustment.* San Francisco: Jossey-Bass.

Spivack, G., & Shure, M. B. (1974). *Social adjustment of young children: A cognitive approach to solving real life problems.* San Francisco: Jossey-Bass.

Steinberg, M. D., & Dodge, D. A. (1983). Attributional bias in aggressive adolescent boys and girls. *Journal of Social and Clinical Psychology, 1,* 312–321.

Whalen, C. K., Henker, B., Collins, B. E., McAuliffe, S., & Vaux, A. (1979). Peer interaction in a structured communication task: Comparisons of normal and hyperactive boys and of methylphenidate (Ritalin) and placebo effects. *Child Development, 50,* 388–401.

White, D. J. (1969). *Decision theory.* Chicago: Aldine.

Zahavi, S., & Asher, S. R. (1978). The effect of verbal instructions on preschool children's aggressive behavior. *Journal of School Psychology, 16,* 146–153.

4 Needed Steps for Social Competence: Strengths and Present Limitations of Dodge's Model

Kim Gale Dolgin
Institute of Child Development
University of Minnesota

I should begin by saying that I find Dodge's model a very reasonable and useful framework within which to dissect social interaction. It is reasonable in that it subjects social cues to the same cognitive processes that we assume are used to interpret nonsocial stimuli; it is useful in that it provides a guide to segmenting the behavioral selection process, a necessity if we are to make sense of complex social decision making. Although the model was developed in order to describe the steps involved in children's selection of aggressive or nonaggressive actions, it can readily be generalized and employed to more broadly delineate the processing steps involved in a wide variety of social decisions.

It is difficult to argue against a model which states that in order to behave appropriately people must first *encode* so that they can *interpret* social cues. Only after having accomplished these processes can they *generate a set of potential responses,* and only then can they *select* and finally *enact* their chosen response. It is also, therefore, difficult to argue against the position that failure to behave appropriately can be caused by failure at any one of these five steps. To determine in individual cases where the lack occurs, Dodge suggests that each of the five processes be observed individually while the other four are held constant.

In addition to supporting Dodge's basic model, I strongly endorse several other points that he makes in his paper. In particular, I believe he is correct in calling for researchers to move past simplistic, single-factor explanations of multifaceted phenomena. Although it is frequently both necessary and desirable to conduct experiments in which just one factor is studied in depth, the leap to developing single-factor theories from these experiments is not warranted.

A second point Dodge stresses is the important influence of context in behavioral decision making. This is a theme which is now generally accepted for most cognitive activities. "Social script" research (e.g., Nelson, 1981; Schank & Abelson, 1977), for example, concerns the influence of context on memory and social knowledge. Given that context is so influential, Dodge feels that predictions of social performance in a specific context can best be derived from assessments which tap that context.

Dodge also calls for research which will lead to precise, rather than vague, predictions as to the effects of particular cognitive processing deficiencies on behavioral selections. Useful predictions are ever the goal of science. The route to such precision lies in fine-grained studies in which one processing step or one stimulus is studied in detail; many of Dodge's own studies are of this ilk.

Finally, Dodge states that much of the decision-making process is unconscious. The cognitive steps are usually unconscious—although we sometimes deliberately ponder our options—and social cues are often subliminally perceived, although they are sometimes sought. Dodge believes that unconscious and conscious processing usually occur in parallel and that they are similar, but he admits that this is a speculative assumption. I feel that many social cues are normally perceived at a purely unconscious level, and that many are consciously uninterpretable even if brought to the perceiver's attention.

The "tongue-show," for example, is a nonverbal social cue performed by humans as well as other primates that indicates an unwillingness by the performer to interact (Smith, Chase, & Lieblich, 1974). Adults will hesitate to interrupt a tongue-showing individual even when it is necessary to do so, even though most are unaware of noticing the display (Dolgin & Sabini, 1982). Even those individuals in our study who remembered seeing a tongue-show did not realize that it was that aspect of the facial expression that discouraged interaction. Because much crucial processing is unconscious, if assessments of sensitivity to social cues are to be accurate they must include measures which tap unconscious reactions to such displays.

Although I am in accord with Dodge's model as it is presented in his paper, it can and should be extended to include issues which it at the present time ignores. This is true both in the case of aggressive behavior and of other social behaviors that the model is generalized to include. This expansion can be accomplished largely by incorporating bodies of knowledge that have been overlooked. In some cases, extensions will require information that we do not yet have. In addition, the model can be better tested, and in such a manner as to determine whether it is step-wise or merely descriptive.

As a developmental psychologist, I was immediately struck by the fact that, as presented, the model is not intrinsically developmental. Although it was designed to describe differences in the social decisions made by children, little mention is made of the important changes in the decision-making processes in children of different ages. Perhaps this is because, in the studies that Dodge reported, the developmental effects were small when compared to those of aggressive tendency. It should be noted, however, that in these studies the subjects' age ranges were narrow.

In any case, 2-year-olds, 7-year-olds, and 14-year-olds surely often differ in the way they arrive at the social behavior they choose, even if they ultimately select the same behavior. If the entire life span is considered, then different competencies in all of Dodge's five steps will be evidenced. These differences will result from changes in perceptual ability, cognition proper (increased ease of recall, improvement in focusing attention, ability to seriate events, etc.), from an increased knowledge of motives, goals, social expectations, and from increasingly differentiated social concepts.

That there are improvements in cognitive capacity is beyond question. Structural psychologists (e.g., Piaget, 1928), of course, believe that cognitive skill emerges through an interaction of maturation and experience, and that many cognitive complexities are beyond young children. Similarly, even though many researchers of the information processing school now believe that during childhood there is little change in basic processing capacity (Siegler, 1983; Simon, 1972), they would agree that improvement in strategy use (e.g., Ornstein, Naus, & Liberty, 1975), metacognitive abilities (Brown, 1978; Flavell & Wellman, 1977), and in the knowledge base (Chi, 1978) result in improved ability to remember, to think, and to make behavioral selections.

These differences in cognitive capacity are particularly important since Dodge states that inappropriate behavior may result from processing overloads (p. 99). When faced with processing overloads, individuals typically revert to more juvenile behavior patterns; if this pattern holds here, then it must follow that older children who behave aggressively due to such overloads do so because younger children are more likely than older children to be aggressive. While this is true, the bulk of young children's aggression is different from that of older children: they are more likely to instrumentally use aggression to obtain some end, whereas older children are more likely to behave in a hostile manner in non-instrumental situations (Hartup, 1974). One could predict, then, that if processing overloads are often responsible for aggressive behavioral selection, then this aggressive behavior should occur predominantly in instrumental contexts.

Comparably, changes in social cognitive ability will influence children's choice of social behavior. For example, children's perspective–taking abilities increase with age (Flavell, Botkin, Fry, Wright, & Jarvis, 1968; Piaget, 1928; Selman, 1980), and this change clearly influences their understanding of others' behavior and thus their behavioral selections. Also relevant are developmental increases in children's abilities to infer motives (even though studies on this topic usually detail children's post hoc descriptions of filmed events rather than their responses to different motives). For example, in a seminal study, Flapan (1968) found that between the ages of 6 and 9 years there was an increase in children's tendencies to interpret actor's thoughts and emotions when asked to describe observed film sequences. Similar findings have been reported by Collins, Wellman, Keniston, and Westby (1978) and Wood (1978). A third important developmental change, particularly relevant to differences in behavioral selection of aggression-prone versus average children, is that during early adolescence children become increasingly aware of the importance of context in influencing a person's behavior (Barenboim, 1977; Lively & Bromley, 1973). As a final example, there is evidence that children's abilities to interpret another's emotional signals increases with age (DePaulo & Rosenthal, 1979; Dimitrovsky, 1964; Girgus & Wolf, 1975; McClusky, Albas, Neimi, Cuevas, & Ferrer, 1975; Zuckerman & Przewuzman, 1979).

A second factor which is not considered by the model is affect. It is common sense that persons will react differently to the same stimulus depending upon their current emotional state. Being angry, for instance, increases the probability of behaving hostilely. Similarly, feeling joy would decrease the likelihood of responding hostilely. Any given child could respond in any of a number of ways to a situation, depending upon her feelings and their intensity.

A third contributing component is that of dispositional bias. In the face of equivalent hostility, some children will respond with aggression while others will attempt to placate their antagonist. Some of this variance can be accounted for by differential likelihoods of perceiving aggressive intent (Dodge, 1980; Nasby, Hayden, & DePaulo, 1980). Still, even if it is true that aggressive children generate fewer responses than typical children, there is no a priori reason why this restricted response set contains only hostile rather than benign alternatives. Dispositional bias is an issue that Dodge raises, but at this time the causes of such a personality trait are not well understood. Some personality correlates of this tendency have been isolated, however. For example, Patterson (1982) found that aggressive boys had difficulty in delaying gratification.

Another issue, one related to dispositional bias, which warrants further attention is that of sex differences in causes and types of aggression. It is well known that it is more common for males to be physically aggressive than females (Feshbach, 1970; Maccoby & Jacklin, 1974; Parke & Slahy, 1983). Some research indicates that boys are more likely to respond to aggressive instigation than girls (Whiting & Pope, 1974), suggesting differences in perceptual or processing bias for social stimuli. Contributing causes of this difference include differential socialization (Bandura, 1973), evolutionarily based tendencies (Lorenz, 1966), and intrauterine (Reinisch, 1981; but see Tieger, 1980) and postuterine hormonal states (Hinde, 1978; Maccoby & Jacklin, 1980). Because of the difficulties of finding aggressive girls to use as subjects, little research has explored the differences in the proximal stimuli or processing differences leading to aggressive action for the two sexes. Even if the model is extended to include other kinds of social behavioral selections, sex differences should be studied.

The final issue that requires more viewing is that of personal history and individual experience. Most persons behave as they do because such behavior has proven adaptive in the past (Bandura, 1977). Modeling of observed parental or sibling aggressive/concilliatory behavior will contribute to response selection (Mischel, 1970; Patterson, 1982). In addition, factors such as divorce (Heatherington, Cox, & Cox, 1979) may in the short run increase the likelihood of aggression. As with most realms of behavior, many individual differences can be accounted for by prior experiences.

A final suggestion that I would make is that Dodge's model be subjected to further testing. The proof that was given for the model was a multiple regression analysis indicating that each of the processing steps contributes to predicting children's competency. While this analysis does demonstrate that each of the steps in his model is present and valid, it does not test if those steps progress in the outlined order. It is this orderly linear processing, which is suggested by the model, that should be more adequately tested. For example, a poor performance in step 2 of the model (interpreting) should better predict poor performance in step 3 (selecting possible behaviors) than in step 1 (encoding): difficulties may begin at any point, but if the steps progress in a regular linear fashion then their effects should always ripple forwards, not backwards. Analyses of covariance or a path analysis would be suitable to test for these forward-moving effects.

Since I am in such accord with Dodge's approach, I'd like to use the remainder of this response to focus in upon one particular aspect of the processing chain which leads to social behavior selection. The steps of the model I will be concerned with are 1 and 2: step 1, again, involves the encoding of social cues, while step 2 involves the interpretation of those cues. Both steps will be discussed simultaneously, since I agree with Dodge that these two steps are quite closely linked and are often difficult to separate. The particular cues to be discussed are those that signal intent. Differences in aggressive and more typical children's abilities to "read" intent cues has been the topic of much of Dodge's research, and some of my own work bears upon this issue.

Dodge presented a literature review which indicated that aggressive children are not as capable as other children at interpreting social intent cues. His own work, for example, indicates that aggressive children are more likely to decide that an ambiguous behavior was indicative of hostile intent, that they are less likely to base their responses upon specific cues, relying instead upon general expectancies (Dodge & Tomlin, 1983, cited in Dodge, this volume), and that they are less willing to spend time searching for cues. Even given this research, there is much yet to know about the encoding and interpretation of intent cues. Differences in this ability might well be correlated with (if not responsible for, in some instances) differences in ability to appropriately select responses in social interactions.

The research that is being conducted is concerned with children's abilities to assess intent. The word "intent" is often used synonymously with "motive," though they are not identical terms (see Gruenich & Trabasso, 1981). To say someone had a motive for doing something necessarily means that they did it intentionally. To say, therefore, that someone acted with "hostile intent" really means that they acted intentionally and with a hostile motive. This distinction often gets swallowed up—as it did, for example, in years of moral development research, where intent and motive were typically confounded—but developing full understanding of the cognitive underpinnings of social behavioral selection involves keeping the two concepts separate. The very first decision one must make in a confrontive situation is whether the offending behavior was intended or whether it was accidental; only in cases where there is a positive assessment of intent does motive correctly come into play. Alternatively, one could first decide whether the action yielded a positive or a negative outcome, and then later assess whether it was or was not intended. If the action were deemed intended, then a hostile motive would usually be inferred. In any case, motive and intent are assessed separately. Very little research has been directed towards understanding the development of the ability to make intent decisions, and almost nothing is known about differences in this ability between aggressive and nonaggressive children.

What do we know about children's abilities to assess intent proper? Most generally, Flapan (1968) and Karniol (1978) found that children become more concerned with describing an individual's intents as they grow older; still, intents were secondary to contextual and situational factors in the behavioral descriptions given by children of all ages. Use and understanding of intention has been demonstrated in children as young as 4 years: Lively and Bromley (1973) found that children of this age provided descriptions of an actors' intents while giving a running commentary about a film of a person waking in the morning, while Shulz (1980) found that 3-year-old children could, under certain circumstances, differentiate between intended actions and mistakes. These findings might be rather method or context specific, however, since, working with children of the same age, King (1971) found that, although they were not overly influenced by severity of outcome when making intent judgments, 4-year-olds failed to differentiate between scenes involving a push and an accidental fall. (King's 5½-year-olds did differentiate between the accidental and the intentional scenes.) Finally, Berndt and Berndt (1975) discovered that the ability to correctly judge an action accidental lags developmentally behind the ability to correctly judge a behavior intentional.

During the past 2 years, Margarita Azmitia and I have been conducting research designed to look at some of the cues that individuals use when assessing intent. To do this, 24 pairs of video tapes, consisting of two different pairs depicting each of twelve broadly selected intent cues, were made. The cues included both affective cues as well as those based upon contextual information. The tapes within a pair varied only in that the embedded cue was altered so that the actor's apparent intent state seemed different in the two pair members. We found that children of different ages were not equally successful at interpreting the cues: while 5-year-olds, for example, correctly differentiated an actor's apparently intentional/apparently accidental behavior only when 4 of the cues—veers, looks of surprise, self-injury, or actor's certain prior knowledge of outcome—were varied, 7-year-olds used these cues and in addition took smiles, frowns, multiple repetitions, sequence violations, verbal assertions of intent, and inanimacy into account. Each of these cues, as well as the other two—glance direction and look of concentration—were used by adults. A slight bias was found at all ages towards assuming an action intentional.

Neither adults nor children were very accurate at describing the information they used to reach an intent decision: typically, invariant information was cited. Contextual information was more frequently cited than affective information. This work is going to be extended to include aggressive children as subjects. This extension will help determine whether aggressive children have relative difficulties in assessing intent or whether the difficulties they experience come from problems with interpreting motive.

As Dodge points out, failure of a cue to influence an individual's behavior can result from at least two sources. First, the cue may have been "missed." This failure to perceive a cue might be caused by overload (e.g., too many things going on at once) or by lack of attention to or interest in an unsalient cue. Alternatively, the cue might have been noted, but either misinterpreted or ignored, either because its meaning was unknown or because it was considered less important than a second, conflicting cue. Some of the subjects we tested, particularly the older subjects (9- and 11-year-olds) informed us that they ignored certain cues—particularly facial expressions—because they felt that they conflicted with contextual evidence (i.e., no adult would really be surprised at a jack-in-the-box, so the expression must have been faked). This is in accord with Bugental, Kasavan, and Love (1970) who found that children will ignore a woman's smile when interpreting messages unless those smiles received support from other channels (e.g., positive tone of voice). A second control study in which the cues are made very salient is in progress. This study will allow us to assess whether failure to use particular cues results from perceptual or cognitive difficulties. In this way, the first two processing steps outlined in Dodge's model will be separated.

Integration of fine-grained studies such as these into Dodge's useful model will further increase our understanding of the social behavioral decision-making process. If, in addition, the model is augmented by incorporating the content areas of developmental cognitive change, transient affective state, dispositional bias, sex differences, and individual experience outlined above, its usefulness will be further enhanced. Whether or not the processing steps are found to proceed in a regular linear order, the model stands as an important taxonomic tool for parsing the cognitive steps that go into the making of social behavioral decisions.

REFERENCES

Bandura, A. (1973). *Aggression: A social learning analysis*. New York: Holt.
Bandura, A. (1977). *Social learning theory*. Englewood Cliffs, NJ: Prentice-Hall.

Barenboim, C. (1977). Developmental changes in the interpersonal cognitive system from middle childhood to early adolescence. *Child Development, 48,* 1467–1474.

Berndt, T. J., & Berndt, E. G. (1975). Children's uses of motives and intentionality in person perception and moral judgement. *Child Development, 46,* 904–912.

Brown, A. (1978). Knowing when, where, and how to remember: A problem in metacognition. In R. Glaser (Ed.), *Advances in instructional psychology.* Hillsdale, NJ: Lawrence Erlbaum Associates.

Bugental, D. E., Kaswan, J. W., & Love, R. (1970). Perception of contradictory meanings conveyed by verbal and nonverbal channels. *Journal of Personality and Social Psychology, 16,* 647–655.

Chi, M. T. H. (1978). Knowledge structures and memory development. In R. Siegler (Ed.), *Children's thinking: What develops.* Hillsdale, NJ: Lawrence Erlbaum Associates.

Collins, W. A., Wellman, H., Keniston, A. H., & Westby, S. (1978). Age-related aspects of comprehension and inference from a television dramatic narrative. *Child Development, 49,* 389–399.

DePaulo, B. M., & Rosenthal, R. (1979). Age changes in nonverbal decoding skills: Evidence for increasing differentiation. *Merrill-Palmer Quarterly, 25,* 145–150.

Dimitrovsky, L. (1964). The ability to identify the emotional meaning of vocal expressions at successive age levels. In J. R. Davitz (Ed.), *The communication of emotional meaning.* New York: McGraw-Hill.

Dodge, K. A. (1980). Social cognition and children's aggressive behavior. *Child Development, 51,* 162–170.

Dodge, K. A., & Newman, J. P. (1981). Biased decision making processes in aggressive boys. *Journal of Abnormal Psychology, 90,* 375–379.

Dolgin, K. G., & Sabini, J. (1982). The tongue-show effects an observer's willingness to interact. *Animal Behavior, 30,* 935–936.

Feshbach, S. (1970). Aggression. In P. H. Mussen (Ed.), *Carmichael's manual of child psychology.* New York: Wiley.

Flapan, D. (1968). *Children's understanding of social interactions.* New York: Teacher's College Press.

Flavell, J. H., Botkin, P. T., Fry, C. L., Jr., Wright, J. W., & Jarvis, P. E. (1968). *The development of role-taking and communication skills in children.* New York: Wiley.

Flavell, J. H., & Wellman, H. M. (1977). Metamemory. In R. V. Kail, Jr., & J. W. Hagen (Eds.), *Perspectives on the development of memory and cognition.* Hillsdale, NJ: Lawrence Erlbaum Associates.

Girgus, J. S., & Wolf, J. (1975) Age changes in the ability to encode social cues. *Developmental Psychology, 11,* 118.

Gruenich, R., & Trabasso, T. (1981). The story as a social environment: Children's comprehension and evaluation of intentions and consequences. In J. Harvey (Ed.), *Cognition, social behavior, and the environment.* Hillsdale, NJ: Lawrence Erlbaum Associates.

Hartup, W. W. (1974). Aggression in childhood: Developmental perspectives. *American Psychologist, 29,* 336–341.

Heatherington, E. M., Cox, M., & Cox, R. (1979). Play and social interaction in children following a divorce. *Journal of Social Issues, 35,* 26–49.

Hinde, R. A. (1978). The study of aggression: Determinants, consequences, goals, and functions. In W. Hartup & J. deWitt (Eds.), *Origins of aggression.* The Hague: Mouton.

Karniol, R. (1978). Children's use of intention cues in evaluating behavior. *Psychological Bulletin, 85,* 76–85.

King, M. (1971). The development of some intention concepts in young children. *Child Development, 42,* 1145–1152.

Livesly, W. J., & Bromley, D. B. (1973). *Person perception in childhood and adolescence.* London: Wiley.

Lorenz, K. (1966). *On aggression*. New York: Bantam Press.

Maccoby, E. E., & Jacklin, C. N. (1974). *The psychology of sex differences*. Stanford, CA: Stanford University Press.

Maccoby, E. E., & Jacklin, C. N. (1980). Sex differences in aggression: A rejoinder and reprise. *Child Development, 51,* 964–980.

McClusky, K. W., Albas, D. C., Neimi, R. R., Cuevas, C., & Ferrer, C. A. (1975). Cross-cultural differences in the perception of the emotional content of speech: A study of the development of sensitivity in Canadian and Mexican children. *Developmental Psychology, 11,* 551–555.

Mischel, W. (1970). Sex-typing and socialization. In P. H. Mussen (Ed.), *Carmichael's manual of social psychology*. New York: Wiley.

Nasby, W., Hayden, B., & DePaulo, B. M. (1980). Attributional bias among aggressive boys to interpret unambiguous social stimuli as hostile displays. *Journal of Abnormal Psychology, 89,* 459–468.

Nelson, K. (1981). Social cognition in a script framework. In J. H. Flavell & L. Ross (Eds.), *Social cognitive development: Frontiers and possible futures*. New York: Cambridge University Press.

Ornstein, P. A., Naus, M. J., & Liberty, C. (1975). Rehearsal and organizational processes in children's memory. *Child Development, 26,* 818–830.

Parke, R. D., & Slahy, R. G. (1983). The development of aggression. In E. M. Heatherington (Ed.), *Socialization, personality, and social development* (Vol. 4). In P. Mussen (Ed.), *Carmichael's manual of child psychology* (4th ed.). New York: Wiley.

Patterson, G. R. (1982) *Coercive family process*. Eugene, OR: Castalia Press.

Piaget, J. (1928). *Judgement and reasoning of the child*. New York: Harcourt, Brace, & World.

Reinisch, J. M. (1981). Prenatal exposure to synthetic progestins increases potential for aggression in humans. *Science, 211,* 1171–1173.

Schank, R. C., & Abelson, R. (1977). *Scripts, plans, goals, and understanding*. Hillsdale, NJ: Lawrence Erlbaum Associates.

Selman, R. L. (1980). *The growth of interpersonal understanding*. New York: Academic Press.

Schulz, T. (1980). Development of the concept of intention. In W. A. Collins (Ed.), *Minnesota Symposia on Child Psychology* (Vol. 13). Hillsdale, NJ: Lawrence Erlbaum Associates.

Siegler, R. (1983). Information processing approaches to development. In J. H. Flavell & E. M. Markman (Eds.), *Cognitive development* (Vol. 3). In P. Mussen (Ed.), *Carmichael's manual of child psychology* (4th ed.). New York: Wiley.

Simon, H. A. (1972). On the developer of the processor. In S. Farnham-Diggory (Ed.), *Information processing in children*. New York: Academic Press.

Smith, W. J., Chase, J., & Lieblich, A. (1974). Tongue-showing: A facial display of humans and other primate species. *Semiotica, 11,* 201–246.

Tieger, T. (1980). On the biological basis of sex differences in aggression. *Child Development, 51,* 943–963.

Whiting, B., & Edwards, C. P. (1973). A cross-cultural analysis of sex differences in the behavior of children aged 3–11. *Journal of Social Psychology, 91,* 171–188.

Wood, M. E. (1978). Children's developing understanding of other people's motives for behavior. *Developmental Psychology, 14,* 561–562.

Zuckerman, M., & Przewuzman, S. J. (1979). Decoding and encoding facial expressions in pre-school-age children. *Experimental Psychology and Nonverbal Behavior, 3,* 147–163.

5 Becoming a Different Person: Transformations in Personality and Social Behavior

Kurt W. Fischer
Donna M. Elmendorf
University of Denver

People change. Over periods of time, they reorganize their behavior so that their personality and social interactions become different in important ways. Also, within any given day, their behavior changes from one moment to the next. Many of these variations involve changes not only in content but also in organization.

We will argue that every individual possesses a number of qualitatively different behavioral organizations. The changes that occur in a person's behavior reflect these different organizations. The most obvious case is probably the organizations that arise with development: As children's cognitive capacity grows, they reorganize their behavior, developing both new skills and new ways of distorting or misinterpreting events in their world. In addition, significant variations in organization occur from moment to moment. Often, these variations are similar to developmental changes, in that they seem to fit along a scale of behavioral complexity similar to a developmental sequence.

We believe that a productive way of analyzing these variations is in terms of transformations—rewrite rules specifying how one behavioral organization changes into another. For example, children develop along a developmental sequence from understanding social categories singly, such as nice (or mean), to understanding the relation between two categories, such as nice and mean. This change involves a transformation in which single categories are coordinated and differentiated to form an overarching relation. One way of describing this transformation is in terms of a rule specifying how single categories can be "rewritten" or changed to form a specific relation between categories.

Moment-to-moment variations in behavior can involve not only such progressive change to a more complex organization, but also the reverse; a person's behavior can change from a relatively advanced organization to a more primitive one. For example, at one moment a child may demonstrate an understanding of the relation between nice and mean, and at the next moment this advanced organization may fall apart, moving backward to single categories: The individual deals with nice or mean but not with the relation between them. We will argue that these regressive changes can also be explained in terms of transformations and that in many cases the regressive transformation rules are simply the reverse of the progressive ones.

A transformational approach requires not only a description of how one organization is reorganized to form another organization, but also an analysis of the kinds of factors that can induce transformations. Factors that will be discussed in this chapter include development of a new capacity, change in the degree of environmental support for a behavior, and change in emotional state. Transformations arising from the development of a new capacity have been studied most extensively; in this chapter, we begin by illustrating how a transformational analysis can explain developmental changes in several types of social-cognitive behavior. We then extend this analysis to variations arising from the degree of environmental support. Finally, we outline a transformational analysis of variations in organization due to emotional state.

The kind of general transformational framework that we are calling for does not exist at present in the behavioral sciences. There is no general framework for analyzing the many types of changes in the organization of human behavior. Some theories of cognitive development provide partial analyses of some types of transformations, and so we will use them to illustrate the transformational approach. For transformations arising from environmental and emotional factors, however, there is much less theoretical and empirical work to build upon. In these cases we have attempted to begin the long process of constructing a transformational approach.

TRANSFORMATIONS FROM DEVELOPMENT: SKILL LEVELS

Children's behavior obviously undergoes vast reorganizations with development, and explanation of these reorganizations is one of the central goals of a transformational approach. The nature of the reorganizations has proven to be a matter of some controversy, however (Fischer & Silvern, 1985). Research has not supported any simple stage theories, such as Piaget's (1957) original hypothesis that reorganizations occur uniformly for the entire mind (Biggs & Collis, 1982; Broughton, 1981; Flavell, 1982). Developmentalists have had to introduce task and context effects into their descriptions of developmental reorganizations, thus adding substantial complexity. Even in the face of this complexity, however, there are straightforward ways to systematically describe developmental reorganizations. Indeed, we will argue that these task and context effects should be introduced directly into the theory and methodology of any transformational framework.

To begin, a precise, detailed description of developmental sequences is essential, because such sequences provide an empirically based portrait of the reorganizations that children actually demonstrate in cognitive development. A sequence provides a series of reorganizations to be explained by a transformational framework. Also, assessment of the sequence can provide a measuring instrument like a ruler for analyzing reorganizations. Thus, the sequences and the methods of assessing them are an important part of a transformational framework.

To provide a precise, detailed description of a sequence, researchers have had to restrict their methods to investigation of *a narrow task domain* for each sequence (Fischer & Bullock, 1981; Flavell, 1972). Restriction to a narrow domain has eliminated many of the methodological difficulties produced by task and context effects (Fischer, 1980). Consequently, researchers have been able to construct precise, detailed descriptions of developmental reorganizations that apply to individual children. Much of the research in the Cognitive Development Laboratory at the University of Denver has involved prediction and testing of sequences within narrow domains. In order to illustrate how such analyses can be done, we will describe three sequences that have been predicted based on a transformational framework for cognitive development and that have been supported by research.

General Method

One central criterion for research on developmental sequences is that a method should be used that provides a direct test of the sequence. In most developmental research, inferences of developmental sequences are based on average differences between age groups in performance on one or a few tasks. Only a few studies have provided direct tests of whether the hypothesized steps in the sequence in fact occur in the expected order for individual children (Fischer & Bullock, 1984; Wohlwill, 1973).

A direct test of a sequence requires independent assessments at several points to determine if the steps follow the hypothesized order. The most frequently recommended method for obtaining these independent assessments has been the longitudinal design, in which the same subjects are tested at several points over a period of time. This method provides independent assessments for testing the sequence, but it is also time-consuming, expensive, and difficult to use.

Strong-Scalogram Method.   An easier direct method for testing sequences is the strong-scalogram technique, in which a separate task is designed to assess every hypothesized step in a sequence (Fischer, Pipp, & Bullock, 1984). In the past, researchers have seldom used this method, but recently a number of investigators have begun to recognize its utility. Even with a cross-sectional design, the use of a separate task for each step provides an independent assessment of the predicted sequence, and of course the method can also be used with a longitudinal design. For a simple, Guttman-type sequence, every subject should pass all steps to a certain point and fail all steps beyond that point, as depicted in the performance profiles in Table 5.1.

In addition to testing the predicted sequence, this method also provides data on the effects of task complexity on performance, because it includes tasks of varying complexity levels. For instance, the investigator can examine the subjects' errors—how performance on the tasks failed varies as a function of the distance of each task from the highest step passed (Roberts, 1981). When a person passes Step 4 but fails Steps 5 through 9, how does his or her performance on the higher steps vary as the tasks become more complex? When one person passes only through Step 2 while another person passes through Step 4, how will their failures at Step 5 be different? In this way, the strong-scalogram method provides a technique for studying the nature of simplification or distortion of complex tasks (how behavior is transformed by an increase in task complexity).

Use of Stories in Pretend Play.   The research reported here used not only the strong-scalogram method but also a standard mode of presentation of tasks. For each developmental step, children were individually shown a pretend story with realistic cardboard dolls, such as the example in Table 5.2, and they were asked to act out a story like the one they saw. The children's stories were recorded on videotape for later scoring. This elicited-imitation, pretend-play procedure proved to be especially useful with young children, who are often difficult to test

TABLE 5.1
The Strong-Scalogram Method:
Profiles for a Nine-Step Sequence

Developmental Sequence of Profiles	Task Devised A Priori								
	1	2	3	4	5	6	7	8	9
0	−	−	−	−	−	−	−	−	−
1	+	−	−	−	−	−	−	−	−
2	+	+	−	−	−	−	−	−	−
3	+	+	+	−	−	−	−	−	−
4	+	+	+	+	−	−	−	−	−
5	+	+	+	+	+	−	−	−	−
6	+	+	+	+	+	+	−	−	−
7	+	+	+	+	+	+	+	−	−
8	+	+	+	+	+	+	+	+	−
9	+	+	+	+	+	+	+	+	+

Note: A plus indicates that the task was passed, and a minus indicates that it was failed.

TABLE 5.2
Example of an Elicited-Imitation, Pretend-Play Story:
Relation Between Intention, Action, and Reaction in Aggression

---

EXPERIMENTER: This story is about Susie pushing Rachel because she wants to take Rachel's ball. Rachel doesn't want to play with Susie because Susie pushed her just so she could take her ball.

(Susie is standing off to the side)

SUSIE: There's Rachel. I want to go push her so I can get her ball.

RACHEL: Hi, Susie. Look at the ball I've got!

SUSIE: (Pushes Rachel and grabs the ball) Gimme that ball! I pushed you because I wanted to take your ball!

RACHEL: (Grabs ball back) Hey! Gimme that back! I'm not gonna play with you because you pushed me because you wanted to take my ball. I don't like to play with kids who push me so that they can take something. Goodbye! (Rachel walks off).

FOLLOW-UP QUESTIONS:

Who acted mean in this story?
What did Susie do that was mean?
Why did Susie push Rachel?
How come Rachel did not want to play with Susie?

---

with traditional procedures (Fischer, Hand, Watson, Van Parys, & Tucker, 1984). Most children found it engaging and cooperated for relatively long periods of time. Also, young children typically spend large portions of their daily lives in pretend play, so the procedure relates to their natural, everyday activities.

The elicited-imitation procedure was highly structured and provided environmental support for high-level performance, in that the demands on the child were clear and the memory requirements were small. The child saw and heard a story and immediately acted out his or her own story. In all of our studies, we also included a second condition, which provided low support and so produced spontaneous behavior: Immediately after the elicited-imitation condition, the child was asked to make up some stories of his or her own using the same dolls and props. The child's stories were recorded on videotape. Because the two conditions assessed performance with high and low environmental support, respectively, it was possible not only to test a developmental sequence but also to determine how performance varied as a function of degree of support.

Three Levels of Social Categories

The three sequences we will describe all involve social categories, but the specific contents differ. The sequences deal with nice and mean social interactions, attributions about aggression, and social roles, respectively. The detailed steps of each sequence hold only for the specific content and task used in the assessment.

However, across the three sequences there is a global similarity in the nature of the reorganizations that children move through. All three sequences follow a similar general outline, in which development moves through three levels for the use of social categories. In addition to providing a global description of the similarities across the sequences, the levels also correspond to large-scale reorganizations posited by several neo-Piagetian theories (Case, in press; Fischer, 1980). Of course, in research documenting these sequences, the exact ages for attainment of a level have varied as a function of condition and domain (Fischer, Hand, Watson, Van Parys, & Tucker, 1984).

At the first level, *single social categories,* children make a doll carry out two or more actions fitting a social category, such as nice, mean, doctor, or mother. For example, a doll acts nice by saying "I like you" and offering candy to another doll. The second doll does not need to do anything at all but can remain a passive recipient of the actions of the first doll.

At the second level, *mappings of social categories,* children relate one social category to another. For example, when one doll acts nice, the second doll acts nice in return. If the interaction is to count as a mapping, the second doll's response must clearly be related to the first doll's nice actions. Otherwise, each doll may be acting nice on its own independently, with no clear relation between the two nice categories. In addition to these relations of similar categories, mappings often relate differing categories, such as mother to child or doctor to patient.

Children construct more complex relations among categories at the third level, *systems of social categories.* For instance, two dolls interact in such a way that each is acting out two social categories simultaneously. One doll does something nice to another while at the same time doing something mean, such as asking to play while hitting. The second doll responds to the first doll's actions in a way that likewise combines both nice and mean behaviors. In another case, one doll acts simultaneously as doctor and father to a second doll, who is his daughter and his patient.

Of course, these three levels do not present the complete picture for the development of social categories, even for data collected with our procedure. First, there are additional levels before and after these three. Second, developmental reorganization in any domain involves much more detail than is represented in the three levels. The several developmental sequences to be described demonstrate both the details of reorganization and some of the additional levels.

Development of Mean and Nice Social Interactions

Social interactions are important for children, and the emotional tone of those interactions is especially significant. In the past, investigators generally neglected the topic of how young children understand interactions and their emotional tone. Researchers have begun to remedy this deficit, providing a portrait of the social-interactive capacities and limitations of preschool children (Fischer, Hand, Watson, Van Parys, & Tucker, 1984; Mueller & Lucas, 1975).

Several developmentally oriented psychodynamic theories have focused on children's ability to process and understand emotions (Kernberg, 1976; Mahler, Pine, & Bergman, 1975; Sullivan, 1953). According to these theories, preschool children have difficulty in integrating opposite emotions, such as nice and mean; and gradually during the preschool and elementary-school years, they develop the capacity for such integration. Recent research has supported this psychodynamic proposition: Young children tend to show a type of emotion-based distortion called affective splitting, in which they divide people and actions in terms of positive versus negative emotions (Harter, 1982). The first sequence we will discuss describes the development of the understanding of nice and mean in social interactions and how these opposite emotions are gradually integrated so that affective splitting is overcome.

Sequence.   In this sequence, children develop gradually from using single categories of nice or mean to relating nice and mean categories in increasingly complex ways. The specific, ten-step sequence tested by Hand (1982) is outlined in Table 5.3, and a more detailed sequence is described in Fischer and Pipp (1984a).

The experiment began with the individual child picking one doll as most like himself or herself. That doll was given the child's name, and then he or she gave names to the other dolls. Testing began with the elicited-imitation condition (using the strong-scalogram method) and continued with the spontaneous condition.

The sequence starts with the level of single social categories. In the first step, active agent, the child does not yet have a true social category, but he or she can make a doll carry out a single nice or mean action. The second step, behavioral category, involves the joining of two or more actions to form a social category for nice or mean. In the third step, shifting behavioral categories, the child makes the doll act out one category, such as mean, and then shifts to making it act out another category, such as nice. The two categories are merely juxtaposed, not related. (In the research testing the sequence, a separate task was designed to test each step in Table 5.3 except Step 3. When children failed the tasks for later steps, such as Steps 6 and 7, they sometimes spontaneously showed Step 3.)

Step 4, one-dimensional social influence with two characters behaving in a similar manner, marks movement to the second level, mappings of social categories. One doll is nice to a second doll, and the second one is nice in reciprocation, with clear evidence that the second doll's nice response is related to the first one's nice actions. A similar mapping occurs for mean behavior. Step 5, one-dimensional social influence with three characters behaving in a similar manner, is the same as Step 4 except that there are now three dolls interacting nicely or meanly.

TABLE 5.3

A Developmental Sequence for Understanding Nice and Mean Social Interactions

Level	Step	Skill	Examples	Mean Age* (in years)
I. Single Social Categories	1	Active agent: A person performs at least one behavior not necessarily fitting a social-interaction category.	Child pretends that self doll picks up a ball or suggests playing with another doll.	2 and older
	2	Behavioral category: A person performs at least two behaviors fitting an interaction category, such as "nice" or "mean."	Child has self doll act nice to another doll, giving it candy and saying, "I like you." The second doll can be passive.	3.0
	3	Shifting behavioral categories: One person performs at least two behaviors fitting the category "nice," as in Step 2, and then a second person performs at least two behaviors fitting the category "mean."	Child has self doll act nice to a second doll, giving it candy and saying, "Let's play." A third doll enters and acts mean to the second one, hitting it and saying, "Give me your ball." In both cases, the second doll can be passive.	3.5
II. Mappings of Social Categories	4	One dimensional social influence: The behaviors of one person fitting an interaction category such as "mean" produce reciprocal behaviors fitting that category in a second person.	Child has a doll say mean things and hit the self doll, who responds by hitting and expressing dislike for the first one. The self doll's behavior is clearly produced by the first one's behavior.	4.1
	5	One-dimensional social influence with three characters behaving in similar ways: Same as step 4, but with three people interacting reciprocally according to a social category.	With three dolls, child has one tease the others, while a second one hits the others. The self doll (who has been both teased and hit) rejects both of the first two because they are mean.	4.6
	6	One-dimensional social influence with three characters behaving in opposite ways: The behaviors of one person fitting a category such as "nice" and those of a second person fitting an opposite category such	With three dolls, child has one share with the others, while a second one hits the others. The self doll responds nicely to the first doll and meanly to the second.	6.9

as "mean" produce reciprocal behaviors in a third person fitting the corresponding categories.

		Description	Example	Age
III. Systems of Social Categories	7	Two-dimensional social influence: Two people interact in ways fitting opposite categories, such that the first one act, for example, both nice and mean, and the second one responds with reciprocal behaviors in the same categories.	Child has one doll initiate friendship with the self doll but in a mean way. The self doll, confused about the discrepancy, declines the friendship because of the meanness. The first then apologizes and makes another friendly gesture, which the self doll responds to accordingly.	7.4
	8	Two-dimensional social influence with three characters: Same as Step 7 but with three people interacting reciprocally according to opposite categories.	With three dolls, child has one doll act friendly to the self doll, while a third one initiates play in a mean way. The self doll acts friendly to the first one and rejects the third, pointing out the latter's meanness. The third then apologizes for being mean, while the first one does something new that is mean. The self doll accepts the third one's apology and rejects the first one, pointing out the change in his or her behavior.	10.0
IV. Abstractions about Social Categories	9	Integration of opposite behaviors in terms of a single abstraction: Two instances of interactions like that in Step 7 take place, and the relations between the two interactions are explained in terms of some general abstraction, such as that intentions matter more than actions.	With three dolls, child has one act friendly to the self doll, while a third initiates play in a mean way. The self doll responds to each accordingly, but then he or she learns that the nice one had mean intentions while the mean one had nice intentions. The self doll then changes his or her behavior to the other dolls to match their respective intentions and explains that he or she cares more about people's intentions than their actions.	10.7

TABLE 5.3

A Developmental Sequence for Understanding Nice and Mean Social Interactions

Level	Step	Skill	Examples	Mean Age* (in years)
	10	Relation of two abstractions concerning opposite behaviors: In interactions where people act in opposite ways to each other, as in Step 9, consideration of one abstraction about the interactions, such as that some people have greater needs than others, is used to modify consideration of a second abstraction, such as that intentions matter more than actions.	Child has two dolls act nice to the self doll to trick him or her into doing their homework for them. The self doll recognizes the trick and rejects both dolls for having a mean intention behind their nice actions. But upon learning the needs that motivated the others, the self doll is nice to the one that had special needs for help with homework, while rejecting the one who was simply lazy. He or she explains that his or her evaluation of their intention to trick was modified by their needs.	16 or older

* The ages for Steps 2 and 4 through 9 are based on the findings of Hand (1982), who assessed each one with an independent task. The age for Step 1 is based on the findings of Watson and Fischer (1977). The age for Step 3 is based on the children who showed it spontaneously in Hand's study. The age for Step 10 is based on the findings of Hand and Fischer (1981) and Fischer, Hand, and Russell (1983).

Note: Portions of this table are reprinted from Fischer, Hand, Watson, VanParys, and Tucker (1984). Copyright (1984), Ablex Publishing Corporation.

At Step 6, one-dimensional social influence with three characters behaving differently, one doll is nice to the self doll while another one is mean to the self doll. In response, the self doll is appropriately nice to the first doll and mean to the second. This step is transitional between mappings and systems. Children can do it relatively easily at the level of systems, because it involves the self doll acting out two opposite social categories at the same time. But because the other dolls act out only one category at a time, it is possible to carry out this task with a complex mapping (Hand, 1982; Jackowitz, 1983).

The level of systems of social categories is fully attained with Step 7, two-dimensional social influence with two characters. One doll acts simultaneously nice and mean to the other doll, who responds in kind. Thus the child has finally achieved a full coordination of opposite emotions in the same interaction. Step 8, two-dimensional social influence with three characters, is the same as Step 7 except that there are now three dolls being both nice and mean to each other.

The final two steps assess later developmental levels, which involve abstractions. At Step 9, a single abstraction integrating two opposite behaviors, the child uses an abstraction to compare two interactions involving simultaneous nice and mean actions. One such abstraction is "Intentions matter more than actions," which leads to the conclusion that someone who tries to be nice and is accidentally mean is in fact better than someone who is superficially nice in the service of a mean intention. Step 10, relation of two abstractions integrating opposite behaviors, involves comparing two interactions in terms of the relation between two abstractions, such as intention and responsibility. For example, a character who acts intentionally to deceive someone can be forgiven if he or she takes responsibility for undoing the deceit, while another character with a deceitful intention who does not take responsibility cannot be forgiven.

Results.   In the main study testing this sequence (Hand 1982), subjects were 72 middle-class children between 3 and 12 years of age. In the strong-scalogram analysis, scalability was nearly perfect, with 70 of 72 children exactly fitting the predicted performance profiles. Some small measurement error would seem to account for the two children who did not fit the profiles. Table 5.3 presents the mean ages of the children at each step. A second study has tested and replicated part of the sequence (Jackowitz, 1983).

Using Skill Theory to Predict Developmental Sequences

Skill theory was designed to predict developmental sequences in any domain. It was used to predict the nice/mean sequence, although the sequence stands as an empirically established finding independent of the theory. To predict and explain developmental sequences, skill theory specifies a number of transformations in the organization of behavior. Thus it is a transformational framework, and it illustrates how transformations can be used to explain changes in behavioral organization. Elsewhere the theory is presented in detail, including an algebraic formulation of the various skill structures and transformations (Fischer, 1980; Fischer & Pipp, 1984b).

However, skill theory is only one model of developmental transformations. Several other theories provide different systems for analyzing transformations (for example, Case, in press; Halford, 1982), although the transformational component is especially salient in skill theory. Consequently, skill theory should be considered only one illustration of a transformational approach.

In addition, the various other theories of cognitive development are designed to explain one limited class of reorganizations—those arising from changes in cognitive capacity. The range of reorganizations discussed in this chapter is much broader than cognitive development. Different approaches may be needed to explain the range of transformations arising from environment and emotion as well as development. Indeed, wherever possible, we have attempted to state our case in terms independent of skill theory. In particular, we have focused on descriptions of transformations that are relatively neutral theoretically, such as empirically supported developmental sequences. Nevertheless, skill theory provides a useful example of how a transformational framework might look.

Developmental Levels.   According to skill theory, children's capacities develop through a series of at least 10 large-scale transformations described in terms of levels. Each level is characterized by a particular structure that defines the general organization of the behaviors that the person can control at that level. Higher level skills represent a differentiation and integration of lower-level skills. Consequently, a child who is functioning at one level within a domain should typically be able to perform the skills characteristic of the preceding levels in the same domain.

The levels develop through a repeating cycle of four levels, which is called a tier. There are at least three tiers: the sensorimotor tier, the representational tier, and the abstract tier. The last level of one tier is also the first level of the next tier. Thus, with three tiers of four levels and two points of overlap, there are a total of ten levels. The structures of the levels are defined in terms of (a) groups of controlled variations in behavior, called sets, and (b) relations between these sets. The transformation for moving from one level to the next involves the combination of at least two skills at the lower level to form a new skill at the higher level. This process is called intercoordination.

The focus of this chapter is the representational tier, and consequently we will use the developmental sequence for representations of nice and mean to illustrate the levels. At the first level within each tier, the structure of a skill is a single set, such as a single representation of an event, an object, or a person. For example, in one single representation of a person, a child makes a doll carry out an action, such as walking or hitting (Step 1). Development occurs within each level as well as between levels. In a more advanced step at the first level, two or more behaviors are grouped together in a behavioral category, as when the child controls the category of mean by combining one doll hitting another with the same doll stealing the other one's ball (Step 2).

The structure of a skill at the second level in the cycle is a mapping, a relation of one set to one or more other sets. With a mapping, a child can relate, for instance, one nice category to another: One doll offers a piece of candy to a second one and says, "Let's play," and the second one reciprocates by taking the candy and saying, "Thank you! You're nice" (Step 3).

A system is the structure of a skill at the third level. The child can relate two aspects of one set to two aspects of one or more other sets. For example, one doll can act both nice and mean to a second doll, who notes the contradiction and in an integrated fashion responds positively to the nice behavior and negatively to the mean behavior (Step 7).

At the fourth level, the structure is a system of systems, involving the relating of two or more systems. This system of systems is identical to the single set of the next higher tier, so that a system of sensorimotor systems is the same as a single representational set, and a system of representational systems is the same as a single abstract set. For instance, in a system of representational systems, the child uses the concept of intention to relate the nice and mean behaviors of two dolls in one interaction with the nice and mean behaviors of two dolls in another interaction (Step 9): "What's important is the reasons why kids do certain things, not what they actually do" (Hand, 1982).

Development through the levels is not the same as development through stages as traditionally construed (Fischer & Bullock, 1981). In traditional conceptions of stage, such as that of Piaget (1957), the entire mind is transformed in a relatively short time to a new stage. In skill theory, what changes in a stage-like fashion is not the entire mind but instead the upper limit on the complexity of skills that the child can construct and control, which is called his or her *optimal level*. That is, children cannot build skills that are at a higher level than their optimal level. To increase the complexity of their existing skills, they must build new skills that remain at their optimal level or below it. Most of the child's behavior does not occur at the optimal level and so does not show stage-like change. It is only the upper limit that shows stage-like discontinuities in the rate of change upon emergence of a new optimal level (Fischer, Pipp, & Bullock, 1984).

Within-Level Transformations.   In addition to the large-scale intercoordination transformations that occur between levels and tiers, there are smaller-scale transformations that occur within a level. It is these microdevelopmental transformations that produce developmental steps within a level, such as those in Table 5.3. Three of these transformations have been used to derive the sequences described in this chapter: compounding, focusing, and differentiation. Each involves a form of combination of two skills at a given level to yield a more complex skill at the same level. The nature of each combination can be expressed as an algebraic rewrite rule (Fischer, 1980).

Compounding refers to the addition of a skill at one level to another skill at the same level to form a more complex skill coordinating all the components of the two initial skills. For example, in the nice/mean sequence in Table 5.3, compounding produces Step 5, one-dimensional social influence with three characters behaving similarly. Two instances of Step 4 are compounded to form Step 5. In one instance of Step 4, for example, a doll named David is mean to a doll named Jason, who responds appropriately with a mean rejoinder. In the second instance, the mean interaction involves Jason and a third doll, named Sean. When these two skills are compounded, the result is a three-way mean interaction, in which, for example, David and Sean are mean to Jason, who responds with appropriate mean actions toward both of them in an integrated story.

In the transformation of focusing, the skills are combined without being integrated. Step 3 in Table 5.3 comes from transforming two Step 2 skills via focusing. One Step 2 skill is a behavioral category for nice, and one is a behavioral category for mean. In Step 3 they are combined by juxtaposition, with the child first acting out the nice category and then shifting focus to act out the mean category.

The third transformation rule is differentiation, the process by which one set (or more) is divided into two separate sets. Differentiation and coordination occur together, so that differentiation typically occurs with one of the other transformations. For example, at Step 5, when Jason responds to the separate mean actions of Sean and David, a differentiation is required between Sean's and David's mean actions. In predicting sequences, however, researchers can use the differentiation rule without having to consider what other transformation may have produced the differentiation. For example, a task that requires the differentiation of two kinds of hitting in a mean category is more advanced than one that merely allows two similar instances of hitting with no clearcut differentiation between them.

Distorting or Simplifying Transformations. When people are faced with a task that they cannot handle, they typically simplify or distort it in some way that allows them to cope with it. The process of simplification seems to involve the application of the developmental transformations in reverse. Fischer, Hand, Watson, Van Parys, and Tucker (1984) describe a number of types of simplifying transformations in preschool children and indicate how these simplifications differ across the three levels of social categories.

In the task with two kinds of hitting, for instance, a child can delete the differentiation, reverting to two similar instances of hitting. In a task that requires compounding, a child can revert to juxtaposing skills via focusing instead of integrating them via compounding. For example, the Step 5 integration of

mean interactions involving three characters can be simplified into two juxtaposed (shift of focus) Step 4 stories, such as one about David and Jason and a
separate one about Sean and Jason. Or it can be simplified even further to form a
Step 3 juxtaposition of a nice behavior and a mean behavior. Of course, a child
also can drop or eliminate some of the sets or subskills, as when the shift between
nice and mean behavior at Step 3 is transformed to a simpler story that is only
about being nice.

One major cause of simplifications and distortions seems to be task complexity. If a task is too complex for children to understand, they must simplify it in
order to deal with it at all, as when Hand (1982) found simplification of a
complex story at Step 6 or 7 into a simpler story at Step 3 (see Table 5.3).
Equally important, simplifications and distortions can arise from emotional factors, as when the content of a task is too frightening for a child. Indeed, the
psychodynamic literature is full of hypotheses about such distorting affective
transformations (Fischer & Pipp, 1984a; Kernberg, 1976; Sullivan, 1953). Yet
researchers have generally neglected this role of emotion, especially in children.
In a later section, we suggest some directions for research on affective transformations in children.

Importance of the Environment.   One of the best documented facts in cognitive research is that environmental factors play havoc with assignments of
developmental stage or step. It is fair to say that unevenness, which Piaget
(1941) called decalage, is the rule in cognitive development (Biggs & Collis,
1982; Fischer & Silvern, 1985; Flavell, 1982). Skill theory builds upon this fact,
and at the same time it builds upon the many data showing that characteristics of
the child are also central in development. It is thus a transactional or collabora-
tional theory, integrating organismic and environmental concepts (Fischer &
Bullock, 1984). Unfortunately, readers sometimes miss this point, making the
mistaken inference that developmental levels occur primarily inside the child.
We wish to review several ways that skill theory mandates inclusion of the
environment in analyses of development. This review will also lay a foundation
for our later discussion of how environmental factors induce transformations in
behavior.

First, skill theory specifies that developmental sequences can be predicted in
detail only for a limited environmental domain, in which all steps involve virtually the same task and procedure (Fischer 1980). That is, the within-level
transformations can be used to predict sequences only within a domain. The
greater the disparity between tasks or procedures, the greater the difficulty in
using the transformations to predict detailed sequences with precision. Although
it is possible to predict across domains when the distance between steps is large
and when environmental influences are similar, such predictions are always a
gamble. With this proviso, skill theory moves the domain-specificity of sequences from an empirical finding to a theoretical postulate.

Second, environmental factors have a fundamental effect on the form of developmental change. For example, it is not meaningful to ask whether developmental change is continuous or discontinuous. Instead, one must ask: What are the environmental conditions under which it is continuous, and what are those under which it is discontinuous? Skill theory predicts that discontinuities will occur upon the emergence of a new optimal level in an individual. That is, under environmental conditions that induce optimal performance, tasks that assess a given level will show spurts in performance when that level emerges. On the other hand, under nonoptimal conditions, performance will typically improve in a gradual, continuous manner (Fischer, Pipp, & Bullock, 1984).

Third, the complexity of the task is a crucial determinant of the level of performance. In a sense, a complex task interferes with high-level performance. Consequently, one task cannot be safely used to assess more than one developmental level. When children encounter a task that is more complex than they can handle, they will simplify it in ways that do not have a one-to-one correspondence with their optimal level (Fischer, Hand, & Russell, 1983; Roberts, 1981; Siegler, 1981). Consequently, a single task is usually a poor tool for assessing a developmental sequence.

Fourth, environmental support routinely facilitates high-level performance. Environmental support includes the provision of materials necessary to carry out a task and the facilitation of recall of essential task components. With such support, children are able to demonstrate capacities that they do not appear to have under other conditions (Hand, 1981; Vygotsky, 1978). This important point will be elaborated in the section on how the environment induces transformations.

Fifth, variations in experience induce important individual differences in developmental sequences. We believe that children routinely develop different specific skills in virtually every domain. Individual differences in developmental sequences are commonplace. Although few studies have used methods that can clearly detect such individual differences, existing evidence supports the hypothesis that such differences do occur (e.g., Knight, 1982). To find universal developmental sequences instead of individual differences, it is necessary to use a highly abstract analysis in terms of general developmental levels instead of a more specific analysis in terms of the actual skills a person uses (Fischer & Silvern, 1985). The developmental sequence for nice and mean interactions in pretend play illustrates a fairly specific analysis, and the description of three levels of social categories illustrates a more abstract analysis.

Development of Attributions about Aggression

One area in which scholars have suggested that there might be individual differences in developmental sequences is aggression, especially attributions about aggression. Aggressive children, it has been hypothesized, tend to distort an ambiguous act by another child in such a way that they assume it is aggressive in intent (Dodge, 1980; Nasby, Hayden, & DePaulo, 1980). For evaluation of any hypothesis about the relation between aggressive behavior and faulty attribution of intention, a detailed portrait is needed of the development of children's understanding of the intentions behind physically harmful acts.

In addition to its relevance to the question of individual differences in sequences, childhood aggression is important in its own right because it constitutes a central social problem. First, conduct disorders, which typically include aggressive behaviors, are one of the most common diagnoses given to children seen in mental health facilities (Rimm & Sommerville, 1977; Stewart, DeBlois, Meardon, & Cummings, 1980). Second, childhood aggression seems to be predictive of problems later in life, unlike many other childhood behavior problems (Kohlberg, LaCrosse, & Ricks, 1972; Lefkowitz, Eron, Walder, & Huesmann, 1977; Robins, 1966). Finally, a fundamental social task for children is learning when it is appropriate to be aggressive and how to modulate the amount of aggression (Feshbach, 1970).

A common hypothesis about aggressive children has been that they suffer from a social-cognitive deficit, such as poor perspective-taking skills (Chandler, 1973; Selman, 1980). That is, they are hypothesized to develop social-cognitive skills more slowly than normal children. However, research suggests a more complex relation between aggression and perspective-taking skills. Aggressive children seem to fall into several types, including some who do lack perspective-taking skills and others who have unusually advanced perspective-taking skills (Selman & Jaquette, 1978; Silvern, 1984; Waterman, Sobesky, Silvern, Aoki, & McCauley, 1981). Those with advanced perspective-taking skills appear to have a general motivation to be aggressive and to use their superior skills to determine effective ways of hurting other people. According to this interpretation, aggressive children do not uniformly develop more slowly than normal children, showing a social-cognitive deficit. Instead, aggressive children fit into several different types, which show different developmental patterns.

A potentially useful approach to studying the social-cognitive correlates of aggression is to analyze children's specific attributions about aggression rather than their general perspective-taking skills. We designed a series of tasks to assess the development of attributions about aggression in the preschool years and to detect individual differences in developmental sequences for these attributions. The study built upon the techniques developed by Hand (1982) for studying the development of nice and mean social interactions. Children were tested with pretend stories about social interactions involving a physically harmful act. In general, physical harm was inflicted on the self doll by another doll, and the self doll made attributions about the reason for the physical harm.

The tasks assessed four different types of intentions behind physically harmful acts: accidental, hostile, prosocial, and instrumental. These four intentions were chosen based on the research literature as well as our experience with preschool children. Besides assessing the development of each of the types of intention, the tasks also could be ordered developmentally in a number of different ways, thus allowing children to demonstrate individual differences in developmental sequences.

A hostile intention was defined as one in which the agent who caused physical harm did so because he or she wanted to hurt the person. In an instrumental intention, the agent of the harm committed the harmful act in order to obtain something from the person harmed. In an accidental intention, the agent who caused physical harm did not intend to do so. In a prosocial intention, the agent of the harm caused it in trying to do something nice to the person harmed, such as trying to prevent some greater harm.

Sequence. For each type of intention, we predicted a developmental sequence of six steps beginning with the level of single representational sets and ending with the level of representational systems, as shown in Table 5.4. Each sequence traced the development of each type of intention from a global undifferentiated aggressive act through more and more differentiated instances of the intention and finally to an integration of positive and negative intentions.

The first step, which was chosen to serve as a floor under the children's performance, required the use of such elementary skills that virtually all children in the study were expected to pass it. Step 6, the last step, was chosen to serve as a ceiling requiring skills that were beyond the capability of virtually all the children in the study. The steps in between these two anchors were expected to be within the capabilities of some but not all the children and thus to form a useful developmental assessment.

One task was used to assess Step 1, and another task was used to assess Step 6. For Steps 2 through 5, four different tasks were included, one for each of the four types of intention. In each of these tasks, the story provided a context constructed to support one of the types of intention. Across the four contexts at each step, the tasks were designed so that amount of physical harm and complexity level were held approximately constant.

The procedures used were the same as those for the nice/mean studies. Children initially chose a self doll, the one that they thought was most similar to themselves, and it was assigned their name. They then chose names for the two other dolls. Children were first assessed in the elicited-imitation condition, in which a separate story was used for each type of context at Steps 2 through 5. Then, children were assessed in the spontaneous condition.

The first two steps involve the level of single social categories (Level 4 single representations). At Step 1, active agent, the child uses a doll to represent a person carrying out a single action, such as hitting. The skill defined in Step 1 becomes more complex at Step 2, behavioral category for physical harm, in that the harm is accompanied by a contextual cue for one of the four types of intention. Through the compounding transformation, the following component is added to the other doll's behavior for each respective context: wanting to hurt the

TABLE 5.4

A Developmental Sequence for Understanding the Intentions Behind Physically Harmful Acts

Level	Step	Skill	Example of Behavior	Mean Age for Each Context (in Years)*			
				Hostile mental	Instru-mental	Pro-social	Acci-dental
I. Single Social Categories	1	Active agent: An agent performs at least one behavior not necessarily fitting the category of nice or mean.	Child pretends that a doll hits self doll.	—	—	—	—
	2	Behavior category for physical harm: An agent performs at least two behaviors that are defined as either nice, mean, or accidental.	Child has a doll do one of the following: (a) act mean to self doll, e.g., hitting self and taking self's candy (instrumental), (b) act mean to self, hitting and saying "I wanna hurt you" (hostile), (c) act nice to self, e.g., pushing self away from a puddle and saying "Watch out" (prosocial), or (d) do something by accident to self, e.g., running backwards and bumping into self (accidental).	3.4	3.4	3.6	3.4
II. Mappings of Social Categories	3	One-dimensional relation between action and reaction: A physically harmful action fitting a behavioral category (nice, mean, or accidental) is responded to with an appropriate reaction.	Child pretends that a doll acts nice, mean, or does something by accident to the self doll, which in turn causes self to either want to play with the other doll (prosocial	4.1	3.8	4.1	4.2

Level	Step	Skill	Example of Behavior	Mean Age for Each Context (in Years)*			
				Hostile	Instrumental	Prosocial	Accidental
	4	One-dimensional relation between intention, action, and reaction: An intention leads to a physically harmful action, which is responded to with an appropriate reaction.	or accidental) or not want to play (hostile or instrumental). Child pretends that a doll hits the self doll because he or she wants to hurt self (hostile), wants to get self's candy (instrumental), wants to stop self from getting hit by a ball (prosocial), or makes a mistake and trips (accidental). Self responds either negatively or possitively depending on the valence of the intention.	4.4	4.0	4.6	4.2
	5	Shifting-one dimensional relations between intention, action, and reaction: I. An intention (hostile or instrumental) leads to a physically harmful action, which is responded to with an appropriate negative reaction. II. Then, ano-	Child pretends that one self doll hits the self doll because he or she wants to get self's candy or to hurt self. Self responds negatively. Then, a third doll pushes self	5.1	5.0	5.0	5.0

ther doll's intention (prosocial or accidental) leads to a physically harmful action, which is responded to with an appropriate positive reaction.

either because he or she wants to stop self from getting hit by a ball or because he or she trips. Self responds either positively or neutrally.

III. Systems of Social Categories

6

Two-dimensional relation between intention, action, and reaction: An intention (prosocial) leads to a physically harmful action, which is misinterpreted and responded to with an inappropriate (negative) reaction. The reaction is then modified as a result of an explanation of the actual intention.

Child pretends that a doll pushes the self doll, who initially responds negatively because self believed the doll intended to do harm. Self changes his or her mind about being mad upon learning that the other doll intended to stop self from getting hit by a ball. There is an indication that the child is simultaneously relating the two intentions of each doll. For example, self doll says, "I shouldn't be mad at you because you weren't trying to hurt me. You just pushed me to do something nice."

*Mean ages are from Elmendorf (1984). There was only one task for steps 1 and 6 instead of the four contexts, and the number of subjects at these two steps was too small to provide an assessment of mean age.

self doll for the hostile context, taking an object from the self for the instrumental context, not seeing the self for the accidental context, and warning the self for the prosocial context.

The next three steps assess development within the level of mappings of social categories (Level 5 representational mappings). At Step 3, one-dimensional relation between action and reaction, the child relates the other doll's physically harmful act to the response of the self doll, who is the one harmed. The physically harmful act is considered negative if the context is hostile or instrumental, positive if the context is prosocial, and either neutral or positive if the context is accidental. The self doll's response to the other doll's harmful act is appropriate to the particular context—negative for hostile or instrumental, and positive for prosocial or accidental.

At Step 4, one-dimensional relation between intention, action, and reaction, the child's social response to physical harm is based on a more refined understanding of the motivation for that harm. The global notion of a hostile, instrumental, accidental, or prosocial act is differentiated to form a more complex skill in which the other doll's specific intention produces an action and the self doll responds appropriately. That is, intention, action, and reaction are differentiated and compounded.

Step 5, shifting one-dimensional relations between intention, action, and reaction, involves a shift of focus from one Step 4 skill to another. Specifically, an intention and action of one other doll is related to a reaction of the self doll, and then separately an intention and action of a second other doll is related to a reaction of the self doll. There are four tasks assessing different contexts at this step, each testing a shift between a positive and a negative intention: from hostile to accidental, hostile to prosocial, instrumental to accidental, or instrumental to prosocial.

Step 6, two-dimensional relation between intention, action, and reaction, marks development of the level of systems of social categories (Level 6 representational systems). The other doll's intentions and actions are related to the self doll's intentions and actions in a way that integrates positive and negative intentions. This task, which is designed to serve as a ceiling on the children's performance, assesses a coordination of the prosocial and hostile contexts. The other doll pushes the self doll to prevent the self from being hit by a baseball, and the self initially mistakes the intention as hostile. Then the self realizes the actual intent and explains his or her mistake.

Results.   Subjects were 48 normal middle-class children ranging in age from exactly 3 years to exactly 6 years; no children were tested younger than 36 months or older than 72 months of age. Four six-step sequences were tested in the study, one for each of the four contexts.

Each of the four sequences fit the predicted developmental pattern: each was highly scalable, and performance moved to higher steps with age. In addition, there was an interaction between context and age. The 3-year-olds showed a higher average step in the instrumental context, and the 4-year-olds showed a higher step in both the instrumental and prosocial contexts. By 5 years of age all differences across contexts disappeared, as virtually all children passed Step 5 for all contexts and failed Step 6. Mean ages for Steps 2 through 5 for each context are shown in Table 5.4; the frequency of children with Step 1 or 6 as their highest step was too small to calculate meaningful mean ages for those steps.

Clearly, the children tested in this study showed different rates of movement through the sequences for the four contexts, with apparent consolidation across the contexts at Step 5. A future study will test for the possibility of differences not only in the speed of development but also in the validity of the specific sequences for specific groups of children. In contrast to the present study, the children in the future study will have been referred for conduct disorders. Highly aggressive children may show different developmental patterns from normal children. For example, certain types of highly aggressive children may naturally develop through only some of the sequences for the four contexts; in others, they may not fit the normal sequence. Also, with a larger sample, we will be able to combine the tasks for all contexts and determine how they order developmentally across contexts. Our expectation is that the developmental orderings across contexts for highly aggressive children will be different from those for normal children. That is, the nature of the developmental transformations these children undergo will differ: they will follow different developmental paths.

Distortions.   In addition to testing developmental sequences, the studies of attributions about aggression and of nice/mean interactions provide data on how children distort tasks that are too complex for them. Data on simplifying distortions are available both from the errors children make on tasks that they fail and from their performance in the spontaneous condition. The nature of these distortions would seem to be especially interesting for the prosocial and accidental contexts, where there is an apparent contradiction between action and intention. Some common types of simplifying distortions for the prosocial context are shown in Table 5.5.

All four of the examples in Table 5.5 seem to involve a reversal of one or more of the transformation rules that produce developmental advance. Correct performance of the task for Step 2 requires combining two actions via the transformation of compounding. In the example of simplifying distortion, one of the two actions is deleted, so that the prosocial part of the behavioral category disappears. The distortion for the Step 3 task involves a different type of reversal of compounding, in which the prosocial action is included but not integrated into the story. The other doll's prosocial action is included in the first part of the story, but the self doll's reaction ignores the prosocial component and is based only on the physically harmful act.

The distortion for the task at Step 4 involves a failure of differentiation, in which a prosocial intention is confused with an accidental one. Such mixing together of two contents that should be differentiated is called condensation or

TABLE 5.5

Types of Simplifying Distortions for the Prosocial Context

Elicited-Imitation Task Administered	Characteristics of Some Types of Simplifying Distortions	Example of Behavior
Step 2 – Behavioral category for prosocial physical harm: One doll pushes the other doll and says "Watch out."	Only one of the two components of the doll's behavior is enacted.	The child omits the statement "Watch out," pretending only that a doll pushes the self doll. The child then categorizes the behavior as mean.
Step 3 – One-dimensional relation between prosocial action and reaction: A doll acts nice to the self doll (as in Step 2), and as a result the self doll wants to play with him or her.	The two components of the nice behavior are not integrated into a behavioral category, so that the self doll's reaction is based on only one aspect of the other doll's behavior.	The child has a doll push the self doll and say "Watch out," but the self doll responds negatively to the push, miscategorizing the behavior as mean despite the statement "Watch out!"
Step 4 – One-dimensional prosocial relation between intention, action, and reaction: A doll pushes the self doll so that self won't get hit by a ball. The self doll acknowledges the attempt to be nice on the part of the other.	Globbing or condensation of prosocial and accidental intentions.	After the child has a doll push the self doll and say "Watch out," the self doll responds to the push as if it were an accident, saying, e.g., "That's O.K., you didn't mean to push me."
Step 6 – Two-dimensional relation between prosocial and hostile intention, action, and reaction: A doll pushes the self doll, who initially responds negatively because of the perceived hostile intent. The self doll changes his or her mind about being mad at the other doll when he or she understands the actual prosocial intent. The self doll simultaneously relates the two possible intentions and reactions; e.g., self doll says, "I shouldn't be mad at you because you weren't trying to hurt me. You pushed me to do something nice."	A shift of focus occurs such that the self doll responds first to the perceived hostile intention and then to the actual prosocial intention without integrating the two.	The child has the self doll respond angrily to the push and the perceived hostile intent. Then, separately, the self doll responds positively to the other doll's prosocial explanation. There is no linking of the two responses; e.g., the child reports that the reason the self doll changed his or her mind about being mad was that the other doll apologized for being mean.

globbing (Fischer, Hand, Watson, Van Parys, & Tucker, 1984). For Step 6 the distortion maintains the primary components of the necessary skill, but their organization is simplified: There is a failure of integration via the intercoordination transformation, and instead the positive and negative components are treated as separate stories juxtaposed via the transformation of focusing.

For all of these types of simplifying distortions, the scalogram method facilitates analysis of how task complexity induces distortion. Other factors that can also lead to distortion include low environmental support and emotional state. These two factors are discussed in later sections.

Development of Social Roles

The domains of social cognition we have studied were chosen in part because they are of interest to children. In their daily play, children spontaneously use social categories like nice, mean, hostile, and accidental. Another area of central interest to children is social roles, the social categories that provide many of the norms that guide everyday behavior. Children seem to be especially motivated to learn about roles of obvious importance, such as girl, boy, woman, man, mother, father, policeman, doctor, and patient. In addition, because many of these roles are so significant to them, children are likely to show major distortions in their understanding and use of the roles. Much of the research in our laboratory has focused on analyzing the developmental transformations and distortions that occur for social roles, and developmental sequences for several roles have been specified in great detail (Fischer, Hand, Watson, Van Parys, & Tucker, 1984; Van Parys, 1983; Watson, 1981). In this chapter, we will not attempt to review all the research but will outline a general sequence for social roles and then describe a type of distortion that seems to arise naturally from children's developing understanding of social roles in the family.

Sequence. The understanding of social roles develops through the three general developmental levels: single social categories, mappings of social categories, and systems of social categories. The first level is behavioral roles, in which children can act out two or more behaviors fitting a role, such as mother or doctor, but cannot relate one role to another. The second level, social roles, brings the understanding of how one concrete role relates to another, such as father to daughter. Children can make a father doll interact appropriately with a daughter doll; both characters participate actively in the interaction in a way that fits the reciprocal roles of father and daughter. The third level, role intersections or combinations, involves the understanding that individual people can simultaneously occupy two roles when they interact. For example, a father can also be a doctor, and his daughter can be his patient. The father can give medical care to his daughter when she is sick, with the interaction simultaneously reflecting father/daughter roles and doctor/patient roles. Table 5.6 depicts a few developmental steps for each of the three role levels.

The results of scalogram analyses strongly supported this sequence across several studies involving different kinds of concrete social roles. Similar sequences were found for the roles of doctor/patient, parent/child, male/female, and adult/child (Van Parys, 1983; Watson, 1981).

TABLE 5.6
A Developmental Sequence of Social Roles

Level	Step	Skill	Example of Behavior
I. Single Social Categories	1	Active Agent: A person performs one or more behaviors, not necessarily fitting a social role.	Child pretends that a doll is walking or eating, as if it were actually carrying out the actions itself.
	2	Active Substitute Agent: An object substituting for a person performs one or more behaviors, not necessarily fitting a social role	Child pretends that a block is walking or eating, as if it were a person or a doll.
	3	Behavioral Role: A person performs several behaviors fitting a social role, such as father.	Child pretends that a father-doll kisses another doll, calls her "daughter," and puts her to bed.
II. Mappings of Social Categories	4	Social Role: A person behaving according to one social role, such as father, relates to a second agent behaving according to a complementary social role, such as daughter.	Child pretends that a father-doll kisses his daughter and builds a tower of blocks with her. The daughter-doll makes appropriate responses.
	5	Social Role with Three Agents: Two complementary roles, such as daughter and wife, are simultaneously related to the first role, father.	Child pretends that a father-doll kisses and plays with a daughter doll and another doll. Both daughter and mother respond appropriately.
III. Systems of Social Categories	6	Intersection of Social Roles for Two Agents: Two separate, agent-complement role relations are coordinated so that one person is in two roles simultaneously and relates to another person in two complementary roles (such as father-doctor with daughter-patient).	Child pretends that a doctor-doll examines a sick patient-doll and also acts as father to the patient, who is his daughter. The patient-doll responds appropriately as both patient and daughter.
	7	Intersection of Social Roles for Three Agents: Three separate agent-complement role relations are coordinated so that one person in two or three roles simultaneously relates to two other people each in the relevant complementary roles (doctor-father-husband with patient-daughter and mother of patient-wife).	Child pretends that one doll is a doctor, father, and husband relating to two other dolls. The second doll is a sick patient and the first doll's daughter. The third doll is the patient's mother and the first doll's wife.

Note: This table is based on Watson (1981).

Family Roles and the Distortions of the Oedipus Conflict. Because family roles are obviously so important to children, the developing understanding of these roles should provide significant insights into the relation between emotional and cognitive development in children. For each of the three levels of family-role development, we have hypothesized a typical type of emotionally relevant distortion of family roles (Fischer, Hand, Watson, Van Parys, & Tucker, 1984).

These distortions are especially clear in the development of the Oedipus conflict. According to Freud (1909/1955), preschool boys develop a desire to take the place of their father in their mother's affections as well as an accompanying set of fears and hostilities toward their father. Eventually, the conflict is resolved at about 6 years of age, when the boy identifies with his father and gives up his desire to take his father's place with his mother. A similar pattern, called the Electra conflict, is hypothesized for girls. Following standard psychoanalytic usage, we will refer to the patterns for both sexes as Oedipal.

Fischer & Watson (1981) have argued that the changing distortions of the preschool period explain the emergence and resolution of the Oedipus conflict in nuclear families. The Oedipal distortions occur in families where the primary emotional bonds are between mother, father, and child and where the parents take primary responsibility for raising the child. In families with a different pattern of social roles, where, for example, another relative plays a major parenting role, the specific role distortions and their emotional concomitants will be different.

At the first level, behavioral roles, children understand each of the family roles separately. Consequently, they do not coordinate the mother role with the father role, and they do not understand the special nature of the relationship between the parents. They understand components of the relationship, such as that Mommy and Daddy sleep in the same bed, but they do not understand the relationship more generally. Crucially, they do not comprehend that men and women can have special love relationships and that because of the children's own gender they will be able to participate in one of the roles in such a relationship. Without this understanding, they cannot experience an Oedipus conflict.

Nevertheless, the limitations of their understandings at this level do produce many cognitive-emotional characteristics that set the stage for the Oedipus conflict. For example, they confuse husband and father roles, and likewise wife and mother roles. They believe that their parents often know what they are thinking. They confuse what they are thinking with what is happening in the real world. And they have poor control of what they are thinking, so that they often frighten themselves with their own thoughts.

With the second level, social roles, the Oedipus conflict blossoms. Children can construct an understanding of the role relationship between their parents: Mommy and Daddy have a special love relationship. But in fact the parents are carrying out two separate roles—parent (mother/father) and spouse (wife/husband). Because children can deal with only one role relationship at a time, they confuse the intersecting parent and spouse roles. That is, they fail to separate mother from wife and father from husband. In addition, children know their own sex, and so they know which role they belong to (Mommy or Daddy). As a result, they believe that they can substitute for the parent of the same sex in the love relationship. That is, the boy can take over the role of the father, or the girl can take over the role of the mother. Because of the children's social-cognitive limitations, they do not consider the larger picture of role relationships: that the parent-child relationship is distinct from the husband-wife relationship, that children do not marry their parents, that the parent will always be much older than the child, and so forth.

The social-cognitive limitations also lead to a number of negative emotional consequences. Children feel hostility toward the parent they wish to replace, and they fantasize about getting rid of that parent somehow. They tend to believe, however, that their parents know what they are thinking, and so they fear that their parents may retaliate for their hostility. Also, because of their difficulty in understanding complex role relationships, they often attempt to monopolize their parents' attention, resenting and interfering with interactions between the parents that do not immediately involve the child.

Resolution of the Oedipus conflict becomes possible with the emergence of the third level, role intersections or combinations. Children come to understand how the categories of parent, spouse, child, male, and female combine to produce the roles in the family. Then they stop confusing the mother/father relationship with the wife/husband one, and they realize that it is not appropriate for a child to take over the spouse role. They also can eliminate most of the confusions from the earlier levels: Children grow older as their parents grow older, children are not supposed to marry their own parents, and so forth.

The development of this level, Level 6 representational systems, also explains other parts of the resolution of the Oedipus conflict. For example, Freud suggested that resolution of the Oedipus conflict leads to both identification with the same-sex parent and formation of a conscience. According to Fischer and Watson (1981), both of these processes are made possible by the capacity for representational systems. The ability to build a system relating representations greatly facilitates the formation of skills for social comparison (Ruble, 1983). Identification requires that the child compare several characteristics in parent and child: This is what my parent is like, and I want to be like this. Similarly, a conscience requires the comparison of one's own behavior to a general social rule or standard.

Of course, environmental influences also affect the course of the Oedipus conflict. Just as the conflict will not arise in families that do not have the appropriate role relationships, it will not be easily resolved in families where the parents relate to the child in an Oedipal fashion, acting as if the child can indeed be a lover of the opposite-sex parent. Also, the degree to which the parents provide support for the child's understanding of family role relationships will affect the speed of emergence and resolution of the Oedipus conflict.

TRANSFORMATIONS FROM ENVIRONMENTAL SUPPORT: FUNCTIONAL AND OPTIMAL LEVELS

Changes in the organization of personality and social behavior occur routinely as a result of variations in environmental support. Behavior becomes more or less complex as the degree of support increases or decreases. These reorganizations have not yet been thoroughly investigated, but existing data are consistent with the position that they can be analyzed in terms of transformations.

As with the analysis of developmental transformations, one useful way of studying these environmental transformations is to carefully analyze variations within a narrow task domain, where orderings can be tested precisely. Indeed, based on the few existing data, we would suggest that environmental transformations within a domain are similar to developmental transformations within a domain. Both types of transformations can be characterized in terms of a developmental scale, even though the environmental transformations do not literally involve development.

In research using the sequences within the three domains discussed earlier— nice/mean interactions, attributions about aggression, and social roles—we and our colleagues have systematically assessed the effects of environmental support. In every study where degree of support has been varied, the developmental level demonstrated by individual children has varied dramatically as a function of support, and likewise the types of errors and distortions have varied. That is, environmental support has produced changes in organization that appear to be generally equivalent to the transformations arising from the development of new capacities. We would like to propose that this apparent equivalence is real: The same types of transformation rules account for both variations arising from development within a domain and those arising from environmental support within the same domain (Fischer, 1979; Fischer & Pipp, 1984a).

Everyday Variations in Level

It is an easy matter to use environmental factors to change the developmental step and level that a child demonstrates (Biggs & Collis, 1982; Bullock, 1983; Feldman, 1980; Flavell, 1982). These effects are often taken as evidence against the existence of developmental stages or levels. However, for an approach that emphasizes how child and environment collaborate to produce behavior, they are consistent with developmental levels: A child's performance on a developmental scale is always affected by both the child's characteristics and those of the environment. A step or level is really a characteristic of a *child-in-a-context*.

Consequently, changes in the environment must affect the child's developmental step, just as changes in the child's abilities must do so.

For a developmental analysis, what is crucial is that in the face of environmentally induced variations, the child's behavior should still be ordered along a developmental scale. Specifically, the child's behavior should show a specific highest step in a given context, with variation in behavior occurring below that step. In a different context, the highest step may vary, but the variations will still show a characteristic upper limit. With this pattern of data, the child demonstrates what Fischer and Pipp (1984a) call a *functional level,* an upper limit on performance within the given context. Of course, changes in context, degree of environmental support, practice, and so forth can change the functional level. So long as these factors do not change, however, the functional level remains consistent. In other words, the child demonstrates what appears to be a competence, but it is specific to the given context.

There may also be order in the variations in functional level. Based on an extension of skill theory, we have hypothesized that the child's functional levels have a limit on them, which is his or her optimal level (Fischer & Pipp, 1984b). Functional levels can vary up to the optimal level but not beyond it. Each child therefore has one optimal level, the upper limit on complexity beyond which he or she cannot construct a skill; but the child has a wide range of functional levels.

Research in our laboratory has tested several predictions based on the functional-level hypothesis. One prediction was that functional level will vary with the degree of environmental support. The research included two different types of conditions for assessing developmental level, as described earlier. The elicited-imitation condition provided strong environmental support for high-level performance, in that children saw a specific story for each developmental step and were immediately asked to give back a similar story. That is, they were shown an appropriate response and were asked to remember the components of the story for no more than a few minutes. The procedure of administering a separate story for each step also guaranteed that children would be exposed to a story at or near their highest step.

The spontaneous conditions, on the other hand, provided weak environmental support for high-level performance. Most of our studies have used at least two different spontaneous conditions, both administered after all the elicited-imitation stories have been given. First, in the free-play condition, each child was asked to make up some stories of his or her own using the props from the elicited-imitation condition. The experimenter left the room, and the stories were recorded on videotape. Second, in the best-story condition, the experimenter returned and asked the child to demonstrate the best story he or she could.

If environmental support affects functional level, then the highest step in the elicited-imitation condition will be consistently higher than that in the spontaneous conditions. This prediction of a gap between high- and low-support conditions has been supported repeatedly in our research (Fischer, Hand, Watson, Van Parys, & Tucker, 1984). The large majority of children have shown a higher step with environmental support than without it. In a study of the nice/mean sequence in Table 5.3, for example, 9-year-olds generally attained Step 7 (Level 6 systems of social categories) in the elicited-imitation condition but only Step 4 (Level 5 mappings of social categories) in the spontaneous conditions (Hand 1982).

Another prediction from the functional-level hypothesis is that the steps shown in the two spontaneous conditions will both demonstrate the same functional upper limit, because they do not seem to differ in degree of support. For the free-play condition, children produced a number of stories that typically represent several different steps in the developmental sequence, while for the best-story condition they produced only one story. If they followed the instructions to give the best story they could in the best-story condition, then according to the functional-level hypothesis, that story should represent the highest step from the stories for the free-play condition.

In every study that has included the two spontaneous conditions, including studies of all three sequences described earlier, this prediction has been strongly supported (Elmendorf, 1984; Hand, 1982; Jackowitz, 1983; Purcell, 1983; Van Parys, 1983; Watson & Fischer,1980). Most children showed the same highest step in the two spontaneous conditions, even though they produced a number of stories in the free-play condition and only one in the best-story condition.

The results appear to demonstrate that differences in environmental support cause variation along a complexity scale that is similar to a developmental sequence. That is, the transformations arising from environmental support seem to be similar to those arising from development. We feel, however, that at least one other test of the construct of environmental support is needed. In addition to high- and low-support conditions, an in-between condition is needed, providing intermediate support. If degree of support causes transformations along a developmental scale, then the functional level for an intermediate-support condition should fall between the levels for the high- and low-support conditions.

Two tests of this third hypothesis are in progress. The intermediate-support condition employs what are called story stems, brief statements about stories that provide some of the essential elements for a given developmental step. For example, a stem for a story involving a hostile intention (Level 5 mapping) could be, "Show me a story about a boy pushing somebody because he wants to hurt him." Preliminary analyses of the data indicate that this condition will indeed produce a functional level intermediate between the low- and high-support conditions (Elmendorf, 1984; Purcell, 1983).

Distortions from Low-Level Functioning

If environmental support has a pervasive effect on developmental level, then one important implication is that degree of support will determine whether a child distorts a given task. That is, when children face the same task under different degrees of support, they will perform differently. If low support moves their functional level below that necessary for the task, they will evidence simplifying distortion in the task even though they show no such distortion with high support. Many of these distortions will have important implications not only for children's understanding but also for their emotional life.

For example, the types of distortion involving attributions about aggression (see Table 5.5) will come and go in children's behavior as a function of degree of support. With high support, a given 5-year-old child will clearly understand the prosocial intention behind the physically harmful act in Step 3, a prosocial mapping between action and reaction. But with low support, the same child will miscategorize the prosocial behavior as mean.

Similarly, for the Oedipus conflict a given child will move in and out of Oedipal distortions as a result of variations in environmental support for high-level understanding of family roles. With high support, a boy will understand that he cannot take his father's place in a love relationship with his mother. But with low support, he will revert to the belief that he can take over his father's role. In this same way, many emotion-laden social-cognitive processes will vary with degree of environmental support (Fischer & Pipp, 1984a).

TRANSFORMATIONS FROM EMOTIONS: VARIATIONS IN LEVEL AND PATH

Not only do emotions follow from specific understandings, as in the Oedipus-conflict example, but they also affect those understandings. That is, emotions are a third factor that leads to changes in the organization of behavior. Researchers have extensively investigated changes arising from the first two factors—cognitive-developmental transformations and environmental ones. But there has been little research on how emotions lead to transformations during the childhood years (Fischer & Bullock, 1984; Sroufe, 1979). Consequently, we will attempt to provide a framework to guide research on emotional transformations.

Emotional transformations seem to take at least two distinctly different forms. In one form they involve variations along a developmental scale of a type similar to the transformations from environmental support. In the other form they involve more massive transformations based on the organizing function of emotions.

Variations in Level Arising from Emotional State

One of the most general phenomena in research on learning and performance is what is often called the Yerkes-Dodson law (Yerkes & Dodson, 1908). The emotional state or level of emotional arousal has a direct effect on the quality of performance. On a given task, performance improves as arousal increases until arousal passes a certain point, and after that point, performance grows worse with greater arousal. Across tasks, the point at which arousal begins to interfere with performance is lower for more complex tasks, higher for simpler tasks.

When applied to development, this law takes a straightforward form: Variations in emotional arousal transform performance along a developmental scale for a given domain. Developmental step moves higher as arousal increases until arousal passes a certain point, and then the step moves lower with further increases in arousal. When children are sluggish, sleepy, or at low arousal for whatever reason, they will show a lower functional level than when they are awake and alert. Likewise, when they are overaroused because of anxiety, excitement, or some other factor, they will show a lower functional level.

Oddly, there has been virtually no research directly testing this hypothesis with children. With newborn infants, on the other hand, a number of investigators have tested it, and the data clearly support the hypothesis (Prechtl & O'Brien, 1982; Wolff, 1966). Newborn behavior seems to regress to lower developmental steps with both low and high arousal states; developmentally advanced behavior occurs only with intermediate arousal.

Informal observations suggest that the same phenomenon occurs with children. A child who is upset, anxious, excited, tired, or sluggish will show a less advanced developmental step in a given domain than one who is at an intermediate level of arousal. One corollary of this hypothesis is that children who are at low or high arousal will demonstrate simplifying distortions more often than those at intermediate arousal. Because the former children are functioning at a lower developmental level, they will not be able to understand social-cognitive tasks that they could handle at intermediate arousal, and the result will be distortions. On the playground, for example, a child who is over- or underaroused will be more likely to distort an incident in which another child accidentally bumps him. The result will be a faulty attribution.

Just as with environmental support, then, variations in emotional state seem to produce movement up or down a developmental scale for a given domain. The scale serves as a useful characterization not only of development within that domain but also of transformations arising from both environmental support and emotional state.

The Organizing Function of Emotions

Besides this effect of arousal within a domain, emotions also have another effect. They transform the general type of organization evident in behavior, with different emotions producing drastically different organizations. Seth Fischer, the $3\frac{1}{2}$-year-old son of one of the authors, showed a reaction that illustrates how a strong emotion can organize behavior. He and I were visiting the Will Rogers Museum in Colorado Springs, which includes a stone tower on top of Cheyenne Mountain. In the tower, tape recordings of talks by Will Rogers were being played continuously. As we approached the tower, which was narrow and a bit eerie, Seth immediately asked if there were any monsters in the tower. Apparently, the eeriness of the tower made him afraid, and like most preschool children, his fear was immediately expressed as a concern about monsters. We began to walk up the stone stairs, with Seth looking generally cautious. After a few steps, he wanted to be carried. When we came to a door in the side of the tower next to the steps, he asked if there were any monsters in there. At several other points, he inquired further about monsters. Apparently, fear was organizing his behavior and leading him to show a concern about monsters. The organizing effect of fear was also evident in several distortions he demonstrated. On the tape recording at one point, Will Rogers used the word "try," and Seth immediately asked, "Who's dying?" A short time later, Rogers used the word "got," and Seth asked, "Who's getting shot?" When we finally left the tower and went back outside on the mountain, Seth's fear quickly subsided, and all the signs of caution and concern about harm disappeared. His fear of the tower transformed the organization of his behavior, and when that fear dissipated, his behavior was transformed back to a nonfearful form.

For a long time, psychodynamic theorists and practitioners have focused on this organizing function of emotion, especially the split between good and bad feelings (Kernberg, 1976; Spitz, 1965; Sullivan, 1953). However, despite this theoretical and clinical work, there is little empirical research on the topic. Recently, some research has begun to appear, especially with infants. A number of developmentalists have investigated how the organizing function of emotion affects specific aspects of early social development, especially with regard to the baby's attachment to the mother (Ainsworth, Blehar, Waters, & Wall, 1978; Mahler, Pine, & Bergman, 1975; Sroufe, 1979). Also, a few experimental psychologists have begun to study how emotions organize memory in adults (Bower, 1981): mood or emotional state has been shown to have a potent effect on the kinds of content people can remember.

Research on children's understanding of opposite emotions is relevant too. The developmental sequence for nice and mean social interactions and Harter's (1982) related work on the development of opposite emotions deal with the organizing effect of emotions—how children initially separate positive and negative emotions and are able to integrate them gradually as they advance cognitively.

As important as this work is, it provides only the bare bones of a beginning for explaining how emotions transform the organization of behavior. Much theoretical and empirical work needs to be done before behavioral scientists will be able to integrate emotions into their theories of behavioral organization (Fischer & Bullock, 1984). One of the central questions about how emotions transform behavior is how they affect developmental paths.

Multiple Developmental Paths

If emotions indeed have a potent effect on the organization of behavior, then one sensible hypothesis is that emotions affect the developmental paths through which people progress. That is, variations in emotional experiences will produce variations in developmental sequences. These variations can take several different forms. First, emotions can produce important individual differences in developmental sequences by transforming a person's basic approach to important issues or contexts. When people have widely divergent emotional experiences, they are likely to develop along substantially different paths. Strong emotional experiences, such as severe child abuse, may be especially likely to induce paths that differ from the modal pattern. Second, within the same person as well, different emotions will lead to different developmental paths. That is, an individual may demonstrate paths specific to emotional states, such as one path (or set of paths) for anger and a different path (or set of paths) for happiness. The person's emotional state transforms his or her behavior from one organization to another. In this case, emotions function somewhat like environmental contexts. Skills tend to be organized in terms of specific contexts or domains—and also in terms of specific emotions (Bower, 1981). Consequently, distinct emotions will lead to separate developmental sequences. Three different phenomena that illustrate the effects of emotions on developmental sequences are multiple personality, the defense mechanism of splitting, and aggression.

Multiple Personality and Child Abuse.   One of the most extreme instances of strongly divergent emotional experiences in childhood arises from severe child abuse. A parent who is sometimes loving and supportive will at another time inflict severe physical harm or sexual abuse on a child. Because of the organizing effect of emotions, a reasonable hypothesis is that child abuse will lead to dissociation or splitting of the child's understandings in terms of the positive and negative experiences with the parent.

Multiple personality is one of the most striking types of dissociation in the clinical literature, and Bower (1981) has pointed out that the separate personalities tend to be organized around highly distinct emotional states. In fact, emotions may produce the momentary transformations from one personality to another.

Using the orientation outlined in this chapter, Fischer and Pipp (1984a) predicted that child abuse would induce multiple personality, and they later came upon a study that provides striking support for it. In a compilation of 100 cases of multiple personality reported in detail by therapists, 97 of the adult patients had experienced severe child abuse (Putnam, Post, Guroff, & Silverman, 1983). In addition, there was a positive correlation between the number of types of abuse (for example, physical and sexual) and the number of personalities in the adult.

This separation of the self into distinct personalities is apparently induced in part by the severe emotional trauma of child abuse. The child seems to construct one personality for dealing with the parent who is loving and another for dealing with the same parent who is abusive. With more types of abuse, the child builds more personalities for dealing with the different emotional situations. Eventually, it seems that constructing different personalities becomes a general strategy for dealing with life's stresses. Throughout his or her life, the person with multiple personality periodically constructs new personalities to deal with new needs that arise. This strategy produces a developmental path that is fundamentally different from those taken by normal people, who have relatively integrated personalities.

Fischer and Pipp (1984a) used skill theory to predict the developmental course of multiple personality. Although there are few developmental data on the disorder, one study does support an important prediction. The ability to construct multiple personalities, they argued, will first emerge with the development of Level 5 representational mappings at about 4 years of age. The construction of multiple personalities requires not only the ability to construct an agency or personality but also the ability to relate two such agencies, because one of the hallmarks of multiple personality is that each personality has a specific relationship with each other one. For example, one personality may repress another, causing it to become unconscious. Or one personality may have full access to the memory of another personality. These relationships seem to require representational mappings, at a minimum. In a recent study of 14 cases of multiple personality, Bliss (1980) found that all 14 patients reported that their multiple personalities first developed between 4 and 6 years of age.

Splitting.   In multiple personality, emotions seem to transform the individual's state from one personality to another. Other types of dissociation and splitting in the clinical literature seem to involve similar transformations, but the organizations involved in the transformations are not completely distinct personalities within the self (Fischer & Pipp, 1984a).

In the defense mechanism of affective splitting, positive and negative emotional experiences become the overriding organizer of the person's world. The shift in organization occurs not only in the self but also in the person's construal of other people with whom he or she is interacting, as illustrated by a common symptom of the psychopathologies of borderline personality or severe narcissistic disorder. Affective splitting is typically a prominent feature of borderline personality or severe narcissistic disorder (Kernberg, 1976; Masterson, 1981). When the patient's mood is different, he or she experiences the therapist literally as a different person. A patient who becomes angry or suspicious, for example, will commonly insist that the therapist is not the same person who was there previously, even though the patient recognizes the obvious physical similarities between the "two" therapists. The change in emotional state leads to a transformation in the patient's perception of the therapist's identity, as if a good therapist has changed into a bad therapist. Presumably, this type of disorder has roots in the patient's emotional experiences in childhood. Abuse by the parent would seem to be a prime candidate, as with multiple personality, although we have not uncovered any solid data bearing upon this hypothesis.

In normal people, less dramatic transformations of a similar type can occur as well. A change in emotional state can lead an individual to react differently to another person or situation, as when Seth's fear led him to react with suspicion to the events in the tower. The difference seems to be that for normal people, the identity of the person or situation typically takes precedence over the emotional change, whereas for borderline or narcissistic patients, the emotional change takes precedence. Also, of course, the patients do not always show affective splitting, just as people with other forms of dissociation and splitting, such as schizophrenia, do not show them all the time. At times, they perceive other people normally.

Aggression.   Another domain in which emotions would seem to lead to different developmental paths is aggression. If hyperaggressive children have a bias to attribute hostile intent to other children, for example, they may be developing along a different path from normal children (Dodge, 1980; Nasby et al., 1980). In the normal path, children may be likely on most occasions to assume that a bump or hit is an accident or at least to gather further information to determine the intent.

Other developmental paths may also lead to problems with aggression. For example, for some families hitting is common, and in some cases it is not viewed as aggressive. It may be a way of getting attention or even of expressing affection. A child who grows up in a family where hitting is normal will of course develop different understandings of the role of hitting in social relations from the child who learns that hitting is an undesirable expression of hostile intent. The measures we have devised for studying the development of attributions about aggression will allow us to begin to test these kinds of hypotheses about developmental paths to hyperaggressiveness.

CONCLUSION: HOW TO BECOME A DIFFERENT PERSON

At different times, individuals act like different persons. That is, their behavior does not exhibit a single organization but shows frequent changes in organization. These changes occur as a result of at least three factors: new abilities, variations in the environment, and variations in emotional state. All such changes can be fruitfully analyzed in terms of the types of transformation rules that are necessary to explain movement from one organization to another—how the organization of one skill can be rewritten to produce the organization of the other. An important goal for psychology is the construction of a general framework for analyzing these various types of transformations.

To outline what such a framework might look like, we have used skill theory to illustrate a transformational analysis of cognitive development. The same limited set of transformation rules are hypothesized to explain both the new skills that children develop and the errors and distortions they show in tasks that are too complex for them. One of the central tools for research within such a framework is the finely graded developmental sequence, which allows analysis of a graded series of transformations within a specific task domain. This sort of sequence provides a powerful method of representing the transformations that occur as children develop new skills in a domain and may also represent their errors and distortions for complex tasks in that domain.

These developmental sequences and the transformations that explain them seem to apply not only to developmental changes but also to changes arising from variations in environmental support and variations in state of emotional arousal. For all three factors (development, environmental support, arousal), when behavior remains within a given environmental domain, the changes can apparently be represented with Guttman-type scales such as those we have described for nice/mean interactions, attributions about aggression, and social roles.

Of course, when the organization of a person's behavior is transformed by any of these factors, it does not change totally. Some aspects of the organization are transformed, while many others remain the same. Examination of the developmental sequences we have described makes this fact especially clear, because later steps always include many of the components from earlier steps.

There is an important limitation to the types of transformations fitting these detailed Guttman sequences: They all occur within a highly restricted environmental context, what we have called a domain. In our research and theorizing, we have expressly excluded the broad classes of transformations that arise from changes in context. This exclusion has been useful, because it has limited the transformations in such a way that it became possible to construct a set of rewrite rules to explain them. Nevertheless, the nature of transformations induced by contextual changes is also of major importance.

When the environmental context changes, it typically induces a substantial transformation in the organization of a person's behavior. The scope of this transformation is often much greater than that of transformations in which the context does not change. In addition, alterations in emotional state can seemingly also induce substantial transformations. The scope of these emotional transformations appears generally comparable to that of environmentally induced transformations, and the two share many similar characteristics. We propose that the processes are similar enough that they can both be called context-induced. That is, there are effectively two types of contexts: environmental ones and emotional ones. In both cases, too, there are components of the behavioral organization that remain stable, even though the transformations in organization are so substantial.

Substantial progress has been made, we believe, in explaining developmental transformations within a context, and it is a straightforward (if time-consuming) task to extend the developmental framework to include within-context transformations arising from environmental support and state of arousal. But the explanation of context-induced transformations is another matter. One of the challenging tasks for those of us who wish to explain the order behind variations in behavioral organization is to build a framework for explaining context-induced transformations.

ACKNOWLEDGMENTS

Preparation of this chapter was supported by grants from the Carnegie Corporation of New York and the Spencer Foundation. The statements made and views expressed are solely the responsibility of the authors. We would like to thank the following individuals for their contributions to the chapter: Daniel Bullock, Helen Hand, Anne Hogan, Elaine Jackowitz, Philip Robbins, Phillip Shaver, Martha Van Parys, and Malcolm Watson.

REFERENCES

Ainsworth, M. D., Blehar, M. C., Waters, E., & Wall, S. (1978). *Patterns of attachment.* Hillsdale, NJ: Lawrence Erlbaum Associates.

Biggs, J., & Collis, K. (1982). *A system for evaluating learning outcomes: The SOLO taxonomy.* New York: Academic Press.

Bliss, E. L. (1980). Multiple personalities. *Archives of General Psychiatry, 37,* 1388–1397.

Bower, G. H. (1981). Mood and memory. *American Psychologist, 36,* 129–148.

Broughton, J. M. (1981). Piaget's structural developmental psychology V. Ideology-critique and the possibility of a critical developmental theory. *Human Development, 24,* 382–411.

Bullock, D. (1983). Seeking relations between cognitive and social-interactive transitions. In K. W. Fischer (Ed.), *Levels and transitions in children's development.* New Directions for Child Development, No. 21. San Francisco: Jossey-Bass.

Case, R. (in press). *Intellectual development: A systematic reinterpretation.* New York: Academic.

Chandler, M. J. (1973). Egocentrism and antisocial behavior: The assessment and training of social perspective-taking skills. *Developmental Psychology, 9,* 326–337.

Dodge, K. A. (1980). Social cognition and children's aggressive behavior. *Child Development, 51,* 162–170.

Elmendorf, D. M. (1984). *The development of preschool children's understanding of the intentions behind physically harmful acts.* Unpublished master's thesis, University of Denver.

Feldman, D. H. (1980). *Beyond universals in cognitive development.* Norwood, NJ: Ablex.

Feshbach, S. (1970). Aggression. In P. H. Mussen (Ed.), *Carmichael's manual of child psychology* (Vol. 2). New York: Wiley.

Fischer, K. W. (1979, June). *Towards a method for assessing continuities and discontinuities in development.* Paper presented at the Fifth Biennial Conference of the International Society for the Study of Behavioral Development, Lund, Sweden.

Fischer, K. W. (1980). A theory of cognitive development: The control and construction of hierarchies of skills. *Psychological Review, 87,* 477–531.

Fischer, K. W., & Bullock, D. (1981). Patterns of data: Sequence, synchrony, and constraint in cognitive development. In K. W. Fischer (Ed.), *Cognitive development.* New Directions for Child Development No. 12. San Francisco: Jossey-Bass.

Fischer, K. W., & Bullock, D. (1984). Cognitive development in middle childhood: Conclusions and new directions. In W. A. Collins (Ed.), *The elementary school years: Understanding development during middle childhood.* Washington, DC: National Academy Press.

Fischer, K. W., Hand, H. H., & Russell, S. L. (1983). The development of abstractions in adolescence and adulthood. In M. Commons, F. A. Richards, & C. Armon (Eds.), *Beyond formal operations.* New York: Praeger.

Fischer, K. W., Hand, H. H., Watson, M. W., Van Parys, M., & Tucker, J. (1984). Putting the child into socialization: The development of social categories in the preschool years. In L. Katz (Ed.), *Current topics in early childhood education* (Vol. 6). Norwood, NJ: Ablex.

Fischer, K. W., & Pipp, S. L. (1984a). Development of the structures of unconscious thought. In K. Bowers & D. Meichenbaum (Eds.), *The unconscious reconsidered.* New York: Wiley.

Fischer, K. W., & Pipp, S. L. (1984b). Processes of cognitive development: Optimal level and skill acquisition. In R. J. Sternberg (Ed.), *Mechanisms of cognitive development.* San Francisco: Freeman.

Fischer, K. W., Pipp, S. L., & Bullock, D. (1984). Detecting discontinuities in development: Method and measurement. In R. N. Emde & R. Harmon (Eds.), *Continuities and discontinuities in development.* New York: Plenum.

Fischer, K. W., & Silvern, L. (1985). Stages and individual differences in cognitive development. *Annual Review of Psychology, 35,* 613–648.

Fischer, K. W., & Watson, M. W. (1981). Explaining the Oedipus conflict. In K. W. Fischer (Ed.), *Cognitive development.* New Directions for Child Development, No. 12. San Francisco: Jossey-Bass.

Flavell, J. H. (1972). An analysis of cognitive-developmental sequences. *Genetic Psychology Monographs, 86,* 279–350.

Flavell, J. H. (1982). On cognitive development. *Child Development, 53,* 1–10.

Freud, S. (1955). Analysis of a phobia in a five-year-old boy. *S.E.* (Vol. 10). London: Hogarth Press. (Originally published in 1909.)

Halford, G. S. (1982). *The development of thought.* Hillsdale, NJ: Lawrence Erlbaum Associates.

Hand, H. H. (1981). The relation between developmental level and spontaneous behavior: The importance of sampling contexts. In K. W. Fischer (Ed.), *Cognitive development.* New Directions for Child Development, No. 12. San Francisco: Jossey-Bass.

Hand, H. H. (1982). *The development of concepts of social interaction: Children's understanding of nice and mean.* (Unpublished doctoral dissertation, University of Denver, 1981.) *Dissertation Abstracts International, 42*(11), 4578B (University Microfilms No. DA8209747).

Harter, S. H. (1982). A cognitive-developmental approach to children's understanding of affect and trait labels. In F. C. Serafica (Ed.), *Social-cognitive development in context.* New York: Guilford.

Jackowitz, E. R. (1983). *A systematic analysis of a particular self-instruction technique for children: An integration of developmental thought and clinical intervention.* Unpublished master's thesis, University of Denver.

Kernberg, O. (1976). *Object relations theory and clinical psychoanalysis.* New York: Jason Aronson.

Knight, C. C. (1982). *Hierarchical relationships among components of reading abilities of beginning readers.* (Unpublished doctoral dissertation, Arizona State University.) *Dissertation Abstracts International,* 1982, *43*(2), 403A (University Microfilms No. DA8216442).

Kohlberg, L., LaCrosse, J., & Ricks, D. (1972). The predictability of adult mental health from childhood behavior. In B. Wolman (Ed.), *Manual of child psychopathology*. New York: McGraw-Hill.

Lefkowitz, M. M., Eron, L. D., Walder, L. O., & Huesmann, L. R. (1977). *Growing up to be violent: A longitudinal study of the development of aggression*. New York: Pergamon.

Mahler, M. S., Pine, F., & Bergman, A. (1975). *The psychological birth of the human infant: Symbiosis and individuation*. New York: Basic Books.

Masterson, J. F. (1981). *The narcissistic and borderline disorders*. New York: Brunner/Mazel.

Mueller, E. C., & Lucas, T. (1975). A developmental analysis of peer interaction among toddlers. In M. Lewis & L. A. Rosenblum (Eds.), *Frendship and peer relations*. New York: Wiley.

Nasby, W., Hayden, B., & DePaulo, B. (1980). Attributional bias among aggressive boys to interpret unambiguous social stimuli as displays of hostility. *Journal of Abnormal Psychology, 89,* 459–468.

Piaget, J. (1941). Le mécanisme du développement mental et les lois du groupement des opérations. *Archives de Psychologie, Genève, 28,* 215–285.

Piaget, J. (1957). Logique et équilibre dans les comportements du sujet. *Études d'Épistémologie Génétique, 2,* 27–118.

Piaget, J., & Inhelder, B. (1969). *The psychology of the child* (H. Weaver, trans.). New York: Basic Books. (Originally published, 1966.)

Prechtl, H. F. R., & O'Brien, M. J. (1982). Behavioral states of the full-term newborn: The emergence of a concept. In P. Stratton (Ed.), *Psychobiology of the human newborn*. New York: Wiley.

Purcell, K. (1983). *Children of divorce: The relationship between cognitive level and children's socio-emotional reactions to divorce*. Unpublished master's thesis, University of Denver.

Putnam, F. W., Jr., Post, R., Guroff, J., & Silverman, E. (1983, April). *One hundred cases of multiple personality disorder*. Paper presented at the American Psychiatric Association Convention, New York City.

Rimm, D. C., & Somerville, J. W. (1977). *Abnormal psychology*. New York: Academic Press.

Roberts, R. J., Jr. (1981). Errors and the assessment of cognitive development. In K. W. Fischer (Ed.), *Cognitive development*. New Directions for Child Development, No. 12. San Francisco: Jossey-Bass.

Robins, L. N. (1966). *Deviant children grow up: A sociological and psychiatric study of sociopathic personality*. Baltimore: Williams & Wilkins.

Ruble, D. N. (1983). The development of social comparison processes and their role in achievement-related self-socialization. In E. T. Higgins, D. N. Ruble, & W. W. Hartup (Eds.), *Social cognition and social development: A socio-cultural perspective*. New York: Cambridge University Press.

Selman, R. L. (1980). *The growth of interpersonal understanding*. New York: Academic Press.

Selman, R. L., & Jaquette, D. (1978). Stability and oscillation in interpersonal awareness: A clinical-developmental approach. In C. B. Keasey (Ed.), *Nebraska symposium on motivation* (Vol. 25). Lincoln: University of Nebraska Press.

Siegler, R. S. (1981). Developmental sequences within and between concepts. *Monographs of the Society for Research in Child Development, 46* (2, Serial No. 189).

Silvern, L. (1984). Emotional-behavioral disorders: A failure of system functions. In E. Gollin (Ed.), *Malformations of development*. New York: Academic Press.

Spitz, R. A. (1965). *The first year of life*. New York: International Universities Press.

Sroufe, L. A. (1979). Socioemotional development. In J. D. Osofsky (Ed.), *Handbook of infant development*. New York: Wiley.

Stewart, M. A., DeBlois, C. S., Meardon, J., & Cummings, C. (1980). Aggressive conduct disorders of children: The clinical picture. *Journal of Nervous and Mental Disease, 168,* 605–610.

Sullivan, H. S. (1953). *The interpersonal theory of psychiatry*. New York: Norton.

Van Parys, M. M. (1983). *The relation of use and understanding of sex and age categories in preschool children*. (Unpublished doctoral dissertation, University of Denver.) *Dissertation Abstracts International*.

Vygotsky, L. (1978). *Mind in society* (M. Cole, V. John-Steiner, S. Scribner, & E. Souberman, Eds.). Cambridge, MA: Harvard University Press.

Waterman, J. M., Sobesky, W. E., Silvern, L., Aoki, B., & McCauley, M. (1981). Social perspective-taking and adjustment in emotionally disturbed, learning-disabled, and normal children. *Journal of Abnormal Child Psychology, 9*, 133–148.

Watson, M. W. (1981). The development of social roles: A sequence of social-cognitive development. In K. W. Fischer (Ed.), *Cognitive development*. New Directions for Child Development, No. 12. San Francisco: Jossey-Bass.

Watson, M. W., & Fischer, K. W. (1980). Development of social roles in elicited and spontaneous behavior during the preschool years. *Developmental Psychology, 16*, 483–494.

Wohlwill, J. F. (1973). *The study of behavioral development*. New York: Academic Press.

Wolff, P. H. (1966). The causes, controls, and organization of behavior in the neonate. *Psychological Issues, 5* (1, Serial No. 17). New York: International Universities Press.

Yerkes, R. M., & Dodson, J. D. (1908). The relation of strength of stimulus to rapidity of habit formation. *Journal of Comparative Neurology and Psychology, 18*, 459–482.

6 Lumping and Splitting in Developmental Theory: Comments on Fischer and Elmendorf

Leonard Breslow
University of Minnesota

Fischer has undertaken the ambitious task of providing a unified account of both cognitive and social development. Somewhat paradoxically, perhaps, this encompassing theory proceeds from the premise that the mind is basically fragmented in nature. Cognition is conceived in terms of context-specific behavior complexes, or skills, and development as the progressive coordination of previously dissociated skills (Fischer, 1980). Starting with situation-specific sensorimotor actions, one behavior comes to be coordinated with another behavior of the same level of complexity; the resultant complex behavior, then, is coordinated with another behavior of the same level; and so on. At a certain point in development, the behaviors are dubbed representations; at a still further point, abstractions. But, within this frankly neobehaviorist framework (Fischer, 1980, pp. 481–483), cognition can never be anything more than increasingly complex situation-specific actions. The primary mechanism for the integration of behaviors in this theory is the developmental process itself in which skills become coordinated with one another to produce skills of a more advanced structural level. Mechanisms for within-level integration are relatively weak, since skills remain essentially domain—if not task—specific throughout development. Certainly, there can be no place in this account for the form of behavior to become abstracted and separated from the content, providing the basis for within-level generalization. But given the disillusionment that has recently surrounded theories that attempt to characterize cognitive development in terms of pervasive abstract structures—in particular, that of Piaget—Fischer might appear to be on safe ground in this regard. The finding of asynchronies across tasks that purportedly measure the same structure (Fischer, 1980; Flavell, 1977) has recently cast doubt on the existence of global structures.

179

However, it is not clear that Fischer's theory is immune to some of the challenges that confront the unity-oriented accounts. First, I question whether the positing of a relation between two behaviors is a sufficiently differentiated characterization of a cognitive structure. The nature of the particular relation coordinating two skills of the same level of complexity may play a differential role with regard to the nature and complexity of the new skill produced. At the very least, the differential effect of the coordinating relation may result in asynchronies, not only in functional level (see below) on different tasks—where asynchrony is sanctioned by the theory—but also with regard to optimal level, where it is not. Worse, one relation may be so much more complex than another that the coordination of two skills of a given level of complexity by means of the more complex relation may produce a skill that is structurally more advanced than the coordination of the same skills by means of the less complex relation.

Second, the mechanism by which skills come to be coordinated remains to be explicitly outlined. Fischer attributes a more central role to the environment in the process of developmental change than does Piaget (Fischer, 1980, p. 484, footnote 3). Further, he indicates that the process by which the environment influences the development of new skills is largely equivalent to the role of the environment in producing within-level fluctuations in performance relative to the child's maximal competence, or optimal level (p.*163*, this volume). However, it is not clear how either of these processes operate. In places, Fischer appears to indicate that new skills are induced or learned directly from environmental stimuli. For instance, he says of a child learning the conservation of the length of a string in a pulley apparatus:

> As she applies the two skills repeatedly to the gadget, the task itself induces the child to notice a connection between them, because the properties of the task make the two skills closely related. Then the child explores the connection and gradually constructs a new, higher-level skill for the conservation of the total length of the cord. (Fischer, 1980, p. 484)

In a second example, he says the child is "induced" by the object to coordinate two previously unrelated skills. If this means that the new skill is acquired by induction, a serious problem arises. Namely, it is not clear how a subject can induce a new concept from the environment either on the basis of its intension or extension, since instantiating or individuating the concept in the environment presupposes that one already knows the concept (cf. Fodor, 1975, pp. 87–97). Based on such arguments, Fodor concludes that "there is a sense in which there can be no such thing as learning a new concept" (*op. cit.*, p. 95).[1] It remains to

---

[1]Contrary to Fodor's contentions, Piaget's theory is not subject to these objections since it is not a learning theory. According to Piaget (1975), the development of a new concept is a largely internal, probablistic process. The environment provides both positive and negative feedback on the results of this process and can provide conditions that maximize the chances that the process will be successful. But there is no sense in which the new concept can be said to be first acquired by induction or observation.

be seen if Fischer can clarify the role of the environment in both interlevel transitions in competence and intralevel fluctuations in performance in an explicit manner that is not open to such objections.

Third, in the notion of optimal level, Fischer (1980; Fischer & Pipp, 1984b; Fischer, Pipp, & Bullock, in press) posits a uniform, task-independent competence characterizing the subject at a given point in development. Optimal level is taken to be related to a central processing capacity limitation. Other theories that have characterized cognitive development in terms of the development of a uniform processing capacity (Case, 1980; Halford & Wilson, 1980; Pascual-Leone, 1970, 1978, 1980) have had to confront problems of task-specificity and individual differences similar to those that have plagued global structuralist theories. Proponents of these theories have provided measures of processing capacity separate from the measures of the structural capacity to be explained by means of the processing capacity construct. These theories have not gone unchallenged (Flavell, 1978; Trabasso, 1978; Trabasso & Foellinger, 1978). It will be necessary for Fischer to operationalize the construct of processing capacity in his theory, to demonstrate the existence of a global, task-independent optimal level, and to demonstrate the dependence of the latter on the former.

Fischer has provided some support for the existence of optimal levels in the form of evidence that, under certain conditions providing subjects with maximal support, high correlations may be obtained in performance on tasks of the same structural level. But in the absence of direct evidence for the existence of corresponding developments of the purported central processing capacity, and for the dependence of changes in optimal level on changes in that capacity, evidence of global levels of optimal capacity could equally support a Piagetian-type global structural model as a separate-structure model, such as advocated by Fischer. Indeed, there is some evidence suggesting that abstract structures may play a role in integrating skills. Children's overgeneralization of transitivity to nontransitive relations suggests that the logical scheme is encoded in an abstract form (Kuczaj & Donaldson, 1982). Also, training research is beginning to demonstrate that the effects of training on one task may generalize to tasks that are phenotypically quite dissimilar in terms of procedures and stimuli, such as from conservation to class inclusion or from conservation to horizontality of water level tasks (Bideaud, 1981; May & Norton, 1981). What is more, these transfer effects may be reversible: that is, training on conservation may transfer to class inclusion, and conversely, training on class inclusion may transfer to conservation (Inhelder, Sinclair, & Bovet, 1974). The reversibility of these nonspecific transfer effects between empirically dissimilar tasks suggests that the effects are mediated by abstract cognitive categories characterizing the similarity between the concepts relevant to the two tasks. The existence of abstract-level categories of this sort, relating disparate contents and skills, is inconsistent with the assumptions of a neobehaviorist model of structural development such as Fischer's. The only generalization operation provided in his theory, the substitution transformation rule (Fischer, 1980, p. 501), can account for only very concrete generalizations between skills that are empirically quite similar. Indeed, in one other neo-behaviorist account of structural development, the possibility of nonspecific transfer effects of training is ruled out in principle (Brainerd, 1979). Thus, in the absence of direct evidence concerning the nature and role of central processing capacity in structural development, Fischer's evidence for the existence of optimal levels may serve to support a model of structural development very different from his own.

In the domain of social development, Fischer has undertaken to grapple with notions that few research psychologists have dared to approach for quite some time—notions such as the unconscious, multiple personalities, and the Oedipal conflict (Fischer, 1980; Fischer, Hand, Watson, Van Parys, & Tucker, 1983; Fischer, & Pipp, 1984a). Social development is encompassed within the same skill theory framework characterizing the development of "cold" cognition. Social behaviors develop in a similar fashion to cognitive behaviors through the coordination of previously dissociated skills. The development of individual differences in social behavior is readily understandable within this framework. According to Fischer, we do not coordinate every skill with every other skill of similar complexity at a given optimal level. Indeed, many skills will remain uncoordinated with one another due to environmental and affective factors, even after we have progressed beyond the requisite optimal level for coordinating them. Thus, two subjects at the same developmental level will show different *profiles* of skills that have been coordinated and that remain dissociated. Personality differences may be conceived in terms of such skill profiles.

Pathological behavior is understood in terms of dissociations of certain sorts. Since dissociation is common to all people to varying degrees, abnormality and normality are taken to be continuous with one another. Further, given that the dissociation of skills is relatively more characteristic of younger than of older persons, one may expect to find cognitive-affective distortions particularly among children. Fischer's account of the Oedipal conflict in terms of the dissociations common among preschool children may be taken as an example of the "psychopathology of normal development."

The extent to which a dissociation constitutes a severe abnormality would appear to depend on both the demands of the environment and the subject's developmental level. Not all dissociations constitute maladaptive behaviors. For example, to fail to integrate certain social skills with certain physical knowledge skills may bring on no negative consequences for many people. However, the failure to integrate the nice and mean behaviors of the same significant individual would be highly maladaptive for virtually all people, given the demands of the social environment in which we live. Such a dissociation would likely result in behaviors that are typically labeled "bizarre" when found in an individual who has already passed the stage at which he could and did integrate skills of comparable complexity to those that remained dissociated. Maladaptive dissociations result from affective and environmental causes according to this model.

From the perspective of the dissociation model, then, symptomatic behavior is an undeveloped competence, an unmotivated failure in adaptation. This view contrasts sharply with the psychoanalytic perspective, according to which the symptom is overdetermined; that is, it is a multiply motivated, multimeaningful, synthetic adaptation (Freud, 1936). The dissociation model may well provide a useful counterweight to some of the interpretive excesses of the psychoanalytic approach. For instance, recent investigations of certain pathological syndromes, such as infantile autism, have placed greater emphasis on the role of cognitive incapacities to explain symptomatic behavior than did previous accounts. The reversal of the pronouns ''I'' and ''you'' by the autistic child, for example, may reflect certain limitations in cognitive processing ability rather than weak ego boundaries (Bartak & Rutter, 1974).

However, while some symptomatic behaviors may best be viewed as dissociations, others are probably more appropriately interpreted as adaptive integrations. Thus, according to one view (Hutt & Ounsted, 1966; Main, 1977), the avoidant behavior of certain infants towards their mothers does not represent a lack of attachment. Rather, it may represent a particular means of maintaining attachment under adverse circumstances. In avoiding looking at the mother, the infant ''cuts off'' (in an ethological sense) expressions of anger towards the mother in order to maintain some proximity to the mother without inciting conflict. Certainly, the proximity that is established involves a very low level of engagement, but it may nonetheless provide the infant with some measure of comfort. Similarly, aggressive behaviors on the part of both infants and older children are often interpreted by clinicians as representing attempts by the child to maintain the only relationship possible with a rejecting parent, an agonistic relationship being more desirable than no relationship at all. Again, contemporary family systems theorists view the family as an adaptive interactive system that actively but unconsciously maintains the symptoms of the ''identified patient''—the family member cast in the role of the symptom-bearer within the system (Bateson, Jackson, Haley, & Weakland, 1968; Haley, 1968). In all of these cases, the symptom is a less-than-ideal solution to the problems confronting the individual (or family) and has many undesirable consequences for that person. Nonetheless, the symptom does serve an adaptive function in all of these cases by integrating diverse opposing forces. For Freud, the symptom was a compromise between the demands of the repressed unconscious and the ego, the ego in turn negotiating the demands of the superego and the environment, as well as needs peculiar to itself (Freud, 1936, 1959, 1968). Later theorists have placed greater emphasis on the ego's own motivations and the role of the environment (Breger, 1974; Hartmann, Kris, & Loewenstein, 1964; Loevinger, 1976; Sullivan, 1953). Certainly Fischer does emphasize the role of the environment as supporting or failing to support optimal level functioning. An unsupportive environment may fail to promote integration of social skills or may even impede integration. However, it is not clear how a model which views pathology as an incompetence and a dissociation can explain how an aversive environment encourages specific forms of integrative, adaptive but pathological responses on the part of the subject.

Fischer's notion of active dissociation (Fischer & Pipp, 1984a) shows potential for explaining the adaptive nature of some symptoms. In active dissociation, two skills are coordinated, but in a peculiar way that keeps them in some sense dissociated even as they are associated. Thus far, Fischer has applied the concept of active dissociation only to the defense mechanism of repression. Again, the primary emphasis is on the dissociative aspects of the symptom. Hopefully, Fischer will extend the notion of active dissociation in the future to account for more elaborate defense mechanisms responsible for adaptive integrations of conflicting tendencies.

Fischer views the concept of active dissociation as relatively similar to the Freudian concept of unconsciousness (Fischer & Pipp, 1984a). In one form of active dissociation, called co-conscious repression, one skill, consciousness A, influences a second skill, consciousness B, with the effect of making B unconscious of A. Historically the notion of unconscious repression has been associated with some thorny theoretical problems (cf., e.g., Sartre, 1965). For example, if one posits a single unitary psyche, then the notion of unconscious repression would appear to lead to a paradox: namely, the paradox that in order to repress an idea from consciousness one has to be aware of it. One alternative to the unitary consciousness model and the paradox of repression is to posit two separate agencies in the mind: Consciousness and unconsciousness become similar to two separate people with motives of their own. If these two people have nothing to do with one another, as in passive dissociation, then there is no reason why they cannot remain unaware of one another. But if the unconscious person wants to make his presence known to the conscious person, and further, to influence the actions of that person, as in unconscious repression and other defense mechanisms, then the conscious person can only resist the unconscious person by recognizing him and his influence. But then we are back to the paradox of repression and have made matters worse by dividing the mind into separate agencies. In order to make the two-person account of repression work, then, one has to introduce a third person in some form. In some places in Freud's writing, this third person was the repressed ego, an agency distinct from the preconscious-conscious ego and the id (Freud, 1952). The third person keeps the unconscious person from influencing the conscious person directly. He allows the needs of the unconscious person to be met through the conscious person, but in such devious ways that the conscious person remains unaware of those needs. Clearly, then, the third person must be aware of the needs and ideas of both the conscious and unconscious persons. This model may clutter the mind, but it does at least preclude the paradox of repression.

Fischer's model would at first appear to resemble the Freudian approach in positing multiple agencies in the mind. One skill, consciousness A, influences a second skill, consciousness B, so as to make B unaware of A. Two emendations of this model would appear to be warranted. First as discussed above, it is difficult to maintain a coherent account of repression in terms of two agencies without admitting a third agency. For what reason would consciousness A want to keep consciousness B unconscious of certain ideas? If the ideas are those of A, these ideas would only pose a threat to B if A were motivated to make B conscious of those ideas. This would result in the contradiction that A would be motivated both to make B conscious and unconscious of his/her ideas. To provide a coherent account of repression, it would be necessary to posit a third agent C, who desires to make his ideas conscious to B, and assign to A the role of mediating between the demands of C and the needs of B.

Second, it is not strictly correct to say that a skill, no matter how elaborate it may be, *is* a consciousness. Skills, at the developmental levels with which we are concerned, are representations or abstractions. But a representation of an emotion is not itself an emotion. Further, since skills are nothing more than complex sensorimotor actions, they must be thought of as behavioral potentialities for the person who performs the actions. Thus, one and the same agent performs all of a subject's social skills, whether those skills are dissociated or coordinated. The "conscious person" and the "unconscious person" represent behavioral capacities of the same person, rather than constituting two separate agents. Finally, who is the third person who coordinates these two skills and allows us to escape the paradox of repression? While it is not altogether clear what the process is by which skills come to be coordinated in Fischer's model, it would appear that the third person is the first person—*singular*. That is, the same individual who plays the role of the conscious "person" and plays the role of the unconscious "person" coordinates those two skills in such a way that when he is playing the conscious person he allows some of the needs of the unconscious person to be met through the conscious person while at the same time keeping the latter unaware of all this. All three "persons" really represent the activity of one and the same person. Thus, while Fischer appears to propose a multiple-agent model of repression, his model must be conceived as a single-agent model if it is to be coherent and consistent with the neobehaviorist premises of the larger theory within which it was conceived. With a unitary-psyche model of repression, however, comes the problem of the paradox of repression: How can one repress an emotion or idea without being aware of it? Indeed, it may ultimately prove to be possible to characterize the process of repression in the context of a unitary psyche without falling into this paradox; and if it is possible, the resultant model would certainly be preferable to the unparsimonious and intuitively unsatisfying model that populates the mind with independent agents.

In conclusion, Fischer has offered us an ambitious theory of cognitive and social development that shows great potential to explain many diverse phenomena in both areas. Fischer's theory already accounts most readily for the dissociated, fragmented aspects of psychological functioning. The problems that remain to be adequately addressed by the theory are some of the same problems that have confronted organismic, unity-oriented theories of cognition and social-emotional functioning. In particular, problems concerned with pervasive cognitive factors, such as optimal level; the mechanism of cognitive structural change; the explanation of the role of adaptive integration in the formation of symptoms; and the theoretical problems adhering to the conception of unconscious repression in the context of a unitary mind still require attention.

REFERENCES

Bartak, L., & Rutter, M. (1974). The use of personal pronouns by autistic children. *Journal of Autism and Childhood Schizophrenia, 4*(3), 217–222.

Bateson, G., Jackson, D. D., Haley, J., & Weakland, J. H. (1968). Towards a theory of schizophrenia. In D. D. Jackson (Ed.), *Communication, family, and marriage: Human communication* (Vol. 1). Palo Alto, CA: Science and Behavior Books, Inc.

Bideaud, J. (1981). Les experiences d'apprentissage de l'inclusion et la theorie operatoire. *Psychologie Francaise, 26*(3–4), 238–258.

Brainerd, C. J. (1979). Markovian interpretations of conservation learning. *Psychological Review, 86,* 181–213.

Breger, L. (1974). *From instinct to identity.* Englewood Cliffs, NJ: Prentice-Hall.

Case, R. (1980). The underlying mechanisms of intellectual development. In J. R. Kirby & J. B. Biggs (Eds.), *Cognition, development and instruction.* New York: Academic Press.

Fischer, K. W. (1980). A theory of cognitive development: The control and construction of hierarchies of skills. *Psychological Review, 87,* 477–531.

Fischer, K. W., Hand, H. H., Watson, M. W., Van Parys, M. M., Tucker, J. L. (1983). Putting the child into socialization: The development of social categories in preschool children. In L. G. Katz (Ed.), *Current topics in early childhood education* (Vol. 5). Norwood, NJ: Ablex.

Fischer, K. W., & Pipp, S. L. (1984a). Development of the structures of unconscious thought. In K. Bowers & D. Meichenbaum (Eds.), *The unconscious reconsidered.* New York: Wiley.

Fischer, K. W., & Pipp, S. L. (1984b). Processes of cognitive development: Optimal level and skill acquisition. In R. J. Sternberg (Ed.), *Mechanisms of cognitive development.* San Francisco: Freeman.

Fischer, K. W., Pipp, S. L., & Bullock, D. (in press). Detecting developmental discontinuities: Method and measurement. In R. Harmon & R. N. Emde (Eds.), *Continuities and discontinuities in development. Topics in developmental psychobiology.* New York: Plenum.

Flavell, J. H. (1977). *Cognitive development.* Englewood Cliffs, NJ: Prentice-Hall.

Flavell, J. H. (1978). Comments, Chapter 4 in Siegler, R. S. (Ed.), *Children's thinking: What develops?* (pp. 97–105). Hillsdale, NJ: Lawrence Erlbaum Associates.

Fodor, J. A. (1975). *The language of thought.* New York: Thomas Y. Crowell.

Freud, S. (1936). *The problem of anxiety.* New York: W. W. Norton. (Originally published 1926)

Freud, S. (1952). *The ego and the id.* New York: W. W. Norton. (Originally published 1923)

Freud, S. (1959). *Beyond the pleasure principle.* New York: W. W. Norton. (Originally published 1920)

Freud, S. (1968). *An outline of psychoanalysis.* New York: W. W. Norton. (Originally published 1940)

Haley, J. (1968). The family of the schizophrenic: A model system. In D. D. Jackson (Ed.), *Communication, family, and marriage: Human communication* (Vol. 1). Palo Alto, CA: Science and Behavior Books, Inc.

Halford, G. S., & Wilson, W. H. (1980). A category theory approach to cognitive development. *Cognitive Psychology, 12,* 356–411.

Hartmann, H., Kris, E., & Loewenstein, R. M. (1964). Papers on psychoanalytic psychology. *Psychological Issues, 4* (2, Whole no. 14).

Hutt, C., & Ounsted, C. (1966). The biological significant of gaze aversion with particular reference to the syndrome of infantile autism. *Behavioral science, 11,* 346–356.

Inhelder, B., Sinclair, H., & Bovet, M. (1974). *Learning and the development of cognition.* (S. Wedgwood, trans.). Cambridge, MA: Harvard University Press (Originally published, 1974).

Kuczaj, S. A., II, & Donaldson, S. A., III. (1982). If the boy loves the girl and the girl loves the dog, does the boy love the dog?: The overgeneralization of verbal transitive inference skills. *Journal of Psycholinguistic Research, 11*(3), 197–206.

Loevinger, J. (1976). *Ego development.* San Francisco: Jossey-Bass.

Main, M. (1977). Analysis of a peculiar form of reunion behavior seen in some daycare children: Its history and sequelae in children who are home-reared. In R. Webb (Ed.), *Social development in daycare.* Baltimore: Johns Hopkins University Press.

May, R. B., & Norton, J. M. (1981). Training-task orders and transfer in conservation. *Child Development, 52*(3), 904–913.

Pascual-Leone, J. (1970). A mathematical model for the transition rule in Piaget's developmental stages. *Acta Psychologica, 32,* 301–345.

Pascual-Leone, J. (1978). Compounds, confounds, and models in developmental information processing: A reply to Trabasso and Foellinger. *Journal of Experimental Child Psychology, 26,* 18–40.

Pascual-Leone, J. (1980). Constructive problems for constructive theories: The current relevance of Piaget's work and a critique of information-processing simulation psychology. In R. H. Kluwe & H. Spada (Eds.), *Developmental models of thinking.* New York: Academic Press.

Piaget, J. (1975). *L'Equilibration des structures cognitives.* Paris: Presses Universitairies de France.

Sartre, J-P. (1965). *The Philosophy of Jean-Paul Sartre.* R. D. Cumming (Ed.). New York: Random House.

Sullivan, H. S. (1953). *Interpersonal theory of psychiatry.* New York: Norton.

Trabasso, T. (1978). On the estimation of parameters and the evaluation of a mathematical model: A reply to Pascual-Leone. *Journal of Experimental Child Psychology, 26,* 41–45.

Trabasso, T., & Foellinger, D. B. (1978). Information processing capacity in children: A test of Pascual-Leone's model. *Journal of Experimental Child Psychology, 26,* 1–17.

7 Children's Comments about their Friendships

Thomas J. Berndt
University of Oklahoma

In many different ways, children demonstrate that their friendships are extremely important to them. They spend a great deal of time with friends (e.g., Ellis, Rogoff, & Cromer, 1981), and report that they are especially happy when they do (Csikszentmihalyi, Larson, & Prescott, 1977). The importance of close friendships is also demonstrated by children's comments about these relationships. Recently, many researchers have interviewed children and asked them a variety of questions about their friendships. The children's answers have provided rich and detailed information about the development of friendships between the preschool period and late adolescence (see Bigelow & La Gaipa, 1980; Damon, 1977; Furman & Bierman, 1984; Hartup, 1975, 1978; Hayes, 1978; Hayes, Gershman, & Bolin, 1980; Selman, 1981; Youniss, 1980). To a large degree, our current understanding of the development of friendships is based on children's statements during interviews of this type.

This paper is primarily a review of several studies in which I investigated children's comments about their friendships. One major theme in the paper reflects the progression in previous research toward the formulation of standardized measures for the assessment of individual children's friendships. After illustrating this progression, I consider the limitations of relying on a single method for examining the development of friendship. By contrast, I also consider the potential value of measures derived from individual interviews for gaining an understanding of the role of friendships in children's development.

AN EXAMPLE OF CHILDREN'S REPORTS ON THEIR FRIENDSHIPS

To provide a context for the presentation of research findings, a concrete example of one child's comments about a particular friendship may be useful. In a
recent study (Berndt, Hawkins, & Hoyle, in preparation), fourth- and eighth-
grade children were individually interviewed. Each child was asked a standard
series of questions about another child who was a close friend. A partial list of
the questions and the answers given by a fourth-grade girl follows:

> Q. How can you tell that Debbie [the name of her friend] is your friend?
> If some kids start picking on me, Debbie always gets in the middle of it and
> yells at the kids and says, "Don't pick on her; she's my friend and you shouldn't do
> that because she didn't do anything wrong."
> Q. What other things show that you are friends?
> She likes almost everything I do, and sometimes she sticks up for me so much
> that I don't know what to do for *her* anymore. I say, "No, Debbie, you don't have
> to do that. I can do it myself," and she says, "I *have* to do it."
> Q. What else?
> We talk to each other and we say, "Mary's jokes weren't that funny," but we
> both had to laugh because we didn't want to hurt her feelings; and if one of us
> makes a joke that isn't funny, we both laugh 'cause we don't want to hurt each
> other's feelings.
> Q. What else?
> Sometimes we play dominoes. If Mary walks in and tries to get into what we're
> doing, and she wrecks it, Debbie will yell and say, "You wrecked it and it took a
> long time to make." I say, "You shouldn't have yelled, Debbie." She says, "I'm
> sorry." She says "I'm sorry" to everything I say.
> Q. What else?
> If I did something wrong to some person and they go around and tell it like a
> rumor—[saying that I did] more than I did—no one would play with me. One day
> that happened, and the rumor got to Debbie and she said, "Tracy [name of child
> being interviewed] didn't do that." Nobody would play with me but Debbie came
> up to me to make me feel better.
> Q. What else?
> She's just nice and makes sure somebody's all right. If someone had the flu and
> the kid looked bad she'd say, "You shouldn't have come to school; you look bad."
> She tells the truth; she doesn't lie.

This friendship was not perfect, however. The girl that I've called Tracy also
had several answers to a question about problems in the relationship:

> Q. "When is it hard to be friends with Debbie?"
> At the beginning, when I first knew her it was hard because she knew this other
> girl and really liked her a lot. I'd say, "Hi, Debbie, can you come over?" and
> sometimes she ignored me.

Being ignored is apparently still a problem occasionally, because the child gave the following response when asked about another time it was hard to be friends with Debbie:

> When she's off with another girl. Like if I wanted to say, "Can you come over?" she'd ignore me and she wouldn't like anyone else but the girl she's with. It happens mostly if I'm out of school and I come back and see there's a new girl she likes more than me. It's hard to go back to her and say, "Hi, Debbie, who's that new girl?"

The responses illustrate, not surprisingly, that there are positive and negative features of even close friendships. The responses also illustrate the amount of detail and the specificity of children's reports about their friendships. I should say explicitly, however, that researchers have not often interviewed children about their actual friendships. More commonly, researchers have examined children's ideas about friendship in general, that is, their conceptions of friendship.

STUDY 1: CONCEPTIONS OF IDEAL FRIENDSHIPS

My first study on this topic was an investigation of children's conceptions of friendship (Berndt, 1978; see also Berndt, 1981c). The study included 96 children from kindergarten, third grade, and sixth grade. There were equal numbers of boys and girls at each grade. Each child was individually interviewed and asked a series of questions about friendship. Two types of questions are most relevant for this paper. First, children were asked about the features of friendship. The specific question was, "How do you know that someone is your best friend?" After the child gave an answer, standard probe questions were used to elicit additional answers (e.g., "How else do you know?"). Second, children were asked about nonfriendship and reasons for the termination of friendship. These questions were "How do you know that someone is not your friend?" and "What would make you decide not to be someone's friend anymore?"

After all the data were collected and the children's answers were examined, a formal coding system was devised. In the research on friendship conceptions, coding systems have varied greatly across studies (see Berndt, 1983; Selman, 1981). Our primary goal when preparing the coding system was to include categories that were as close to the content of children's answers as possible. We ultimately defined eight categories that were mutually exclusive and exhaustive. The categories can be described best by providing both a definition and one or two examples of responses that fit each category:

1. *Play or association*—playing together or spending time together (e.g., "we play dominoes together," and "he always calls me up").

2. *Prosocial behavior*—the friends' generosity and helpfulness toward each other (e.g., ''she lets me use her stuff,'' and ''we help each other with our homework'').

3. *Aggressive behavior*—fighting or teasing (e.g., ''he always bothers me,'' and ''she calls me names'').

4. *Intimacy and trust*—the friends' willingness to disclose personal information to each other and their confidence that the information will be kept confidential (e.g., ''I can talk to her about my problems,'' and ''he'll keep a secret if you tell him'').

5. *Loyalty*—a friend's support for you when you are around other children or adults (e.g., ''if other kids were picking on me, he'd tell them to stop it,'' and ''she won't spread rumors about me''). Many of the statements in the interview quoted earlier referred to loyalty.

6. *Faithfulness*—the friend's dependability: the friend won't leave you for someone else (e.g., ''he wouldn't have a party and leave me out,'' and ''she wouldn't ignore me when she's around her other friends'').

7. *Definitional*—comments about aspects of a relationship that are basic to the definition of a friendship: the friend knows you well, likes you, and says that he or she is your friend (e.g., ''he says I'm his best buddy,'' and ''we like each other a lot'').

8. *Personal attributes*—aspects of the friend's personality that affect the friendship (e.g., ''she has a good personality,'' and, from the earlier interview, ''she's honest'').

The same categories were used for the questions about the features of friendship and about the termination of friendships. For the questions about friendship termination, the answers in each category referred to the absence or the violation of the positive features of friendship. For example, children said a friendship would end if a child did not play with them, always teased them, or was unfaithful to them. Present-absent scoring was used for each category. That is, children received scores of 1 or 0 for each category, based on whether or not they used the category when answering the questions. Children received one set of scores for the questions on friendship features and a second set for the questions on friendship termination. The coding was done with 87% agreement between two coders.

Previous research suggested that children's conceptions of friendship change with age (e.g., Bigelow, 1977). The proportion of children in our study who gave answers in each category for each type of question is shown in Table 7.1. Across all grades and both questions, the category used most frequently was play or association. Friends were expected to play together or spend lots of time with each other. If they stopped spending time together, their friendship was expected to end. This category was used equally at all ages and by both sexes.

TABLE 7.1
Proportion of Children at Each Grade Using Each Category for the
Questions on Friendship Features and Friendship Termination (Study 1)

Category	Friendship Features (Termination)		
	Kindergarten	3rd	6th
Play or association	.69 (.62)	.69 (.69)	.59 (.59)
Prosocial behavior[a]	.28 (.15)	.56 (.31)	.68 (.22)
Aggressive behavior[b]	.03 (.53)	.12 (.88)	.12 (.88)
Intimacy and trust[a,b]	.00 (.03)	.03 (.03)	.41 (.28)
Loyalty[a,b]	.00 (.00)	.06 (.15)	.31 (.65)
Faithfulness	.00 (.34)	.00 (.22)	.03 (.41)
Definitional[a]	.50 (.47)	.62 (.34)	.28 (.28)
Personal Attributes	.03 (.12)	.03 (.09)	.12 (.25)

[a]significant at .05 for friendship features.

[b]significant at .05 for friendship termination.

By contrast, four other categories were used more often by older than younger children when answering one or both questions. Sixth graders were more likely than third graders or kindergartners to mention intimacy and trust as a feature of friendship; they also were more likely to mention the lack of intimacy and trust as a reason for the termination of friendships. These results illustrate a growing recognition that motives, thoughts, and feelings can and should be shared with close friends (cf. Selman, 1981). The results also support previous hypotheses that intimacy becomes an important feature of friendship during adolescence (see Berndt, 1982; Sullivan, 1953).

Sixth graders mentioned loyalty as a feature of friendship and disloyalty as a reason for the termination of friendships more often than younger children. These findings are also consistent with previous research (e.g., Bigelow, 1977). The other categories that increased with age were references to prosocial behavior as a feature of friendship and references to aggressive behavior as a reason for the termination of friendships. These findings are more difficult to interpret, because previous data on age changes in concerns with a friend's prosocial and aggressive behavior are mixed (see Berndt, 1982).

Finally, answers referring to the basic definition of friendship—you know someone, you like them, and they say they are your friend—decreased with age. One plausible explanation for the decrease is that older children took the definition of friendship for granted and so emphasized other features that they viewed as more crucial for a close or satisfying friendship.

Only one category varied significantly with sex. Roughly half the girls (46%) mentioned a friend's unfaithfulness as a reason for the termination of friendship, but only about a fifth (19%) of the boys did so. Comparable sex differences were reported by Bigelow and La Gaipa (1980) and by Coleman (1980). Many writers have suggested that girls have more intimate friendships than boys (e.g., Douvan & Adelson, 1966). More girls (17%) than boys (6%) mentioned intimacy and trust, but this difference was only marginally significant.

Taken together, the results of the study suggest that the most important developmental change in friendships is the emergence of concerns with intimacy and loyalty during adolescence. Nevertheless, this study and the previous research established only that intimacy and loyalty are important in adolescents' conceptions of friendship. No direct evidence was obtained on the features of actual friendships in childhood and adolescence. In addition, a potential methodological problem was the use of a coding system devised after examination of the children's responses. Conclusions could be drawn more confidently if the coding system was applied to the responses given by a new sample of children.

STUDY 2: FEATURES OF ACTUAL FRIENDSHIPS

The next study also included 96 children from the kindergarten, third, and sixth grades, divided evenly between boys and girls. The children again were individually interviewed and asked a series of questions about friendship. In contrast to the children in Study 1, these children first were asked to name a best friend. Then they were asked questions about the features of that friendship: "Why do you say that he is your best friend?" and "How else do you know that he is your best friend?" Children were also asked questions about the termination of an actual friendship: "Has anything ever happened that made you break up with a best friend? What was that?" About a third of the children (39%) said they had never broken up with a best friend, so they were asked a hypothetical version of the same question.

Children's answers to the questions about the termination of friendship were coded into the same eight categories as in Study 1. The eight categories included most of the answers to the questions about friendship features, but three categories were added: (a) similarity (e.g., "we like the same things"); (b) duration of friendship (e.g., "we've been friends since second grade"); and (c) conflict resolution (e.g., "we get into fights but we always make up"). These categories reflect features of actual friendships that were rarely mentioned when children discussed abstract conceptions of friendships.

When the data on the proportion of children using each category were analyzed, the major findings in the first study were replicated (Table 7.2). Older children referred more often to intimacy and loyalty in friendships, although the age change for loyalty was significant only for the question on friendship termination. Older children more often mentioned prosocial behavior as a feature of

TABLE 7.2
Proportion of Children at Each Grade Using Each Category for the
Questions on Friendship Features and Friendship Termination (Study 2)

Category	Friendship Features (Termination)		
	Kindergarten	3rd	6th
Play or association[a]	.53 (.36)	.88 (.32)	.75 (.22)
Prosocial behavior[a]	.38 (.03)	.69 (.17)	.69 (.12)
Aggressive behavior[a]	.06 (.83)	.06 (1.00)	.41 (.66)
Intimacy or trust[a,b]	.00 (.00)	.03 (.21)	.38 (.12)
Loyalty[b]	.03 (.00)	.03 (.00)	.16 (.19)
Faithfulness[b]	.00 (.00)	.00 (.29)	.06 (.22)
Definitional[a,b]	.50 (.22)	.28 (.08)	.22 (.03)
Personal attributes	.09 (.07)	.16 (.03)	.03 (.22)
Similaritiy	.03	.09	.19
Duration	.09	.25	.09
Conflict resolution	.00	.06	.16

[a] significant at .05 for friendship features
[b] significant at .05 for friendship termination

friendship, and they gave fewer answers referring to the basic definition of friendships.

In contrast to Study 1, there was an increase with age in comments about unfaithfulness. There also was an increase with age in comments about aggressive behavior as a feature of friendship. These comments referred to the *absence* of aggression between good friends. At all ages, however, aggressive behavior was mentioned frequently as a reason for the termination of friendships. References to friends' play or association were also common at all grades, but the proportion of children making such comments peaked at third grade. Sex differences were not found for any category on either question.

The differing results for Studies 1 and 2 clarify which categories show replicable age changes and which do not. The increases with age in comments about intimacy and loyalty appear to be most reliable and most significant (cf. Selman, 1981; Bigelow & La Gaipa, 1980). The increase with age in comments about prosocial behavior is consistent with the statements of other writers about the growing importance of mutual responsiveness and equality in adolescent friendships (see Berndt, 1982), but it is not consistent with a few previous studies (e.g., Bigelow, 1977; Furman & Bierman, 1984).

The age and sex differences that were not replicated across questions and studies may be attributed partly to the modest reliability of measures based on children's answers to a small number of open-ended questions. A more basic problem with the measures is that there is little evidence on their validity. Although some researchers view children's statements about friendship primarily as an index of their social cognitive level, the statements are most often used as a basis for conclusions about the characteristics of actual friendships. The children in Study 2 were asked about an actual friendship, but their answers must depend to some degree on their verbal fluency, their cognitive sophistication, and other factors besides the nature of their friendships. To demonstrate the validity of measures derived from interview responses, evidence on the relations of these measures to other data on children's own friendships is required.

STUDY 3: CHANGES OVER TIME IN COMMENTS ABOUT FRIENDSHIP

The next study was designed to provide several types of data on the validity of measures derived from interviews on friendship. The study included 90 children drawn fairly equally from the fourth and eighth grades. These grades were chosen because previous theory and research suggested that major developments in friendship occur during the age range that they span (see Berndt, 1982).

In the fall of a school year, each child was paired with a close friend. The pairings were based on the children's responses to a brief sociometric question-naire. The children first wrote down the names of their best friends in their grade. Then they were asked to indicate how much they liked each child of the same sex in their grade by circling a number ranging from 1 for "don't like" to 5 for "like very much, as much as a best friend." Children were considered close friends if one or both of them named the other as a best friend and their ratings of liking on the 5-point scale averaged 4.0 or better (see Berndt, 1981a, 1981b). These criteria were established because the combination of best-friend nominations and ratings of liking was assumed to allow more accurate identification of close friends than could either measure by itself (cf. Hallinan, 1981). In this study, roughly 75% of the pairs of friends had nominated each other on the sociometric questionnaire; their ratings of liking for each other averaged 4.7 on the 5-point scale. Thus most children were paired with a very close friend.

Friendship Interview.   Shortly after the questionnaires were completed, each child was interviewed individually. Children first were asked a standard series of open-ended questions about the personality and social behavior of the friend with whom they were paired. Then they were asked three types of questions about the friendship itself: (a) how they could tell that their partner was their friend; (b) what they liked best about being friends with him or her; and (c) what they did not like about being friends with him or her (or times when it was hard to be friends). After children gave one response to each type of question, they were asked if they could supply any additional information. Probing continued until children gave at least three responses or said that they could not think of anything else. The interview quoted at the beginning of this paper illustrated the procedure and some fairly typical answers to the questions.

The children's statements about their friendships were coded into one set of categories for positive comments and a second set of categories for negative comments. Four of the positive categories were taken directly from previous studies. These categories were play or association, prosocial behavior, intimacy, and similarity. Some other categories were combined or modified, usually because responses fitting those categories were rare and, therefore, scores for the categories probably would be low in reliability. The category that originally was called lack of aggressive behavior was broadened to include the category originally called conflict resolution. Then the category was renamed, "absence of conflicts." The original categories for loyalty and faithfulness were combined, because both these categories focused on the connections between a pair of friends and the larger group of other friends, classmates, and adults. The category that originally referred to the defining elements of friendship was redefined as "liking and friendship." Because comments about the duration of a friendship were relatively rare, they were included in this category. Finally, a new category was created for comments about how much fun or how exciting it was for the friends to spend time together. This category was called "stimulation value" (after Bigelow, 1977).

Most of the categories for negative comments were comparable to the positive categories. Corresponding to the similarity category, for example, was a dissimilarity category. References to a lack of prosocial behavior and to frequent hostile or aggressive behavior were included in a single category, however, called "presence of conflicts." In addition, when children referred to a lcak of stimulation in the friendship, they usually meant that the friend was boring or dull. These comments were included in a separate category referring to the friend's personality. Because the personality categories are tangential to the topic of this paper, they will not be described in detail. It is necessary only to mention that, like the friendship categories, they were divided in one set for positive comments and a second set for negative comments.

A series of close-ended questions followed the open-ended ones. For these questions, children rated how positively they viewed their friendship with their partner. There were two questions for each of five features of friendship: prosocial behavior, aggressive behavior, intimacy, loyalty, and similarity. For example, one question on intimacy was "How often does your partner talk with you about problems that are important to him or her?" Children responded on a 5-point scale ranging from never (1) to very often (5).

There was a parallel series of close-ended questions about four aspects of the friend's personality: prosocial behavior toward peers in general, aggressive behavior toward peers in general, popularity, and academic ability. Finally, the interview included five close-ended questions about the frequency of play or association between the friends. An example is, "How often do you spend time with your partner when you have free time during the school day?" A 5-point scale was also used for responses to these questions.

Both the sociometric questionnaires and the interviews on friendship were repeated during the spring of the same school year, about 6 months later. During the spring interviews, children were asked about their current relationship with the same partner that they had had in the fall, regardless of whether or not they had remained close friends. We anticipated that some of the friendships identified in the fall would become weaker or end by the spring. If the changes in friendships shown by the sociometric data were matched by changes in the measures derived from the interviews, the validity of the interview measures would be confirmed.

Effects of Time, Grade, and Sex on Interview Responses.   As expected, the children who were close friends in the fall did not always remain close friends in the spring. A friendship score was created for each pair of children by considering whether or not the children had nominated each other as best friends and how highly they had rated their liking for each other. These scores did not vary with grade or sex, but they decreased between the fall and the spring. Actually, the fourth- and eighth-graders' friendship were fairly stable over the 6-month period; 69% of the pairs that were formed in the fall still met the criteria for a close friendship in the spring. Nevertheless, there was a general decline between the fall and the spring in the strength of the children's friendships.

The changes in friendship were accompanied by dramatic changes in children's comments during their individual interviews (Table 7.3). Positive comments about the friendships were less frequent in the spring than in the fall; negative comments about the friendships were more frequent in the spring than in the fall. Comparable changes were found for comments about the friend's personality, although the decrease in positive comments was only marginally significant. Similarly, mean ratings on the close-ended questions decreased over time, indicating that children became less positive about the friendship and the friend's personality. Children also rated their play or association with their partner as less frequent in the spring than in the fall. In sum, all the measures derived from the interviews reflected the weakening in friendships over time.

Surprisingly, the decline in friendships was shown by all categories and items to roughly the same degree. When the separate sets of categories and ratings

TABLE 7.3
Mean Scores for Reports on the Friendship and the
Friend's Personality at Each Time (Study 3)

Measures	Time	
	Fall	Spring
Positive friendship categories	1.20	1.10
Negative friendship categories	.48	.60
Positive personality categories	.67	.57
Negative personality categories	.39	.50
Ratings of friendship	2.85	2.69
Ratings of friend's personality	2.87	2.73
Ratings of play or association	11.17	9.33

were examined in repeated-measures analyses of variance, the interactions of Time with Category (or Rating) were rarely significant. In other words, no single measure seemed to be especially sensitive to the changes in friendships. The only exception was for negative comments about the friendship. The increase in negative comments was particularly great for the category of disloyalty and unfaithfulness. A common example of this category was, "she's gotten new friends that she likes more than me." Of course, some children said that they made new friends whom they liked more than their original partner.

The changes over time in children's interview responses did not differ greatly for fourth- and eighth-graders or for girls and boys. These findings further support the validity of the interview measures, because the sociometric data also suggested that the changes in friendships between the fall and the spring were not significantly greater for one grade or for one sex than another.

For a few measures, grade differences were apparent both in the fall and in the spring. Eighth-graders mentioned the intimacy of their friendships more often than fourth-graders, confirming the age trend found in the two previous studies. Eighth-graders also commented more often on the stimulation value of their friendships. By contrast, on the close-ended questions eighth-graders did not rate their friendships as more intimate than did fourth-graders. Eighth-graders did give lower ratings for their similarity to their friends and their friends' prosocial behavior toward them. They also reported less frequent play or association with their friends. These results are not easily interpreted, but they may indicate that the two age groups differed in their use of the rating scale, with the younger children generally giving more positive ratings than the older children.

Sex differences in the interview measures were rare but were consistent with previous research. Girls mentioned the intimacy of their friendships more often than did boys; at eighth grade, girls rated their friendships as more intimate than did boys. As in Study 1, girls made more comments than boys about their friends' disloyalty and unfaithfulness. These findings add some support to earlier conclusions that girls' friendships are more intimate and more exclusive than boys' friendships and, as a result, that girls worry more about rejection by friends than do boys (e.g., Douvan & Adelson, 1966; Eder & Hallinan, 1978). Nevertheless, the differences between boys' and girls' friendships should not be exaggerated. In general, the similarities outweigh the differences.

Additional evidence on the validity of the interview measures was obtained by correlating them with the friendship scores based on the sociometric data. The number of significant correlations was relatively small in the fall, probably because all children were close friends with their partners and, therefore, their friendship scores had a restricted range. The range in friendship scores was greater in the spring, as was the number of significant correlations.

Children who were better friends in the spring made more positive comments about their friendships (Table 7.4). Close friends commented especially often on the frequency of their play or association with each other, and their liking for

TABLE 7.4
Correlations of Friendship Scores with Positive
Comments During Spring Interviews (Study 3)

Category	4th	8th	All
		Grade	
Total Positive Comments	.57**	.29	.49**
Play or association	.47*	.30	.41**
Prosocial behavior	.30	-.13	.09
Intimacy	.40	.40	.26
Similarity	.64***	.06	.40**
Absence of conflicts	.32	.03	.20
Loyalty and faithfulness	.19	.31	.23
Liking and Friendship	.35	.30	.33*
Stimulating play	-.02	-.05	-.06

*$p < .05$
**$p < .01$
***$p < .001$

each other. Overall, they also commented frequently on their similarity with each other, but this correlation was significant only for fourth-graders. No other correlations between the interview measures and the friendship scores varied significantly with grade.

Children who were closer friends did not make fewer negative comments about the friendships during the spring interviews (Table 7.5). Apparently, this null result was due to the positive correlation of friendship scores with comments about the dissimilarity between the friends. When considered along with the positive correlation for the similarity category, the dissimilarity correlation suggests that close friends knew and mentioned both how they were alike and how they were different from each other. The significant correlations for the other negative categories are more easily interpreted. Children did not consider themselves close friends when their relationships lacked intimacy or they were disloyal or unfaithful toward each other.

TABLE 7.5
Correlations of Friendship Scores with Negative
Comments During Spring Interviews (Study 3)

Category	4th	8th	All
		Grade	
Total Negative Comments	-.07	-.19	-.16
Lack of play or association	-.07	-.32	-.22
Lack of intimacy	-.33	-.28	-.30*
Dissimilarity	.33	.24	.31*
Presence of conflicts	.17	.16	.15
Disloyal or unfaithful	-.22	-.33	-.30*
Disliking	-.38	-.14	-.27

*$p < .05$

Finally, children who were closer friends, as judged from their sociometric data, rated their friendship more positively on the close-ended questions (Table 7.6). Of all the interview measures, the strongest correlate of friendship scores was the 5-item scale for ratings of the frequency of play or association between the friends. In addition, better friends gave higher ratings for prosocial behavior, intimacy, and similarity. The negative correlation for the absence of conflicts implies that close friends fight with or tease each other more than children who are not close friends, perhaps because nonfriends seldom interact with each other. On the other hand, the negative correlation was nonsignificant, so this hypothesis must be treated as tentative.

Taken together, the findings from this study suggest that children's answers to open-ended questions provide valid measures of their friendships. The measures derived from the children's answers reflected the changes in their friendships over time and the relative strength of their friendships in the spring. The validity of the measures derived from the close-ended questions was confirmed in the same ways.

Nevertheless, the two types of measures were not equivalent. For example, the increase during adolescence in the intimacy of friendships was indicated by children's spontaneous comments but not by their ratings on the close-ended questions. Conversely, children's ratings of their play or association with friends decreased with age, but the frequency of spontaneous comments about play or association did not change significantly.

The discrepancies in results for the measures based on the open and close-ended questions could be attributed to the modest reliability of both types of measures. The scores derived from the open-ended questions had a fairly re-stricted range, because the frequency of responses in any particular category usually was low. Only two close-ended questions were used for most of the features of friendship, limiting the reliability of these measures. From this per-spective, the strong correlations between the spring friendship scores and the

TABLE 7.6
Correlations of Friendship Scores with Ratings
of Friendship Features in the Spring (Study 3)

| Feature | Grade | | |
	4th	8th	All
Mean Ratings	.36	.43*	.41**
Prosocial behavior	.54**	.28	.44**
Intimacy	.33	.31	.33*
Similarity	.51*	.37	.45**
Absence of conflicts	-.37	-.02	-.17
Loyalty	.04	.53*	.29
Play or association	.77***	.51*	.66***

*$p < .05$
**$p < .01$
***$p < .001$

ratings for play or association may be attributed to the high reliability of the 5-item scale for play or association.

Close-ended questions possess an intrinsic advantage over open-ended questions in that they can be scored quickly and easily. One disadvantage of close-ended questions is that the answers of children who misunderstand a specific question are difficult to detect. Exploring the reasons for children's answers is also difficult when purely close-ended questions are used.

A combination of open- and close-ended questions may yield the advantages of both alternatives. The strategy used in the next study was similar to that discussed extensively in the literature on cognitive development. There has been a continuing debate in this literature over whether a child's level of cognitive development can be assessed more accurately from their judgment on a structured task or their explanation for their judgment (see Brainerd, 1977; Larsen, 1977). One compromise position is to argue that judgments and explanations furnish complementary information. Therefore, in nonsocial as well as social cognitive research, it may be valuable to obtain both types of information.

STUDY 4: FRIENDSHIPS AS SOCIAL SUPPORTS

Our next study differed from the previous ones not only in the interviewing procedure but also in its conceptual framework. Instead of focusing entirely on what children perceived as important features of their friendships, the study was designed to explore the degree to which friendships serve as social supports for children. The concept of social support has been mentioned frequently in recent psychological research, although most studies have examined the supports available to adults in their social networks, or the degree to which adults function as supports for children (cf. Gottlieb, 1981), rather than the supportive functions of friendships or other peer relationships during childhood and adolescence. Nevertheless, many hypotheses about the contributions of friendships to children's development are consistent with a view of friendships as effective social supports for children.

Actually, the new focus on social support did not require major changes in the features of friendship that were examined. In the current literature, social supports generally refer to interpersonal relationships which convince people that they are cared for and loved, esteemed and valued, and able to rely on other people for advice and material aid (Cobb, 1976). Most of the features of friendship that children mentioned in previous studies, such as friends' prosoical behavior toward each other, fit this broad definition of social support.

Interview Format and Content.   The major changes in the new study related to the interviewing method itself. As in Study 3, children were asked questions about their relationship with a particular partner, who was mentioned by name, but each question referred to a specific feature of friendship. For example, one question about play or association was, "Do you ever spend your free time with (name of partner)?" If children said "yes," they were asked how often they did so. They responded on a 4-point scale with labels ranging from *once in a while* to *very often*. By treating a "no" response as the lowest point on the scale (1), children's responses were converted to ratings on a scale from 1 to 5. These ratings provided sensitive measures of children's judgments about their relationships.

After children reported their judgment on a specific question, they were asked to explain their response. For example, they were asked why they spent free time with their partner, or why they did not. Unlike in previous studies, the interviewers did not probe these answers extensively. The goal was simply to obtain one clear explanation for the children's judgments.

To increase the reliability of the data, five questions were included for each of six features of friendships. Features were chosen that seemed important in theory and in past research. As was just mentioned, one feature concerned the play or association between the friends. The other five features are listed next with sample questions:

Prosocial behavior: "If (name of partner) got a new game or a new toy, would he or she share it with you?" and "Does (name of partner) try to help you when you can't do something by yourself?"

Absence of conflicts: "Do you ever feel like it's hard to get along with (name of partner)?" and "Do you ever get into fights or arguments with (name of partner)?" Although these questions refer to how often conflicts arise, they were reverse-scored, so that higher scores reflect fewer conflicts. Thus higher scores indicate better relationships, as on the other features.

Intimacy: "If you told (name of partner) a secret, could you trust him or her not to tell anyone else?" and "When you have a problem at home or at school, do you talk to (name of partner) about it?"

Loyalty and faithfulness: "If you were picking partners at school, would you and (name of partner) try to pick each other?" and "If other kids were teasing you, would (name of partner) tell them to stop it?"

Self-esteem and attachment: "When you do a good job at something, does (name of partner) tell you that you did?" and "If (name of partner) had to move away, would you miss him or her?"

All but the last feature are familiar from previous studies. The last one was suggested by Sullivan's (1953) comments about the importance of friendships in the validation of self-worth, and Hartup's (1975) comments about the parallels between parent-infant attachments and friendships. Self-esteem and attachment were treated as a single feature because they both refer to the emotional support provided by a friend. In retrospect, however, treating them as two separate features might have been wiser.

Because there were five questions for each of six features, the entire interview included 30 questions. The average length of an interview was between 15 and 20 minutes.

Research Design. For the study, approximately 120 children from the second, fourth, sixth, and eighth grades were interviewed. The goal in choosing these grades was to test the new interview format across a fairly broad age range. Prior to the interview, each child completed the sociometric questionnaire described previously (Study 3). Children's best-friend nominations and ratings of liking were used in combination to pair each child with a close friend, using the criteria for friendship stated earlier.

In addition, most children were paired with a classmate who was not a close friend. Children were considered merely as classmates if they did not name each other as best friends and their average ratings for each other ranged from 2.0 to 3.0. In other words, these children liked each other less than did close friends, for whom the average rating of liking was always greater than 4.0. Children were not considered as classmates if either one gave the other a rating of "1," meaning that they disliked the other.

Some children could not be paired with a classmate because their own ratings of other children and the other children's ratings of them yielded average ratings that were either too high or too low for the classmate condition. In addition, a few children received ratings of 0 from most other children. Children were told to rate another child 0 if they did not know who the child was. In some cases, the children receiving many ratings of 0 were newcomers to the school.

Children not paired with a classmate were interviewed only about one close friend. The remainder of the children were interviewed about a friend and a classmate, using the same set of questions in random order.

Judgments about Friends' Support. The first step in the analysis of children's judgments was to determine the reliability of the measures for each feature of friendship, and for the total scale. (The same analyses were done for reports on classmates, with comparable results.) Reliability was estimated by Cronbach's alpha, a measure of internal consistency or the degree to which items from a single scale are intercorrelated. An alpha greater than .70 is generally considered adequate for research purposes; standardized IQ and achievement tests have reliabilities of .90 or better (Nunnally, 1978).

For the entire sample, four features had alpha coefficients greater than .70. These features were play or association, prosocial behavior, intimacy, and loyalty. The coefficient for conflict resolution was .64 and that for self-esteem and attachment was .54. The low coefficient for self-esteem and attachment may reflect the lack of strong relations between the two aspects of this feature.

The coefficient alpha for the entire interview, based on the mean scores for each of the six features, was .89. The values for the alpha coefficient were equally high when the analyses were done separately for second-, fourth-, sixth-, and eighth-graders (alphas = .88 to .93). This high degree of internal consistency was confirmed by factor analyses. For the entire sample, the six features loaded on a single factor that accounted for 70% of the variance. Separate analyses for each grade also yielded single-factor solutions except at eighth grade, where there was a second, specific factor on which only conflict resolution loaded highly.

The factor analyses and the estimates of internal consistency suggest that the strength or quality of friendships is unidimensional. At least as perceived by children and adolescents, good friendships are good on all features and poor friendships are poor on all features. The same conclusion was suggested by the analyses in Study 3 of the changes in interview responses over time. In that study, most of the interview measures showed the decline in friendships between the fall and the spring to roughly the same degree.

On the other hand, the correlations between feature scores were not so high that the features could be considered equivalent. The distinctions between features were most evident in the analyses of the differences in scores for friends versus classmates, younger versus older children, and boys versus girls. As expected, children generally gave more positive answers when talking about a friend rather than a classmate. Across all features, the mean score for friends was 3.59 and the mean score for classmates was 2.45. The friend–classmate difference accounted for 38% of the variance in the children's responses (as estimated by eta-squared).

The mean scores derived from the interviews about friends did not vary significantly between second and eighth grade. Nevertheless, there were differences between grades for specific features (Figure 7.1). The only significant change with age was the increase in the reported intimacy of friendship. Because the age trend for intimacy has now been shown in multiple studies with multiple methods (cf. Diaz & Berndt, 1982), it can be regarded as one of the best-documented facts about the development of friendships.

On most features, the mean scores from the classmate interviews decreased with grade (Figure 7.2). The decreases were significant for the features of play or association, and intimacy. These trends indicate that the differentiation between friendships and other relationships increases with age, because as scores for friends increased or remained stable, scores for classmates dropped (see also Furman & Bierman, 1985; Selman, 1981). By contrast, scores for the absence of conflicts with classmates increased with age, indicating that older children perceived that they had fewer conflicts, even with classmates, than did younger children. Because a trend in the same direction was found for reports on friendships, it can be regarded as a general decrease in aggressiveness or argumentativeness, rather than a change specific to friendship.

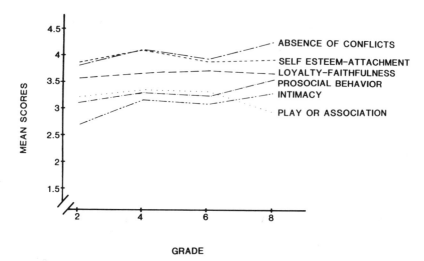

FIG. 7.1.   Mean scores for each feature from interviews about close friends (Study 4).

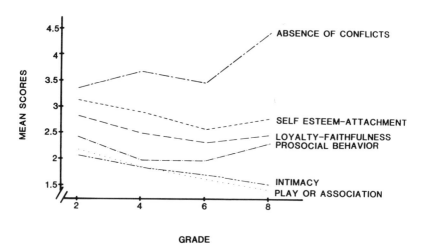

FIG. 7.2.   Mean scores for each feature from interviews about classmates who are neither close friends nor children who are disliked (Study 4).

Finally, there were no significant differences in boys' and girls' reports on their friendships. For reports on classmates, the sex difference was significant for only one feature at one grade. Second-grade boys reported more conflicts with their classmates than did second-grade girls. Recent reviews suggest that this difference in reports matches a difference in children's actual behavior (see Hyde, 1984).

In summary, the results of this study illustrate that reliable measures of friendship can be derived from children's answers to structured questions. The results also demonstrate the validity of the friendship measures, because scores on the measures were higher for close friends than for classmates who were not close friends. In addition, the grade differences in scores for specific features were consistent with previous theory and research.

CONCLUSIONS

In all the studies discussed thus far, the features of friendship were determined primarily by asking children to talk about their own relationships. For many people, obtaining information about children's friendships from the children themselves is intuitively appealing. As in the example quoted at the beginning of this paper, children's ways of phrasing their comments and their word choices are often humorous and fascinating at the same time. In addition, children's comments often include concrete details that precisely define the situation or the context for an event. Children also reveal their feelings about people and events in vivid, colorful language.

By contrast, some psychologists look with suspicion on data obtained from interviews with children. These psychologists emphasize the problem of social desirability biases, that is, children saying what they think an adult wants to hear rather than disclosing their true feelings or describing what actually happened in some situation. Moreover, these psychologists emphasize the limitations on children's understanding. Children may not know or be able to report what events had the greatest influence on the formation and maintenance of their friendships. Because of these limits on what children can and will report, interviews with children are not regarded as an appropriate method for examining the features of their friendships. Rather than relying on the subjective perspective of children, researchers are urged to rely on their own, more objective perspective.

In recent research, there have been two major alternatives to the interview method for investigating children's friendships. First, researchers have attempted to train children in the social skills that are assumed to contribute to good friendships (see Asher & Renshaw, 1981; Ladd & Mize, 1983). Many different skills have been selected as targets for training, but three common targets are (a) being able to initiate a friendly social interaction with an unfamiliar peer; (b) behaving in a cooperative way toward the peer; (c) quickly and amicably resolving conflicts that arise during social interactions with the peer (see, e.g., Oden & Asher, 1977). The selection of skills for training has been done either on theoretical grounds or, more commonly, on the basis of previous research that examined the behavior of popular children—children with many friends. If children who are included in a social-skills training program show an increase in the number of friends that they have, researchers generally assume that their hypotheses about the skills that are important for good friendships have been supported.

Social-skills training programs frequently include interviews with children. During these interviews, children are asked how they would respond to hypothetical social situations that illustrate social conflicts or problems. In contrast to the studies described in this paper, the interviews are not intended to assess the features of children's actual relationships with peers. Furthermore, they are not intended to explore children's own ideas about the social behaviors or interactions that contribute to the success of a relationship. Instead, the interviews are designed to assess the children's awareness and understanding of the social skills that the researcher has already selected as important targets for training. That is, the interviews serve primarily as a pretest, a means of measuring children's skills prior to the training program. When described in this way, such interviews clearly reflect the researcher's perspective rather than the child's perspective on the important features of successful peer relationships.

The second major alternative to the interview method is observation of children's actual behavior when they are engaged in an interaction with a friend. In some cases, observations have been conducted in settings structured by an experimenter, as friends worked together on specially designed tasks. Most often, these studies have focused on a single feature of friendship, friend's prosocial behavior toward each other. A few studies have confirmed the hypothesis suggested by common sense and by the research on children's conceptions of friendship, that close friends will help and share with each other more than nonfriends (e.g., Berndt, 1981a; Newcomb & Brady, 1982). Other studies have demonstrated that, during middle childhood, friends help or share with each other less than nonfriends under certain conditions (e.g., Berndt, 1981b; Staub & Noerenberg, 1981). Friends appear least likely to share with each other when they view themselves as in competition with each other. It is worth noting explicitly that the existence of competition between close friends was not strongly evident in children's own comments about their friendships.

In other observational studies, conversations between friends were recorded as the friends engaged in free play (e.g., Gottman, 1983). Then the transcripts of the conversations were coded for indicators of several social processes that were presumed to be important for the formation of friendships. For example, children were expected to become closer friends if their conversations were marked by the "establishment of a common-ground activity." In other words, the children agreed on an activity to do together. This type of research again represents an emphasis on the researcher's perspective, because the social processes selected for intensive investigation are chosen by the researcher rather than directly suggested by the children under observation.

Of course, researchers are not committing an error when they make their own judgments about the important features of friendship. These judgments are tested in research and they can either be confirmed or disconfirmed. By the same token, researchers are not committing an error when they use interviews to obtain children's own judgments about their friendships. The reliability and validity of these judgments can and should be tested in research.

Moreover, both methods can be used with profit in a single study. When convergent results are obtained with the two types of methods, the validity of both types is supported. In one of the studies described earlier (Berndt & Hawkins, in preparation), the interviews with children about their friendships were complemented by observations of friends' interactions as they worked together on a structured task. The task was similar to one that in previous research had shown the existence of competition between friends. As expected, fourth-graders competed more on the task when their interview responses indicated that they were better friends with each other. By contrast, eighth-graders whose interview responses indicated that they were better friends competed less and shared more with each other. The contrast between the two grades is consistent with previous hypotheses that competition between friends gives way to sensitivity and mutual responsiveness during adolescence (see Sullivan, 1953; Youniss, 1980). Moreover, the findings from this study attest to the value of using multiple methods, involving both subjective judgments by the child and objective observations by a researcher, to explore the development of friendships.

Nevertheless, the interview method has some distinct advantages that should not be overlooked. These advantages can be conveyed succinctly by quoting from another interview. One eighth-grade boy from Study 3 (Berndt & Hawkins, in preparation) was explaining why his friendship with another boy was not as good in the spring of the year as it had been in the fall:

"He doesn't like to do things that we want to do. We always used to have stickfights, but he doesn't do that anymore. He things it's too babyish. But I asked him once and he said 'no'; one of the more popular kids asked him and he said, 'I guess so.' He'd rather be with the more popular kids."

In other words, the friendship is not as good as it had been originally because the boys find it harder to establish a common-ground activity (Gottman, 1983). The boy's response demonstrates that the processes previously examined by recording friends' conversations can also be examined by analyzing children's comments during an interview.

The boy's response goes further, however, in explaining why he and his former friend have trouble establishing a common-ground activity. Apparently, the friend is a social climber, wanting only to do activities that make him seem mature, or to do activities with the more popular children. The boy's comments illustrate an influence on friendship that is not obvious in studies focused exclusively on the interactions of two friends who are separated from their peer group. In short, the comments both support a current hypothesis about friendship and suggest a new hypothesis to be examined more carefully in future research.

Besides its value in hypothesis generation, the interview method has several practical advantages for future research. First, interviews that allow children to rate specific features of their friendships on structured scales are easy to administer and score. Responses to individual questions can be combined to form reliable and valid measures of friendship. If the interview also allows children to explain the basis for their judgments, it can clarify why a particular relationship is close or distant. Such an interview may be useful in clinical work with individual children. If a child appears to have difficulty forming and keeping good friendships, for example, both the magnitude and the probable sources of the difficulty can be explored during an interview. Of course, interviews with the other children whom the child nominates as friends may be equally or more illuminating.

The efficiency of the interview method is important for other reasons as well. Instead of asking a child questions about just one of his or her friendships, an interviewer could ask the child about all of his or her closest friendships. In this way, researchers could shift from a focus on dyadic friendships to a focus on a child's friendship network, without sacrificing information about the specific features of particular friendships.

Interviews with children about their friendship network could be a valuable component of new designs for research on friendship. Up to now, friendship has been the dependent variable in most research. That is, researchers have explored developmental changes in friendships themselves. Many of the most important hypotheses about friendship, however, include friendship as an independent variable. These hypotheses concern the effects of friendships on children's development. As mentioned earlier, friendships can be viewed as social supports that enable children to deal more effectively with problems in their lives. The supportive functions of friendship can be illustrated with one final quote from an interview with an eighth-grade girl. In describing one of the best things about her friendship with another girl, she said:

"She has the same problems I do. Her parents are divorced and my parents were divorced and now they're back together, but they're not married. She understands what I mean by it. I have problems with my parents. My mother and me are close, and my father and me are starting to get close and my mother's jealous—and that is what happens to Janet [her friend] a lot."

Data that demonstrate the supportive functions of friendships are scarce. To obtain these data, sensitive measures of the features of friendship are needed. Perhaps the best method for obtaining these measures is to ask children to comment on their own friendships. With new and improved interviewing procedures, answers to the old questions about the influence of friendships may be found. Researchers then may understand more clearly why friendships are important to children and why promoting good friendships should be an important goal for those adults who work with children.

ACKNOWLEDGMENTS

The research reported in this paper was supported in part by grant number 1R01MH38093 from the National Institute of Mental Health and by a grant from the Spencer Foundation. The author would like to thank Jill Devenport, Jacquelyn Hawkins, Sally Hoyle, Bridgett Perry, and Julie Watson for their assistance in the collection, coding, and analysis of the data reported.

REFERENCES

Asher, S. R., & Renshaw, P. D. (1981). Children without friends: Social knowledge and social skill training. In S. R. Asher & J. M. Gottman (Eds.), *The development of children's friendships.* Cambridge, England: Cambridge University Press.

Berndt, T. J. (1978, August). *Children's conceptions of friendship and the behavior expected of friends.* Paper presented at the meeting of the American Psychological Association, Toronto.

Berndt, T. J. (1981a). Age changes and changes over time in prosocial intentions and behavior between friends. *Developmental Psychology,, 17,* 408–416.

Berndt. T. J. (1981b). The effects of friendship on prosocial intentions and behavior. *Child Development, 52,* 636–643.

Berndt, T. J. (1981c). Relations between social cognition, nonsocial cognition, and social behavior: The case of friendship. In J. H. Flavell & L. D. Ross (Eds.), *Social cognitive development: Frontiers and possible futures.* England: Cambridge University Press.

Berndt, T. J. (1982). The features and effects of friendships in early adolescence. *Child Development, 53,* 1447–1460.

Berndt, T. J. (1983). Social cognition, social behavior, and children's friendships. In E. T. Higgins, D. N. Ruble, & W. W. Hartup (Eds.), *Social cognition and social development: A socio-cultural perspective* (pp. 158–189). England: Cambridge University Press.

Berndt, T. J., Hawkins, J. A., & Hoyle, S. G. (in preparation). *Stability and change in childhood and adolescent friendships.*

Bigelow, B. J. (1977). Children's friendship expectations: A cognitive-developmental study. *Child Development, 48,* 246–253.

Bigelow, B. J., & LaGaipa, J. J. (1980). The development of friendship values and choice. In H. C. Foot, A. J. Chapman, & J. R. Smith (Eds.), *Friendship and social relations in children.* New York: Wiley.

Brainerd, C. J. (1977). Response criteria in concept development research. *Child Development, 48,* 360–366.

Cobb, S. (1976). Social support as a moderator of life stress. *Psychosomatic Medicine, 38,* 300–314.

Coleman, J. C. (1980). Friendship and the peer group in adolescence. In J. Adelson (Ed.), *Handbook of adolescent psychology.* New York: Wiley.

Csikszentmihalyi, M., Larson, R., & Prescott, S. (1977). The ecology of adolescent activity and experience. *Journal of Youth and Adolescence, 6,* 281–294.

Damon, W. (1977). *The social world of the child.* San Francisco: Jossey-Bass.

Diaz, R. M., & Berndt, T. J. (1982). Children's knowledge of a best friend: Fact or fancy? *Developmental Psychology, 18,* 787–794.

Douvan, E., & Adelson, J. (1966). *The adolescent experience.* New York: Wiley.

Eder, D., & Hallinan, M. T. (1978). Sex differences in children's friendships. *American Sociological Review, 43,* 237–250.

Ellis, S., Rogoff, B., & Cromer, C. C. (1981). Age segregation in children's social interactions. *Developmental Psychology, 17,* 399–407.

Furman, W., & Bierman, K. L. (1984). Children's conceptions of friendship: A multimethod study of developmental changes. *Developmental Psychology, 20,* 925–931.

Gottlieb, B. H. (Ed.). (1981). *Social networks and social support.* Beverly Hills, CA: Sage.

Gottman, J. M. (1983). How children become friends. *Monographs of the Society for Research in Child Development, 48,* (3, Serial No. 201).

Hallinan, M. T. (1981). Recent advances in sociometry. In S. R. Asher & J. M. Gottman (Eds.), *The development of children's friendships.* Cambridge, England: Cambridge University Press.

Hartup, W. W. (1975). The origins of friendship. In M. Lewis & L. A. Rosenblum (Eds.), *Friendship and peer relations.* New York: Wiley.

Hartup, W. W. (1978). Children and their friends. In H. McGurk (Ed.), *Issues in childhood social development.* London: Methuen.

Hayes, D. S. (1978). Cognitive bases for liking and disliking among preschool children. *Child Development, 49,* 906–909.

Hayes, D. S., Gershman, E., & Bolin, L. J. (1980). Friends and enemies: Cognitive bases for preschool children's unilateral and reciprocal relationships. *Child Development, 51,* 1276–1279.

Hyde, J. S. (1984). How large are gender differences in aggression? A developmental meta-analysis. *Developmental Psychology, 20,* 722–736.

Ladd, G. W., & Mize, J. (1983). A cognitive-social learning model of social-skill training. *Psychological Review, 90,* 127–157.

Larsen, G. Y. (1977). Methodology in developmental psychology: An examination of research on Piagetian theory. *Child Development, 48,* 1160–1166.

Newcomb, A. F., & Brady, J. E. (1982). Mutuality in boys' friendship relations. *Child Development, 53,* 392–395.

Nunnally, J. C. (1978). *Psychometric theory* (2nd ed.). New York: McGraw-Hill.

Oden, S., & Asher, S. R. (1977). Coaching children in social skills for friendship making. *Child Development, 48,* 495–506.

Selman, R. L. (1981). The child as a friendship philosopher: A case study in the growth of interpersonal understanding. In S. R. Asher & J. M. Gottman (Eds.), *The development of children's friendships.* England: Cambridge University Press.

Staub, E., & Noerenberg, H. (1981). Property rights, deservingness, reciprocity, friendship: The transactional character of children's sharing behavior. *Journal of Personality and Social Psychology, 40,* 271–289.

Sullivan, H. S. (1953). *The interpersonal theory of psychiatry.* New York: Norton.

Youniss, J. (1980). *Parents and peers in social development.* IL: University of Chicago Press.

8 Comments on Berndt: Children's Comments About Their Friendships

Ellen Berscheid
University of Minnesota

> *To a large degree, our current understanding of the development of friendship is based on children's statements during interviews. . .*

Berndt, this volume

To a large degree, our current understanding of the development of any relationship, whether between children or adults, friendship or marital, or anything else, is based on people's comments about that relationship. Sometimes these comments are spontaneously given, other times they are elicited in interviews, and perhaps most frequently they are obtained in response to written questionnaire items. Despite the fact that the individual's self-reports of the nature and causes of his or her relationship represent the most usual source of data about all aspects of relationships, their interpretation is never unproblematic. One is reminded of this eternal verity reading through Berndt's programmatic studies of children's comments about their friendhips, for one frequently finds oneself asking, "What do these comments really mean? What do they signify?"

We can be fairly confident that these comments represent the children's true perceptions of the nature of their relationship and of the factors that may have caused it to be initiated and maintained. Such perceptions are not unimportant. At the least, they guide the individual's behavior within the relationship. In this sense, then, it may matter little whether Joe *truly* likes Jim and supports his most cherished beliefs and values as long as Jim thinks so; knowledge of that perception is crucial to predicting Jim's immediate behavior toward Joe.

The problem lies in remembering what these comments do *not* signify. Specifically, it is always tempting to assume that self-reports are veridical with reality, or, that they serve as an adequate substitute for reports made by external observers of the relationship. Unfortunately, observers who evaluate the actual degree to which Joe likes Jim, or the actual degree to which they disclose to each other, might find a number of discrepancies, of greater or lesser degree, between their observations and each partner's report of the nature of the relationship. Thus, and to expand upon Jesse Bernard's (1972) observation about marital relationships, there is "*his* relationship," "*her* relationship," and "*their* relationship" as viewed by an external observer. Understanding of relationship dynamics, including prediction of the developmental course of the relationship, probably lies somewhere in the triangle of these views.

The special status of self-report data in the study of relationship phenomena has been extensively discussed elsewhere (e.g., see Harvey, Christensen, & McClintock, 1983), as have the relative advantages and disadvantages of "insiders'" versus "outsiders'" views of a relationship (e.g., Olson, 1977). Here, it is perhaps sufficient to observe that many of the questions raised by these comments of children can be answered only by obtaining complementary data from external observers. Such data would allow us to determine the extent to which the children's comments about the sharing, the support, and so on that they receive from their friends agree or disagree with external observations.

Undoubtedly, there will be discrepancies between the two sets of reports. (The likely nature of some of these is known, at least within adult relationships. For example, husbands and wives generally assume that they share more attitudes than they really do, and people who like one another, for whatever reason, also tend to assume attitude similarity (see Berscheid & Walster, 1978).) The extent and nature of such discrepancies between partners' and observers' reports of the nature of their relationship is of considerable significance for predicting the likely course of the relationshp. One need only consider the cartoon of the wife who says to her husband sprawled in his undershirt, beer can in hand, and glued to the TV, "I wonder if you ever *were* the man I thought you were!" He probably never was. Where the discrepancies between perception and reality are severe, one suspects the relationship may suffer a different fate than where the friendship is grounded on more accurate perceptions of the partner and the relationship.

At the least, the number, nature, and pattern of discrepancies between insiders' and outsiders' reports may provide insight into the dynamics of a specific relationship as well as into the development course of children's relationship experiences and skills. With respect to this last, is it the case that as children grow older, there are fewer discrepancies between their perception of the nature of the relationship and that of observers? Are there differences in the areas in which perceptions are *not* likely to be veridical in children of different ages (e.g., in self-disclosure as opposed to degree of social support)?

Knowledge of the variances between what is and what is perceived to be also may provide some indication with children, as with adults, of the degree to which the individual's comments about his or her relationship are drawn primarily from the individual's "social theories" about the nature of friendship *in general* rather than from the actual pattern of interaction characteristic of that specific relationship. That the children in Berndt's studies have already well developed cognitive schemas of friendship is suggested by the striking correspondence between the factors he identifies as characteristic of the children's comments and those identified in a study conducted by Sternberg and Grajek (in press) of adults' reports of the nature of their close relationships with "loved" persons. Thus, one wonders—in adults' reports as in children's reports—about the extent to which the reports are a reflection of two alternative processes. In one, another is, first, and for whatever reason (perhaps because of the exigency presented by experimenters' demands to name a "friend"), categorized as "friend" and, then, the other and the relationship are given attributes commonly associated with "friend" and "friendship." In the other, the report of a specific relationship is responsive to its actual properties, even when these vary from the individual's notions of what most friendships are or ought to be.

In this respect, further information about the children who fell through the cracks of Berndt's studies might be helpful. For example, in Study 3 (in which changes over time and comments about actual relationship were examined), 25% of the children who had nominated another as a close friend had not also given that person a high rating of liking. Who were these children? What differentiates them from the others? Do their general theories of friendship differ (e.g., a "friend" need not be liked)? Similarly, in Study 4, almost one-third of the children could not be paired with a classmate who was *not* a close friend because they gave high ratings of liking to all of their classmates, or, conversely, disliked many of their classmates and were disliked in return, or because they simply did not really know who their classmates were. It would be interesting to contrast these children's general conceptions of friendship with those who could be paired with a best friend.

If people's descriptive comments about the nature of their relationship do not necessarily reflect the facts of the matter, their comments about *why* they are in that relationship (or why they are friends with another) are even more suspect for several reasons. One of these derives from experience in asking adults why they "like" another. Usually the answers refer to qualities of the other that seemingly *elicit* attraction, such as the other's "honesty," "generosity," "sense of humor," and so on. Were one to take these reports at face value, the psychology of interpersonal attraction would consist merely of all the positive adjectives in the dictionary and a statement that those who possess these qualities tend to be liked. In actuality, of course, the situation is far more complex. Specifically, in focusing on the characteristics of the other (O), what these self-reports of the determinants of attraction and friendship tend to leave out are, first, characteristics of the person himself or herself (P) that cause the person to like most everyone (or no one), as well as P × O factors, or interactions between P and O characteristics that lead to attraction (e.g., attitude similarity).

Perhaps most prominently, however, what our self-reports often overlook is the causal role the social environment (E_{soc}) and the physical environment (E_{phys}) plays in the initiation, maintenance, and termination of relationships (see Kelley et al., 1983). When seeking the *raison d'etre* of any relationship—child or adult—it is tempting for laypersons and investigators alike to look for its causal determinants within the confines of the relationship (in P, O, and P × O factors) rather than in the external context in which the relationship is embedded. These contextual factors, however, form the banks and the bed, if you will, of the relationship as it flows through time and space, affecting both its nature and its course. Nevertheless, at least within the adult relationship and attraction literature, the causal role of the social and physical environments, as well as their interaction with factors internal to the relationship, has been almost wholly ignored by investigators (see Berscheid, in press).

Partly, environmental factors have been ignored because the determinants of attraction have been investigated largely within the confines of the laboratory where the two persons involved have met (and evaluated) each other at the request of the experimenter and expect never to see each other again. Thus, the physical context of the short-term relationship examined is standardized to an experiment in an academic setting and the relationship is encapsulated from the individual's actual social environment. Unlike developmental psychologists, only recently have investigators of adult relationships begun to study relationships *in vivo* and *in situ,* where consideration of the role environmental factors play in relationship development is not only possible but mandatory.

In other part, however, the role of environmental factors has been overlooked because they so rarely appear in individuals' reports of their rationale for relationship initiation and maintenance. These accounts and rationales, both with respect to adult relationships (e.g., Sternberg & Grajek, in press) and child peer relationships (e.g., Berndt, in press), tend, as previously noted, to refer to such things as the "sharing of deeply personal ideas and feelings" and "receipt and provision of emotional support to the other" (Sternberg & Grajek, in press). It is tempting to conclude, then, that these factors are not only descriptors of the relationship but determinants of it; that is, to conclude that if O had *not* provided sharing and emotional support to P, there would be no "friendship."

It is possible, however, that such behaviors sometimes *follow* the establishment of a relationship, and then constitute a reasonable rationale for it (to oneself and to others), rather than represent causal determinants of the relationship. For example, if you ask Susan why she married Harry, one is likely to get answers that refer to Harry's dispositional characteristics, such as his "honesty," his "kindness," and "generosity," or, answers that refer to certain aspects of the interaction pattern characteristic of the relationship, such as "We like to do the same things" and "We do a lot of work for the Republican party." The fact of the matter, however, may be that the *real* reason she married Harry is that she wanted to get married and he is the only man she knew at the time and he happened to ask her. Thus, an important causal factor was E_{soc}, or an impoverished social network, and its interaction with P characteristics (e.g., she just lost her job and flunked out of school and had no place to live), as well as O characteristics (e.g., Harry's overtures). Harry may indeed be honest, kind, and generous, but these are not the primary reasons that she signed the marital contract. (These personal characteristics of Harry may have constituted necessary conditions, of course, but not sufficient, and in some circumstances, they may not even be necessary.)

Thus, when people are asked *why* Joe is their best friend or Harry is their husband, it seems reasonable that children, like adults, will ferret around for some of the good qualities associated with the partner and with their relationship. And one need not assume that a social desirability bias is responsible for this tendency. Presumably, all of us would like to think that we have some very good reasons for choosing the mates, dates, and friends we *do* choose, and that we whisper these justifications to outselves in the dark of night even when researchers are not around and social desirability considerations are not salient. Furthermore, and as this implies, most of us like to think we *had* a choice, although few of us have the smorgasbord of opportunities the literature on interpersonal attraction tends to assume. What our self-reports tend to overlook, then, is that many of our relationships come about by default, fate, and chance— or influential constellations of social and physical environmental variables— rather than by conscious and deliberate choice. Thus, the explanations we offer for why Joe is a friend may indeed truly constitute some of the reasons the relationship is maintained, but they may not be the critical ones (e.g., there is no one else around) and, further, these factors may have played a very small role in the actual establishment of the relationship.

Social desirability, of course, probably *does* play some role in these self-reports, as Berndt discusses. If so, it might be interesting to ask children who they perceive within their class to be best friends and to ask them the basis upon which they make their judgments. In children's relationships, again as in adult relationships, we probably are less likely to justify other people's choices in the same ways we do our own. It is probably more socially permissible, for example, to refer to mundane factors as determinants of others' friendships. For example, when persons in Susan's social circle are asked to tell why Susan married Harry, they are probably more likely than she (although this is an hypothesis in need of test) to refer to the fact that Harry is filthy rich and happened to ask her to marry him just when she had flunked out of school and lost her job.

In sum, it has been argued that studies which systematically examine partners' self-reports of the nature and causal determinants of the initiation and maintenance of their relationship with another constitute a necessary first step to understanding the initiation and developmental course of relationships. Prudence dictates, however, that those reports not be taken to signify the *actual* nature of the relationship, at least as determined by outside observers. Nor should we expect such reports to adequately reflect the causal conditions that are responsible for the relationship's existence and maintenance. Many of these, it has been argued, lie in social and physical environments surrounding the relationship—in such mundane physical circumstances as sharing the first letter of one's surname with another in an alphabetical classroom seating arrangement (e.g., Segal, 1974) or in an impoverished social network that confines one's friendship choice to a single other person. And, like fish surrounded by water who rarely think to mention the role it plays in their existence, we cannot expect that many of us will be aware of, or think to report, the sometimes cosmic role our social and physical environments, and the flukes of fate and circumstance they sometimes present, play in the most intimate and valued aspects of our lives.

REFERENCES

Bernard, J. (1972). *The future of marriage*. New York: Bantam.

Berscheid, E. (in press). Interpersonal attraction. In G. Lindzey & E. Aronson (Eds.), *Handbook of social psychology* (3rd ed.). Reading, MA.: Addison-Wesley.

Berscheid, E., & Walster, E. (1978). *Interpersonal attraction* (2nd ed.). Reading, MA.: Addison-Wesley.

Harvey, J. H., Christensen, A., & McClintock, E. (1983). Research methods. In H. H. Kelley. E. Berscheid, A. Christensen, J. Harvey, T. L. Huston, G. Levinger, E. McClintock, A. Peplau, & D. R. Peterson. *Close relationships*. San Francisco: Freeman.

Kelley, H. H., Berscheid, E., Christensen, A., Harvey, J., Huston, T. L., Levinger, G., McClintock, E., Peplau, A., & Peterson, D. R. (1983). *Close relationships*. San Francisco: Freeman.

Olson, D. H. (1977). Insiders' and outsiders' views of relationships: Research strategies. In G. Levinger & H. L. Raush (Eds.), *Close relationships: Perspectives on the meaning of intimacy*. Amherst, MA.: University of Massachusetts Press.

Segal, M. W. (1974). Alphabet and attraction: An unobtrusive measure of the effect of propinquity in a field setting. *Journal of Personality and Social Psychology, 30,* 654–657.

Sternberg, R. J., & Grajek, S. (in press). The nature of love. *Journal of Personality and Social Psychology: Interpersonal Processes*.

9 Understanding the Developing Understanding of Control

John R. Weisz
University of North Carolina at Chapel Hill

> *"Practice makes perfect."*
> *"If at first you don't succeed, try, try again."*
> *"When the going gets tough, the tough get going."*
> *"Anything worth doing is worth doing well."*

With maxims like these we counsel persistence in our children, and sometimes in our peers and ourselves. Yet, a moment's reflection reveals limitations of these familiar sayings. For example, we have all faced tasks at which practice makes mostly weary, and perfection remains elusive; need I mention those piano lessons some of the more ham-handed of us were nudged into by our parents, or the dashed hopes of countless budding prima ballerinas whose petite frames were done in by the ravages of puberty? A major problem with these maxims, like most, is that in their succinctness they oversimplify; they do not, and of course cannot, take into account the range of situations people may actually encounter, nor of the fact that in many of those situations the maxim in question is simply bad advice. Perhaps it is partly in reaction to such situations that our culture has developed a downbeat counterpart to most upbeat maxims, thus permitting the construction of such balanced, bipolar maxims as:

If at first you don't succeed, try, try again	. . . .	If at first you don't succeed, quit.
When the going gets tough, the tough get going.	. . . .	No use butting your head against a stone wall.

219

| Anything worth doing is worth doing well. | . . . . | Anything not worth doing is not worth doing well. |

Children, and adults for that matter, caught in a world of such bipolar maxims, are often forced to make decisions as to which pole offers the better advice in a given situation. If at first we don't succeed, should we persist or quit? Now that the going has gotten tough, what *should* we do? Many of these judgments should, and evidently do, depend in part on a judgment about the degree to which we can cause events to occur as we intend—that is, a judgment about our prospects for control. If we judge that we can control relevant events we have a stronger basis for persistence than if we judge control to be impossible or unlikely. Moreover, if we judge *correctly,* we enhance our ability to allocate energy appropriately and effectively.

There is evidence that judgments about control do, in fact, relate to voluntary response initiation and to task persistence among adults and children (see, e.g., Bandura, 1977; Dweck, 1975; Lefcourt, 1976; Seligman, 1975). In addition, perceived control is sometimes found to be related to actual task effectiveness and school achievement (Lefcourt, 1976; Stipek & Weisz, 1981), sometimes to key attributional patterns (Dweck & Goetz, 1978; Harvey, 1981), and sometimes to affective states such as fear in infants (Gunnar, 1980; Gunnar-von Gnechten, 1978) and depression in adults (Abramson, Seligman, & Teasdale, 1978; Alloy & Abramson, 1979). The notion that a perceived *lack* of control can undermine motivation, perseverance, and performance quality is central to learned helplessness theory (Abramson et al., 1978; Seligman, 1975) and to self-efficacy theory (Bandura, 1977, 1981). Perceptions of control may also influence the course of intellectual development. In the "performance theory of cognitive development" being developed at the Max Planck Institute by Paul Baltes, Michael Chapman, and Ellen Skinner, control beliefs are seen as determinants of the use, and expansion, of intellectual competencies (Skinner & Chapman, 1983).

If judgments about control influence persistence, motivation, affective state, performance effectiveness, and possibly even aspects of cognitive development, it seems important to understand how those judgments are formed and how the processes involved differ over the course of development. This one objective guides much of the research that is discussed here. With this research, my colleagues and I hope to enhance our understanding of control judgments within the age range of about 5 years through young adulthood. Within this range, we are trying to answer such questions as, (1) How do people judge the degree of control that is possible in various situations? (2) How do the processes involved differ (and in what ways do they *not* differ) as a function of developmental level? and (3) How do these judgmental processes relate to beliefs, affect and/or behavior in developmentally significant domains outside the realm of control per se? The research I present here deals primarily with questions 1 and 2, but includes some preliminary evidence bearing on question 3.

DEFINING CONTROL

At this point, we need to define control—a risky enterprise, since any definition is likely to collide with someone's theory. Nonetheless, we will work from the following provisional attempt: Control means causing an intended event. Working from this definition, if we are to judge an individual's capacity for control we must gauge that individual's capacity to cause an event consistent with his or her intentions. This seemingly simple definition is designed to be at least roughly compatible with the perspectives of the Max Planck group (Skinner & Chapman, 1983), self-efficacy theory (Bandura, 1981), and the reformulated version of learned helplessness theory (Abramson et al., 1978). Implicit within the definition are two important distinctions. First, control is distinguished from the likelihood of an intended event. An intended event may or may not be likely, quite independently of whether the individual plays a causal role; in the absence of a causal role, the individual does not exert control, even if the outcome eventually experienced is precisely what the individual intended. This brings us to a second distinction: Causality alone is also not control. Most "locus of control" questionnaires for adults and children focus in part or in full on judgments about the causality of events. In most such questionnaires, a judgment that one is the cause of unintended or undesirable outcomes (as well as intended or desirable outcomes) is classified as a sign of "internal" or "personal" control. As Figure 9.1

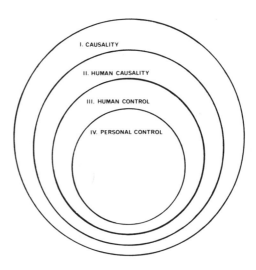

FIG. 9.1.   Some levels of causality. I. Caused events. II. Events subject to human agency. III. Events subject to human agency consistent with intent. IV. Events subject to personal agency consistent with intent.

suggests, this classification would not be consistent with the present definition of personal control.

The figure depicts four classes of events within the domain of causality. Class I, *caused events,* is the most general. It may include all events in the natural world; whether we believe that this is the case depends on whether we believe that some events can be random in the sense of being "uncaused."[1] Regardless of our position on this philosophical issue, it seems clear that Class I represents a very large domain of events. A subset of the events within Class I is designated as Class II: events that can be caused (in full or in part) by at least some people. Events fall within Class II if they are subject to human agency and regardless of whether they can be made to occur in harmony with people's intentions. Thus, a coin toss falls within Class II because it is subject to human causality, even though people cannot cause the event (heads or tails) to occur in an intended direction. Those events that can be caused (in full or in part) by at least some people in an intended direction qualify for Class III: Human control. Of course, not all events that are subject to human control in this sense can be caused by a given individual in harmony with that individual's intent. Events which can be influenced by the individual in this way fall within Class IV: Events subject to the personal control of the individual. Thus, according to this pictorial model and our provisional definition, causality does not necessarily imply control, but control does imply causality of a certain type, that is, the capacity to cause events consistent with one's intentions.[2]

Lay Definitions—Talking to Children About Control

So much for the academician's definition of control. What do real people, especially real children, in the real world have to say about control and what it is? How do they construe it? What examples of it come to mind? Do their answers resemble the definition given above? Perhaps more importantly, do children have any concept of control that they can verbalize? At this point, I cannot offer any very definitive answer, but I can convey something of the flavor of what we are finding in ongoing interviews with 5- to 13-year-olds. The interviews involve

---

[1]Later in this paper, when I refer to "random" events as being "noncontingent," I am not endorsing indeterminism. I am not arguing that such events as weather and the outcome of a coin toss are noncontingent in the sense of being "uncaused." Instead, the argument is that we are not likely to know enough about the causal forces involved in such events to render them predictable or to influence them in an intended direction. In other words, such events are considered noncontingent in an epistemological sense—i.e., they are events determined by causal patterns that are, for us, unknowable.

[2]The present definitions of (and conceptual distinctions among) contingency, competence, and control, differ slightly from those I have used previously. The changes reflect continuing efforts to (1) refine my own thinking about these matters, and (2) use language as harmonious as possible with that of other investigators in the area.

eight different ways of asking for definitions and examples of control. Among the younger children, as expected, we get a substantial number of "I don't knows," and a good deal of silence; but most of the children, even at age 5 and 6, answer at least one or two of our queries in a meaningful way. The answers convey a certain "gestalt" with respect to children's everyday notions about control. Rather than summarize via means, I will quote representative answers from some of our youngest interviewees, then some of our older ones.

> *#1—Girl, aged 5:* "Like when you're going fast and you pull over to control your bike."
> *#2—Boy, aged 5:* "When you drive a car, pushing on the gas pedal."
> *#3—Boy, aged 5:* "Control is when you control your arms."
> *#4—Girl, aged 6:* "Something you can do whatever you want with."
> *#5—Girl, aged 6:* "When you're mad at somebody and you don't hit them. If they punch you then you say don't do that and you don't punch them back. You control yourself."
> *#6—Boy, aged 6:* "When you're steering a car or a motorcycle, by your hands."
> *#7—Boy, aged 10:* "Like my sister; she was acting wild when I was the babysitter, and I had to get her under control."
> *#8—Boy, aged 10:* "Power; you have power, like if you're in control of a plane."
> *#9—Boy, aged 13:* "Being able to take charge of a situation."
> *#10—Boy, aged 13:* "When you make something turn out the way you want it to."

Of course, I saved #10 for last, because this 13-year-old's definition conforms so nicely to our provisional definition; it involves the two key concepts of causality and intentionality, and it is worded very much like our own definition. The other definitions and examples are useful in rounding out the picture of how children construe control. First, they suggest that "control" is not some foreign notion that is too abstract or remote to have any meaning for children. Instead, most of the children we have interviewed—even the 5- and 6-year-olds—do have *some* idea of what the term means and many make at least a rough approach to the notion that control means causing intended events. The responses quoted above and the other answers we have received seem to focus especially on three uses of the term: control over inanimate objects such as machines (see #1, 2, 6, and 8), interpersonal control (see #3 and 5), and self-control (see #6). It is not difficult to imagine the kinds of scenarios that may have familiarized our young interviewees with these uses of the term; it is especially easy to imagine parental urgings toward greater self-control—as in the case of child #3, whose arms may well have caused him trouble. Regardless of how these children developed their concepts and examples, it does appear that the notion of control, in some construction or other, has made its way into their lives.

METHODOLOGICAL EMPHASES

Generalized versus Situation-Specific Control

By asking our young subjects to focus on specific examples of control, we reveal an emphasis that should be made explicit. Some researchers study control in a relatively global, trans-situational sense, while others take a more situation-specific approach. These two approaches are best construed as poles marking a continuum. At the general end lies research in which people's estimates of control are assessed via (a) such broad questions as whether their lives are working out the way they want (Lachman, 1985), or (b) summary scores such as those generated by most locus of control questionnaires. At the situation-specific end of the continuum lies research in which people are asked to confine their control judgments to one specific activity or outcome (e.g., Alloy & Abramson, 1979). In general, the research we discuss here ranges from highly- to moderately-situation-specific in its orientation. We will focus primarily on studies of control judgments in narrowly circumscribed situations, and secondarily on control judgments with respect to such moderately restricted domains as school performance. We will not be dealing with constructs so broad as locus of control or a "sense of control over one's life."

Phenomenological versus Objective Assessment

The research to be reviewed here also takes a position on a second methodological continuum: phenomenological versus objective. The phenomenological approach (see Peterson, 1980) can be traced at least as far back as Lewin's (1951) field theory and Heider's (1958) not-so-naive "naive" psychology. The perspective emphasizes subjective, psychological reality and the question, "What does the individual perceive to be true." From the phenomenological perspective, what the person perceives to be true *is* reality for that person. The question of whether the individual's perception accords with some more objective, external reality is not necessarily regarded as irrelevant; but the individual's phenomenology has center stage, with primary attention directed to the subjective perceptions, how they are formed, and what they correlate with in the individual's life. Perhaps the most familiar example of this approach is locus of control theory and the cascade of research on "internality," "externality," and the correlates thereof (e.g., Lefcourt, 1976; Rotter, 1966). In fact, many of the life outcomes mentioned in locus of control scales involve such an uncomputable blend of personal and external causation that perceptions of control could not fairly be tested for accuracy anyway. For these situations, since they do not permit precise analysis of an individual's "true" control, the phenomenological approach makes perfectly good sense.

A contrasting approach to the study of control has been labeled the objective orientation (Peterson, 1980). Researchers who adopt this orientation, focus, of necessity, on situations and events for which actual control can be assessed to some reasonable approximation. The intent is usually to probe for errors and/or gauge accuracy of control judgments. Events that are more or less purely chance-controlled or purely skill-controlled may be studied within this orientation (e.g., Ayerhoff & Abelson, 1976; Langer, 1975). Or investigators may design situations in which they can calibrate the degree of control their subjects have (e.g., Alloy & Abramson, 1979).

Much of the research that we examine here is focused on errors and their implications—on questions of veridicality in control judgments. This research obviously tackles the problem of control from the objective end of the phenomenological-objective continuum. Other research that we will discuss deals with situations in which actual control is difficult to gauge with precision; this research is somewhat more phenomenological in tone, but even it tends to assume a certain "appropriate strategy" for gauging control. So the overall approach adopted here could be described as leaning toward the objective pole of the continuum.

HOW TO MAKE A VERIDICAL CONTROL JUDGMENT

If we are to emphasize relatively situation-specific judgments about control and concern ourselves with their veridicality, we need to pose a key question from the outset: How can people accurately assess their capacity to control specific events? We can draw a few suggestions from the model shown in Figure 9.1.

Contingency

Events lying outside Class III in Fig. 9.1 can be regarded as inherently uncontrollable. Our shorthand for such events will be the term *noncontingent*. Accurately judging the contingency of a target event can enhance one's ability to make a veridical control judgment. Contingency judgments may involve not only the gross distinction between totally noncontingent events (e.g., a snowstorm, in Class I, or a roll of the dice, in Class II) and those subject to some human influence, but also more refined distinctions among various levels of contingency. These more refined distinctions need to be made, of course, because within the realm of contingent outcomes the *degree* of contingency can vary widely, for example, from the extremely low level at which presidential election outcomes are contingent on each individual voter's behavior, to the extremely high level at which the volume of a stereo is contingent on the behavior of the individual whose hand is on the control knob. To make matters slightly more complex, we must note that outcomes which are highly contingent on the behavior and attributes of some people may not be equally contingent for all people. For example, employment interviews where the interviewers are biased may be highly contingent for certain racial or gender groups but not for others. For this reason, we need to introduce the term *relevant people* into our thinking about contingency. We may thus define contingency as the degree to which an event can be controlled (i.e., causally influenced in an intended direction) by variations in the behavior or attributes of relevant people.

Competence

Although event contingency has sometimes been treated as virtually synonymous with control in the psychological literature, Figure 9.1 suggests that an additional factor may need to be considered before an individual's level of control can be gauged accurately. We will label that factor *competence,* and we will define it as the individual's capacity to manifest the attributes or behavior on which the intended event is contingent. For events that are completely noncontingent, competence plays no role; one cannot be competent at, say, roulette or weather. However, for events that involve some degree of contingency, an individual's level of competence with respect to relevant attributes or behavior will determine whether the event also lies within Class IV (Fig. 9.1), and if so, the degree to which personal control can be manifest. (Whether the individual *will* exert control, and whether the individual experiences a subjective perception of control, depends also upon the individual's probability of action, which may involve questions of motivation and values [Skinner, 1985]; but these matters will not concern us here, since our discussion is focused on the individual's *capacity* to exert control.)

The Interplay of Contingency and Competence

I am suggesting (building on an earlier analysis, in Weisz & Stipek, 1982) that contingency and competence both need to be assessed if we are to accurately judge an individual's capacity to exert control. To illustrate how each factor sets limits on the impact of the other, let us consider the matter of journal reviews. Suppose that a prestigious journal in a prominent field—say, child development—has a new editor. Let us further suppose that this individual, widely reputed to be fair-minded, selects associate editors who are fair and even-handed, and that together they select consulting editors and ad hoc reviewers who are good judges of what merits publication. Publication in this journal will thus be highly contingent on characteristics of the individual authors' behavior as investigators and writers. However, this high level of contingency may or may not mean that a particular author will have a high level of control over publication in the journal. The degree to which an individual can exert control here will depend on his or her competence to do the kinds of research and writing on which publication is contingent. Now suppose that, years from now, there is a transition to a less fair-minded and less careful editorial team, with the effect that publication is less contingent upon the quality of research and writing than was previously the case. This will mean a net reduction in the individual's prospects for control, even though that individual's competence has remained unchanged; whatever the individual's competencies as researcher and writer, those competencies will be less relevant to publication than before. In this example and elsewhere, the relationship between contingency and competence can be described as follows: Contingency defines the relevance of attributes and behavior to an intended event, and competence defines the degree to which the individual can manifest the relevant attributes and behavior. Control is thus construed as a joint function of contingency and competence (the nature of this "joint function" will be discussed in a later section). An accurate judgment about an individual's capacity to control an event is thus thought to depend on accurate assessments of, (a) the contingency of that event, and (b) the competence of the individual.

Kindred Notions from Control Theorists

The notion that two factors such as contingency and competence are relevant to control may represent a sort of rough synthesis of several theoretical perspectives. Some of these perspectives are identified in Table 9.1. The first entry in the table comes from Virginia Crandall (1971). She has argued that certain items on children's locus of control scales make it impossible to know why children respond "externally." A child, she notes, who indicates that he cannot prevent an adverse outcome from occurring may do so because, "he feels incompetent to prevent failure" (i.e., low competence) or because, "he sees no relationship

TABLE 9.1
Conceptual Distinctions Similar to Contingency - Competence

Control Theorists:	Contingency-Related Concepts	Competence-Related Concepts
1. Crandall (1971)	Relationship between own behavior and unpleasant event	Competence to prevent failure
2. Bandura (1977)	Responsiveness of the environment	Efficacy in achieving the required behavior
3. Abramson, Seligman, & Teasdale (1978)	Universal helplessness-- i.e., no one's responses can produce the desired outcome	Personal helplessness-- i.e., others can generate the response needed to produce the desired outcome, but I cannot
4. Gurin (1980)	Environmental responsiveness	Personal competence
5. Brim (1980)	Action-outcome expectancy	Sense of self-confidence
6. Skinner & Chapman (1983)	Causality beliefs	Agency beliefs

between his own behavior and that unpleasant event" (Crandall, 1971, p. 5; i.e., resembling our notion of low or no contingency).

The other entries in the table reflect distinctions that bear at least a rough similarity to Crandall's. For example, Bandura (1977), in proposing his "self-efficacy theory," noted that people may feel a sense of futility and quit trying to exert control, for either of the following reasons: (a) "because they lack a sense of efficacy in achieving the required behavior" (p. 204; from the present perspective, this perception could be described as one of low competence), or (2) "they may be assured of their capabilities but give up trying because they expect their behavior to have no effect on an unresponsive environment or to be consistently punished" (p. 204–205; from the present perspective, this perception resembles one of low or no contingency). Abramson et al. (1978), in their reformulated learned helplessness theory, propose a distinction between *personal helplessness* and *universal helplessness*. Individuals suffering from personal helplessness are said to believe that no response in their repertoire can produce the desired outcome, but that "a relevant other" could generate a response that would produce the outcome; from the present perspective, this set of beliefs seems to involve a low level of personal competence relative to others. Individuals suffering from universal helplessness, by contrast, are said to believe that the desired outcome is not contingent on any response that they can generate, or on any response "in the repertoire of any relevant other" (Abramson et al., p. 53; from the present perspective, this belief seems to involve a low level of event contingency). Another entry in the table is from Gurin (1980), who (building on earlier factor analytic work by Gurin, Gurin, Lao, & Beattie, 1969) has criticized Rotter's I-E scale for allegedly confounding "personal competence" and "environmental responsiveness" (p. 8). Brim (1980) has underscored the importance of distinguishing between "one's sense of self-confidence" and "the action-outcome expectancy" (p. 4). Finally, Skinner and Chapman (1983) have argued that beliefs that one can control an outcome "imply (a) causality beliefs of the form, Condition Y results in outcome X, and (b) agency beliefs of the form, 'I have or can produce condition Y.'" (p. 3). Skinner and Chapman identify their notions of causality and agency beliefs as "similar in most respects" to the present notions of contingency and competence beliefs, respectively.

Certainly, none of the contrasts suggested by these several control theorists maps perfectly onto the present distinction between contingency and competence. However, the *rough* convergence of these various perspectives is worth noting. It does suggest that a number of people who have thought about these matters believe that an understanding of control will require an understanding of, (1) the susceptibility of intended events to human influence and (2) the capacity of the individual to manifest the forms of human influence that are relevant. Are these two general notions best captured by the concepts of contingency and competence as defined here? In the long run, perhaps not. However, I believe that the processes of contingency judgment and competence judgment are useful topics for study in their own right, particularly from a developmental perspective. And it does seem likely that studying these processes and their correlates, together with the ways people *use* contingency and competence information, can add something to our understanding of how people reason about control.

A RESEARCH AGENDA

Working from this perspective, several of us have been conducting research, and surveying the research of other groups, that seems to have a bearing on the developing person's developing understanding of control. Thus far, we have focused on the early elementary through young adult years, and we have attended to three separable cognitive processes:

1. *Contingency judgment.* Judging the degree to which intended events are contingent upon variations in people's attributes and behavior.
2. *Competence judgment.* Judging the capacity of individuals to manifest attributes or behaviors on which intended outcomes are contingent.
3. *Integrating contingency and competence information.* Combining information about outcome contingency and personal competence in a manner that leads to judgments about control.

Research on the development of these three processes is still in progress. What I can do here is convey the flavor of the few studies done to date, and some of the thinking underlying, and provoked by, those studies.

DEVELOPMENT OF CONTINGENCY JUDGMENT

In studying contingency judgment it is possible to focus on circumstances in which a variety of animate or situational factors limit actual contingency (e.g., Alloy & Abramson, 1979) or on conditions in which actual contingency is limited by chance or random factors (e.g., Langer, 1975). We have recently begun research in the first category, but the work I would like to discuss here deals with the second—specifically, noncontingency due to chance. It is this latter category within which our research began. Our thinking about chance-based noncontingency profited considerably from the theoretical work of Piaget and his colleagues, particularly Barbel Inhelder (see, e.g., Piaget, 1930; Piaget & Inhelder, 1975). Their account depicts development as partly a process of dispensing with exaggerated perceptions of contingency. One of the central themes is that children come to understand the noncontingency of chance events only by comparing them with events that are non-random. Non-random events entail causal sequences that are logically reversible; this is true of motor actions such as opening a door, and of mental operations such as adding 3 to 5. The outcome of, say, a coin toss, by contrast, involves such complex and inscrutable causal patterns that it is not logically reversible, and adults therefore regard it as chance, noncontingent.

To understand nonreversibility as a defining characteristic of noncontingent events requires, first, a grasp of reversibility, which, according to Piaget and Inhelder, does not emerge until middle childhood (concrete operations). Prior to this time, children are in Stage 1 of the Piaget-Inhelder model, unable to distinguish between contingent and noncontingent events. They manifest "phenomenalism," the vague perception that events which are temporally proximate are causally linked, and they manifest "efficacy" or "dynamism," which Flavell (1963) defines as, "a dim sense that the inchoate feelings of effort, longing, etc., which saturate one's actions are somehow responsible for external happenings" (p. 142).

In Stage 2 of the Piaget-Inhelder framework, children come to compare reversible and nonreversible operations and thus grow to appreciate the "differentness" of chance events. These children can distinguish, in a gross way, between contingent events and events that are noncontingent due to chance. However, children at this level are not able to generate predictions about or interpretations of noncontingent events that require probabilistic thought. Such thought is said to develop in Stage 3, roughly coincident with the formal operations stage; it then becomes possible not only to recognize the noncontingency of chance events, but also to reason in terms of combinations and permutations, and to make accurate interpretations and logically appropriate predictions regarding such events. Experiments bearing on Piaget and Inhelder's notions have dealt primarily with probability concepts (e.g., Fischbein, 1975; Piaget & Inhelder, 1975). However, the Piagetian theorizing also seems related to the subject of interest here: age differences in judgments about contingency between intended events on the one hand, and variations in people's attributes and behavior, on the other (see a relevant review by Sedlack & Kurtz, 1981).

Focusing our initial research on children's judgments about chance events offered two advantages appropriate to the initial stages of research on contingency judgment. First, Piaget and Inhelder's work afforded a theoretically rich framework within which to think about our data. Second, chance events, unlike most non-chance events, involve a stable, knowable level of contingency—that is, zero; thus, when people make judgments about such events we can evaluate the accuracy of their judgments.

Study 1: Contingency Judgments in the Laboratory

The initial study (Weisz, 1980) was designed to meet two objectives: (a) to test a procedure designed for the assessment of contingency judgments in young children, and (b) to probe for preliminary evidence of the kinds of developmental differences suggested by the Piagetian literature. The procedure was simple. Kindergarteners and fourth-graders played a game of chance. Afterward, they were asked questions about the game that were intended to reveal perceptions of contingency or noncontingency.

Procedure. Each child was shown 20 white cards, each with either a blue spot or a yellow spot on one side. The child then counted out five yellows and five blues, turned them all over, and mixed them up thoroughly. Asked how many yellows and how many blues were in the newly mixed deck, all the children answered correctly. The experimenter then lined up five poker chips in front of the child, and the two played a game with the following rule: The child drew a card from the deck, held face-down by the experimenter, and if the child drew one with a yellow spot (blue for half the children), he or she won a chip (chips were exchanged for prizes later). There were five rounds of this game. After each of the five draws made by the child, the card drawn was returned to the deck, the deck was reshuffled, and it was placed in an open briefcase just out of the child's line of vision. (This allowed the experimenter to control winnings, by surreptitiously using two decks, one with all yellow spots and the other with all blue. The procedure was evidently undetectable; there were no signs of suspicion.) Half of the children at each grade level won four chips out of the five tries; and the other half won only one chip. This variation was introduced to probe for signs of self-serving bias in children's contingency judgments (discussed below).

How children explained outcomes. After their five draws, children were asked some open-ended questions. The experimenter asked what she should say to a child who, "asked me how to be *sure* to pick the right card *every* time." The experimenter also described what had happened when two other (fictitious) children played the game; one of the children, she said, "didn't win even one chip," and the other child "won five chips—he/she got the right color every time." After each account, the child was asked to explain why that particular outcome might have occurred. Answers to the three open-ended questions were categorized by raters as either not codable (e.g., no answer), or as reflecting perceived noncontingency (e.g., "It's just luck," "It just happens—no reason," in response to the last two questions) or perceived contingency (e.g., "He wasn't paying attention," or "She tried real hard").

On all three questions, there were more "not codable" responses among the younger children than among the older ones. Thus, I have limited confidence in the findings obtained. However, the findings are suggestive. Although the first question did not yield any significant grade level differences, the two questions calling for an explanation of very high and very low winnings yielded highly significant effects. As Table 9.2 shows, not one kindergartner gave a noncon-

TABLE 9.2
Perceived Contingency and Noncontingency on Two Minimally Structured Questions

Question A: Why did a (fictitious) child pick the wrong color every time?

	Kindergarteners	Fourth-Graders
Perceived noncontingency	0	11
Perceived contingency	9	6

Question B: Why did a (fictitious) child pick the right color every time?

	Kindergartners	Fourth-Graders
Perceived noncontingency	0	15
Perceived contingency	12	3

Note: For both tables, $p < .01$ (two-tailed Fisher exact tests). From Weisz (1980).
Copyright (1980) by the American Psychological Association. Reproduced by permission.

tingency response to either question; yet, a majority of fourth-graders gave noncontingency responses to both questions. This pattern seems consistent with Piaget and Inhelder's notion that by middle childhood boys and girls can make at least a gross identification of chance outcomes as noncontingent, but that in early childhood they cannot.

How children predicted future outcomes.   The experimenter also probed for contingency judgments in a more structured way than with the open-ended questions. In structuring these probes, we relied on a defining property of contingent outcomes, that is, they are influenced by variations in people's behavior and attributes. To assess the judged impact of such variations on these noncontingent outcomes the experimenter asked the children to make predictions. She lined up rows of five chips in front of the child and asked the child to show how many chips out of five the following groups and individuals would win if they were to play the same card game the child had just completed:

1. "Most kids older than you."
2. "Most kids younger than you."
3. A child "who got to practice lots of times before trying to win chips."
4. A child "who didn't get to practice picking the cards at all."
5. A child who "was very careful and tried very hard to pick the yellow (blue) cards and win chips."
6. A child who "didn't try very hard at all—he/she picked cards very quickly and did not seem to care what color he/she got."
7. A child who "was very smart."
8. A child who "was not very smart."

The children's predictions were analyzed in pairs that formed logical counterparts. Questions 1 and 2 (older vs. younger) were analyzed together, as were questions 3 and 4, 5 and 6, and 7 and 8. To interpret the predictions, we relied on the inferential process illustrated in Fig. 9.2. The figure shows prediction patterns that reflect perceived noncontingency with respect to questions 3 and 4 (i.e., practice vs. no-practice); it is a way of plotting predictions bearing on the maxim, "practice makes perfect." People who believe that outcomes (say, winnings in the card game of Study 1) are influenced by such behavior as practice, should make predictions that fall somewhere off the diagonal. In other words, off-diagonal predictions should reflect a judgment that the outcomes are contingent on variations in practice. By contrast, predictions that fall on the diagonal should be made by people who believe that practice does *not* make perfect, nor does it matter in the least. I should emphasize that this strategy for tapping contingency judgments was designed to take as sophisticated a form as we thought very young children could comprehend. Investigators such as Shaklee and Mims (1981), working with children somewhat older than our youngest age group, have studied a relatively complex array of strategies for

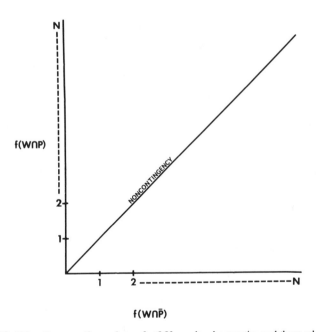

f(W∩P̄)

FIG. 9.2. Does practice make perfect? If people who practice and those who do not, have equal opportunity to win, the judged contingency of outcomes on practice can be inferred from predictions for the two groups. If the predicted frequency of winning with practice [f(W∩P)] is identical to the predicted frequency of winning without practice [f(W∩P̄)], then a judgment of noncontingency can be inferred. Other prediction patterns (i.e., off-diagonal predictions) imply judged contingency.

TABLE 9.3
Does Practice Make Perfect? A Conjoint Information Approach to Contingency Judgment

		Win W		Lose $\bar{W}$
Practice [P]	a.	$f(P \Omega W)$	b.	$f(P \Omega \bar{W})$
No Practice [$\bar{P}$]	c.	$f(\bar{P} \Omega W)$	d.	$f(\bar{P} \Omega \bar{W})$

Where, a. $P \Omega W$ = People who practice win
      b. $P \Omega \bar{W}$ = People who practice lose
      c. $\bar{P} \Omega W$ = People who do not practice win
      d. $\bar{P} \Omega \bar{W}$ = People who do not practice do not win

Four ways of judging contingency

Strategy 1.	"Cell a only":	$f(P \Omega W)$
Strategy 2.	"Cell a vs. Cell b":	$f(P \Omega W)$ vs. $f(P \Omega \bar{W})$
Strategy 3.	"Sum of diagonals":	$[f(P \Omega W) + f(\bar{P} \Omega \bar{W})]$ vs. $[f(P \Omega \bar{W}) + f(\bar{P} \Omega W)]$
Strategy 4.	"Condit. probability":	$P(W/P)$ vs. $P(W/\bar{P})$

From Weisz, Yeates, Robertson, and Beckham (1982). Copyright (1982) by the American Psychological Association. Reprinted by permission of the publisher.

contingency (or "event covariation") judgment, as illustrated in Table 9.3. The approach we have used is less rich than the Shaklee-Mims approach in the information it yields but it appears to offer the special advantage of being understandable by very young children.

Prediction patterns for the questions about practice were similar to the patterns found for the age and intelligence questions. Overall, our young subjects expected older, more practiced and more intelligent children to win more chips than their younger, less practiced, and less intelligent counterparts. However, when we followed up on a significant interaction involving grade level, we found that only the kindergarteners passed Tukey's test for statistically significant differences. In other words, kindergarteners' expected outcomes on the card game showed very strong effects of age, practice, and intelligence, but fourth-graders' expected outcomes did not.

Children's predictions regarding the effects of effort did not show quite the same pattern. The relative sophistication shown by the fourth-graders on the other questions eroded quickly when they were confronted with the stark contrast between a child who tried hard and a child who not only did not try hard but did not even seem to care. On this pair of questions, both groups judged outcomes to be highly contingent on effort.

The preceding analyses were focused on the magnitude and variance of the pairwise predictions. Table 9.4 presents a somewhat different perspective on the same data. The table shows the number at each grade level who predicted some difference versus no difference as a function of age, practice, effort, and intelligence. Predictions of no-difference (i.e., on-diagonal predictions), of course, should be made by people who fully understand the noncontingency of the outcomes. As Table 9.4 suggests, most fourth-graders, like most kindergarteners, were unwilling to take their reasoning quite this far. A number of fourth-

TABLE 9.4
Number of Children Making Various Contingency Judgments

Contingency-Related Factor	Grade Level[a]	Predicted Winnings Compared	
		Different	Same
Age (older vs. younger child)	K	20	2
	4	14	9
Practice (child with practice vs. child without practice)	K	22	0
	4	18	5
Intelligence (smart vs. not smart)	K	22	0
	4	15	8
Effort (try hard vs. not try)	K	20	2
	4	22	1

[a]The only significant grade effect was on intelligence x^2 (1) = 7.08, $p < .01$. From Weisz (1980). Copyright (1980) by the American Psychological Association. Reprinted by permission of the publisher.

graders did show these logically appropriate predictions, and most fourth-graders predicted *smaller* differences than did kindergarteners; but the fact remains that most fourth-graders judged that there would be *some* difference in outcome as a function of age, practice, intelligence, and effort.

A particularly interesting subgroup of the sample were those children who had explicitly identified outcomes on the card games as luck- or chance-determined. The 17 children who had made such statements on at least one of the minimally structured questions described earlier would seem to be a step ahead of the remaining youngsters. However, even these more ''enlightened'' children made predictions suggesting contingency. Of the 17, only one went on to predict precisely equal winnings in each group of the four pairwise comparisons. Six of the children made the perceived contingency error (i.e., off-diagonal predictions) on all four of the pairwise comparisons; four made the error on three comparisons, three made the error twice, and one made the error once. These children were fourth-graders; they were thus at an age appropriate to what Piaget and Inhelder (1975) designated as Stage 2 in the developmental framework discussed above. At this level, they described children as being capable of gross qualitative distinctions between chance and non-chance outcomes, but not of precise probabilistic predictions based on the noncontingency of chance. These findings are reminiscent of that notion. Here, 16 of 17 children who could identify the outcomes as being determined by chance or luck failed at least once to make predictions that followed logically from that identification.

Self-serving biases?   I noted earlier that half the children in each age group won four chips out of five tries, while the other half won only one chip, and that this variation was introduced to probe for signs of self-serving bias in children's judgments. There is considerable evidence of such biases in adults' judgments (see Greenwald, 1980). For example, adults are more likely to judge that outcomes are contingent on their behavior when the outcomes are desirable (e.g., high winnings) than when the outcomes are undesirable (e.g., low winnings). By introducing high and low winnings into our procedure, it was possible to test for preliminary evidence of judgmental differences in children as a function of outcome valence. The study revealed glimmers of such effects, but nothing dramatic. When explaining the outcomes of the hypothetical child who won no chips, those children in the sample who had won only one chip were marginally more likely than the four-chip children to use noncontingency explanations; that is, children who had higher winnings perceived higher levels of contingency. In addition, when predicting outcomes for a child who had practiced and one who had not, kindergarteners who had won only one chip predicted larger differences than the four-chip children. Perceived effects of practice were thus greatest among those who had had no practice and had done poorly, that is, the group for whom lack of practice might be used to conveniently explain away low winnings. Overall, the evidence of self-serving bias was modest and was confined largely to kindergarteners, the group whose understanding of noncontingency was weakest.

Contingency errors and just world beliefs.   The study included one attempt to determine whether children's judgments in our laboratory task were related in any way to their judgments about real life events. A few weeks after the laboratory task, children were interviewed by a second experimenter who administered a "Just World Questionnarie." The questionnaire was patterned after one developed by Rubin and Peplau (1975); it was designed to yield an index of the degree to which children perceived events in the world, both good and bad, as contingent upon the behavior of the people who experienced those events, that is, with good behavior leading to good outcomes and bad behavior leading to bad outcomes. Half the questions were keyed so that a yes implied high contingency (e.g., "Do good things usually happen to good people?"); half the items were keyed in the reverse direction (e.g., "Do robbers often steal things without getting caught?"). Considerable variability, and an interesting correlational pattern was found among the fourth-graders. The questionnaire yielded a total score for perceived contingency in the form of just world beliefs. We computed a companion score for perceived contingency on the laboratory task by summing the differences across the four pairwise predictions—that is, the difference between a child's perception for an older versus younger child, added to the difference between a practiced versus unpracticed child, and so forth. Among kindergarteners, virtually all of whom perceived the laboratory task as highly contingent, the laboratory and just world contingency scores correlated .24 (*n.s.*); but among fourth-graders, who showed much greater variability in their judgments on the card task, the two contingency scores correlated .61. Among this group, perceived contingency on our laboratory task evidently bore a strong relationship to perceived contingency in the real world.

Overall, the results suggested that these youngsters in middle and early childhood, respectively, did differ in their judgments about the noncontingent card game outcomes. Kindergarteners appeared to believe strongly that outcomes on this guessing game were highly contingent on the behavior and characteristics of the individuals who played it. Fourth-graders were able to identify the outcomes as noncontingent when we asked them for causal explanations, but they showed significant lapses in two respects. First, they seemed to believe as strongly as did the kindergarteners that variations in effort would influence outcomes. Second, most of them incorrectly predicted that variations in age, practice, and intelligence, would have at least a slight influence on outcomes. The overall pattern seemed to suggest a sort of illusory contingency, pronounced at the kindergarten level, and still lingering in milder forms in the fourth grade.

Study 2: Illusory Contingency at the State Fair

This first study was limited in its implications, for a number of reasons. One of the most important was that it relied on a single laboratory task designed specifically to make the chance-controlled nature of outcomes as self-evident as possible. There are many naturally occurring noncontingent outcomes in the real world which are not so designed; these may well evoke quite different reactions from children than those we witnessed. It seemed useful to try to determine whether the developmental pattern seen in Study 1 was confined to such specially simplified laboratory tasks, or whether it might also be found in more naturally occurring settings. For this reason, the second study in the contingency series (Weisz, 1981) was focused on questions like those of Study 1, but set in a revved-up, cacophonous world where illusions are actively promoted: the North Carolina State Fair.

Interviewers lurked near games of chance along the state fair midway. They found such purely chance-determined games as an electronic horse race on which participants placed bets, and a giant dice throw in which the object was to make a die face of a certain color end up on top. As children completed the games and turned to reenter the midway, they were approached and questioned by our interviewers, provided they and their parents gave consent. Children were first asked whether they had won the prize they wanted or not. Then they were asked "Why do you think it turned out that way?" "What caused you *to win/not to win* the prize you wanted?" and "How good are you at (name of the chance activity) compared to most other kids your age?" Children were also asked to make predictions like those in the previous study. To give the child practice at making predictions, the interviewer held up five fingers and said "Suppose you were to try (*the chance activity*) five times. How many times do you think you would win the prize you want?" Using the same procedure, the child was asked to predict the winnings (out of five tries) of (a) a first-grader and a tenth-grader, (b) a "smart kid" and a "kid who is not very smart," (c) one who "tried really hard and really concentrated" and one who "hardly tried at all and didn't even pay much attention to the game," and (d) one who "got to practice all he/she wanted" and one who "did not get to practice at all."

One of the most upsetting things about our work on the midway was the absence of very young children. They may have been at the fair, but they stayed away from the chance activities in droves. When families appeared, it was usually the parents who actually participated, as if outcomes in these chance activities were contingent on age. A few children younger than six did try chance games, and their parents did give consent; but these children either proved unable to concentrate over the din of the midway, or unable to comprehend the content of the interviews. Consequently, our sample ranged in age from 6 to 14 years. A division at the median formed age groups of 6 through 10, and 11 through 14. Thus, the younger age group in this second study incorporates the ages of the older group in Study 1. This fact should be borne in mind as we turn to the results.

How children explained their outcomes.   The first analysis focused on children's answers to the question about why they had won or failed to win the prize they wanted. The answers were coded as reflecting perceived contingency (e.g., "I'm not that good at the games because I don't play them much"), noncontingency (e.g., "Just luck"), or not codable, using procedures like those of Study 1. We found significant age group differences, with a majority of the younger group giving perceived contingency answers and a majority of the older group giving noncontingency answers. All of the children in the younger group who identified their outcome as noncontingent were older than eight.

How children compared themselves to others.   Children had been asked how good they were at the chance game compared to other kids their age. The intent was to see how often they would rate themselves "the same as other kids" (a noncontingency judgment) or better or worse (contingency judgments, since one can only be better or worse than others on a contingent task). The answers did not differ as a function of age group; only a minority of younger (30%) and older (39%) children answered correctly that they were the same as their peers in ability at the task.

How children predicted future outcomes.   Children's predictions for hypothetical others were analyzed like the predictions in Study 1. Group means relevant to these analyses are shown in Table 9.5. The predictions of the younger group showed "honestly significant differences" as a function of grade level, intelligence, effort, and practice, whereas the predictions of the older group did not show significant differences on any of the four pairwise predictions.

TABLE 9.5
Predicted Winnings on Children's Paired Prediction Questions

	Grade 10	Grade 1	Smart	Not Smart	Try	Not Try	Practice	No Practice
Children aged 6–10	3.16	1.58	3.25	1.61	3.30	1.09	3.78	1.54
Children aged 11–14	2.23	1.55	1.88	1.59	2.18	1.18	2.43	1.55
Children who lost	2.49	1.49	2.52	1.67	2.16	1.40	2.88	1.42
Children who won	2.91	1.64	2.48	1.53	3.31	.87	3.32	1.68

Characteristics of Hypothetical Child

From Weisz (1981). Copyright (1981) by the American Psychological Association. Reprinted by permission of the publisher.

Another aspect of the data in Table 9.5 may be conceptually significant: the differential impact of grade, intelligence, effort, and practice on the predictions of the two age groups resulted almost entirely from age group differences in predictions for the higher levels of the four characteristics; that is, older and younger children differed significantly in their predictions for hypothetical others who were in the tenth grade, were intelligent, tried hard, and had practiced; but there were no age group differences in predictions for hypothetical others who were in the first grade, were not very smart, did not try hard, or had not practiced. What might this mean? One possibility is that children across a fairly broad age range assume that there are certain baselines for outcomes even under conditions of low ability, low effort, and so forth; that is, that no matter how low in age, intelligence, effort, and experience, children may sink, they are still expected to win at certain minimal levels. The impact of developmental change, according to this reasoning, would be seen primarily in the judgments children make about hypothetical others who are not covered by this baseline assumption, that is, children who are above minimal levels of age, intelligence, and so forth. One hunch about this pattern that may be worth pursuing is that the ''baseline assumption'' is actually one part of a nascent chance concept; that is, chance may be partly construed as that invisible force which insures that even inept, inexperienced, and lazy people still win *something!*

As in Study 1, I looked for evidence of self-serving bias in the prediction data. This was done via a comparison of predictions made by children who had won the prize they wanted and children who had not. The two rows at the bottom of Table 9.5 show these data. Across the four pairs of predictions, only one—the try versus not-try predictions—differed significantly as a function of children's winnings. In essence, winning children saw effort as more influential in determining outcomes than did losing children.

Again, as in Study 1, I assessed the frequency of perfectly logical predictions—that is, the frequency with which children predicted the same winnings for hypothetical others of the first and tenth grade, others who tried hard and who did not, and so forth. As in Study 1, the frequency of such predictions was low, even though the mean age of the present sample was considerably higher than in the earlier study. As Table 9.6 shows, only in predictions about the first- versus

TABLE 9.6
Number of Children Making Various Contingency Judgments

Characteristics of Hypothetical Child	Age (in years)	Predicted Winnings		Significance Test
		Same	Different	
10th grade vs.	6-10	4	26	
1st grade	11-14	9	12	χ^2 (1) = 4.09*
Smart vs.	6-10	6	24	
not smart	11-14	5	16	χ^2 (1) < 1 (ns)
Try vs.	6-10	4	26	
not try	11-14	4	17	χ^2 (1) < 1 (ns)
Practice vs.	6-10	5	25	
no practice	11-14	5	16	χ^2 (1) < 1 (ns)

Note: The "Same" column shows the number of children who predicted that performance outcomes would be identical for a 1st and for a 10th grader, for a smart and for a not smart child, and so on. The "Different" column shows the number of children who predicted different outcomes for a 1st and for a 10th grader, and so forth. *$p < .05$. From Weisz (1981). Copyright (1981) by the American Psychological Association. Reprinted by permission of the publisher.

tenth-grader did our older group show significantly more sophistication than the younger group, and even there, a majority of the older group predicted different winnings for the two hypothetical children. Overall, the pattern shown in Table 9.6 suggests that the midway games were powerful in evoking at least *some* illusory contingency in most of the sample, young and old.

Another analysis probed whether this was the case for those "sophisticates" in our sample who had explicitly identified their outcomes as caused by "luck." By and large, the answer was yes. Of the 16 sophisticates, only five predicted precisely equal winnings in all four of the paired predictions. Of the remaining 11, one child made differential predictions once, three did so twice, and seven made differential predictions all four times. Some of the predictions made by these children were accompanied by comments that seemed revealing—comments that suggested an effort to grasp the noncontingent nature of luck. One child, for example, predicted no wins for the "not very smart" child, and one win for the smart child "if lucky." Another predicted five wins for the child with practice and two wins for the child with no practice, then added, "and *that* by luck only."

Overall, the findings seem to reveal age differences in understanding. However, the understanding achieved by even the older group must certainly be described as incomplete. Like many adults (cf. Abramson & Alloy, 1980; Langer, 1977), our mostly adolescent older group proved susceptible to a subtle form of illusory contingency: the belief that factors related to contingent outcomes (factors such as grade level, practice, etc.) will be associated with at least *slight* outcome differences. Attribution theorists should take note of the fact that even those youngsters explicitly attributing their outcomes to luck tended to make such contingency judgments. This suggests the possibility that children, unlike a number of attribution theorists (e.g., Weiner, 1979, and myself), may not really construe luck as an uncontrollable cause.

Study 3: Concurrent Predictions about Contingent and Noncontingent Outcomes

The prediction data of Studies 1 and 2 pose a significant problem of interpretation, one that we need to consider at this point. In both studies, older subjects predicted smaller differences as a function of grade level, practice, and so forth, than did younger subjects; this was interpreted as evidence that older subjects were less susceptible to illusory contingency. An alternative interpretation, though, is that older subjects may have simply been showing that they are more conservative predictors in general, that is, they may anticipate smaller effects of grade level, practice, and the like, than do younger children, regardless of whether the target activity is a chance or skill task. In other words, the age differences found in Studies 1 and 2 might be attributable to differences in predictive style. A third study (Weisz, Yeates, Robertson, & Beckham, 1982) was conducted to explore this possibility.

We asked people at four levels of maturity (kindergarten, fourth grade, eighth grade, and college) to make contingency judgments like those of Studies 1 and 2, but this time for both chance and skill outcomes. Our reasoning was that if we found the same age group effects with both chance and skill outcomes, then the effects could be attributed to age group differences in predictive style, not differences in the ability to judge contingency. However, if the kinds of age group differences found in Studies 1 and 2 were more pronounced with chance than with skill tasks, then we could infer developmental differences in the ability to gauge contingency.

The chance task and procedure was similar to those of Study 1, except that subjects (rather than drawing blindly from a deck of cards) were asked to indicate which of two cards placed face-down on a table contained a spot of the designated color (blue or yellow). The skill task involved similar stimulus materials, but it was designed to make memory and concentration appear relevant to outcomes. Subjects were asked to try to memorize a large number of paired associates, that is, 36 different line drawings (adapted from the Matching Familiar Figures Test), each paired with a colored spot (blue or yellow). After a series of study periods, subjects were given pairs of cards to choose between, as in the chance task, but each card had one of the line drawings on the visible side. Subjects were asked to select the card from each pair that had a spot of the designated color on the opposite side. In reality, the pictures were so complex and numerous, and they differed in such minor details, that it would be difficult for anyone to be absolutely certain about any specific memory. Nonetheless, our subjects at all age levels seemed convinced that memory and concentration were highly relevant to outcomes in the skill task.

How subjects predicted future outcomes.   After playing the chance game, and after playing the skill game, subjects were asked to predict the winnings (maximum = 6) of other players at each game. With questions similar to those of Studies 1 and 2, we asked the subjects to predict the winnings of a player one grade level below their own, a player one grade level above their own, a player who got to practice, one who did not practice, a player who tried hard, one who did not try hard, a player who was smart, and one who was not smart. The prediction patterns are shown in Figure 9.3.

The first thing to notice in the figure is the evidence supporting the response style effect discussed at the outset. This evidence appeared in the older/younger, smart/not smart, and practice/no practice predictions, but not in the try/no try predictions. Perceived differences as a function of age, intelligence, and practice, all grew increasingly modest with increases in the subjects' level of maturity, and this trend was present in predictions of chance *and skill* outcomes. However, this narrowing of predicted differences was significantly more pronounced for chance outcomes than for skill outcomes. In other words, the evidence also pointed to real developmental increments in the ability to judge the relative contingency of the skill and chance outcomes. The one exception to this trend was seen in the older/younger predictions. Here, predictions for the chance *and skill* task showed an orderly convergence across predictors' levels of maturity, such that kindergarteners showed extreme "older versus younger" differences while college students predicted no differences at all. A bit of reflection convinced us that this trend actually represented good judgment on the part of our subjects. We had asked them to predict outcomes for individuals one grade level higher and one grade level lower than themselves. Comments by some of our older subjects about their skill task predictions indicated that they regarded the 2-year age difference as too trivial to have a significant influence on task performance. And of course they were right. A 2-year difference is likely to influence skill task performance a great deal among young children, but not among college students. In an unusual way, then, this pattern of predictions strengthens our confidence in the findings overall, since it suggests that our subjects were attending to and really thinking about their predictions.

As in Studies 1 and 2, we also examined the frequency of perfectly logical prediction patterns. Because a chance and skill task were involved here, we focused on the frequency with which subjects predicted precisely *equal* winnings on the chance task despite differences in hypothetical players' age, intelligence, effort, or practice, *and* predicted *different* winnings on the skill task as a function of differences in age, intelligence, effort, or practice, For example, a subject who predicted that a smart player would win more than a not-very-smart player on the skill task but that the two would win the same amount on the chance task

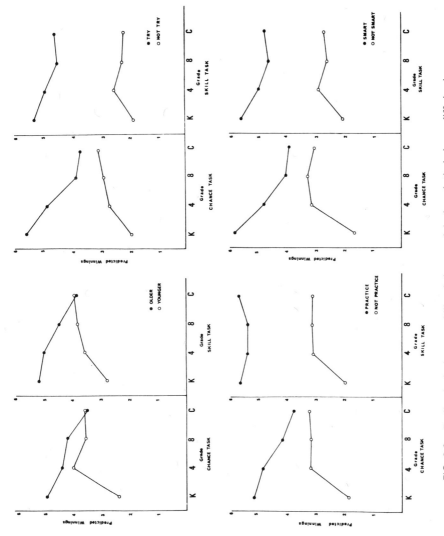

FIG. 9.3. Predicted winnings at a skill and chance task by hypothetical players differing in age, effort, practice, and intelligence. (Source: Weitz, Yeates, Robertson & Beckham 1982, pp. 901–902.)

243

would be classified as having shown a "logical" prediction pattern; all other smart/not smart prediction patterns would be classified as "illogical." Our analysis of the older/younger predictions showed no age group differences in the frequency of "logical" patterns—probably, for reasons discussed above, because, "logical" patterns with respect to these predictions would not actually be very logical for the older subjects. In the other three areas (i.e., intelligence, effort, practice), however, the frequency of logical patterns rose sharply with increases in subjects' level of maturity. Across the three areas, the mean percentage of logical prediction patterns was 0% for kindergarteners, 7% for fourth-graders, 53% for eighth-graders, and 53% for college students. A striking feature of these findings, one shown in Figure 9.4, was the absence of differences between eighth-graders and college students. This fact suggests that whatever major developmental gains are to occur in the emergence of contingency reasoning may have already taken place by early adolescence.

Comparing chance and skill tasks.   The experiment also yielded some evidence on the order in which certain key distinctions between contingent and noncontingent outcomes may be comprehended. We asked seven questions dealing with such distinctions after subjects had completed the skill and chance tasks. The percentage of correct answers to each question increased monotomically from kindergarten through college. We next sought to find what might be called the developmental "break points" for each question; we calculated chi square tests for each, comparing the frequency of correct answers among kindergarteners versus fourth-graders, then fourth- versus eighth-graders, then eighth- versus college—looking for the points at which significant shifts in the frequency of correct answers occurred. We found that none of the questions were answered at better than chance levels by kindergarteners, but that fourth-graders (as well as our older subjects) could correctly answer the following four questions:

1. In which of the two games does it help *to try hard?*
2. In which of the two games is it *just a matter of luck?*
3. In which of the two games does it help *to remember well?*
4. In which of the two games is it *just guessing?*

For these four questions there was a significant improvement from kindergarten to fourth grade. For a fifth question there was significant improvement from kindergarten to fourth grade, then another significant improvement from fourth to eighth grade. This question was

5. In which of the two games does it help *to be smart?*

For a sixth question the only significant difference was between the fourth- and eighth-graders:

  6. In which of the two games would you *get better as you get older?*

Finally, on a seventh question there was significant improvement between fourth and eighth grades, and again between eighth grade and college:

  7. In which of the two games does it help to get *to practice a lot?*

From this pattern it appears that among the aspects of the chance-skill distinction to be learned early may be the use of such chance-like tags as "luck" and "just guessing," and the differential importance of effort ("try hard") and *task-specific* skill ("remember well"). Recognition of the differential role of a broadly relevant but *general* attribute (being "smart") may emerge somewhat later. Most difficult of all, or at least most delayed in our data, was the recognition of the relative impact of somewhat abstract phenomena that could not be observed directly in the activities themselves (i.e., getting older and practicing a lot). These findings suggest some potentially useful hypotheses for future study.

Overall, the data from these three studies present a picture of development roughly similar to that hypothesized by Piaget and Inhelder (1975).[3] We found little evidence that pre-elementary-school children could distinguish between contingent and chance outcomes in any way. The elementary-age children seemed to be aware of the chance-contingent distinction at a gross qualitative level, but unaware of some of its most important logical (predictive) implications. Young adolescents and college students showed a definite ability to distinguish between contingent and chance events; the predictions of a modest majority at these higher levels of maturity reveal a recognition of the precise logical implications of the distinction (i.e., differential predictions for skill, "same" predictions for chance).

The errors made by the youngest subjects could not be described as random. Nearly every kindergartener predicted *some* performance difference as a function of age, intelligence, effort, and practice, on the chance task. This uniformity

---

[3]The three contingency studies described here deal with judgments made for hypothetical others. One might reasonably ask whether similar developmental trends would be observed in contingency-related judgments made for *self*. Faith Quintavell and I recently completed a study in which we asked first-, third-, and fifth-graders to predict future outcomes for others and for themselves at a marble machine game in which they had just received a random sequence of outcomes. In addition to paired prediction questions like those of Studies 1, 2, and 3 (above), children predicted their own future winnings under conditions of high and low effort, and under conditions in which they were allowed practice and not allowed practice. The age-related declines in perceived contingency on these self-prediction questions were actually stronger and more significant statistically than the age-related declines in perceived contingency for hypothetical others.

seems to suggest a consistent belief that the chance outcomes were contingent. These data, together with the more anecdotal reports of Piaget (e.g., 1930, 1960), suggest that such a belief may indeed be quite pervasive in early childhood and that it may succumb only very slowly to the onslaught of logical operations. Why would young children err so consistently in the direction of perceived contingency? One might argue that these errors are stimulated by a powerful motive for causal agency and/or by the aversiveness of a perception that one has no control (see White, 1959; Langer, 1977). Yet, motivational explanations alone seem unlikely to account for the consistency and pervasiveness of the young child's errors. Even the young child's motivation for food, as powerful as it is, certainly does not cause the child to regard all objects as edible.

One possibility, very speculative but interesting, is that illusory contingency in young children may be a cognitive phenomenon that has evolved partly through a process of natural selection. Let us imagine, for example, a prehistoric population of infants and young children whose cognitive limitations prevented them from accurately distinguishing between contingent and noncontingent events. Suppose that some of these youngsters tended to err randomly, showing behavior that conformed to the law of effect only when they happened to perceive events as contingent. Suppose that a second group erred most often in the direction of perceived noncontingency and thus showed a persistent nonresponsiveness to real contingencies in the environment. Suppost that a third group erred most often in the direction of perceived contingency and thus showed a strong responsiveness to environmental events, including physical events affording opportunities for cognitive development and social events affording opportunities to respond to caregivers in ways they find rewarding. Certainly, such youngsters would over-respond, but they might also profit more than the other groups from situations where contingency does prevail. Members of this hypothetical third group, despite their intellectual limitations, would seem to have had an adaptive edge over members of the other two groups. Would such highly "contingent-responsive" youngsters actually have been more likely to survive and contribute to the species gene pool than other youngsters. Perhaps the possibility is worth pondering.

Whatever the cause of the apparent early bias toward illusory contingency, we also need to explain why the bias persists so long—well into middle childhood for a majority of our samples, and even (in weakened form) into the college years for some. The bias may linger in part because certain key cognitive developments cannot be hurried (see Piaget and Inhelder, 1975), because even mature contingency concepts are prototypic rather than definitional (see Rosch & Mervis, 1975; Weisz et al., 1982), or because at least some achievement/skill cues are associated with most chance events (Langer, 1975, 1977). It may also be that typical socialization within many western cultures may contribute to prolonged illusory contingency. Such traditions as the tooth fairy myth, the Santa Claus myth, and a goodly portion of Judeo-Christian religious training—not to mention the maxims quoted at the beginning of this paper—convey forceful messages about the degree to which the outcomes that people experience are contingent on their attributes and behavior.

Contingency Awareness and Energy Allocation

Earlier in this chapter I suggested that accurate judgments about control could enhance people's ability to allocate energy appropriately. Recent evidence from Nicholls and Miller (in press) supports this idea, at least for the kinds of contingency-related control judgments described in this section. Nicholls and Miller used procedures patterned after Weisz et al. (1982), but they also used a detailed interview procedure to classify their kindergarten through eighth-grade subjects according to their level of comprehension of the distinction between the skill and chance variants of the task. The most mature children in this classification system were those who clearly understood the noncontingency of the chance outcomes—the fact that effort could not influence such outcomes—and who appropriately attributed skill outcomes to effort and chance outcomes to luck. Children at this mature level of comprehension, compared to children at lower levels, actually allocated more time to their performance on the skill task and less time to their performance on the luck task. This difference seems to demonstrate in a very concrete way that comprehension of this particular aspect of control can enhance judicious energy allocation.

A Limitation of the Contingency Data

Finally, a word about one significant limitation of the data reviewed thus far. These data suggest that most preadolescents are unable to identify chance outcomes as completely noncontingent. If this is the case, then it follows from the reasoning presented earlier that preadolescents would have difficulty in accurately judging their prospects for control *in those situations where contingency of outcomes is limited by the influence of chance*. This range of situations may be fairly broad. Chance factors can enter into such diverse, predominantly non-chance outcomes as school grades, social acceptance, and sports (particularly if we consider the role of chance in determining such attributes as intellect, physical attractiveness, and agility!). In this respect, the findings reviewed above are relevant to many of the everyday control judgments made by children. However, Connell (1978, 1980) found in constructing a children's perceived control measure, that elementary school children did not make systematic attributions to luck or chance for their academic, social, and sports outcomes (Harter, 1982). They frequently acknowledged that they did not know what controlled these outcomes; this prompted Connell to include an *Unknown* dimension in his scale. The possibility that chance, per se, may not enter into most children's thinking about control over many important everyday outcomes suggests the need for more research. In particular, it serves as a reminder that we need to study the development of reasoning about sources of noncontingency other than chance. Such sources (e.g., powerful others, unalterable situations) may conceivably be more important, more salient, and easier to judge accurately than such an abstract, intangible force as chance.

DEVELOPMENT OF COMPETENCE JUDGMENT

We turn now to the development of competence judgment. I can give this area less extensive coverage than contingency, in part because some of the most important theory and research was described by Susan Harter (1982), in recent volume of this series. Most of the theories bearing on the development of competence judgment appear to generate similar developmental predictions, at least for the period from infancy through middle childhood. Even psychoanalytic theory depicts infants and young children as having a quite exaggerated sense of their own competence or potency—in fact, a sense of "omnipotence." Freud (1957) referred to the tendency of parents to regard their infant as " 'His Majesty the Baby,' as once we fancied ourselves to be" (p. 49). Ferenczi (1913) described four stages in the evolution of omnipotence; he and Freud posited a developmental trend in the direction of increasingly modest and accurate self-assessments as reliance on the pleasure principle gives way to increasing reliance on the reality principle. In a similar vein, Piaget (1960) wrote of the infant's feeling, "that he is commanding the world" (p. 153), and of a developmental decline in this feeling as the child, striving to overcome gaps and contradictions, adopts a view of self and the world that is less and less a reflection of the child's wishes, and more and more a reflection of objective reality. There are other reasons to anticipate developmental increments in accuracy. Nicholls (1978, 1979), has suggested that the ability to assess one's competence relative to that of other persons requires, (a) the ability to perform seriation, (b) the capacity to see one's performance and position from a detached perspective, and (c) the ability to relate temporally separate outcomes to one another. These abilities only emerge with development, and are evidently only consolidated during the elementary school years. For a different set of reasons, Bandura (1981) has also suggested that "self-efficacy" estimates will grow more modest and more accurate through the childhood years.

Actual research on competence judgment, at least the research with people old enough to give verbal reports, tends to involve two general constructions of the concept. Competence is often construed in relative terms, as when an individual's capacities are judged in comparison to some reference group (see, for example, Nicholls, 1978, 1979). At other times, competence is construed in absolute, or criterion-based terms, as when judgments are made about the upper limit of accomplishment an individual is capable of when doing his or her best (see, e.g., Bandura, Adams, & Beyer, 1977). Both constructions of competence can be tested in at least approximate ways for veridicality, and both seem to be appropriate foci for developmental research. It may also be useful to study developmental change in relative preference for and relative accuracy of these two approaches to competence assessment. At this time, however, most of the evidence relevant to our present analysis reflects the relative, social-comparative approach to gauging competence.

Some Data on the Direction of Developmental Change

Thus far, cross-sectional evidence from the period of early through late child-hood certainly suggests that levels of perceived competence grow increasingly modest with development. My first encounter with developmental differences of this sort came in unpublished parts of two studies of hypothesis testing behavior (Weisz & Achenbach, 1975; Weisz, 1977). In both studies, children ranging in mental age from $5\frac{1}{2}$ to $9\frac{1}{2}$ years took part in a concept formation task in which prearranged feedback insured that all received exactly the same level of "success." The only competence-related differences in these studies involved children's use of hypotheses and strategies, and these differences, of course, showed the older children to be more competent. After completing "the game," each child was asked to move a sliding arrow along a scale to indicate how good he or she was at the game, "compared to other kids in your school." A rating at the top of the scale was said to mean "the best in your school." In both studies, there was a highly significant decline in self-ratings with increasing mental age. Children at the lowest mental age level gave themselves ratings near the top of the scale, whereas children at the upper mental age levels placed themselves about three fourths of the way up the scale, on the average. In a more recent study, Faith Quintavell and I had first-, third-, and fifth-graders play a game in which they tried to coax marbles out of a machine by pushing colored buttons. All children received marbles on a random 50% of their trials. Afterward each child used a rating scale to answer the question, "How good are you at this game, compared to other kids your age?" Despite equal winnings at all grade levels, self-rated competence declined sharply from first to third to fifth grade. Developmental trends in magnitude of self-assessed competence within such non-cognitive domains as sociometric status (Ausubel, Schiff, & Gasser, 1952) and physical strength (Goss, 1968) resemble the trends found with the problem solving tasks just described.

Nicholls (1978) collected self-ratings of competence more broadly defined than in the case of the preceding studies. He focused on children's assessments of their general reading ability. Nicholls showed children aged 5 through 13 an array of 30 line drawings of faces, arranged vertically on a sheet of paper. He told the subjects that these faces represented a rank ordering, with the top face representing the best reader in their class. He then asked the children, "Now, can you show me how good you are at reading? Which one is you?'' Nicholls found that children's self-rated competence grew generally more modest as their age level increased. As can be seen in Table 9.7, the mean rating of 13-year-olds was 15, precisely the mean that would be obtained if all children rated themselves accurately. To assess accuracy more directly, Nicholls calculated correlations between the 7- to 13-year-olds' own self-ratings and teacher ratings of the children's reading competence (no teacher ratings available for 5- and 6-year-olds). This procedure obviously is not a perfect test of accuracy, but it does compare the children's perceptions to an important external validity criterion. The results are shown in Table 9.7. The self-ratings of children younger than age nine did not correlate significantly with teacher ratings; from age nine onward, though, all teacher-child correlations were significant, and the correlations for 12- and 13-year-olds were remarkably high. The general direction of Nicholls' (1978) findings is roughly consistent with developmental trends found in studies of self-assessed strength (Goss, 1968), toughness (Freedman, 1975), social characteristics (Phillips, 1963), and sociometric status (Ausubel et al., 1952).

Harter (1982) has studied perceived personal competence more broadly construed than in the studies just cited. Her Perceived Competence Scale for Children is designed to assess self-perceptions of cognitive, social, and physical competence via three separate subscales, and to assess ''general self-worth'' independently of any specific competence domain. The questions involve a ''some kids-other kids'' format designed to minimize social desirability effects. For example, one item reads, ''Some kids often forget what they learn,'' but ''Other kids can remember things easily.'' Children are asked to make two judgments: (a) Which kind of kid is most like me, and (b) Is the characteristic of that kind of kid ''really true for me'' or only ''sort of true for me?'' Thus, each question yields a four-point scale. Harter's measure seems to represent a blending of the ''relative'' and ''absolute'' constructions of competence discussed above.

In contrast to the findings described earlier, Harter has found no significant age differences in mean perceived competence on any of her subscales (see Table 9.7). Interestingly, though, her samples only extend downward to the third-grade level, that is, to about age 9. This age is the point above which Nicholls' (1978) data did not show significant developmental differences, and it corresponds to the mental age ceiling of the Weisz and Achenbach (1975) and Weisz (1977) samples. Thus, the Harter findings do not directly contradict or support the implication of these other findings, that self-assessed competence may decline in magnitude over the 5 to 9 year age period. In fact, Betty Rintoul, at North Carolina, recently checked to see whether developmental effects would emerge when the Harter scale was administered to first-, third-, and fifth-graders. To enhance comprehension (Harter does not recommend the use of her scale with children below the third grade), Rintoul administered the scale by reading it, item-by-item, to the 180 children. She found significant grade level differences

TABLE 9.7

Age/Grade Differences in Magnitude and Validity of Self-Rated Competence in Two Studies

		Nicholls (1978)[a]--Self-Rated Reading Competence [1=highest, 30=lowest]							
Age (in years)	5	6	7	8	9	10	11	12	13
mean rating	3.1	5.1	9.1	9.0	11.9	13.8	11.6	12.9	15.1
Teacher r	-	-	.21(ns)	.27(ns)	.58	.71	.57	.80	.78

	Harter (1982)[b]--Perceived Competence Scale for Children [4=highest, 1=lowest]						
Grade Level	3rd	4th	5th	6th	7th	8th	9th
mean rating	3.0	2.9	2.7	2.7	2.6	2.6	2.6
Teacher r	.28	.32	.50	.55	.31	.66	.73
Ach r	.27	.40	.45	.45	.29	.44	.54

[a]Nicholls' study included 144 children from Wellington, New Zealand. His validity criterion (Teacher r) was the correlation of children's self-ratings with the ratings teachers gave them. In his child scale, low ratings = high perceived competence.

[b]Harter's study included samples from four states in the U.S. The data shown here are from her California sample (N=746). Her validity criteria included correlations with teacher ratings (Teacher r) and with achievement test scores (Ach r). In her child scale, high ratings = high perceived competence.

on the social, cognitive, and general self-worth subscales. In each case, the only substantial difference was a decline in perceived competence from first- to third-grade.

Harter tested children's self-perceptions for accuracy against two criteria: teacher ratings and standardized achievement test scores. She focused on children's *cognitive* competence subscale scores, in part because teachers felt most confident about their judgments of this particular competence domain. As Table 9.7 shows, the child-teacher correlations increased monotonically from third through sixth grade, dipped at the seventh, and resumed their increase thereafter. The table shows a similar trend in the correlations between children's cognitive competence ratings and their percentile scores on the combined reading, language, and math portions of the Iowa Test of Basic Skills. Harter interprets the seventh-grade dip in both correlational trends as a reflection of uncertainties brought on by junior high school entry. This transition, she argues, brings with it an unfamiliar school structure, an array of different teachers (evaluators), and a new social hierarchy. "It may well be," Harter suggests, "that those seventh-grade adolescents lose their ability to make realistic judgments about their cognitive competence" (1982, p. 96).

Harter notes an interesting parallel between this seventh-grade dip and Connell's findings (with the same sample) on the Unknown dimension of his perceived control scale (Connell, 1980). Scores on this measure of *uncertainty* as to just *what* is responsible for cognitive outcomes showed a steady decline from third to sixth grade but a dramatic increase in the seventh grade. The Harter and Connell findings suggest that the accuracy of self perceptions of competence, at least in the cognitive domain, may be strongly influenced by life transitions that provide confusion and uncertainty. (Nicholls [1978] did *not* find the pattern identified by Harter and Connell, but Nicholls' subjects were from New Zealand, where social and school realities are different than for Harter's and Connell's young Americans.) Overall, the findings serve to remind us that, however important *normative* developmental trends may be in determining the veridicality of perceived competence, veridicality is also apt to be influenced by a variety of other factors. Any comprehensive picture will need to include the role of significant social stressors, situational constraints, and pervasive life circumstances, of which entry into seventh grade is but one example.

Some Data and Theory on Determinants of Developmental Differences

The evidence on the developmental course of self-assessed competence is preliminary at best. Even more preliminary is our knowledge about the *determinants* of development in this area. Some of the research on this issue has been guided by theoretical perspectives like those of Nicholls (1978, 1979), who has attempted to identify specific cognitive activities necessary for accurate self-assessment. As noted earlier, Nicholls (1978) stressed the importance of the ability to seriate, to take a perspective outside of oneself, and to relate temporally separate outcomes to one another. There is evidence that each of these abilities requires years of development to be consolidated, and that the three skills are not fully operational until middle childhood. It is this age level at which Nicholls' (e.g., 1978, 1979) first finds significant correlations between children's self-ratings and the ratings of their teachers. This finding is in harmony with Nicholls' views, but more empirical work will be needed if we are to determine whether the three specific cognitive developments flagged by Nicholls (1978) are actually necessary conditions for accurate self-assessment.

Some investigators have focused on developmental changes in social comparison processes. Without the information gained via such processes, it seems unlikely that such cognitive skills as perspective-taking ability and seriation could lead to accurate rankings of one's own competence relative to that of others. There is considerable evidence that children do not spontaneously use information on peers' performance to make comparisons with their own performance, until about the age of seven or eight (Ruble, Feldman, & Boggiano, 1976; Ruble, Parsons, & Ross, 1977; Veroff, 1969). In a recent study, Ruble, Boggiano, Feldman, and Loebl (1980—Study 2) tried to provide kindergarten, second-grade, and fourth-grade children with incentives toward social comparison of abilities. They reasoned that comparison might be most likely when they made the usefulness of comparative ability information clear to children. The task was a ball-throwing game; children judged whether they could beat the other players, and the accuracy of their judgments influenced their winnings. Surprisingly, these presumably enhanced incentives did not lead to increased use of comparison information by younger children. In fact, effective social comparison was found only among fourth-graders. This finding suggests that it may not be appropriate to attribute previous developmental findings to age differences in the *motivation* for social comparison. In fact, children as young as 5 to 6 years show some *interest* in comparing their behavior with that of others (Dinner, 1976; Frey & Ruble, 1983). It may be, then, that effective social comparison requires cognitive abilities (e.g., the ability to focus on self and others concurrently from the perspective of a detached observer) that are simply not in place until the age of seven or eight. On the other hand, Ruble et al. (1980) caution against premature conclusions, noting, for example, that Masters (1971) has found children's self-reinforcement behavior to be influenced by social comparison even at nursery school levels. At this point, social comparison does seem likely to be an important element in effective self-assessment of competence, but there is a good deal more work to be done before we understand how, and why, the relevant comparison processes change with development.

Taking a somewhat different tack, Stipek and her colleagues (Stipek, 1981, 1984; Stipek & Hoffman, 1980a,b; Stipek et al., 1980) have focused on the steps needed to *eliminate* the self-assessment errors made by 3- to 6-year-olds. These young children generally make exaggerated self-ratings that do not correspond to their teachers' ratings of them. However, under certain conditions, even kindergarteners have shown that they can make ratings of their *classmates'* ability that are significantly related to teacher ratings of those classmates (see Stipek, 1984). In addition, under carefully arranged laboratory conditions, children as young as four who overestimate their own ability levels may generate more realistic expectancies for classmates whose performance they observe (see Stipek in press). However, Stipek (1984) found that even judgments about *other* children were overblown when the "judges" were to receive a reward contingent upon good performance by the other child. The first two findings suggest that cognitive egocentrism may undermine young children's self-assessments. The third finding is reminiscent of Piaget's (1930) argument that young children confuse their desires (in this case, the desire for the other child to perform well) with reality.

Mounting evidence on children's causal reasoning may also enhance our understanding of young children's competence assessment errors. Kun (1977), for instance, has identified a "halo scheme" in young children; an example of the scheme is the common finding that young children perceive effort and ability as varying directly with constant levels of an outcome. As Kun (1977) notes, this finding "implies that a child will perceive himself as very competent if he succeeds after considerable exertion but not so capable if success was attained without much effort" (p. 872). This and other evidence indicates that young children often use faulty rules in judging competence from information about effort and outcomes. The use of, say, a halo scheme could certainly explain some instances of disagreement between the competence judgments of children and the corresponding judgments of adults (e.g., teachers), for whom the halo scheme is the epitome of illogic.

A general implication of Kun's (1977) findings is that adults may employ a quite different concept of ability, or competence, than do children. This, in turn, suggests that to understand developmental change in competence judgment, we may need to understand the development of the basic competence concept. Nicholls and Miller (1984) have offered a three-stage developmental account of the concept of ability, drawing on many of the findings cited in this section. Their earliest stage, the "ego-centric level," is one in which children fail to distinguish between task difficulty and ability, but can differentiate tasks on the basis of their own perceived likelihood of success; to the extent that such children have any sense of their own ability, it relies heavily on their subjective impressions as to what tasks they can master (see also, Stipek et al., 1980). At stage 2, the "objective level" (attained somewhere between 5 and 8 years), more difficult tasks are perceived as requiring more ability, but the distinct contributions of task difficulty and ability to outcomes are not distinguished. At stage 3, the "normative level," ability and task difficulty are differentiated, and social comparison information can be used to form ability judgments. This last stage is said to emerge at about 7 years. The Nicholls-Miller formulation may prove a useful stimulus to research on the conceptual underpinnings of competence judgment.

A conceptual factor identified by Dweck (1981) may continue to influence self-assessments even after major cognitive milestones have been passed. Dweck distinguishes between *entity* and *incremental* models of intellectual competence. People of any age who subscribe to entity models perceive intellectual competence as a relatively fixed entity, more or less stable over time. By contrast, those who subscribe to incremental models construe intellectual competence as improving over time and with practice. According to Dweck, a number of consequences flow from an individual's endorsement of one or the other model. For example, an entity model should lead one to reduce effort following failure (particularly if the failure follows high effort), since that failure would be viewed as an indication of one's present *and future* competence. An incremental model might trigger *increased* effort following failure, since the failure could be read as information about present competence that can be used to enhance future competence.

The overall impression that emerges from much of the literature in this area is that as in the case of contingency reasoning, certain cognitive developmental milestones may need to be attained in order to establish baseline conditions for accurate competence judgment. These cognitive developments, at least some of which seem to be in place by middle to late childhood, are apt to be necessary but not sufficient conditions for veridical judgment. Once the milestones have been attained, individual variations in veridicality may well be determined largely by a broad array of factors that are not, strictly speaking, cognitive-developmental in nature—factors so diverse as to include social stereotypes, vicarious experience (Bandura, 1977), susceptibility to beneffectance (Greenwald, 1980), and even affective state (Lewinsohn, Mischel, Chaplin, & Barton, 1980).

INTEGRATING CONTINGENCY AND COMPETENCE INFORMATION

Thus far I have argued that actual control is a function of contingency and competence, and that a veridical control judgment requires accurate information about both. Our discussion has focused on age differences in the ability to generate such information. We now turn to a related question: How (if at all) do people at various ages *use* contingency and competence information when they form judgments about control? Let us begin by considering some ways the two kinds of information *might* be used. Figure 9.4 shows two idealized heuristic models, one involving additive effects of contingency and competence, the other involving multiplicative effects. At a simple level, the two models generate relatively similar predictions. To illustrate, suppose we return to our earlier

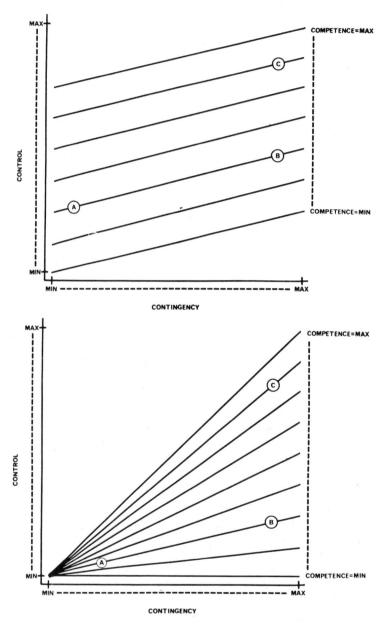

FIG. 9.4.   Additive (top) and multiplicative (bottom) models for the integration of contingency and competence information in judgments of control.

256

discussion of journal publication. We can imagine three individuals, shown in the figure as *A, B,* and *C. A* has a very modest level of competence as researcher and writer and has submitted to a journal in which review procedures are not very refined, and in which publication decisions are thus not very contingent on quality. *B* has the same level of competence as *A,* but has submitted to a journal in which publication is highly contingent on quality. *C* has submitted to the same journal as *B,* but is more competent than both *A* and *B.* Both the additive and multiplicative models generate the view that control will be lowest for *A* and highest for *C.* But what about *judged* control? Do people actually gauge control in a manner resembling either model?

Control Judgments by College Students

Our first efforts to answer this question took the form of four studies on judgmental processes among college students (Weisz, Gregg, Olasov, & Beckham, 1985). In the two studies most relevant to this chapter, we provided students with contingency and competence information in the context of brief vignettes, then asked them to judge the degree of control the vignette protagonists would have over intended outcomes. We tried to sample some significant life domains; one of our vignettes involved a job interview, another involved a college essay assignment, and a third involved an argument with a friend. Contingency and competence were varied as orthogonal factors, with each having two levels. For example, in the college essay vignette, the professor who grades the essays was described as either (1) a diligent reader who grades the essays carefully and fairly, so that, "grades depend heavily on essay quality" (high contingency), or (2) a lazy professor who just skims the essays so that, "grades have relatively little to to with essay quality" (low contingency). Competence was varied by specifying that the protagonist ("George") was either "very good," or "not very good" at writing essays. Each student fell into one cell of the 2 (contingency) × 2 (competence) design for each vignette. The student's task with each vignette was to judge the amount of control the protagonist (e.g., George) would have over the outcome (e.g., the essay grade received). In a second study, students were asked to imagine that they themselves were the protagonists in these vignettes. The results for several hundred college students across these two studies of prospective control judgments can be summarized quite simply. (Results were more complex in later studies, when we specified outcomes, then asked students to make post hoc control judgments.) Prospective control judgments showed patterns generally consistent with Figure 9.4. Across academic, job, and social situations, both contingency and competence information had highly significant main effects on control judgments. The students anticipated the most control when contingency and competence were both high, and the least control when contingency and competence were both low.

Control Over Pac Man—Developmental Data

To know what college students do when judging control is not necessarily to know what adolescents and children do. In recent studies, we have cut a braoder developmental swath, sampling the judgments of young adults (many, but not all, college students), adolescents, and elementary-school children. An initial question concerned whether both contingency and competence information would be used at all by people at the two younger age levels. The evidence reviewed thus far suggests that the consolidation of at least certain kinds of contingency and competence judgment may be taking place from middle childhood through early adolescence. If this is the case, then the ability to *apply* contingency and competence information to yet another judgment, for example, to a judgment about control, might well require additional skills that lie beyond the reach of most elementary-school children. The interview data discussed earlier suggest that elementary-school children may have at least a rudimentary concept of control, but whether such children see contingency and competence as relevant to that concept is certainly an open question. One could also question whether or not adolescents, and even young adults who are not all in college, would show patterns of reasoning like those of the college students in Weisz et al. (1985).

In our first effort to tackle these questions, we asked children (aged 6–10), adolescents (12–16), and young adults (18–25) to make control judgments about a domain in which all had experienced some outcomes, and under similar circumstances: Pac Man. This video game operates with similar rules for participants of all ages, and its surge of popularity in the early 80s insured that most "people on the street" would have some exposure to it. The study began with interviews in video arcades but was eventually extended to other public settings, such as shopping malls and parks. We interviewed people who had previously played Pac Man, asking them (in random order):

1. In Pac Man, how much does getting points depend on the players and what they do? (Contingency)
2. How good do you think you are at Pac Man? (Competence)
3. How much control do you have over getting points when you play Pac Man?
4. How much do you like to eat raisins?

Question 4 was not mere foolishness. We included it, in part, to insure that all of the younger subjects had understood the preliminary instructions on the use of 7-point rating scales; we asked all the child and adolescent subjects to explain their raisin question rating, and we dropped the data for those whose rating and reason did not correspond logically. Only two children, both in the 6 through 11 year group, failed this comprehension test. The raisin question was included for a second reason: to provide a check against the possibility that any correlations among contingency, competence, and control ratings might be merely artifacts of a generalized tendency to give high, or low, ratings across the scales. After completing about 50 interviews with each of the three age groups we calculated the correlations shown in Table 9.8.

Note first the relative absence of positive correlations involving raisin preference. While there may be information of value to nutritionists here (e.g., raisin preference was negatively correlated with age in the youngest group), there was no indication of the kind of rating scale response bias discussed above. Other coefficients in the table show that control ratings were significantly related to both the judged contingency of the Pac Man game and the self-assessed competence of the interviewees, at all three age levels. Competence was correlated somewhat more strongly with control than was contingency at the upper and lower age levels, while the reverse held true in the middle age group. Despite these variations, it seems reasonable to conclude that for interviewees in all three age groups, control ratings were related at a respectable level to judged con-

TABLE 9.8
Pac Man Correlation Coefficients for Three Age Groups

Ages 6-10 (N = 51)

	Age	Experience	Contingency	Competence	Control
Experience	-.092				
Contingency	.022	-.117			
Competence	-.293*	.203	.469***		
Control	-.165	.022	.299*	.493***	
Raisins	-.658***	.033	.064	.206	-.020

Ages 12-16 (N = 44)

	Age	Experience	Contingency	Competence	Control
Experience	.253				
Contingency	.102	.113			
Competence	-.098	.424**	.185		
Control	.013	.053	.645***	.482***	
Raisins	.315*	.090	.126	-.079	-.045

Ages 18-25 (N = 50)

	Age	Experience	Contingency	Competence	Control
Experience	-.049				
Contingency	.018	.178			
Competence	.169	.229	.155		
Control	.073	.203	.346*	.579***	
Raisins	-.070	-.169	-.357*	-.238	-.210

*$p < .05$
**$p < .01$
***$p < .001$

tingency and competence. One other aspect of these data deserves some comment. Among the children, but not among the adolescents and adults, contingency and competence ratings were correlated with one another. Perhaps this finding reflects a sort of "halo" or "glow" effect such that high contingency is seen as implying high competence, or vice versa; or perhaps the conceptual distinction between the two constructs is not entirely clear to children in the elementary school years. In any event, the correlations for the two older groups suggest that they had little difficulty disentangling the concepts of contingency and competence.

One additional question was asked of these Pac Man data: Did the control judgments of subjects at any of the age levels appear to reflect contingency and competence information used *in combination?* One way of addressing this question is to ask whether contingency and competence together accounted for more of the variance in perceived control than did either factor alone. To find out, I squared the Pearson rs between contingency and control and between competence and control, then compared these r^2 values to the R^2 obtained by squaring the multiple correlation linking control to contingency and competence combined. For the 6–10 year-olds, the results were as follows:

Age 6–10 years

r^2 contingency/control................. = .090
r^2 competence/control................. = .243
R^2 contingency, competence/control...... = .249
[p value for R^2 increment = n.s.]

What these numbers show is that among the 6 to 11 year-olds about 24% of the variance in perceived control over Pac Man was accounted for by the young players' perceived competence alone, and that combining perceived competence with perceived contingency adds almost nothing to the variance accounted for. The result for the adolescent group was quite different:

Age 12–16 years

r^2 contingency/control................. = .416
r^2 competence/control................. = .232
R^2 contingency, competence/control...... = .552
[p value for R^2 increment = .01]

Thus, for the adolescents, the variance in perceived control was better accounted for by contingency and competence information in combination than by either, considered separately. This also proved true for the young adults:

Age 18–25 years

r^2 contingency/control................. = .120

r^2 competence/control . . . . $= .335$
R^2 contingency, competence/control . . . . . . $= .403$
[p value for R^2 increment $= .05$]

What these data suggest is that contingency and competence information were used somewhat differently by the 6–11 year-olds than by the older groups. For the older groups, but not for the children, perceived control was a function of perceived contingency and competence *in combination,* over and above the influence of either factor considered in isolation. Something integrative appeared to be happening among the older groups that did not happen among the children.

The Interplay of Contingency and Competence: Developmental Vignette Data

The Pac Man data tell us something about how people's own contingency and competence assessments correlate with their control judgments. Another approach to studying this judgmental process is to provide people with contingency and competence information and examine the impact of that information on their subsequent control judgments. This procedure seems to bear a rough conceptual similarity to certain logical reasoning tasks popularized by Inhelder and Piaget (1958). The kinds of additive or multiplicative reasoning reflected in Figure 9.4 might be compared, for example, to the reasoning called for in a conservation of liquid task. On this task, pre-operational children often focus on a single aspect of the perceptual array (water in the beakers, etc.), most often, height. The ability to attend to two dimensions concurrently, say, height and breadth, evidently does not emerge until the elementary school years. If this sort of physical/perceptual analogy is an appropriate parallel to the use of contingency and competence information, then we might anticipate that elementary-age children can integrate contingency and competence information, recognizing the potentially compensatory relationship that the two dimensions have with one another. On the other hand, one might see in Figure 9.4 a set of intellectual demands more appropriately compared to the combinatorial reasoning of formal operations; one might thus anticipate that reasoning such as that depicted in Figure 9.4 would not emerge until adolescence. Finally, of course, it is conceivable that at no age level do people perceive contingency and competence as contributing to control in anything like an additive *or* multiplicative fashion; however, our data from college students, described above, casts doubt on this possibility.

In our attempt to test the various possibilities, we carried out more "people on the street" interviews. People ranging in age from 6 to 25, were stopped in shopping malls and other public places and asked to respond to simplified vignettes roughly similar to those of the college student studies. For continuity with our Pac Man study, we included one vignette dealing with a video game. It indicated that, "Cris is trying a new video game." The game was described as one in which either "The player makes most of the moves, and getting points depends mostly on what the player does" (high contingency), or in which "The machine makes most of the moves, and getting points depends mostly on what the machine does" (low contingency). Cris was described as "very good at the moves she gets to make in this game" (high competence) or as "not very good at the moves she gets to make in this game" (low competence). The second vignette indicated that, "Susan is having a big argument with her friend. Her friend thinks that Susan has been saying bad things about her behind her back. Susan knows this is not true." Susan's friend was described as "paying close attention to what Susan says" (high contingency) or as a person who is very stubborn and "won't pay attention to what Susan says" (low contingency). Susan was described as either "very calm, she is very good at explaining things when she is in an argument" (high competence) or as, "very nervous, she is not very good at explaining things when she is in an argument" (low competence). A third vignette stated, "Students in George's class all have to write special reports." George's teacher was described as one who "reads the reports very carefully, so grades usually depend on how good the reports are" (high contingency), or as one who "does not read the reports very carefully, so that grades often do not depend on how good the reports are" (low contingency). George was described either as "very good at writing reports" (high competence), or as "not very good at writing reports" (low competence).

The people interviewed were divided into three age groups: 6 to 11, 12 to 17, and 18 to 25. To be included in the final sample, interviewees had to meet two requirements. First, they had to pass a comprehension check designed to tap at least a rough understanding of control and an ability to use a rating scale. Several interviewees, (most from the youngest group), were dropped for failure to pass this comprehension check. The second requirement for sample membership turned out to be more demanding. After making their ratings on a given vignette, each interviewee relinquished the printed vignette and answered questions listed on a memory check-sheet, testing recall of the specific contingency and competence information given in that particular vignette. People in the youngest age group failed these memory checks quite often. More then one-fourth of the original 6 to 11 year group failed one or more of the memory tests, while only a few of the 12 to 17 year-olds and the 18 to 25 year-olds did so. When subjects failed one memory check, the data for that particular vignette were dropped. All data were dropped for those individuals missing two or more memory checks. Replacement interviews were conducted to insure that age would be balanced across the experimental groups and that sample numbered 120, with 5 males and 5 females in each of the three age groups receiving one of the four 2 (contingency) $\times$ 2 (competence) vignette combinations. These dropping and replacement procedures, of course, mean that the results presented below pertain only to people who showed that they had attended closely enough to remember the contingency and competence information.

Interviewees judged how much control the key actor in each vignette (Cris, Susan, George) would have over the outcome in question (other ratings were also made, as discussed below). Mean control ratings, and all significant effects, are shown in Tables 9.9, 9.10, and 9.11. The tables indicate that contingency information had a significant effect on control ratings in all of the vignettes. Competence, by contrast, had a significant effect on perceived control in the video and argument vignettes, but a negligible effect on the class report ratings. Contingency and competence also entered into differing interactions across vignettes. It is apparent from these data that the subjects used the two kinds of information in somewhat different ways, depending on the content and context of the situation they were asked to envision. It is also apparent that influence of contingency and competence information in these situations did not differ greatly from one age level to the next.

The data are also presented graphically, in Figures 9.5 and 9.6, to facilitate comparison with the two models shown earlier in Figure 9.4. The comparisons are, of course, extremely rough, given that only four data points are generated by each study. However, the figures do at least suggest variations that may arise when contingency and competence information are combined. The video game data (Fig. 9.5, top) show a pattern that roughly resembles the additive model. The argument data (Fig. 9.5, middle) suggest a more multiplicative pattern, one that may be quite reasonable in this particular context. One feature of the multiplicative model in Figure 9.4 that I find conceptually attractive is that at extremely low levels of contingency variations in competence have relatively little impact, and at extremely low levels of competence variations in contingency have relatively little impact. This is an appealing feature because it is consistent with two significant realities: (1) When outcomes are completely noncontingent, individual differences in actors' competence make no difference in their prospects for control; and (2) When an actor is completely incompetent, the question of how contingent an outcome is is not relevant to his or her prospects for

TABLE 9.9
Control Ratings for Cris in the Video Game

	Low Competence	High Competence
Low Contingency	2.57	3.60
High Contingency	4.43	6.07

Effects
Contingency: F (1, 96) = 53.06, $p < .0001$
Competence: F (1, 96) = 20.09, $p < .0001$

Gender X Age X Competence: F (2, 96) = 5.89, $p < .01$ [For females, at the lowest age level competence makes no difference, but at the middle and upper age levels, higher competence = higher control; for males, at the lowest age level higher competence = much higher control, but at the middle and upper age levels, higher competence = moderately higher control.]

TABLE 9.10
Control Ratings for Susan in the Argument

	Low Competence	High Competence
Low Contingency	3.53	3.50
High Contingency	3.63	5.40

Effects

Contingency: F (1, 96) = 9.00, $p < .01$
Competence: F (1, 96) = 6.76, $p = < .05$

Contingency X Competence: F (1, 96) = 7.29, $p < .01$ [When contingency is low, competence makes no difference; when contingency is high, competence makes a big difference.]

control. Such reasoning may have entered into responses on the argument vignette. If we look closely at the "low contingency" condition in that vignette, we see a virtual "*no* contingency" instruction. Susan's friend is described, not as being *unlikely* to pay attention, but as one who "won't pay attention to what Susan says." Perhaps the interviewees reasoned that if Susan's friend will not listen, then Susan's competence in arguments is not likely to help her at all.

Finally, we come to George and his class report. Frankly, I am puzzled by this pattern of findings. The pattern is unlike what we have found in the college student studies described above—studies in which we used a similar vignette. I am tempted to attribute the finding to the general perversity of data, turning against me just before the Minnesota Symposium. As I read the class report vignette in its four incarnations, I see no reason why George's competence at writing should not enhance his control in this situation. However, several of the interviewees who accepted our invitation to explain their ratings reacted differently. Common among this group were responses indicating that actual control lay in the *teacher's* hands since she, after all, was the one who assigned grades.

TABLE 9.11
Control Ratings for George on the Class Report

	Low Competence	High Competence
Low Contingency	2.87	3.76
High Contingency	5.60	5.53

Effects

Contingency: F (1, 96) = 46.61, $p < .0001$
Competence: F (1, 96) = 1.60, $p = .21$

Age X Contingency: F (2, 96) = 3.59, $p < .05$ [Contingency makes a big difference at the low and high age levels, but only a slight difference at the middle age level.]

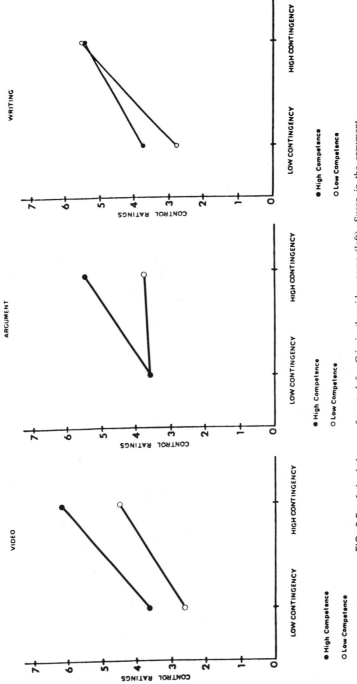

FIG. 9.5. Judged degree of control for Cris in the video game (left), Susan in the argument (middle), and George with the class report (right).

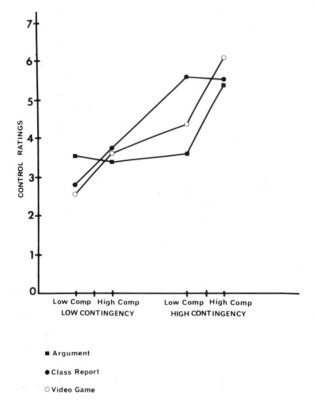

FIG. 9.6. Judged control in the video game, argument, and class report vignettes, as a function of contingency and competence information.

My only hunch about these findings, then, is that something about the vignette wording made the impression of teacher control so strong as to either undermine attention to competence information or actually make George's competence seem irrelevant.

In Figure 9.6, the data from all three vignettes are combined. The figure offers an opportunity to compare trends across vignettes. It also shows something rather obvious, but worth noting nonetheless: in all three vignettes, contingency and competence information were combined rather consistently when low levels of both attributes or high levels of both attributes were involved; the variation across vignettes occurs under conditions in which differing levels of the two attributes are mingled.

Perhaps the most notable finding of the study is a non-finding: age played virtually no role in this particular form of control reasoning. There were no main effects of age, and age entered into only two interactions, neither one of noticeable theoretical significance. To be sure, age entered into the findings at an earlier level. It influenced comprehension of the rating task to a slight degree, and it was strongly related to memory for vignette information. However, given adequate comprehension, and memory for the information, people at all three age levels appeared to use the information in rather similar ways. This suggests that the kinds of control reasoning studied here may be roughly analogous to the kinds of conservation reasoning mentioned earlier, with both involving skills that take shape during the elementary-school years. I should add, though, that the 6–11 year group averaged 9 years of age. This leaves open the possibility that the kinds of reasoning seen here in our youngest group might not be found among early-elementary-age children.

CONTROL, RESPONSIBILITY, AFFECT, AND HELPLESSNESS: BEGINNING TO TRACE CONNECTIONS

The research described thus far has been focused on cognitive/judgmental processes related to control. A long-term objective of this research program is to better understand the influence of such processes on affect and behavior. We are just beginning to focus on these patterns of influence. As a part of that process, we asked interviewees in the developmental vignette study just described to make three judgments in addition to their control ratings. To put these judgments into context, we need some brief background on a topic of special interest to me as a clinical psychologist: depression in children and adults.

In a widely-cited analysis of depression among adults, Abramson and Sackeim (1977) identified what has come to be called the "depression paradox." The paradox is that depressed adults tend to anticipate little control over aversive events in their lives but they often feel personally responsible, nonetheless, when such events occur. Most clinicians who work with children and adolescents in states of depression would agree that this so-called "paradoxical" pattern often characterizes their young clients as well, perhaps to an even greater degree than is the case with adults. It seems to me that this pattern of reasoning might be explained in part as a function of the differential impact of contingency and competence on perceptions of control and responsibility.

The evidence reviewed in this chapter suggests that for people to judge that they have a high level of control may require a relatively high degree of perceived contingency and perceived competence. But what about responsibility? How is it assessed? Responsibility is often equated with control, hence the view that perceived responsibility without perceived control is "paradoxical." However, my impression is that the two entities are not judged in the same manner. I suspect that responsibility is often attributed primarily on the basis of perceived contingency, with relatively little attention to perceived competence. To illustrate, let us suppose that a graduate student is called upon to give a seminar presentation to a group of peers and a high-powered professor or two. This student has severe public speaking anxiety, has never been competent as a speaker, and knows this quite well. Moreover, the student is not particularly knowledgeable or insightful about the topic to be addressed. However, neither the student nor others in the seminar have any doubt that the outcome of this process, that is, how well the presentation goes and is received, will be highly contingent on the behavior and attributes of the presenter. Suppose the presentation is delivered and that it is a disaster. Will the student presenter feel that he or she ever had a high level of control in this situation? Probably not, because control seems to require both contingency *and* competence, and the student feels a distinct lack of competence. Will the student feel responsible for the way things turned out? Yes, I would guess, because I suspect that responsibility in such cases is attributed largely on the basis of outcome contingency. If the outcome is thought to be contingent on the actor's behavior, the actor will feel responsible. This, of course, can be made an empirical question, so we need not rely simply on my opinion. We turn now to the evidence generated in the vignette study described earlier.

In the video game, argument, and class report vignettes described above, the question about control was accompanied by three additional questions, one focused on responsibility and two focused on seemingly allied emotions, pride and shame. In the class report vignette, for example, interviewees were asked "How responsible will George be for the grade he gets?" "If George gets a good grade how proud should he be?" and "If George gets a bad grade how ashamed should he be?" Ratings on the seven point scales accompanying these questions showed similar main effects on the video and class report vignettes. Responsibility, pride, and shame, were all rated significantly higher in the high contingency conditions than in the low. By contrast, there were no significant effects of competence. The argument vignette showed a somewhat more complex pattern. The findings just described for the video game and class report vignettes were replicated, but only for female interviewees. For males, contingency seemed to make little difference in this particular vignette. This gender difference may have resulted partly from difficulty on the part of male interviewees in identifying with the characters and content of the argument vignette. In addition to this gender $\times$ contingency interaction, there was a significant competence effect on the shame ratings; interviewees, especially males, rated Susan's shame higher if she was lower in competence at arguments. Overall, the findings suggest that in at least some situations perceived responsibility, pride, and shame may be strongly influenced by contingency but not by competence. This, in turn, suggests that in some situations people who perceive outcome contingency as high but their own competence as low may feel both responsibility and shame for adverse outcomes that they feel unable to control. These data suggest that such reasoning may not be confined to depressed people, nor to adults.

Our findings with the video game and class report vignettes, combined with the earlier developmental data on contingency judgment, raise some interesting possibilities for study in the realm of affect. One example concerns developmental differences in responses to adverse outcomes. The vignette data suggest that in at least some situations, elementary-school-aged children resemble adolescents and young adults in their *use* of contingency information. Such information may sometimes be a strong determinant of attributed responsibility and the associated response of shame when things turn out badly. Findings reviewed earlier in the paper suggest that elementary school aged children do *not* resemble adolescents and young adults in their *generation* of contingency information. The children appear considerably more likely to overestimate the degree to which events are contingent, even to the extent that they fail to recognize the inherent uncontrollability of totally noncontingent, chance events. This combination of reasoning patterns in children may pose a special risk: When adverse outcomes occur noncontingently, children may be especially likely to perceive contingency where it does not exist, attribute personal responsibility accordingly, and feel shame where it is unwarranted. There is some evidence indicating that elementary school-aged youngsters are prone to blame themselves for adverse outcomes in school even when the outcomes are administered by adults in ways designed to be blatantly and transparently unfair (e.g., Gray-Little, 1980). Clinicians working with children who are mourning the death of a loved one are often warned to watch out for unrealistic feelings of responsibility and self-blame (cf. Wahl, 1958). Such feelings are also reported in early and middle childhood among youngsters whose parents have divorced (Wallerstein & Kelly, 1980).

This reasoning can be expanded to suggest a developmental perspective on learned helplessness and perceived control. The reformulated helplessness model (Abramson et al., 1978) suggests that if I fail repeatedly and/or saliently to exert control, two forms of helplessness are possible. I may conclude that others could succeed where I cannot—from the perspective of this chapter, this involves a perception that I am low in competence relative to others; this cognitive pattern is called *personal helplessness*. Alternatively, I may conclude that neither I nor others could succeed in this situation—from the perspective of this chapter, this involves a perception that the intended outcome is noncontingent; this cognitive pattern has been labeled *universal helplessness*. The evidence reviewed above suggests that judgments of personal competence tend to be inaccurate and inflated through early childhood, and that young children would be less likely than older children and adolescents to conclude that they are incompetent, even in the face of repeated failures (see, e.g., Stipek, in press). Several lines of evidence (especially the work of Nicholls, Ruble, Dweck, and their colleagues, cited earlier) suggest that the kinds of competence-related reasoning that seems to be required for authentic personal helplessness may be relatively unlikely until the mid-elementary years. Young children may experience personal help-lessness, but perhaps not so readily as older children, adolescents, and adults.

If universal helplessness requires a capacity to perceive noncontingency, then that particular form of helplessness may also need to be viewed through a developmental lens. Our data suggest that, at least for the kinds of outcomes we have studied thus far, the ability to detect or perceive noncontingency may be almost out of reach until very late childhood. In the elementary years there seems to be a growing awareness that not all outcomes are equally contingent; but a recognition that some outcomes can be completely and inherently noncontingent is something we have not seen until very late childhood and early adolescence. Thus, it may be that one of the key cognitive prerequisites for universal help-lessness does not take shape in a stable way until about the time children make the transition to adolescence.

To summarize, much of the evidence surveyed here suggests that reactions to adverse events, particularly those involving repeated failure to exert control, may vary with developmental level. In the preschool and early elementary school years, learned helplessness in either of the cognitive forms described by Abram-son et al. (1978) may be relatively unlikely; the cognitions seemingly required for both forms are evidently difficult for such children to muster. In the mid to late elementary-school years, personal helplessness may be increasingly likely, as children become increasingly capable of gauging their competence relative to others, and increasingly capable of perceiving themselves as less than "the best." The late elementary and junior high school years may mark a newfound susceptibility to universal helplessness, and thus a capacity to experience both forms identified by Abramson et al. In keeping with these ideas, there are some data which suggest that susceptibility to helplessness may increase as children mature. Rholes, Blackwell, Jordan, & Walters' [1980] found that children in the early elementary years showed few signs of helplessness in response to experi-mentally-induced failure, but that older elementary children were quite suscepti-ble to helplessness.

It is possible, then, that one drawback of maturity is an increased susceptibili-ty to learned helplessness in a broader array of forms. Perhaps this is an example of what Nicholls and Miller (1984) call "development and its discontents." On the other hand, the cognitive developments involved may offer some adaptive advantages. As we suggested in our earlier discussion of maxims, unbridled, unthinking persistence is no virtue. A key developmental task is learning to distinguish between situations where persistence pays and situations where it does not. Without a capacity to understand and accurately gauge one's own competence and the contingency of events, these control-related discriminations would be difficult indeed. Finally, returning to affect, we should not forget that the emerging capacity to identify noncontingency, which may foster a suscepti-bility to universal helplessness, can also be our ally, protecting us from unwar-ranted feelings of responsibility and self-blame.

PRIMARY AND SECONDARY CONTROL: A NASCENT TWO-PROCESS MODEL

Thus far, we have focused on the development of judgments about control and its components, construed in more or less traditional ways. We turn now, briefly, to a less conventional perspective on control, one that several of us are now trying to nurture into empirical respectability, but that is still too embryonic to have stimulated much research to date. This embryonic perspective is the two-process model of control recently detailed by Rothbaum, Weisz, and Snyder (1982) and Weisz, Rothbaum, and Blackburn (1984a,b).

According to the model, there are two braod processes by which individuals may seek a sense of control. Individuals may pursue control by (1) attempting to change existing realities so as to bring them into line with their wishes (a more or less "traditional" definition of control), or by (2) attempting to accommodate to existing realities in order to effect a more satisfying fit with those realities. These two processes have been labeled *primary control* and *secondary control*, respectively. The two processes are described in overview form in Table 9.12. Note that both primary and secondary control conform to the provisional definition given at the beginning of this chapter—that is, control means causing an intended event. In primary control, the intended event is some modification of objective conditions; in secondary control, the intended event is some modification of one's orientation toward those conditions—that is, internal change that affords control over the impact of objective conditions on the self while leaving those conditions unchanged.

According to our model, both primary and secondary control can assume varied forms. Some examples are shown in Table 9.13. As the table indicates, people may try to predict accurately, align themselves with powerful others, get into harmony with fate or chance, or interpret events, for reasons that we regard as reflecting primary control or for reasons we regard as reflecting secondary

TABLE 9.12
Primary and Secondary Controls: An Overview

Type of Control and General Strategy	Typical Targets for Causal Influence	Overall Objective
Primary (Influence existing realities)	People, objects, events, circumstances, symptoms, problems	Enhance reward (or reduce punishment) by modifying realities to fit self
Secondary (Accommodate to existing realities)	One's expectations, wishes, goals, perceptions, attitudes	Enhance reward (or reduce punishment) by accommodating oneself to fit realities as they are

Adapted from Weisz, Rothbaum, and Blackburn (1984a). Copyright (1984) by the American Psychological Association. Reprinted by permission of the publisher.

TABLE 9.13
Types of Primary and Secondary Control

Type of Control	Process	Description
Predictive	Primary	Attempts to accurately predict events and conditions so as to select strategies that are most likely to make realities fit the self's needs, wishes, goals, etc.
	Secondary	Attempts to accurately predict events and conditions so as to control their impact on the self--e.g., to avoid uncertainty, anxiety, or future disappointment.
Illusory	Primary	Attempts to influence or capitalize on chance, so as to increase the likelihood that fate will fit one's needs, wishes, goals, etc. (e.g., riding a lucky streak).
	Secondary	Attempts to associate or "get into synchrony" with chance, so as to enhance comfort with and acceptance of one's fate.
Vicarious	Primary	Attempts to emulate the behavior, values, etc. of powerful individuals, groups, or institutions, so as to modify realities as they do.
	Secondary	Attempts to associate or closely align oneself with other individuals, groups, or institutions, so as to share psychologically in the control they exert.
Interpretive	Primary	Attempts to understand or construe existing realities so as to master them (e.g., figuring out the nature of a problem in order to solve it).
	Secondary	Attempts to understand or construe existing realities so as to derive a sense of meaning or "purpose" from them, and thus enhance one's satisfaction with them.
Selective Attention	Primary	Attempts to focus attention on elements of a problem, so as to solve it.
	Secondary	Attempts to focus attention away from a problem area, so as to avoid or minimize the unpleasant thoughts and feelings associated with it.

Adapted from Rothbaum, Weisz, and Snyder (1982). Copyright (1982) by the American Pyschological Association. Reprinted by permission.

control. Thus, assessing the reasons or goals underlying an individual's behavior is a crucial step in judging whether the behavior reflects a pursuit of primary or secondary control, or whether it actually represents relinquished control. This makes the assessment of primary, secondary, and relinquished control particularly difficult, because it means that reliable and valid classification will be difficult to achieve via direct observations or reports of behavior alone.

These difficulties notwithstanding, efforts to operationally define primary and secondary control may yet prove worthwhile. The two-process model may possibly have useful applications to such settings as schools, where successful adaptation may depend in part on the youngster's capacity to distinguish between appropriate targets for primary control (e.g., grades, sports) and for secondary control (e.g., school rules, authority of the teacher). The two-process model does, to a certain extent, broaden the range of what can be thought of as control, and it may provide a way of distinguishing between forms of compliance and submission that involve feelings of (secondary) control and those that involve feelings of relinquished control. Thus, operationally defining components of the model may help us uncover aspects of the control-school behavior relationship that are significant but understudied.

A Preliminary Questionnaire Approach to Primary and Secondary Control

In the first effort to operationally define these concepts for research with children, Cameron (1983) developed a questionnaire measure for use with fifth- and sixth-graders. Her Children's Primary-Secondary Control (CPSC) Scale, consisted of 15 school scenarios. Every scenario posed a control-relevant dilemma and three possible courses of action with a rationale for each. The three course of action/rationale combinations for each item were designed to reflect primary, secondary, and relinquished control, respectively. Children were asked to rate the likelihood that they would respond as described in each of the alternatives. Thus, an estimate of the child's self-reported propensity for all three approaches to control could be obtained.

Cameron (1983) investigated the relationship between CPSC Scale scores, on the one hand, and measures of her 95 fifth- and sixth-graders' academic achievement and behavior problems, on the other. The school achievement information included grade point averages and California Achievement Test (CAT) scores. The problem incidence reports came from parents who completed the Child Behavior Checklist (Achenbach & Edelbrock, 1983). Parents and teachers also completed rating forms designed to gauge the students' primary, secondary, and relinquishing control. Overall, Cameron found that the various relinquishing control scores were negatively correlated with a number of achievement measures and positively correlated with internalizing behavior problems (e.g., sadness, anxiety). When significant, correlation coefficients involving primary control scores showed primary control to be negatively correlated with achievement and positively correlated with internalizing behavior problems. By contrast, secondary control scores showed few significant correlations with achievement or behavior problems; in the few cases where they were significant, the correlations showed secondary control to be positively related to achievement and negatively related to behavior problems.

This exploratory study suggests that a strong emphasis on primary control may be associated with some undesirable correlates in the realm of school achievement and behavior at home. It also suggests that fifth- and sixth-graders who tend to endorse "giving up" in control dilemmas may show poorer school achievement and more parent-reported behavior problems than children who do not often endorse relinquishing control alternatives.

The paucity of significant correlates of secondary control may have resulted from measurement and sampling limitations in Cameron's investigation; certainly the CPSC Scale is only a preliminary measurement device. However, it is also possible that secondary control has few real correlates in the domains of academic achievement and behavior problems.

Preliminary though they are, these findings do suggest a possibility worth pursuing in future research: Behavior that involves compliance and yielding may have somewhat different correlates depending on whether it is associated with a sense of relinquished control or secondary control. We all know that schools and homes present the child with many situations in which submissiveness, compliance, or "going along" with such existing realities as rules, and the authority of teachers or parents, is expected. In these situations, the pursuit of primary control—for example, defying the rule, or disobeying the teacher or parent—may often be maladaptive for the student, and may (Cameron's data suggest) sometimes be associated with negative achievement and behavior correlates. Yielding, by contrast, may or may not have unpleasant correlates, depending on the motives and cognitions that accompany it. When yielding is linked to a sense of relinquished control, to feelings akin to helplessness, it may indeed be accompanied by undesirable correlates in the areas of academic achievement and behavior problems. However, when yielding is linked to motives and cognitions that afford a sense of secondary control, there may be few negative correlates. This, at least, is a possibility that may bear further study if we are to understand the range of forms that the child's sense of control may take, and the implications of those forms.

DEVELOPING AN UNDERSTANDING OF CONTROL: SUMMING UP

Now it is time to sum up. In this chapter we have worked from a provisional definiton that equates control with the capacity to cause intended events. I have suggested that these intended events may take two general forms: (1) modification of objective conditions so as to bring them into line with one's wishes (primary control); and, (2) accommodation to objective conditions in ways designed to enhance one's goodness of fit with those conditions and thus influence their subjective impact (secondary control). Focusing mainly on primary control, I have suggested that accurate judgments about one's capacity for control will depend on one's ability to (1) assess the degree to which target events are contingent on people's behavior or attributes, (2) gauge one's own competence to manifest the relevant behavior or attributes, and (3) retain such contingency and competence information and use it in logically appropriate ways. Evidence thus far indicates that there are pronounced developmental differences in some of these abilities. Taken together, these individual differences suggest that youngsters at different developmental levels may differ in their capacity to gauge their prospects for control, and thus to judge appropriate targets for persistence. The findings also point to possible developmental differences in cognitive and affective responses to outcomes—particularly in attributions of responsibility, pride, and shame. Finally, I have suggested that youngsters may differ from one another in their relative inclination toward primary control, secondary control, and relinquished control, and that these individual differences *may* be related to individual differences in the areas of school development and behavior problems. Overall, I have tried to indicate that an understanding of the developing child's developing understanding of control may be enriched by two potentially complementary processes: analyzing control judgments into component processes, and broadening our perspective on the multiple forms that a "sense of control" may take.

ACKNOWLEDGMENT

Some of the research reported here was supported by grants from the National Institute of Mental Health (1-R01-MH-34210-01 and 1-R03-MH-38450-01).

REFERENCES

Abramson, L. Y., & Sackeim, H. A. (1977). A paradox in depression: Uncontrollability and self-blame. *Psychological Bulletin, 84,* 838–851.

Abramson, L. Y., Seligman, M. E. P., & Teasdale, J. D. (1978). Learned helplessness in humans: Critique and reformulation. *Journal of Abnormal Psychology, 87,* 49–74.

Achenbach, T. M., & Edelbrock, C. S. (1983). *Manual for the Child Behavior Checklist and Revised Child Behavior Profile.* Burlington, VT: Queen City Printers.

Alloy, L. B., & Abramson, L. Y. (1979). Judgment of contingency in depressed and nondepressed students: Sadder but wiser. *Journal of Experimental Psychology: General, 108,* 441–485.

Ausubel, D. P., Schiff, H. M., & Gasser, E. B. (1952). A preliminary study of developmental trends in socioempathy: Accuracy of perception of own and others sociometric status. *Child Development, 23,* 111–128.

Ayerhoff, F., & Abelson, R. P. (1976). ESP and ESB: Belief in personal success in mental telepathy. *Journal of Peronality and Social Psychology, 34,* 240–247.

Bandura, A. (1977). Self-efficacy: Toward a unifying theory of behavioral change. *Psychological Review, 84,* 191–215.

Bandura, A. (1981). Self-referent thought: A developmental analysis of self-efficacy. In J. H. Flavell & L. Ross (Eds.), *Social cognitive development: Frontiers and possible futures.* New York: Cambridge University Press.

Bandura, A., Adams, N. E., & Beyer, J. (1977). Cognitive processes mediating behavioral change. *Journal of Personality and Social Psychology, 35,* 125–139.

Brim, O. G. (1980). *How a person controls the sense of efficacy through the life span.* Paper presented at the Social Science Research Council Conference on the Self and Perceived Personal Control Through the Life Span. New York.

Cameron, A. M. (1980). *Understanding children's academic and behavior problems: A comparison of the one- and two-process models of perceived control.* Unpublished doctoral dissertation. University of North Carolina, Chapel Hill.

Connell, J. P. (1978). *Manual for the Multidimensional Measure of Children's Perceptions of Control.* University of Denver.

Connell, J. P. (1980). *A multidimensional measure of children's perceptions of control.* Unpublished manuscript, University of Denver.

Crandall, V. C. (1971). *Discussant's comments*—symposium on developmental aspects of locus of control expectancies, at Annual Convention of the American Psychological Association, Washington, D.C.

Dinner, S. H. (1976). Social comparison and self-evaluation in children (Doctoral dissertation, Princeton University, 1976). *Dissertation Abstracts International, 37,* 1968B. (University microfilms No. 76-22, 634)

Dweck, C. S. (1975). The role of expectations and attributions in the alleviation of learned helplessness. *Journal of Personality and Social Psychology, 31,* 674–685.

Dweck, C. S. (1981). *Discussant's comments*—symposium on the development of achievement motivation, at the biennial meeting of the International Society for the Study of Behavioral Development. Toronto, Canada.

Ferenczi, S. (1913). *Contributions to psychoanalysis.* Boston: Badger.

Fischbein, E. (1975). *The intuitive sources of probabilistic thinking in children.* Boston: Reidel.

Flavell, J. H. (1963). *The developmental psychology of Jean Piaget.* New York: Van Nostrand Reinhold.

Freedman, D. G. (1975). The development of social hierarchies. In L. Levi (Ed.), *Society, stress, and disease (Vol. 2): Childhood and adolescence.* London: Oxford University Press.

Freud, S. (1957). On narcissim: An introduction. In *Collected Papers* (Vol. 14). London: Hogarth.

Frey, K. S., & Ruble, D. N. (1983, April). *What children say to each other when the teacher's not around: Self-evaluation and social comparison in the classroom.* Paper presented at the biennial meeting of the Society for Research in Child Development, Detroit.

Goss, A. M. (1968). Estimated versus actual physical strength in three ethnic groups. *Child Development, 39,* 283–290.

Gray-Little, B. (1980). Race and inequity. *Journal of Applied Social Psychology, 10,* 468–481.

Greenwald, A. G. (1980). The totalitarian ego: Fabrication and revision of personal history. *American Psychologist, 35,* 603–618.

Gunnar-von Gnechten, M. R. (1978). Changing a frightening toy into a pleasant toy by allowing the infant to control its actions. *Developmental Psychology, 14,* 157–162.

Gunnar, M. (1980). Control, warning signals and distress in infancy. *Developmental Psychology, 16,* 281–289.

Gurin, P. (1980). *The situation and other neglected issues in personal causation.* Reported in Thematic Minutes V of the Social Science Research Council Conference on the Self and Perceived Personal Control Through the Life Span. New York.

Gurin, P., Gurin, G., Lao, R. C., & Beattie, M. (1969). Internal-external control in the motivational dynamics of Negro youth. *Journal of Social Issues, 25,* 29–53.

Harter, S. (1982). The perceived competence scale for children. *Child Development,* 87–97.

Harvey, D. (1981). Depression and attributional style: Interpretations of important personal events. *Journal of Abnormal Psychology, 90,* 134–142.

Heider, F. (1958). *The psychology of interpersonal relations.* New York: Wiley.

Inhelder, B., & Piaget, J. (1958). *The growth of logical thinking from childhood to adolescence.* New York: Basic Books.

Kun, A. (1977). Development of the magnitude-covariation and compensation schemata in ability and effort attributions of performance. *Child Development, 48,* 862–873.

Lachman, M. (1985). Personal efficacy in middle and old age: Differential and normative patterns of change. In Glen H. Elder, Jr. (Ed.), *Life-course Trajectories and transitions, 1968–1980.* Ithaca, N.Y.: Cornell University Press. Pp. 188–213.

Langer, E. J. (1975). The illusion of control. *Journal of Personality and Social Psychology, 32,* 311–328.

Langer, E. J. (1977). The psychology of chance. *Journal for the Theory of Social Behavior, 7,* 185–207.

Lefcourt, H. M. (1976). *Locus of control: Current trends in theory and research.* Hillsdale, NJ: Lawrence Erlbaum Associates.

Lewin, K. (1951). *Field theory in social science.* New York: Harper.

Lewinson, P., Mischel, W., Chaplin, W., & Barton, R. (1980). Social competence and depression: The role of illusory self-perceptions. *Journal of Abnormql Psychology, 89,* 203–212.

Masters, J. E. (1971). Social comparison by young children. *Young children, 27,* 37–60.

Nicholls, J. G. (1978). The development of the concepts of effort and ability, perception of academic attainment, and the understanding that difficult tasks require more ability. *Child Development, 49,* 800–814.

Nicholls, J. (1979). *The development of perception of own attainment and causal attributions for success and failure in reading.* Unpublished manuscript, Victoria University, Wellington, New Zealand.

Nicholls, J. G., & Miller, A. T. (1984). Development and its discontents: The differentiation of the concept of ability. In J. G. Nicholls (Ed.), *The development of achievement motivation,* Greenwich, CT.: JAI Press. Pg. 185–218.

Peterson, C. (1980). *The sense of control over one's life: A review of recent literature.* Unpublished manuscript, University of Pennsylvania, Philadelphia.

Phillips, B. N. (1963). Age changes in accuracy of self-perceptions. *Child Development, 34,* 1041–1046.

Piaget, J. (1930). *The child's conception of physical causality.* London: Routledge & Kegan Paul.

Piaget, J. (1960). *The child's conception of the world.* Totowa, NJ: Littlefield, Adams.

Piaget, J., & Inhelder, B. (1975). *The origin of the idea of chance.* New York: Norton.

Rholes, W., Blackwell, J., Jordan, C., & Walters, C. (1980). A developmental study of learned helplessness. *Developmental Psychology, 16,* 616–624.

Rosch, E., & Mervis, C. B. (1975). Family resemblances: Studies in the internal structure of categories. *Cognitive Psychology, 7,* 573–605.

Rothbaum, F., Weisz, J. R., & Snyder, S. S. (1982). Changing the world and changing the self: A two-process model of perceived control. *Journal of Personality and Social Psychology, 42,* 5–37.

Rotter, J. (1966). Generalized expectancies for internal versus external control of reinforcement. *Psychological Monographs, 1* (Whole No. 609).

Rubin, Z., & Peplau, L. A. (1975). Who believes in a just world. *Journal of Social Issues, 31,* 65–89.

Ruble, D. N., Boggiano, A. K., Feldman, N. S., & Loebl, J. H. (1980). Developmental analysis of the role of social comparison in self-evaluation. *Developmental Psychology, 16,* 105–115.

Ruble, D. N., Feldman, N. S., & Boggiano, A. K. (1976). Social comparison between young children in achievement situations. *Developmental Psychology, 12,* 192–197.

Ruble, D. N., Parsons, J. E., & Ross, J. (1977). Self-evaluative responses in children in an achievement setting. *Child Development, 47,* 990–997.

Sedlack, A. J., & Kurtz, S. T. (1981). Review of children's use of causal inference principles. *Child Development, 52,* 750–784.

Seligman, M. E. P. (1975). *Helplessness: On depression, development, and death.* San Francisco: Freeman.

Shaklee, H. (1976). Development in inferences in ability and task difficulty. *Child Development, 47*, 1051–1057.

Shaklee, H., & Mims, M. (1981). Development of rule use in judgments of covariation between events. *Child Development, 52*, 317–325.

Skinner, E. A. (1985). Action, control judgments, and the structure of control experinece. *Psychological Review, 92*, 39–58.

Skinner, E. A., & Chapman, M. (1983, April). *Control beliefs in an action perspective.* Paper presented at the biennial meeting of the Society for Research in Child Development, Detroit.

Stipek, D. J. (1981). Children's perceptions of their own and their classmates' ability. *Journal of Educational Psychology, 73*, 404–410.

Stipek, D. J. (1984). Young children's performance expectations: Logical analysis or wishful thinking? In J. Nicholls (Ed.), *The development of achievement motivation.* Greenwich, CT: JAI Press. Pp. 33–56.

Stipek, D. J., & Hoffman, J. M. (1980a). Children's achievement-related expectancies as a function of academic performance histories and sex. *Journal of Educational Psychology, 72*, 861–865.

Stipek, D. J., & Hoffman, J. M. (1980b). Development of children's performance-related judgments. *Child Development, 51*, 912–914.

Stipek, D. J., Tannatt, L., & Sanborn, M. (1980). *Children's perceptions of competence in school.* Paper presented at the meeting of the American Educational Research Association, Boston, MA.

Stipek, D. J., & Weisz, J. R. (1981). Perceived control and children's academic achievement: A review and critique of the locus of control research. *Review of Educational Research, 51*, 101–137.

Veroff, J. (1969). Social comparison and the development of achievement motivation. In P. C. Smith (Ed.), *Achievement-related motives in children.* New York: Russell Sage.

Wahl, C. W. (1958). The fear of death. In H. Feifel (Ed.), *The meaning of death.* New York: McGraw-Hill.

Wallerstein, J. S., & Kelly, J. B. (1980). *Surviving the breakup: How children and parents cope with divorce.* New York: Basic Books.

Weiner, B. (1979). A theory of motivation for some classroom experiences. *Journal of Educational Psychology, 71*, 3–25.

Weisz, J. R. (1977). A follow-up developmental study of hypothesis behavior among retarded and nonretarded children. *Journal of Experimental Child Psychology, 24*, 108–122.

Weisz, J. R. (1980). Developmental change in perceived control: Recognizing noncontingency in the laboratory and perceiving it in the world. *Developmental Psychology, 16*, 385–390.

Weisz, J. R. (1981). Illusory contingency in children at the state fair. *Developmental Psychology, 17*, 481–489.

Weisz, J. R., & Achenbach, T. M. (1975). The effects of IQ and MA on hypothesis behavior in normal and retarded children. *Developmental Psychology, 11*, 304–310.

Weisz, J. R., Gregg, L., Olasov, B., & Beckham, J. C. (1985). *The teflon president and the depression paradox: Some informational determinants of perceived control and responsibility.* Unpublished manuscript, University of North Carolina, Chapel Hill.

Weisz, J. R., Rothbaum, F. M., & Blackburn, T. C. (1984a). Standing out and standing in: The psychology of control in America and Japan. *American Psychologist, 39*, 955–969.

Weisz, J. R., Rothbaum, F. M., & Blackburn, T. C. (1984b). Swapping recipes for control. *American Psychologist, 39*, 974–975.

Weisz, J. R., & Stipek, D. J. (1982). Competence, contingency, and the development of perceived control. *Human Development, 25*, 250–281.

Weisz, J. R., Yeates, K. O., Robertson, D., & Beckham, J. C. (1982). Perceived contingency of skill and chance events: A developmental analysis. *Developmental Psychology, 18*, 898–905.

White, R. (1959). Motivation reconsidered: The concept of competence. *Psychological Review, 66*, 297–323.

10 Comments on Weisz: "Understanding the Developing Understanding of Control"

Linda Heath
Loyola University of Chicago

One issue that has puzzled humankind throughout the ages is that of control. Humans seem to be driven to understand their world and what makes it work, and further they seem to need to believe that they play some role in it all—that somehow they can exercise control over their actions, their bodies, and their environments. A whole host of gods and spirits have been posited to wield control over those events that are seemingly uncontrollable. But in designing these gods, people have shrewdly built in an element of human control. If one needs rain for the crops, one prays to Dementer or Ceres or does a rain dance, depending on one's location in time and space. If one wishes to have a healthy child, one sacrifices to the fertility god, or lights a candle, or visits a genetic consultant. The explanations for control and causation have varied over the years, but the search for them has never diminished.

It is somehow fitting that psychologists are now puzzling over human's puzzlement over control. Clinical psychologists are examining the role that control perceptions play in depressive disorders, social psychologists are addressing the question of attributions for control, and developmental psychologists are examining the formation of control perceptions. The work in all these areas of psychology indicates that learning to make accurate assessments of control is a difficult task, not only for children but also for adults (Wortman, 1976). And understanding the process by which control perceptions develop is useful for understanding problems that arise from inappropriate control perceptions. The work that Weisz has presented at this symposium, therefore, has important implications for psychologists seeking to understand the understanding of control among adults, as well as children.

279

One aspect of Weisz' work that is particularly intriguing to me as a social psychologist is his depiction of causality as represented by concentric circles. The outermost circle contains all caused events, both those caused by human forces and those beyond human causation. The circle immediately within that contains events that are caused at least in part by some people. Within that circle is another subset that contains only those events that can be caused in an intentional way by some people, and finally, the innermost circle contains events that can be personally controlled by the individual. An accurate assessment of causality, therefore, would require proper placement of events in the appropriate circle. Further, an accurate assessment of personal control requires recognition of the distinction between the innermost circle and the outer circles of causation.

This depiction of causality might imply a developmental sequence for gaining perceptions of control that would have important implications for understanding control perceptions and misperceptions among adults. Could it be that children start out in the innermost circle, believing that they have vast amounts of personal control, and that the developmental process is really one of coming to recognize the outer layers of causality? As Weisz has mentioned, Piaget (1960) noted that infants feel that they are "commanding the world" (p. 153) and make increasingly more modest assessments of their role in the causal scheme. Similarly, Freud described the progression from reliance on the pleasure principle to the reality principle, which carries with it the movement of many events from the innermost to outer circles of causation.

This perception of omnipotence held by young children is not at all unreasonable. In a sense, an infant wields more control than he or she probably ever will again. What adult has enough control over his parents to convince them to rise at 4 a.m. to fix him a snack? What adult can bring an early end to a boring dinner party by fidgeting, whining, and spilling her milk? In keeping with Weisz' working definition of control, children can cause things to come about in line with their intents.

But gradually children learn that there are limits to their power. Perhaps the first step is simply to transfer the omnipotence to someone else (perhaps a parent), thus recognizing the second concentric circle. And perhaps then they recognize that some things cannot be willed by any person and finally that some things are simply not caused by people. If this is the developmental path, then noncontingency and randomness or chance should be the last piece fit into the control puzzle. And, as such, it could have important implications for both children and adults.

Being a researcher, I decided to collect some data to test this hunch. I borrowed the neighbor's children, ages 4 and 7, and asked them some questions to see if their understanding of control in any way fit the outward path through the concentric circles. Not surprisingly, the 4-year-old was already beyond the innermost circle of thinking that everything was caused by her wishes and actions (if, indeed, she had ever been there). When asked if she could make it stop raining, she said "No," and neither could her mother. Only God can make it stop raining. If she hurt herself, she could not make herself well, and neither could her mother. (So much for parental omnipotence.) Only a bandaid could make her well. She cannot make dice roll the way she wants because they just go where they want to. Is luck equivalent to chance for this 4-year-old, as Weisz has suggested? It is hard to say, because she defined luck as "when you get two pieces of candy and the other kids don't get any because they were mean," and yes, you can make yourself lucky "by getting candy."

Her 7-year-old brother answered somewhat differently. No one can make it stop raining. No one. If he is hurt, a doctor, not a bandaid makes him well, and dice do not decide where to go, it just happens. Luck is when good things happen to you, and no one can make himself lucky, it just happens. Obviously, I do not claim great scientific merit for these off-the-cuff interviews with two children, but the idea I am entertaining is that noncontingency, the outermost circle, is the last piece to be fit into the puzzle of perceived control. If this is so, it could also be the aspect of control most vulnerable to distortion and misperception, even among adults.

Ellen Langer (1975) has demonstrated the powerful illusion of control under which many adults operate, particularly in any situation that has overtones of skill or control. For example, people who are given the opportunity to practice a game of chance, or to pull a lever or select a card themselves, believe they have some degree of control, although, if pushed, logically they understand the random nature of the task (Langer, 1975). Witness the gamblers pulling slot machine levers or selecting lottery numbers. In a recent interview, a winner of the Illinois state lottery explained how she took the numbers that formed her birthdate and age and added or subtracted 2 from each number to arrive at the winning number. (The number 2 was her personal fudge factor.) Logically, of course, she recognized the random nature of lotteries. Even adults apparently have a hard time accepting the slings and arrows of outrageous fortune.

This reluctance of humans to accept randomness or noncontingency has been addressed in several theoretical formulations. Brehm (1966), for example, has proposed a reactance dynamic, whereby people strive to re-establish control when control is threatened. Abramson, Seligman, and Teasdale (1978) have suggested a reformulation of the learned helplessness hypothesis that incorporates attributions for lack of control as mediators between uncontrollable events and negative emotional states among humans. According to this reformulation, when people are faced with noncontingency, they attribute that noncontingency to a cause. The placement of these attributed causes on the dimensions of stability, universality, and globality coincide with the different circles of causality proposed by Weisz.

This same quest to make sense of life events is evident in Wortman and Dintzer's (1978) critique of the reformulated learned helplessness hypothesis and in Taylor's (1983) theory of cognitive adaptation. For example, Taylor proposes the search for meaning, mastery, and enhancement of self-esteem as the main themes in the readjustment process following a personally threatening event. Meaning and mastery are particularly relevant to this discussion of control. Basically, the search for meaning revolves around answering two main questions: What caused the event to happen? What does my life mean now? Mastery, on the other hand, involves "gaining control over the event and over one's life" (Taylor, 1983, p. 1161). In all of these formulations, a central point is the reluctance of human beings to accept noncontingent events as falling neatly into the outermost circle of causality. People seem to have an amazing antipathy for accepting randomness as the final cause.

There is a curious sidelight to this reluctance of humans to accept randomness as reality. People faced with negative life events often cope better if they believe, however erroneously, that they controlled the events that led to the negative situation (although not the negative event itself). Spinal cord patients, even those injured in freak accidents, cope better if they believe they controlled events that led to the injury (Bulman & Wortman, 1977). Rape victims regain their sense of security faster if they believe some behavior on their part led to the rape (Medea & Thompson, 1974). Parents of children with leukemia cope better if they attribute the disease to some error on their part (such as marital infidelity) rather than to fate or chance (Chodoff, Friedman, & Hamburg, 1964). Even cancer patients cope better if they attribute the disease to some controllable source (such as diet or being hit by a frisbee) no matter how illogical (Taylor, 1983). And, faced with a reoccurence of the disease, rather than give up control, patients simply shift to another "cause" of the disease or shift their focus of control to another aspect of the disease (such as controlling reaction to chemotherapy [Taylor, 1983]).

Recall that our working definition of control requires intentional causation. It is important to note that the focus of control among victims is on the events leading to the negative event, not on the negative event itself. For example, rape victims cope better if they intentionally caused the event leading to the victimization (for example, if they purposely hitchhiked as opposed to being stranded by car failure prior to the victimization) (Janoff-Bulman, 1979). This in no way implies that they set out intentionally to be raped. Rather, this type of control means that, because the rape is at one level attributable to an act of volition, that act can be avoided in the future, re-establishing a sense of security. Similarly, cancer victims who attribute their cancer to diet can alter their diets and believe they will thereby avoid a reoccurence of the disease. So although control (i.e., intentional causation) does not apply to the victimization itself, control over the precipitating events does provide psychological benefits.

In the same way that children avoid assessing outcomes as noncontingent, so do adults. Sometimes this reluctance to accept impotence is beneficial to adults, and, as Weisz has suggested, perhaps to children. But in other situations this aversion to noncontingency could have negative consequences. For example,

Beck (1967) has suggested that manic disorders might really be reactions to misperceptions of control. The manic person struggles and struggles to control some event that is, in fact, uncontrollable. And this same reluctance to accept the uncontrollable might lead some people to a life of crime.

My colleagues David Ward, Candace Kruttschnitt and I are currently interviewing inmates convicted of violent offenses in the state's maximum security prisons. The data from this project are still in the coding stage, and consequently my comments are based on my impressions from the interviews I conducted, rather than on statistical analyses. One issue of concern to us in this research is the relationship between control perceptions and criminal behavior. A plethora of research in social psychology indicates that perceiving no control over the environment results in negative affect and decreased performance. In areas ranging from uncontrollable noise (Glass & Singer, 1972) to geriatric institutionalization (Rodin & Langer, 1977) to dormitory structure (Baum & Gatchel, 1981) to possible rape victimization (Heath, 1983), lack of control results in negative mood and maladaptive behavior. Similarly, the sociological literature offers explanations such as blocked opportunities (reflecting lack of control) to explain criminal behavior. Do criminals see themselves as hapless pawns in an unresponsive world and turn to crime in frustration or as an attempt to gain control over the world?

From previous work concerning the demographic correlates of locus of control, I hypothesized that the prison population would be filled with externals, people who viewed themselves as having little personal control over events in their lives. Having now spent countless hours behind bars, I am fairly confident that the statistical analyses *will* reveal significant differences between our prison population and the matched comparison group in regard to control, but in the opposite direction. Far from being passive pawns of a greater causal scheme, the inmates I interviewed believe they can control events in a wide range of areas, and very often they are right! For example, one inmate did not like his mother seeing a particular man. Many people would see that as a situation beyond a son's control. This son, however, simply robbed a jewelry store, kidnapped his brothers and sisters, moved them to Indiana, brought them a house there with the proceeds of the previous evening's work, and insisted that if his mother wanted to be with her children, she move to Indiana and leave the boyfriend behind. And she did. Although unemployment, noisy neighbors, and unrequited love might engender feelings of lack of control in most of us, the inmates come up with quite effective and generally illegal ways to take control in these situations.

Another of Weisz' concepts, secondary control, is also evident in our prison population. Weisz and his colleagues (Rothbaum, Weisz, & Snyder, 1982) have proposed that, in addition to controlling events (which they term primary control), people can also gain a type of control by being able to predict the event, understand the event, or identify with a powerful other. They refer to these types of control as secondary control. This, too, is evident among the inmates I interviewed. In regard to school, most inmates report they *could* have been straight A students if they had wanted to. But they did not want to. They had better things to do with their time. Thus, they establish predictive control, rather than lack of control. Even in regard to imprisonment, most inmates accept it as an inevitable result of the career they have chosen. Some even establish slush funds on the outside *prior* to arrest, to provide them with money during incarceration.

On the other end of the continuum are adults who perceive *no* control in their lives. A few inmates do fit this description. Chance, bad luck, and other people caused them to lose jobs, commit crimes, and get caught. And because they accept no responsibility for and perceive no control over their misfortunes, they make no attempts to alter their behavior. So, residing squarely in either the innermost or the outermost of the concentric circles can prove problematic for adults. In fact, this pattern led my colleague Steve Brown and me to propose a therapeutic model centered around assessment of control (Brown & Heath, 1984).

Weisz' work has convinced me that understanding the developmental process of control, and, perhaps more importantly, the clear conceptualization that is necessary for such developmental work, may have important implications that range far beyond children and developmental psychology. The levels of causation represented by the concentric circles and the work that has been done charting the developmental process by which control perceptions are formed provide important insights into the costs and benefits of accurate control perceptions among adults. Beyond advancing the field of developmental psychology, Weisz' work helps social psychologists fit peices into the puzzle of control among adults.

REFERENCES

Abramson, L., Seligman, M. E. P., & Teasdale, J. (1978). Learned helplessness in humans: Critique and reformulation. *Journal of Abnormal Psychology, 87,* 49–74.

Baum, A., & Gatchel, R. J. (1981). Cognitive determinants of reaction to uncontrollable events: Development of reactance and learned helplessness. *Journal of Personality and Social Psychology, 40,* 1078–1089.

Beck, A. T. (1967). *Depression.* Philadelphia: University of Pennsylvania Press.

Brehm, J. (1966). *A theory of psychological reactance.* New York: Academic Press.

Brown, S., & Heath, L. (1984). Coping with critical life-events: An integrative cognitive-behavioral model for research and practice. In S. Brown & R. Lent (Eds.), *Handbook of counseling psychology.* New York: Wiley.

Bulman, R., & Wortman, C. (1977). Attributions of blame and coping in the "real world": Severe accident victims react to their lot. *Journal of Personality and Social Psychology, 35,* 351–363.

Chodoff, P., Friedman, S., & Hamburg, D. (1964). Stress defenses and coping behavior: Observations in parents of children with malignant disease. *American Journal of Psychiatry, 120,* 743–749.

Glass, D. C., & Singer, J. E. (1972). *Urban stress.* New York: Academic Press.

Heath, L. (1983). *Dealing with the threat of rape: Reactance or learned helplessness?* Unpublished manuscript.

Janoff-Bulman, R. (1979). Chracterological versus behavioral self-blame: Inquiries into depression and rape. *Journal of Personality and Social Psychology, 37,* 1798–1809.

Langer, E. (1975). The illusion of control. *Journal of Personality and Social Psychology, 32,* 311–328.

Medea, A., & Thompson, K. (1974). *Against rape.* New York: Farrar, Straus, & Giroux.

Piaget, J. (1960). *The child's conception of the world.* Totowa, NJ: Littlefield, Adams.

Rodin, J., & Langer, E. J. (1977). Long-term effects of a control-relevant intervention with the institutionalized aged. *Journal of Personality and Social Psychology, 35,* 897–902.

Rothbaum, F., Weisz, J. R., & Snyder, S. S. (1982). Changing the world and changing the self: A two-process model of perceived control. *Journal of Personality and Social Psychology, 42,* 5–37.

Taylor, S. (1983). Adjustment to threatening events: A theory of cognitive adaptation. *American Psychologist, 38,* 1161–1173.

Wortman, C. (1976). Causal attributions and personal control. In J. Harvey, W. Ickes, & R. F. Kidd (Eds.), *New direction in attribution research.* Hillsdale, NJ: Lawrence Erlbaum Associates.

Wortman, C., & Dintzer, L. (1978). Is an attributional analysis of the learned helplessness phenomenon viable?: A critique of the Abramson-Seligman-Teasdale reformulation. *Journal of Abnormal Psychology, 87,* 75–90.

11

Adult Social Cognition: Implications of Parents' Ideas for Approaches to Development

Jacqueline Goodnow
Rosemary Knight
Judith Cashmore
Macquarie University

Studies of cognitive development benefit from exploration across a range of content areas and age levels, with the results from one age level or domain supplementing and challenging proposals based on results from another. This paper describes such an effect. The research started with questions related to parents' ideas about childhood and parenting, using this domain as a step towards filling gaps in accounts of adult cognitive development and of socialization. The end-result was a questioning of the way cognitive development is usually described, for both adults and children and for both "physical" and "social" cognition.

The two main research questions are as follows: (a) How can we describe parents' ideas? What domains or dimensions will differentiate among parents or be useful to work with? (b) What conditions will be related to change or variation in parents' ideas? We shall be presenting some results related to both questions.

The broader picture concerns both practical and theoretical implications. To explore the practical use of knowledge, we have chosen a specific case, one in which altering parents' ideas has been a route to improving interactions with premature infants. That case raises as well the theoretical issue of relationships between ideas and overt actions.

The main theoretical implications however, have to do with our understanding of what cognitive development covers and how it came about. We brought to the adult work some particular models or expectations, based largely on work with children, found they did not fit well with the adult data, and came to consider that we should re-examine and modify our original assumptions.

One of the main modifications has to do with creating a larger space for value, function, and affect: in short, for factors other than simply taking information into account. In fact, we have come to propose that models of cognitive development place their stress on information and on intrinsic curiosity largely because they have concentrated on content areas where "social" factors play a relatively small part. With the move to "social" cognition, the need for change in the usual models becomes more apparent.

Also in need of a second look is the distinction between "physical" and "social" cognition. We plan to offer one more set of answers to that perennial question: What is "social" about "social" cognition? To anticipate, we plan to suggest some other ways in which we may make distinctions among domains of thought.

To trace the way we reached these end states, we shall begin with a brief background section, covering two starting points: (a) some reasons for being interested in parents' ideas, and (b) some general models or expectations that we brought to the adult work, borrowed in the main from work on cognitive development in children. This section is followed by three research sections. Each describes a specific study together with the possibilities it offered for further work and the questions it raised about our original expectations. The final sections look at a practical extension and at the general changes we suggest for approaches to cognitive development.

STARTING POINTS

Some Reasons for Interest in Parents' Ideas

An interest in parents' ideas is now to be found in diverse forms and in several places, with Macquarie being one of them. A general picture of the work may be gained from the chapters in Sigel (1985), from a review article by Goodnow (1984), and from a recent paper by Russell (1983) concentrating on ideas and actions.

For our own part, one general reason for interest was the wish to gain a broader picture of cognitive development. There have been in recent years a number of expansions on the classical picture, using that term to refer to knowledge based on Piagetian models: the move towards "everyday" or "real" tasks, the exploration of contextual effects, the very interest in "social" cognition itself and its building of links between developmental and social psychology. We hoped to add to that expansion by giving attention to two gaps that seemed especially glaring. One of these was the relative lack of knowledge about adult cognitive development, added to by a lack of continuity between accounts of adult cognition and child cognition. The other was the relative lack of connection between the literature on cognitive development and the literature on socialization. With a background sense of these gaps, we began looking more carefully at work on adult cognitive development and on socialization. Both roads led to parents' ideas about development and parenting. Following that direction, we must add, was all the more attractive because it held out the promise of some applied aspects and of being a fruitful training base for students.

Adult Cognitive Development. One particular difficulty in approaches to adult cognitive development, and in linking work on children with work on adults, is that the one is usually described in terms of positive change, the other in terms of deterioration and decay. As Flavell noted, we know relatively little about adult change of a positive kind (Flavell, 1970). One of the "new looks" in development, in fact, consists of more benign proposals.

Some of these proposals concentrate on aspects of ability. We may, for instance, regard adult life as a period of gaining wisdom and expertise (Baltes, Dittman-Kohli, & Dixon, in press). That view, together with the proposal that some aspects of ability are at least maintained over age, combines well with arguments for adult change as based on specific experience and environmental demand (e.g., Baltes & Labouvie, 1973; Baltes & Willis, 1976; Labouvie-Vief, 1982; Schaie, 1973).

The evidence for adult growth, however, is not startling in studies of ability as measured by psychometric tests. The problem may lie in the nature of the measures. We may do better, for instance, if we look at changes in social cognition, on the assumption that this domain may be more readily linked to changes in life-situation. An example is Epstein's work (1981) on women law-yers, re-entering the paid labor force and developing forms of competence they had not previously displayed. In such cases, change occurs in self-esteem and in what is seen as possible. Some further examples are to be found in Mortimer and Simmons' (1978) review of work on adult socialization, and in work by Feldman and her colleagues on changes in ideas about sex roles with changes in one's position in the family life-cycle (Abrahams, Feldman, & Nash, 1978; Feldman, Biringen, & Nash, 1981). The notion that parents' ideas might provide a further example comes from Flavell (1970). Building on work by Stolz (1967), he suggested that parenting was a form of experience that might well produce evidence of positive change in adult thought, with ideas becoming over time more differentiated and more in line with reality.

For us, Flavell's (1970) suggestion was especially attractive because of its link to some broader descriptions of "culture" and possible adult socialization. These descriptions are in terms of prevailing ideas about human nature and development. Historians and psychologists, for instance, have used such ideas as a way of describing the difference between one historical period and another (e.g., Ariès, 1962; Kessen, 1979; Lomax, Kagan, & Rosenkrantz, 1978; Pinchbeck & Hewitt, 1969, 1973). Anthropologists and psychologists have used them to describe differences among contemporary cultures (e.g., Hamilton,

1982; Whiting, 1963) and the nature of cultural change as a traditional culture becomes "modern" (Whiting & Marshall, 1976). From such work, it seemed a small next step to regard parents' ideas as changing to fit with parental experience.

The Socialization of Children.   For a number of scholars, the starting-point for an interest in parents' ideas has been an interest in parents' behaviors, and a growing awareness of the lack of data about ideas that may influence those behaviors (Dix & Grusec, 1985; Hess, in press; McGillicuddy-de Lisi, Sigel, & Johnson, 1979; Parke, 1978). The awareness has been prompted in part by noting the lack of continuity between work with children and work with adults. Most current work with children, for instance, is marked by an acceptance of the notion that the effect of events upon children is mediated by the schemas or constructions children use to interpret events. That understanding of children is not reflected in research with parents (Dix & Grusec, 1985; Grusec & Dix, 1982). Parke (1978) in fact has described most psychologists, in their analysis of mother-infant interactions, as treating the mother as if she were at the same level of cognitive complexity as the infant.

The awareness of a lack of data on parents' ideas does not, however, reflect simply an extension of approaches generated by research with children. An important further source is the emergence of some particular results. A case in point is the finding (Dix & Grusec, 1985; Grusec & Dix, 1982) that mothers' responses to children's behaviors are particularly affected by the way mothers divide behaviors into groups or categories (e.g., dividing "misdemeanors" into active misdeeds, such as fighting, and failures to be prosocial, such as not sharing). Such data prompt a search for parents' categories, and for their ideas about how behaviors in different categories are best treated (Grusec, personal communication).

Some General Expectations about Development

Having decided to work on parents' ideas, we needed to find a way to begin. To the work, we brought some inter-related expectations, strongly affected by work with children:

  (a) that change would be more likely than no change over the course of parenting;
  (b) that the basis for change would be a response to new information. This expectation carries with it the assumption that parenting provides information one can absorb, and the assumption that people are interested in new information;

(c) that the direction of change would be positive, in the sense of ideas moving towards greater clarity or differentiation, or towards a "better fit" with the lessons of experience;

(d) that the task might best proceed by exploring parents' ideas in three areas: ideas about goals or ends; ideas about conditions affecting the reaching of goals; and ideas about how to assess the nature or current state of a child.

These are the expectations we shall keep returning to in the course of looking at results. We shall briefly spell out their background.

The Expectation of Change.   Change seemed likely for several reasons. In general, adults do not present the kind of barrier we usually think of as holding back children's cognitive development: namely, a lack of intellectual capacity to absorb the information provided. It also seemed probable that if any change occurred in adults' ideas about people, parents' ideas about children and parenting were good candidates for change. Parents are in many ways novices; children are important to them; their children's behaviors are not completely predictable. All these are conditions that seem to invite some re-thinking. Finally, parental change fitted with the feeling—on the part of the two of us who are parents— that our ideas had changed in the course of parenting, and with a view of adults as developing their own "personal constructs" (Kelly, 1955).

The Basis of Change.   We started with a strong bias towards information as the major base of change. Like Flavell (1970), we were sympathetic towards Stolz's (1967) discription of parenthood as a period of "reality-testing": a time when ideas about children and parenting were checked, affirmed, modified, or discarded. That type of proposal has a great deal of intuitive appeal. It fits also with a prevailing image of children's cognitive development as based—most of the time—on an active interest in information and an accommodation of ideas to the events encountered. Finally, it fits with longitudinal data on the way parents change their ideas about their children's abilities as feedback becomes available from school performance (e.g., Entwisle & Hayduk, 1978, 1981).

The Direction of Change.   Apart from occasional cases of "regression," we usually think of development as being in a positive direction.

The Description of Parents' Ideas.   We faced from the start the need to find dimensions and content areas that would allow measures of change and variation. That search was in many ways our first encounter with gaps within conventional definitions of what cognitive development covers. We simply did not have available to us a ready-made language or framework that meshed neatly with ideas parents might hold about the nature of children or the nature of parenting.

We decided to start by checking through the literature on parents for suggestions about variations in ideas (Goodnow, 1982, 1985a). We also asked: What do parents themselves appear to be thinking about or using as a base when they interpret behaviors? What is the nature of such parental work? The combination of questions led us to a division of parents' ideas into three very broad domains: ideas about goals or "end-products", ideas about conditions that affect the reaching of goals, and ideas about how to assess the material one is working with (roughly, the use of omens, cues, or signs to assess a child's nature or current state).

The first domain overlaps with a literature often phrased in terms of "values." The second overlaps with a literature on attributions and on the perceived influence of heredity and environment. The third is the more novel. It reflects largely the everyday observation that parents spend a great deal of time and effort in locating signs that will help them to determine how well a child is doing or to predict a child's future. Fischer and Fischer (1963) in fact regarded such "divining" as one of the most salient characteristics of parents in Orchardtown, U.S.A. These parents, in the Fischers' description, regarded children as a collection of partially hidden "potentials." They also regarded themselves as having the obligation to "divine" that potential and then to arrange the environment so that potential could be maximized. We believed that some attempts at predicting, "divining," and evaluating occur among all parents and we were eager to have this part of parents' work represented in our approaches to their ideas.

Within each of the three domains, we also expected that one of the most useful steps would consist of locating *categories of behaviors;* that is, coming to learn how parents grouped behaviors, regarding some—for example—as more desirable, more attainable or as having more predictive value than others. That expectation, one may note, may be regarded as a follow-through from work on social cognition with children. Within work on moral reasoning, for instance, one helpful step has been the recognition that children differentiate among "misdeeds," regarding some behaviors as violating "social" rules while others violate "moral" rules (e.g., Nucci, 1981; Turiel, 1978). We expected to find parents' groupings or categories to be equally useful.

Overall, as the preceding statements imply, our original expectations were for positive change to be likely, for information to be its basis, and for some broad areas of content to be useful markers of change and variation. We shall now see how those expectations worked out in practice.

STUDY 1: IDEAS ABOUT AGE AND DEVELOPMENT

To the extent that parents hold any kind of informal theory of development, they should entertain some ideas about the relationship of behavior to age. That they do so is suggested by comments about children being "smart for their age," being "late bloomers," or "normal for their age." To such suggestions that parents have ideas about age-norms, we have added the possibility that they also entertain ideas about the stability of behavior over time, regarding some behaviors as fleeting while others are likely to mark some enduring quality. In a very broad sense, one might say that these ideas are aspects of parents' "developmental scripts" or "developmental scenarios." They may be expected to form an important basis to parents' task-setting and to their assessments of how well a child is progressing.

What conditions are likely to affect ideas about age-related behavior? We began with the goal of combining differences in cultural background with some differences in individual experience.

The notion that cultural background makes a difference to ideas about the nature of childhood is widespread. Combining variations in cultural background with variations in individual experience is a step less often taken. One such study is Ninio's (1979) comparison of ideas about early development held by mothers in Israel who came from two cultural groups and who varied also in the age of their child (1 or 3 years). The study we shall concentrate upon is Australian (Goodnow, Cashmore, Cotton, & Knight, 1981, 1984). The adults in the sample were mothers. Half the sample was born in Australia; half born in Lebanon (the children of these mothers spoke at home either only Arabic or a combination of Arabic and English). All of the mothers were enrolling a child for the first year of school (the child was between 4:9 and 5:5 years old). For half the sample, this child was the first to enter school; for the other half, not the first. This degree of contact with the school system and the implied difference in years of parenting was the factor reflecting the parents' experiences in parenting. To it may be added also differences in years of education (0 to 19 years in the Lebanese-born group). In general terms, we expected that experience with the Australian school system, and with any school system, would move the expectations of the Lebanese-born mothers towards those held by the Australian-born.

"Timetables"

Mothers were asked whether they expected a child to master each of 40 behaviors at ages 4–5 years, before 4, or after 6. The specific behaviors are much the same as those used in the study by Hess, Kashigawi, Azuma, Price, and Dickson (1980) and were generously lent in advance of publication by Robert Hess. The results may be simply stated. First, mothers did differentiate among behaviors; that is, they expected certain ones earlier than others. The only significant factor was cultural background. Mother's education, child's gender, and child's birth order had no effect. The two cultural groups differed most strongly in their age-expectations in the two areas found by Hess et al. (1980) to discriminate between mothers in the U.S.A. and in Japan: "verbal assertiveness" (e.g., "asks a question when in doubt," "can express a preference or opinion if asked"), and "social skills with peers" (e.g., "gets own way by persuading others," "initiates friendships," "is sensitive to the feelings of others"). Mothers in the U.S.A. and Australian-born mothers expected skills in these areas at an earlier age than was expected by the Japanese or the Lebanese-born.

The cultural difference was also the only factor yielding a difference on two open-ended questions about timetables. After describing an average day for the child in question, mothers were asked: "Does your child have any tasks around the house or in his or her room? And will that be the same when the child is a year older?" The Australian-born mothers assigned more tasks, often commenting on the value of early training. They also mentioned more changes in tasks from one year to the next, often adding the rationale that the child would be "a year older." In contrast, the Lebanese-born mothers assigned fewer tasks (although minding a younger child received more frequent mention than from the Australian-born). The Lebanese-born also mentioned either no planned change or a change based on the need of the mother (e.g., "My next baby will be born by then and I shall need the help").

Results and Expectations.   How well do these results fit our original expectations and reasons for interest?

The most rewarding result is that ideas about timetables turn out to be a rich area for exploring ideas about development and for broadening our notions of what cognitive development may cover. As a start, it has been possible to locate some of the ways in which parents differentiate among behaviors, expecting some at earlier ages than others, and to relate these groupings to differences in national background.

The exploration of ideas about age, however, need not be restricted to ideas about age-norms. On the contrary, a number of aspects of developmental scenarios emerged as promising.

One is the extent to which a parent expects that a *change in age is sufficient* for a change in tasks or skills, arguing, for instance, that "she will be older, so . . . ." or "now that he is 10, ..." Such arguments might reflect an age-oriented culture, or the reliance of novices on a single cue that is easy to use. A second possibility is the extent to which a parent considers that *"earlier is better."* We have come to recognize that, within the Lebanese and a number of other cultures, the attitude towards household skills is often one of acquiring them when needed, rather than believing that "earlier is better." Furthermore, within certain cultures experience may alter this aspect of ideas about age. In a current study of household tasks by Goodnow and Delaney, for instance, an Australian-born mother provides an example, describing why she gives few tasks to her third child: "I used to think you had to start it all when they were young, but now I'm more relaxed. I didn't start as early with the second as with the first, and they've both turned out all right." The third area for possible change is the particular set of behaviors to which a parent—in the light of experience—would now attach the notion of "earlier is better" rather than the idea that "you can wait." In effect, change could occur in the *content areas seen as requiring an early start*.

Finally, we would now suggest, for any study of timetables, the need to consider the *band of ages* that a parent would find as acceptable for the appearance of a behavior. That is, we would propose looking not only for the usual expected age, but also for the lower and upper limits: the ages at which appearance would seem "oddly early," and non-appearance "worryingly late." Such a band would build on Bell and Harper's (1977) proposal that parents judge behavior on the basis of a "zone of reference," adding the notion that it is the zone or band that is open to change.

In effect, we emerged with a number of ideas about possible ways of describing variation and change in parents' ideas. We did not, however, emerge with evidence of effects from mothers' individual experience and the information it provides. Perhaps the results for expected stability will be different.

Stability

To explore this content area, we asked mothers: "If a child is like this at age 6, what do you think is likely at age 12? Do you think it is likely to last, or to change?" The behaviors ranged from aspects of ability to aspects of style. In terms of relevant factors, the results may be even more simply stated than those for age-norms. *All* mothers, regardless of cultural background, expected "desirable" qualities (e.g., "understands easily," "is organized") to last, and "undesirable" qualities (e.g., "is easily upset by mistakes") to change.

That type of result has been taken further by Rosemary Knight, asking mothers and fathers of children aged 4, 7, and 10 years to make a judgment about the likelihood of change in a quality from ages 6 to 12 years, and to state how satisfied they were with the child's current progress in the same area. The qualities again covered a mixture of "cognitive," "social," and "style" qualities (e.g., "understands easily," "expresses love and affection," "is well-mannered," "tries hard," "has a sense of humor").

Knight's (1983) result takes the form of a strong canonical correlation between perceived stability and degree of satisfaction with current progress: $R^2 = .81$, for mothers, $R^2 = .79$ for fathers. Knight's data also yielded no significant effects from other factors: the age or gender of the child, or the gender of the parent. The sample was "Anglo" and restricted to a middle socioeconomic range, so that the effects of culture or socioeconomic status do not arise.

Results and Expectations.   Once again, the most positive result turns out to be the indications of interesting content areas to explore. This time, the promising content area consists of the *"predictive value"* that parents and others assign to behaviors. Stability judgments, we suspect, are part of a more general set of explorable ideas about sequence and prediction: ideas about necessary prerequisites, for instance, about "critical periods," or about the significance of various "signs" at one age for development in another.

The unexpected aspect of results is the way they point towards the role of need or function. Believing that things will improve—a position of "developmental optimism"—is useful. It allows one to continue with the task of parenting. In contrast, the picture does not look promising for any effect from individual experience on parents' ideas about stability. In fact, demand—the need to believe—appears to be the major factor combined with some attention to the quality of particular behaviors.

Some further results, however, keep alive the possibility that "values" and "needs" are not the only processes involved, and that parents are taking into account information about some other features of behavior. Within the stability expectations, one item ("is energetic and active") showed a clear sex difference (higher expected stability from mothers of preschool girls than for mothers of preschool boys). Such a quality is less stereotypic of girls than of boys, and mothers may note its appearance in a girl as indicating more of an "inbuilt" dispositional quality than they would for its appearance in a boy. This particular effect does not emerge with any clarity in Knight's (1983) study. The type of effect, however, is consistent with results from attribution theory, and is being explored further by Lisa Bird from the University of Wellington in New Zealand.

Stronger evidence comes from Dix and Grusec (1985). They have reported two important studies. In both, parents of children aged 4, 8, and 12 years were asked to give their attributions for behavior presented in vignette form. Study 1 sampled mothers and fathers, and negative behaviors: either actual misconduct (stealing, lying, fighting) or failure to be prosocial (not sharing, not helping, being insensitive). Study 2 sampled mothers only, but covered both negative and altruistic behaviors (helping, sharing, showing concern). We shall note for the moment one particular result, highlighted by Study 2. Dix and Grusec (1985, p. 227) noted that

> type of child behavior . . . was a significant determinant of every social influence we measured. Altruistic responses were seen as more stable, general, intentional, controllable, and more the result of dispositions in the child than were either failure to be altruistic or active misdeeds. Given the identical situation, why should parents think that sharing the cookies is more intentional, controllable, and dispositional than not sharing them; or that helping pick-up spilled items is more intentional, controllable, and dispositional than not helping?

Dix and Grusec (1985, p. 227) suggest that one factor is the parents' recognition that altrusitic behavior is "undertaken at a cost to the child, while failure to be altruistic and active misconduct actually provide benefits." Behavior that is not in one's own obvious self-interest, as models for adult behavior suggest

(Jones & Davis, 1965; Kelley, 1972), may be especially likely to be thought of as stemming from a disposition.

Implications

We have already pointed to some interesting and explorable content areas. What we now wish to emphasize is the extent to which the results raise questions about the impact of individual experience and the information it provides.

At this point, we have two challenges to the notion that parents' ideas change in response to the information they gain in the course of normal parenting. The first is suggested by the significance of cultural background for developmental timetables, coupled with the insignificance of differences in mothers' education, child age, or child gender. Such an effect suggests that at least in this content area parents are working less from "personal constructs" (Kelly, 1955) than from schemas provided for them by others. In absorbing such *ready-made schemas,* they may be said to be responding to information, but without the degree of thought or individualization that the notion of "personal construct" or "reality testing" implies. To use a term from Shweder (1982), the ideas seem to be somewhat "pre-packaged."

The second is the appearance of a possible double basis to parents' ideas. On the one hand, there is the information gained in the course of parenting (although evidence for that is not yet compelling). On the other is the presence of *a functional basis.* Ideas about stability, for instance, may reflect what one needs to believe in order to continue with the task of parenting. It is the possibility of a functional basis that we had underestimated. Once alerted to it, other compatible evidence became easier to find. Pharis and Manosevitz (1980), for instance, have compared two groups of young adults: a group about to be parents, and a group with no current intention to be parents. The former emerged as judging babies to be less difficult, less disruptive of one's life, and competent at an earlier age than did the latter. For people about to be parents, minimizing the problems probably has a functional value; for people who do not yet wish to be parents, maximizing the problems has value. A second example comes from a study by Hess, Price, Dickson, and Conroy (1982). Mothers and teachers in full-day preschool centers were alike in expecting earlier competence than did teachers in half-day centers. One suspects also that grandparents—for similar reasons of lesser need or responsibility—would also have relaxed developmental timetables.

Recognizing a larger role for need or necessity, however, does not mean that these factors can have undisputed sway over ideas. The behaviors expected early by parents might be the behaviors they especially value. We would not, however, want to accept value as the only factor. In the normal course of events, feasibility should surely be taken into account. All told, an early expectation probably combines ideas about value, feasibility, and the possible dangers of starting "late," allowing some competitive behavior to creep in. The general task is really not one of arguing for information versus need or value as single factors, but of sorting out the way they interact and the conditions that at times give one a stronger weighting than the other.

As a more immediate step, what has arisen is the possibility that if we wish to explore further the effects of individual experience, we may need to shift to some other content area within parents' ideas, that is, to ideas other than developmental timetables or perceived stability. These are areas where we now know that the effects of culture and of a functional basis are strong. We chose parents' ideas about parental influence and responsibility.

STUDY 2: IDEAS ABOUT PARENTAL INFLUENCE AND RESPONSIBILITY

Some time ago, Kohn (1963) suggested that parents' ideas about methods might be more amenable to change than their ideas about what they thought children should be. People read books, magazines, or columns of advice to parents, he argued, for advice on how to achieve goals that remained unexamined. In addition, he proposed, the historical changes noted by scholars such as Bronfenbrenner (1958) were predominantly changes in ideas about methods rather than changes in values.

Within the general rubric of ideas about methods for child-rearing, we may place two specific sets of ideas. One refers to divisions of labor: in the present case, divisions of labor between parents. The second refers to ideas about the amount of influence one has over various aspects of development. The work of Knight (1981, 1983) combines attention to both aspects. It extends some earlier work on ideas about divisions of labor by Russell (1979), and on perceived influence by Goodnow et al. (1981) and by Russell and Russell (1982). It is linked also to an argument by Freeburg and Payne (1967) to the effect that knowledge about parents' perceptions of their influence is in short supply, surprisingly so given the importance psychologists usually assign parental influence.

Knight's main sample (Knight, 1983) contains 60 couples with children (all first-born) aged either 4, 7, or 10 years. The sample was intended to capture variations in experience represented by being a mother rather than a father, by years of parenting, and by the first-born being a boy or a girl.

Divisions of Labor

If children were in school, parents were asked: "Does your child get very much help with schoolwork or homework?" If children were not yet in school, the question became: "Do you expect to give help?" If the answer was yes, the next question was: "Who helps (or is likely to help)?" At age 4, 89% expected to help; the modal expectation was that both parents would help (57% both, 31% mother, 12% father). For parents of 7-year-olds, the percentage of parents helping had dropped to 53%; the modal pattern had become one of it being mostly mother's work (26% both; 63% mothers; 11% fathers). The same pattern applies for parents of 10-year-olds: 68% reported giving help; 24% of these reported help from both parents, 65% from mothers, 11% from fathers.

Results and Expectations. We could propose several explanations for Knight's (1983) results on divisions of labor. The one we offer is in terms of a *shift from an idealized picture,* based on experience providing information about the feasibility or the difficulty of an original hope. That proposal has some generalization value, that is, it could apply beyond ideas about divisions of labor. We can, in fact, apply it immediately to some further data of Knight's (1983) on parents' estimates of children's positions in their school class.

Knight (1983) asked parents to rate children on progress in school: as one of the best in the class, above the middle, in the middle, below the middle, near the bottom. Parents of 7-year-olds gave most of their answers to the top two rankings (76%). Parents of 10-year-olds were less enthusiastic (50% in the top two ranks). At both age levels, the remainder of the ranked positions were mostly "in the middle" (20%, 32%). (It needs to be remembered that these parents were volunteers, and were not the total sample of parents in a class, a factor that could account for an apparent bias towards high expectations but not for the age difference.)

The shift appears again to be from one of original high hopes to a more realistic picture. That type of change, with an important addition, accounts as well for a finding by Entwisle and Hayduk (1978, 1981) in a longitudinal study of parents' expectations of children's marks over the first years of primary school. Within a middle-class group, these expectations did change towards a more realistic picture. The important feature to Entwisle and Hayduk's (1981) work is that the basis for change was specified. It lay in the mothers' greater knowledge of how marks had to be distributed: that is, in their awareness of the mean and the range. Mothers did not necessarily change their views about a specific child's ability. Acquisition of *knowledge about the range of possibilities*—the nature of the competition in this case—seems then a promising aspect of ideas to link with increasing experience.

Perceived Influence

In two studies, parents have stated that their influence over children declines as the child grows older, particularly once the child enters school (Knight, 1981; Newson & Newson, 1976). These statements were made in response to open-ended questions about influence in general. To take such possibilities further, Knight (1983) selected behaviors and qualities to represent three domains: social (e.g., "expresses love and affection," "is well mannered and well-behaved"), cognitive (e.g., "understands easily," "catches on quickly," "is able to think things out, to reason and solve problems"), and style (e.g., "is not easily distractible and holds interest in tasks," "is imaginative and creative—e.g., at painting or making-up stories"). Later item analyses showed that the parents used two categories: one covering the investigator's "cognitive" and "style" groups, the other covering "social" behaviors.

Parents rated each quality for how much influence they felt they had over it. They also rated each item for the amount of influence they perceived teachers had over it, a check on whether a characteristic was seen as open to all forms of influence or as differentially open to the influence of particular people.

Results and Expectations.   Once again, we emerged with some interesting ways to describe parents' ideas and the way parents differentiate among behaviors. We have already mentioned that on item analysis parents used two categories, dividing behaviors into "social" and "cognitive" domains. A further basis for categorization comes from comparing parents' perceptions of their own influence with their perceptions of teachers' influences. The comparative ratings yielded three groups:

1. A group where parents' ratings of their own influence far exceeded the influence they attributed to teachers. These were predominantly the "social" items.
2. A group where parents perceived the influence of parents and teachers to be equal or close to equal. These items referred to general aspects of ability and achievement (being curious and interested, for example, thinking things out, trying hard, expressing things easily in words, catching on quickly).
3. A small group where parents perceived the influence of teachers to exceed their own. This group covered two specific school skills ("doing well at ' "is not easily distractible and holds interest in tasks").

With a knowledge of that type of grouping, it would now become interesting to ask—as one step—whether teachers give the same ratings, or whether they see their influence as exceeding that of parents in more than the two specific areas that this group of parents allotted them. As in attribution studies, a position of responsibility for development, combined with greater opportunities for observation, may alter one's perceptions of influence and of feasibility.

The unexpected result was again one of *limited evidence for experience.* With one clear exception, we did not find data supporting the notion that experience in parenting would change parents' ideas about the extent of their influence. Child age (and child gender) were not significant effects.

The exception is related to whether the parent is a mother or a father. Mothers and fathers were highly similar on items in the ''cognitive/style'' area. They were also close to alike in their perception of teachers' influence (mothers gave teachers somewhat more credit for influence overall). They differed clearly, however, on items in the ''social'' area (mothers perceiving their influence as higher than fathers saw theirs). On a 5-way analysis of variance, the interaction between domain, parent gender, and parent/teacher influence was significant.

This interesting interaction takes an important step towards unravelling any effects from experience. It also points up, however, the need to be cautious in one's inferences. In this particular case, we have at last signs of an effect from the type of parental experience. We cannot yet tell, however, whether the mother/father difference reflects experience, responsibility (and the need to believe in one's influence), or both.

Implications

As with the study on ideas about age and development (timetables and stability), we need to review progress in two directions: (a) finding ways of describing parents' ideas, preferably ways that might reflect change and broaden our picture of cognitive development, especially among adults; (b) locating conditions and processes that might be related to change.

As with the first study, we are again doing well with the task of finding interesting ways to describe parents' ideas, ways that open some fresh vistas in the description of cognition. As with the first study, we are also presented with some puzzling questions about the effects of individual experience and the information it provides. These are critical questions if we are to think of cognitive development as based less on structural change than on change in one's knowledge and one's opportunities to test ideas. In other words, these are questions of particular importance for exploring adult cognitive development.

The questions are threefold: (1) Are there other studies supporting the notion that mothers and fathers will differ in their ideas, in ways that seem attributable to different types of experience in parenting? (2) Is it likely that change requires particular forms of experience? The difference between mothers and fathers, for example, or between 4 and 7 years of parenting, may not be sufficient to bring about a difference in ideas about parental influence. These two questions are directed towards accounting for why differences are not as easy to find as we expected. The third looks toward accounting for any differences we do locate. (3) How far can we attribute differences in ideas to differences in experience?

Possible Effects from Experience and Information.   Bear in mind that the general case for positive cognitive changes among adults rests on relating changes in ideas to changes in experience. Knight's (1983) finding of one area of difference between mothers and fathers is a promising sign. It cannot, however, stand alone. Can we add to it other data reporting differences between mothers' and fathers' ideas that seem attributable to differences in experience? There are some.

One comes from work by G. Russell (1983). Fathers—after they take on a larger share of caregiving—recognize that the task of parenting is more demanding, less straightforward, and more isolating than they had expected. In this respect, experience seems to move fathers' perceptions closer to mothers' perceptions.

A second result comes from Stolz (1967). She reports a difference between mothers and fathers in the frequency with which parents attributed their actions to beliefs or values as against "other influences" (e.g., the pressure of a particular time or place, or previous experience with trying to follow through on a general belief with a particular child). "Other influences" were mentioned by mothers in 63% of their statements about reasons, compared with fathers' 53%, an apparently small difference but statistically significant. The recognition that one's ideas about "good" parenting need to be set aside as not feasible at particular times—treated as ideals rather than practicalities—seems likely to reflect experience.

A third result comes from a large-scale study at E.T.S., reported by McGillicuddy-de Lisi (1982) and by Sigel, McGillicuddy-de Lisi, and Johnson (1980). It is again in the form of a difference in the relationship between ideas and actions. Mothers and fathers were similar in their beliefs about the way children learn. They differed, however, in the degree to which their ideas were linked to observed actions. The relationship was significant for fathers but not for mothers (.15 compared with .10 in a path analysis reported by McGillicuddy-de Lisi, 1982). On the two tasks used as measures of actions, mothers also displayed behavior that was more task-specific than did fathers. For mothers, in fact, correlations for types of action across the two tasks were not significant (Sigel, 1982), suggesting again that mothers are more inclined than are fathers to follow the demands of a specific situation rather than general principles.

In effect, the most promising signs of difference in ideas related to variations in experience lie in the greater differentiation of ideas with experience: a differentiation that appears in ideas about means or methods rather than about goals. People involved in daily caregiving are less inclined to believe that general principles can be followed through with specific children in specific situations. The nature of an expert's learning, it appears, lies in the addition of many qualifications to an idea: "it all depends." A lesser knowledge seems to allow also a simpler link to action.

The Critical Aspects of Experience.   Suppose we assume for the moment that any differences observed between mothers and fathers are the result of differences in experience. We would next need to ask: What are likely to be the critical aspects of experience? Given the small evidence to date for mother/father differences, we have not taken that question very far at all. We would draw attention, however, to a specific prpposal for how differences might emerge. On the basis of studies of families where care is truly shared by mothers and fathers (Russell, 1982a, 1982b; G. Russell & Radin, 1982), Russell and Radin have proposed that changes in fathers' ideas do not come from any simple increase in exposure to children, from "helping mothers," or from "holding the fort" until the mother returns. Change occurs only, it is argued, when fathers assume real responsibility for an area (G. Russell & Radin, 1982). Until that happens, the need to reevaluate one's ideas is apparently not sufficiently strong.

Isolating Experience as the Critical Factor. We are still not sure when mother/father differences are the result of differences in experience and when they represent differences between males and females, regardless of experience in parenting. This problem of inference gives one pause, regardless of whether one's primary interest is in mother/father differences per se or if one is using mother/father comparisons as prime markers for the effects of experience.

The same problem of inference, we may note, arises also when we analyze the effects of a child's age. Suppose, for instance, that it were firmly established that the parents of 7-year-olds perceive themselves as having less influence over child development than do parents of 4-year-olds. Could we infer that the difference reflects an effect from experience? Or is there a prevailing belief in our culture—common to all parents and to non-parents—that the younger the child, the more malleable?

The way round the problems of inference does not lie in shifting to longitudinal studies. Some problems would arise regardless of whether a design was longitudinal or cross-sectional. A more feasible solution seems to lie in the selection of particular content areas. There are, for instance, content areas where parents' ideas diverge from folklore. Folklore, for instance, favors a belief in "maternal instinct." Mothers' lesser belief in it than fathers' (G. Russell, 1979) must then reflect some other factor: the reality of finding oneself uncertain, or the wish to believe equally in fathers' competence.

There are also content areas where there is no prevailing folklore but where parents differ among themselves. Knight's (1983) finding that mothers rate teachers as more influenctial than fathers do is an example.

Both types of content area will be essential if we are to untangle several sources of change in parents' ideas or if we are, on a broader scale, to explore differences in ideas in relation to differences in experience.

STUDY 3: IDEAS ABOUT THE NATURE OF LEARNING

In this last section dealing with specific studies, we wish to draw upon a study by another graduate student at Macquarie: Andrew Reiner (Reiner, 1982). The work is a longitudinal study of an "alternative" school established as a parent cooperative. It was not originally intended to be an analysis of change in parents' ideas about the way children learn, but turned out to provide some very helpful information about the nature and conditions of development and to prompt some questions one might ask in any study of change.

Who is Interested in Changing their Ideas?   You might expect that parents who start or join an alternative school will hold some non-traditional views about education and will be open to learning more about the value of a progressive approach. For some parents, that was true. A number had read widely on the issue of "progressive" education, and continued to do so. For many, however, the primary interest was not in changing their own ideas. The motivation lay in a sense that their own schooling had been an unhappy experience, one they would not wish their children to repeat. For some, the push came from recognizing that their child was deeply unhappy at school and not achieving, a situation overcoming a strong initial distrust.

In effect, even people who were alike in having taken the same action—an unusual action at that—were not alike in their openness to new information or in their wish to alter their views. The result is one more reminder of the need to qualify any image of adults as eagerly and happily readjusting their ideas in the light of new information. It is also a reminder of the presence of individual differences—at all ages—in the degree of interest brought to cognitive change.

Is Change Always Positive?   We have so far looked for change only in the direction of "positive" effects, with positive defined in terms of greater depth, more subtlety, more differentiation, or taking account of several factors and perspectives. This is not always the case. In Reiner's (1983) account, a number of parents and teachers, faced with ideas or situations more "progressive" than they had expected, tended to retreat into less differentiated ideas.

An illustration comes from the first few weeks of the new school. The two teachers appointed had assumed that parents would know that the critical first step was the establishment of good feeling between teachers and children, and that activities would be relatively unstructured, with most of the initiative for any particular activity coming from the child. The parents, perhaps to their own surprise, found the result deeply disturbing and soon began asking the children what they had "done" each day and expressing to the School's Council concern that the teachers were "not doing anything," and that the classrooms needed more "order" and "structure" and less "chaos."

That type of conflict occurred over and over again, either between parents and teachers or among parents, with a number of teachers and parents moving back to more "conventional" ideas and to more fixed positions.

Were there then no people who changed towards being more "progressive?" Under what conditions? A few teachers and parents did so, after an initial period of doubt about whether "progressive" education could every really work. Among the parents, those who changed were those who spent a large amount of time in the classroom. They were impressed with changes in children's attitudes, especially in the degree to which they were becoming self-managing, enthusiastic, imaginative, and helpful to each other. These changes in children, however, were difficult to communicate to people who came in briefly and saw only the surface "chaos." In effect, the evidence that could lead to a change of ideas was not highly visible. For one other parent whose ideas changed in major fashion—from being initially appalled to being enthusiastic—the evidence that overcame her original ideas was the obvious happiness and interest in reading shown by her young son, whose unhappiness and failure to read had been the spur to her willingness to try any alternative.

The point of both stories—the concern about children "not doing anything" and the cases of change—lies in the way they point to *the availability and the visibility of information* as conditions affecting whether or not change occurs in one's ideas.

Are Some Ideas More Amenable to Change than Others?   We have suggested so far that one large factor in the occurrence of change is the extent to which maintaining an idea fits a particular need or demand: it is self-protective, ego-enhancing, effort-sustaining. We now wish to point to a further possibility. Some ideas may be more deeply ingrained than others. Some may be part of a broader set of ideas, with the effect that information directed towards one has to counter not just the evidence sustaining that particular idea but also the weight of evidence supporting the rest of the set. To change what may seem to us to be a "single" idea may amount almost to a change in one's larger "world view."

We shall use Reiner's (1983) material and concepts to make those possibilities more specific. Some ideas about learning and about children, he argues, are so ingrained in today's thinking that they are extremely difficult to "think away" or to "unthink." Some of these ideas are part of a Protestant ethic: primarily, the notion that people—children especially—cannot be trusted to manage their own learning. They will "become lazy," "stop working when things get hard," "prefer to do nothing." The same ethic assumes that what is "good" for one is not likely to be pleasant. More specifically, learning will be predominantly tedious and will require forced drill.

Other *ingrained ideas* are part of what has been called "modern consciousness" (Berger, Berger, & Kellner, 1974). These ideas cover:

— the central place given to "work," so much so that most other activities and occasions (leisure, weekends, holidays) are defined as time away from "work";
— the sharp line drawn between "work" and "play";

— the assumption that the value of any present activity rests in its preparation for the future: only the future, in fact, justifies one's present actions;
— the assumption that learning proceeds best by breaking a subject matter into small components, placing these in sequence, and working one's way through a carefully controlled sequence;
— the assumption that learning requires a "teacher," an "expert";
— the assumption that any achievement can be improved; a better way, a higher level of product, can always be found;
— the need to judge by way of visible products, preferably products that can be quantified.

The ideas least likely to change, Reiner (1983) proposes, are those that are part of today's "modern consciousness," using that term to incorporate the Protestant ethic. They are also, to take the argument a little further in a fashion proposed by Berger et al. (1974), those ideas that are continually sustained by the social structures or institutions encountered in everyday life. It is difficult, for example, to accept as valuable a schoolday with no set class periods, no set "snack time" or "lunch time," as long as one continues to live in a world where segmentation of time and keeping to a schedule are taken for granted. To give up such ideas, in the analysis of Berger et al. (1974), calls for the equivalent of religious conversion.

SOME PRACTICAL IMPLICATIONS

In the last two sections of this paper, we wish to bring out some implications: implications for deliberately changing adults' ideas and for the way we view cognitive development (among adults or children).

We shall start with some work on altering parents' ideas. That direction of work provides a good testing ground for hypotheses about adult cognitive change. It is also a reminder that intervention has been in some studies an explicit reason for studying parents' ideas. The hope is that altering ideas may prove to be a way of changing behavior that can apply to a range of practices and a range of ages, as well as being more amenable to change than are some other conditions affecting practices: conditions such as income level, for example (Schaefer & Edgerton, 1985; Sigel, 1985). One might, for instance, work towards a change in knowledge about developmental timetables as a way of reducing the unrealistic expectations thought to be a factor in child abuse (Parke, 1978; Spinetta & Rigler, 1972), or towards a change in the perceived capacity to influence cognitive or scholastic achievement, thought to be a factor in the lower school achievement of some cultural groups (cf. Ghuman, 1975; Radin, 1972).

There are risks in any program of parent education. There is, for instance, the risk of programs being used as ways to eliminate cultural differences rather than to respect them, and to strengthen the dependence of parents on the advice of experts. For this and for pragmatic reasons, it is essential that we regularly ask: Do parents' ideas really need changing? And what have we learned that could be helpful to remember in working towards change?

We have already suggested two general points. One is that it would be unrealistic to expect any easy change in ideas where parents had a vested interest in maintaining particular views. The other is that it would be wise to consider the compatibility of new information with ideas already held. That second type of factor is especially highlighted in a study by Frankel and Roer-Bornstein (1982). Among people from the Yemen, many of the traditional explanations for events in pregnancy and birth were ''magical'' in nature. The new information stressed physical explanations. Young Yemenite mothers apparently ended in a state of suspension. When asked about miscarriage, for instance, they ''failed to offer any explanation. A magical tradition may have been rejected, but nothing else seemed to take its place as an explanatory construct'' (Frankel & Roer-Bornstein, 1982, p. 15). Such a limbo-like state hardly seems desirable.

Suppose we take a specific case. Robyn Dolby and her colleagues have been working in a Sydney hospital with the parents of preterm babies. In addition to finding that parents benefit from watching and discussing videotapes of their babies being tested on the Brazelton scale (Dolby, English, & Warren, 1982), they have isolated a particular problem in the interaction between babies and parents. The babies often display marked motor activity, with arms and legs moving at a rapid rate. To clinicians, the activity often signals a form of distress: the infant cannot bring itself to a resting state; the movements are rigid or piston-like. In an adult, a comparable state is an agitated tiredness: one is too ''wound up'' to relax. To parents, however, the activity is a sign of vigor, even though the infant may be crying, and most parents take no steps to bring the activity to a stop. In fact, some take pride in the way such activity shows how ''strong'' the infant is.

Intervention in such counter-productive interactions seems desirable for both parent and infant: the infant is clearly distressed; the parent finds the infant's crying both stressful and puzzling. In intervening, however, it is helpful to recognize that the parents' interpretations will not be easy to set aside. In discussions with Dolby, it becomes clear that the interpretation of motor activity as distress is counter-intuitive for most parents. For parents of preterm babies, the activity is also reassuring. What they fear in their babies is a continuation of the weak, passive state they have already observed. To simply say, then, that the activity is not a ''healthy'' sign is likely to be ineffective. Parents would not wish to hear such a message. Nor is the message compatible with the rest of their informal knowledge, with its equation of ''activity'' with ''vigor'' and ''strength,'' an equation reinforced by the language and the visual images encountered every day.

Robyn Dolby is finding that, under these circumstances, the most effective steps towards change lie in demonstrating the effects of swaddling: the infant relaxes, ceases to cry, and may even smile. Only after the parent has been demonstrated a technique that brings another desired result—a happily relaxed child—does any discussion of the meaning of the child's activity seem appropriate or useful. That order of help remains to be checked, but it has a very good fit with what we have learned about the importance of functional or affective bases to parents' ideas.

In effect, Dolby's approach brings out several aspects of intervention. One is that it is directed first towards ideas proposed as most open to change: that is, ideas about "how to," about means rather than ends or values. A second is that it highlights the need to ask: What kind of information would be compelling?

Two Caveats to this Picture of Practical Implications.   The preceding comments may appear to suggest that the link between ideas and actions is a simple one, and that "actions" are all we wish to change.

There are, in fact, many sources of "slippage" between ideas and actions, operating against finding any isomorphism between the two (Goodnow, 1985). To state some of those briefly: (a) Ideas are often general, actions have to be specific to a time, a place, a task and a particular child; (b) Ideas often describe what is "good" in principle, actions more often involve specific cost-benefit assessments. In terms of advice to parents, such discrepancies may well mean that "general" advice may not be found helpful or lead to change in actions. General advice may also be set aside in favor of taking an inexpensive action even though it is perceived as having a low likelihood of payoff, or avoiding an action that is theoretically "good" but costly in time, effort, or emotion.

The comments on intervention may also seem to suggest that the only relevant consequence of parents' ideas—and change in their ideas—lies in an effect upon parents' actions, with these actions then seen as the major or the only determinants of the way children develop. That suggestion needs qualifying on several counts.

First, it seems quite likely that children discount a number of specific parental actions ("that's just Mum losing her cool again," to use a statement recently heard) and that they often respond to parents' intentions rather than to specific actions. Second, stress on a direct link between parental actions and child outcomes ignores the importance of an intervening step: namely, the child's perception of the parents' positions (Cashmore & Goodnow, 1985).

Finally, reservations about too heavy a stress on parents' "actions," and on changing their "actions," stem from the way that "actions" seem to be defined in terms of "deeds," excluding "words" and implying that "words" are unimportant or are not "deeds." We would like to stress the importance of parents' words. Words provide the categories of activities (e.g., "work" and "play") and of people ("nice" and "not nice," "poor" and "well-off," "family" and "not family" etc.) that soon become taken for granted and hard to change. Parents' stated interpretations also provide children with the reasons that soon become part of the way children see the world: "you clean your teeth because . . . , you work hard at school because . . . , you respect your parents because . . . , you give money to the poor because . . . ." Such words and statements seem seldom to be studied, however, as forms of parental "action." If they were fully regarded as such, we might see more advice to parents explicitly directed towards ways of making their values clear; ways of altering their statements so that they achieve a goal of importance to them, namely, "getting their message across." Such forms of intervention might alter not only the impact of parents' ideas but also, by putting parents' ideas into a shape that can be looked at and reflected upon, alter the ideas themselves.

SOME THEORETICAL IMPLICATIONS

We started this round of research with several expectations drawn from prevailing approaches to cognitive development in children: expectations of change as probable, as positive, and as taking the form of constructions based on an individual's lively interest in information and his or her own active interactions with objects and people. We also started with the expectation that three broad content areas of ideas (roughly ends, means, and assessments of progress) would provide a promising base for the exploration of parents' ideas.

We may now stand back and review those expectations, especially those dealing with the probable basis of change. The adults present us with a picture of people who are not omnivorous for information. In fact, they are often resistant, with the degree of resistance to change particularly marked for some "ingrained" ideas. They also show fewer signs of readiness for growth than anticipated, and the ideas they hold are often related to functions or situation demands: sustaining effort, enhancing self-esteem, making life with children more bearable or more rewarding. Overall, there is not so far any strong evidence of any inherent push towards moving from one level of thought to another: the type of motor or motivation often proposed for change in children's thought.

We had expected to make some changes in the course of bringing a model based largely on "physical" cognition to a content area that is "social." The contrasts with our expectations, however, were more than expected. They raise four questions:

1. *Does the model drawn from children's cognitive development simply not hold for adults?* We shall be proposing that one difficulty in answering this question is the relative lack of continuity in tasks (and their interest value) across the life-span. A further difficulty is the nature of the child model.
2. *Does the child model we normally use need modifying?* If so, in what ways? We shall be proposing that modification is needed to the expectation of change, to the emphasis on individual constructions, to the image

of information as readily available, and to the degree of attention given to incentives for acquiring or providing information.

3. *How did we come to use such a limited model for expectations about development?* We shall be proposing that classical Piagetian models take the form they do because they are based largely on knowledge domains where "social" factors are minimal.

4. *Is the division of knowledge domains into "physical" and "social" cognition the most effective division?* Based largely on our answers to question (3), we shall be proposing some alternatives.

We shall take up each of these questions in turn.

Adult Thought and Children's Thought: Discontinuous?

Most of the literature on adults' reasoning is not in accord with the prevailing pictures of children's development. Adult reasoning, for instance, is usually described as based on short-cuts, prone to error, and dedicated towards saving effort. That is not the classical Piagetian child (or, we think, the Vygotskian child).

It is possible that adults lose curiosity as they grow older and no longer wish to put effort into better ideas except in special domains. Certainly the Piagetian literature begins to discuss motivation, in the form of interest in a particular subject matter, in the context of adolescence (cf. Piaget, 1972).

It is also possible, however, that there is more continuity than might appear. One problem in deciding about that is a dearth of research that takes the same topics of thought across a wide age-span. In part, topics of interest do change. The constancy of weight, for instance, once resolved as a problem, probably ceases to be an active topic of thought. There are, however, topics that remain of interest throughout the life-span, even though their specific form may change. There are also some characteristics of thinking that may be followed across a long age-span.

Those claims may sound easy to make but hard to implement. What might such topics and dimensions be? We shall start with one dimension (the quality of thought) and then consider some promising content areas.

The Quality of Thought.   Attention to the quality of thought is extremely prominent in studies of children. In fact, one might describe the essence of the Piagetian approach as a concern with change in the quality of thought.

At the moment, work on adult social cognition seems to show less concern with differences in quality than with changes in content. The striking exception is work by Sameroff and his colleagues (cf. Sameroff, 1975; Sameroff & Feil, 1985). In their view, a parent might start from a "categorical," single-factor explanation (e.g., "just a contented baby" or "just a difficult child") and shift to one that is multi-factor or "perspectivistic" (e.g., "she was slow getting started and I was inexperienced and there was no one around to help"). The approach comes from Piagetian accounts of child development.

It is not clear why the type of approach Sameroff exemplifies is under-represented in work on adult thought, when compared with work on children's thinking. It is almost as if the assumptions exist that changes in quality will be of most interest when there are changes in capacity, and that, until old age strikes, changes in capacity are not the issue in adult development. In fact, as we have seen in the results comparing mothers with fathers, it may be the quality of ideas—in that case, the degree of conviction and of differentiation—that is the major aspect of change.

Categories of Behaviors. Psychologists have always been interested in the nature of categories or groupings, with attention shifting from the way people categorize objects to the way they group people or, more recently, situations (cf. Forgas, 1982). Work with parents' ideas about children brings out the importance of considering the way people group behaviors. Parents clearly distinguish among behaviors, regarding some as more acceptable, stable, or dispositional than others (Dix & Grusec, 1984; Goodnow et al., 1984). They also appear to regard some as more significant than others, a point made by Dix and Grusec (1985) for social behaviors and by Schieffelin (1979) for language behaviors.

The clearest counterpart in work with children is work on "moral" development, with attention paid to the way children distinguish among various types of "transgressions" or "rule-violations" (cf. Much & Shweder, 1978; Nucci, 1981; Turiel, 1978). These studies, in Shweder's (1982) analysis, contain gaps, gaps related primarily to the way categories may be linked together, and to our knowledge of the sources that give rise to the development of some categories rather than others. The same gaps might well be explored in work on parents' categories.

Developmental "Scripts" or "Scenarios." We use these terms to describe the pictures people have of how the course of life is laid out: pictures that include "milestones," what may be expected at various ages, how one moves from one "stage" or "state" to another, when the best and the hardest times of one's life will be. Parents, charged with the responsibility to see that their children follow a particular set of life-course scenarios, perhaps spend more time thinking about developmental sequences and timetables than other adults do. Neugarten and Hagestad (1975), however, present us with the argument that a major part of all adult thinking consists of measuring oneself and others against expected times and progressions: for leaving school, "settling down," having children, finding a job, retiring, dying.

This type of content area appears underrepresented in work on children's cognitive development. What developmental scenarios do they have in mind? How are they acquired? What distinguishes one from another? Such questions are not unanswerable. They do move us, however, towards regarding age-span cognitive development in a new light. It may well consist of changes in the nature and the clarity of the paths one sees as connecting various parts of one's life, especially those leading from the present to the future. Such a definition of cognitive development is contained, for instance, in Bronfenbrenner's (1977) approach to the ecology of childhood, Tyler's (1978) stress on the perceptions of paths and options as a way of describing individual differences, and Poole's (in press) adaptation of Tyler's views to analyze adolescents' perceptions of progressions from school to work.

Relationships across Generations.   Suppose we have found some topics that are of interest across a number of age groups. Are we then limited to asking whether several age groups (e.g., a "child" and an "adult" generation) are similar? That would be a narrow view of continuity. We could readily add a check on the way one age group perceives the thinking of the other.

At the moment, close attention to cross-generation agreement and cross-generation perceptions is largely the province of sociologists, with little actual data on perception as a mediating step (cf. Bengston & Troll, 1978; Troll & Bengston, 1979).

A gap-filling step is described in Cashmore and Goodnow (1985). It consists of comparing parents' statements about the qualities they see as important for their 12- to 14-year-olds to acquire, with children's statements about the qualities they themselves see as important and about the qualities they see their parents as stressing. That type of work brings out an interesting result: for most qualities, the best predictor of the adolescents' positions is their perception of the parents' positions. The exceptions to this perceived agreement with parents are qualities where parents and adults seem to have different vested interests ("being neat" and "being obedient"). The result underlines again the importance of considering both information and interests as determinants of ideas. It also demonstrates the way one may use a single content area to explore not only the presence of similarity but also its basis.

Overall, there is no shortage of promising topics that would allow us to ask more precisely about similarities in adult and child thought and about the extent to which the same model of development might apply. We shall make only restricted progress, however, if at the same time the child model does not come up for review.

Modifying the Traditional Child Model

For us, the traditional model is the Piagetian model, with its emphasis on children individually and rationally building up a picture of their world—constructing reality—on the basis of their driving curiosity and their active exploration of that world. The main restraint on change is the individual's capacity to take in information that is readily available. The model is thought to apply equally to the understanding of the "physical" and the "social" domain, that is, to a world of objects and a world of people.

We still have a great deal of respect for the Piagetian model, even while we work for expansions and qualifications. One familiar re-examination takes the form of asking whether the same model fits equally well the domains of "physical" and "social" cognition. We would like to set that aside for the moment and ask instead: Based on what we have seen of adult thought, what would we now wish to add to the picture of how change comes about? What questions would we now raise, starting from the assumption that the factors affecting adult thought must have some representation in our picture of children's thinking?

We suggest a second look at (a) the expectation of change, (b) the emphasis on individual constructions; (c) the notion of information as readily available; and (d) the need to consider motives and incentives for either acquiring or providing information.

The Expectation of Change and Improvement.   We started the adult research with an expectation that adults would be interested in new ideas and in "fine-tuning" their ideas to fit with new information. We have come to see the need for an alternative model, one proposing that parental ideas and practices display more continuity than change (Roberts, Block, & Block, 1981). A simple choice between two working models (change or no change) is not the task to be faced. The real problem turns out to be a question of specifying particular conditions that produce change, the particular ideas that are more or less likely to be altered, and the people who are more or less interested in change.

We have now begun to consider that the child model may display an excessive interest in change, with less attention given than is warranted to the maintenance of ideas or to resistance to change. There is room for a shift in emphasis. The Piagetian model does contain a place for assimilation: a process by which the thinker resists new information, protecting himself or herself from instability or chaos, from being pulled in too many different directions by new material. Assimilation, however, seems to have been a far less studied process than the accommodation looked for in training studies or studies of environmental effects. There is also a place for resistance to change in the discussion of adolescence and the achievement of formal operational thought. In the face of wide individual differences in the occurrence of this achievement and large effects from the type of material being thought about, Piagetian theory (Piaget, 1972) has come to include a role for motivation and interest. The inclusion recognizes both the effect of specific experience and the effort involved in improving one's ideas. It is difficult to believe, however, that children do not—at least in some domains—proceed in just the same pragmatic, expedient way that adults seem to most of the time. We would now be encouraged to look for "adult-type" procedures and heuristics in children's work. We would also, in any theory, look more carefully for accounts not only of the way new ideas are acquired but also of the way old ideas are maintained and new ideas resisted.

The Emphasis on Individual Constructions.   The individual in classical Piagetian theory is relatively solitary. His or her own activities count most in the construction of ideas, with other people playing primarily the role of offering discrepancies that can lead to some modification of the original thought.

In our adult research, however, we have found a number of widely-shared ideas, with individual differences less apparent than would be expected from the diversity of parenting experience. One possible explanation is that the apparent diversity of experience still allows a number of achieved ideas to be like one another. An alternate way of looking at the pattern is to begin considering some ideas as not being achieved at all on the basis of individual construction. One might consider three possibilities:

1. information gained from an individual's direct interactions with the targets of thought (people or objects), and from active thought;
2. information received in more passive fashion from others, peers or adults: "pre-packaged" in Shweder's (1982) terms. Ideas acquired in this fashion might be particularly expected to be shared by members of a group, to be "collective representations" (Shweder, 1982);
3. information gained and validated in the course of negotiations and discussions with one's peers. This is, for instance, the type of source stressed by Youniss (1982) in his analysis of children's acquisition of moral judgments.

As the references to Shweder (1982) and Youniss (1982) indicate, the second and third sources of ideas are now becoming visible in the literature on children's thinking. Also emerging in that literature is a closer attention to the specific ways in which meanings are "negotiated" (Youniss, 1982) or "cultural messages" transmitted (Much & Shweder, 1978; Shweder, 1982).

The debate between Shweder (1982) and Youniss (1982) is concentraded on children's acquisition of moral reasoning. It can well extend beyond that area. As Damon (1983) notes, all social relationships and social cognitions involve "the transmission of culture." So also does the acquisition of ideas about the nature of "intelligent behaviors" (Goodnow, 1976). In fact, the sociological literature on negotiated meanings and cultural transmission covers every area of knowledge. For developmental psychologists, the problem is one of bringing general ideas into specifiable form, and of working out *which ideas* are likely to be more individually versus socially constructed, and more actively versus passively acquired.

Information: How Readily Available? Work on parents' ideas brings a reminder that information is not always available in a form that prompts further thought. It brings also a question about the availability of information for children.

Availability in the research studies we have reported first surfaced in Reiner's (1983) comments on variations in the "visibility" of evidence to parents in an alternative school. Other material with adults contains the same theme. It is, for instance, part of Clarke-Stewart's (1978) work on the kind of advice that is presented to parents in "primers for parents." It is especially prominent in reminders by Sameroff and his colleagues that "expert" advice may not encourage differentiated thought (e.g., advice to the effect that "nothing can be done with children like this"), and that the evidence often encountered by parents may not allow them to choose among alternative explanations. A child who is healthy and "progressing well," for example, may confirm a variety of hypotheses about the source of success: from a belief in magic to a belief in the quality of one's genes or one's parenting (cf. Sameroff, 1975; Sameroff & Feil, 1985).

Does a picture of limited information also apply to children's thought?

The classical tradition—for physical or social cognition—points us towards a view of the environment as benignly offering all the information needed, with the main restrictions on change coming from the individual's capacity to absorb or the extent to which information has been cast into an absorbable form. Once one begins to look at ideas about the social world, however, it seems more and more doubtful that such an open state exists. Adults often have vested interests in children holding to particular views about the world, and in managing the social ideas they are exposed to. Increasingly, scholars are suggesting that similar factors may apply to the ideas children are encouraged to develop concerning all events. One such proposal is Glick's (in press) argument that adults may deny opportunities for the kind of experimentation needed to explore a new idea, or may present "rigged" information. In hiw view, our accounts of the world of information children meet have been too benign. A related but broader proposal is that knowledge—about either the social or physical world—is seldom presented in "neutral" form (as available to all). It is instead often tagged as "owned," as "belonging" to particular people (cf. Foucault, in Sheridan, 1980). For psychologists, an example is the way people often present ability in mathematics as being more "natural," "relevant," or "appropriate" for girls than for boys. That "ownership" tag is one we now recognize as affecting children's ideas about the sources of skill and the level of skill they acquire (Parsons, Adler, & Kaczala, 1982).

Motives for Acquiring or Providing Information. The section on availability of information has already raised the issue of motives as affecting the providing of information. The outside world, we have suggested, is not as disinterested in the child's acquisition of ideas as the classical picture may suggest. We shall concentrate at this point on the need to give more stress than the classical picture normally does to motives or incentives for acquiring and changing ideas.

Within the adult research we have reported, a recurring theme has been the extent to which ideas are linked to their functions. It is useful, for instance, to believe that "good" behaviors will last and "less desirable" behaviors will change (Goodnow et al., 1984) or that one has most influence over the qualities regarded as most important (Knight, 1983). A stress on function, in fact, seems to turn up regularly in discussions of parents' ideas, especially among historians and anthropologists. As an historian considering changes in ideas about child labor, for instance, Rosenkrantz (1978) points to evidence that a preceding factor was a decline in the need for such labor and a rise in the extent to which children competed with adults in a shrinking labor market. As an anthropologist, Irvine (1982) takes two psychologists to task for using the term "ideology" in referring to parents' ideas, without specific attention to the "function" of those ideas in the general society. Minturn and Lambert (1964) make that point specific by arguing that the size of one's living space is a major factor in one's child-rearing practices and in one's ideas about the needs of children.

Where is the equivalent emphasis on function, interest, or value in descriptions of children's thinking? The model of wide-ranging curiosity, of intrinsic motivation, has been our major guide. It may well need some qualification. That possibility we had thought novel. It emerges, however—a point we had not noticed until recently—in Flavell's first model of social cognition. Individuals may vary, he suggested, in the extent to which they feel "disposed" to learn more about themselves or about others and in their "awareness . . . of when and why one might or should try to take readings of such objects" (Flavell, 1977, pp. 121–122).

Where might such proposals lead us? A simple choice between two models— an intrinsic interest in new information, and an interest based on need, function or motivation—would not be productive. The task to be faced is one of working out the conditions under which the two types of process interact or predominate. At the moment, the clearest example of such a research direction appears to lie within attribution theory, with its double consideration of attributions as based both upon ego-enhancement and upon the opportunities for gaining information (cf. Dix & Grusec, in press).

Also to be faced is the task of finding *a place for affect* in one's models of cognitive development, applied either to children or to adults. It is not feasible to start considering motives or functions and then not proceed to considering affect. Locating a place for affect, however, is not easy in discussions of cognition (Goodnow, 1984). In fact, that is one of the dilemmas that seems to pervade the papers in this symposium. We all seem to be finding that once we move into "social" cognition, we are faced more rapidly than usual with motives and, as part of that confrontation, with affect. It might be said, overall, that psychologists have placed most of their emphasis to date on relationships between thinking and acting. The time has come to look at "the trinity" of thinking-acting-feeling (Flavell & Ross, 1981). What we are adding is the proposal that the same "trinity" might well be thought of as occurring in areas of "physical" cognition also.

Sources for a Limited Model of Cognition

Given the number of modifications suggested for the model we carried over from research with children, we have come to ask: How did such a limited model come to prevail? (We consider it as not having been confined to our own thinking.) The question is not purely historical. It has, on the contrary, led us to think about the general nature of knowledge domains and about the value of a distinction between "physical" and "social" cognition.

Briefly, we wish to propose that a model of development that stresses intrinsic curiosity, freely available information, and minimal interference or help from others arises when we pay attention to some particular content areas. These are areas where:

— Other people have *few vested interests* in making sure that particular ideas are acquired. Outside school settings, for instance, people may not care greatly about the extent to which one has absorbed the current state of knowledge about dinosaurs, rocks, or transport systems. They do care, however, about the acquisition of some particular ways of defining "responsibility," "obligation," or "belief in God," and they are prepared to put effort into the management of information so that those particular ways of thinking are acquired.

— Other people have an interest but consider that information does not need to be managed because the *ideas are expected to be acquired easily or without effort on their part.* The perceived ease of acquisition may have several sources: the world may be seen as full of relevant information, for instance, or recovery from error may not be seen as difficult. Whatever the source, the overall impact is one of little help or interference from others.

— A number of *alternative views do not conflict with one another.* In the face of few conflicting perspectives, for instance, the decisive factor in choosing among ideas may well come to be "logical necessity" rather than expedience or compromise.

— *It is feasible to acquire information by direct manipulation of the material.* It is feasible, for instance, to squeeze clay, drop pebbles, or rearrange materials. In fact, this may be the only way to gain information. Some other physical materials may not be so available for experiment. People also are not so readily available. They may, in fact, become irritable with one's attempts to "pull strings" or to experiment in the interest of defining limits.

Those several possibilities—few vested interests and a lesser assigned importance, a trust in learning as likely to occur, the absence of many conflicting views, and the feasibility of experimentation—seem to us to hold for such knowledge areas as conservation of amount, weight, volume, or number. It is the prominence of such topics in the classical Piagetian tradition, we suggest, that helps give rise to the classical stress on individual constructions, intrinsic motivation, and an inherent push for progression from one level to another. In areas of knowledge where the same features do not apply, the same model may also become less appropriate.

Knowledge Domains: "Physical" or "Social?"

We have suggested, in the preceding section, that particular models of cognitive development have varying degrees of fit with particular content areas of knowledge. We have also suggested some ways of distinguishing among knowledge domains.

What impact do those distinctions among domains have on a currently prominent distinction: that between "physical" and "social" cognition? A variety of ways in which "physical" and "social" cognition differ has already been proposed (cf. Flavell & Ross, 1982). We are now ready to add to these. In fact, we are now at a point of proposing that other distinctions may take precedence and may make the "physical"–"social" distinction at best a form of shorthand.

We have already suggested that knowledge areas vary along several dimensions: in the extent, for example, to which they involve vested interests in particular views, confidence that learning will take place, the likelihood of encountering conflicting views, and the feasibility of direct experimentation or direct questions. We may easily add to those features. All topics, for instance— regardless of the "physical" or "social" tag—seem to vary in the extent to which they are likely to be thought about throughout life. The constancy of an object's weight, for instance, is a topic that seems likely to be mastered and then not actively thought about again. It becomes "taken-for-granted." The constancy and the nature of friendship, however, may be another matter. All topics also—again regardless of the "physical" or the "social" tag—seem likely to vary in the extent to which they offer incentives for "good-enough" as against "complete" thinking-through. Finally, topics for thought are likely to vary in the extent to which useful information is available. The availability may reflect "the state of the art" or the presence of vested interests (one's own or those of "significant others").

What we call the "social domain" or "social cognition," we suggest, contains more topics that are thought about throughout life, more topics for which information is not freely available, more topics that call for juggling a variety of "weak" cues rather than allowing direct experimentation (inviting the use of "short-cuts" such as judging from stereotypes), more topics that evoke an "evaluative" stance, and more topics where vested interests are strong.

Such dimensions for describing different knowledge domains, we suggest, may at times coincide with "physical"–"social" distinctions. They need not coincide. It is possible, for instance, to see an area such as the acquisition of ideas about time or space as being, in some cultures, areas of high social importance, marked affect, regular concern about progress, and carefully managed information. In similar fashion, there are undoubtedly areas of "social" cognition where one may be able to use the procedures that usually apply in "physical" areas. In some contexts, for instance, it is feasible to use direct personal questions as a way of learning about people, or to alter their work environments to determine effects. Such contexts may be especially liable to occur whenever people move towards the status of objects, or whenever the relationship of people (as in a legal context) contains an accepted departure from the usual methods of gaining information about people from people.

A FINAL COMMENT

We began with a specific interest in parents' ideas about development and parenting, an interest that seemed quite properly labeled as "adult social cognition." We began also with the general goal of placing this research in a broader context and of using it as a way to broaden the usual picture of what cognitive development covers and how it proceeds.

The first goal was the more readily achieved. We have emerged with both data and a number of promising possibilities for further research. The area is clearly viable and profitable, both in terms of the information it adds to our knowledge of parenting and socialization and in terms of its use as a vehicle for exploring changes in adult thought that are positive rather than deteriorating in quality.

The second goal has required the more thought. We have found it necessary to look more closely at continuities and discontinuities between descriptions of children's thinking and descriptions of adult's thinking. Some of the discontinuity, we suggest, is more apparent than real. Much of it suggests a "revisionist" look at classical models of children's cognitive development, with modifications in the direction of paying more attention to received and negotiated knowledge, to the availability of information, to the impact of motives and incentives for acquiring or providing information, and to the role of affect.

We also found it necessary to look more closely at the distinction between "physical" and "social" cognition, and at the way particular models of cognitive development are related to particular features of a knowledge domain. A model that sees change as based primarily on omnivorous curiosity, active experimentation, and information limited only by one's capacity to absorb it, for instance, may best fit knowledge areas where people are happily left to their own devices. It will fit less well—regardless of whether the area is "physical" or "social"—whenever the nature of the material or the intervention of other people cuts down the possibility of experimentation or leads to information being provided in more managed form.

All told, the effort underlines the value and the feasibility of exploring areas such as parents' ideas about development, both in their own right and as ways of increasing our understanding of adult cognitive development and cognitive development in general: child or adult, "physical" or "social."

ACKNOWLEDGMENTS

This work was financially supported by research grants from the Australian Research Grants Committee and the Macquarie University Research Committee. For intellectual support, we happily acknowledge our debt to several colleagues: in particular, Graeme Russell, whose related but independent studies of parents' ideas have been a challenge, a knowledge base, and an important reminder of the importance of fathers; Ailsa Burns, for keeping us mindful of families as a whole; Andrew Reiner, for keeping before us the need for large views of society; Robyn Dolby, for reminders of relevance; Joan Grusec and Kay Bussey for consistent intellectual challenge.

REFERENCES

Abrahams, B., Feldman, S., & Nash, S. C. (1978). Sex role self-concept and sex role attitudes: Enduring personality characteristics or adaptations to changing life situations? *Developmental Psychology, 14*, 393–400.

Ariès, P. (1962). *Centuries of childhood*. London: Jonathon Cape.

Baltes, P. B., Dittman-Kohli, F., & Dixon, R. A. (in press). New perspectives on the development of intelligence in adulthood: Toward a dual-process conception and a model of selective optimization with compensation. In P. B. Baltes & O. G. Brim Jr. (Eds.), *Life-span development and behavior* (Vol. 6). New York: Academic Press.

Baltes, P. B., & Labouvie, G. V. (1973). Adult development of intellectual performance: Description, explanation, and modification. In C. Eisdorfer & M. P. Lawton (Eds.), *The psychology of adult development and aging*. Washington, DC: American Psychological Association.

Baltes, P. B., & Willis, S. L. (1976). Toward psychological theories of aging. In J. E. Birren & K. W. Schaie (Eds.), *Handbook on psychology of aging*. New York: Reinhold-van Nostrand.

Bell, R. Q., & Harper, L. V. (1977). *Child effects on adults*. Hillsdale, NJ: Lawrence Erlbaum Associates.

Bengston, V. L., & Troll, L. (1978). Youth and their parents: Feedback and intergenerational influence in socialization. In R. M. Lerner & G. B. Spanier (Eds.), *Child influences on marital and family interactions: A life-span perspective*. New York: Academic Press.

Berger, P. L., Berger, R., & Kellner, H. (1974). *The homeless mind*. Harmondsworth: Penguin.

Bronfenbrenner, U. (1958). Socialization and social class through time and space. In E. E. Maccoby, T. M. Newcomb, & E. L. Hartley (Eds.), *Readings in social psychology*. New York: Holt, Rinehart & Winston.

Bronfenbrenner, U. (1977). Toward an experimental ecology of human development. *American Psychologist, 32,* 513–531.

Cashmore, J. (1982). *Factors in agreement between parents and children on values and sources of skill.* Unpublished doctoral thesis, Macquarie University.

Cashmore, J., & Goodnow, J. J. (1985). Agreement across generations: A two-process model. *Child Development, 56,* 493–501.

Clarke-Stewart, K. A. (1978). Popular primers for parents. *American Psychologist, 33,* 359–369.

Damon, W. (1983). *Social and personality development: Infancy through adolescence,* Melbourne, Australia: Edward Arnold.

Dix, T. H., & Grusec, J. E. (1985). Parent attribution processes in child socialization. In I. E. Sigel (Ed.), *Parental belief systems.* Hillsdale, NJ: Lawrence Erlbaum Associates.

Dolby, R., English, B., & Warren, B. (1982). *Brazelton demonstrations for mothers and fathers: Impact on developing infant-parent relationships.* Paper presented at 3rd International Conference on Infant Studies, Austin.

Entwisle, D. R., & Hayduk, L. A. (1978). *Too great expectations: The academic outlook of young children.* Baltimore: Johns Hopkins University Press.

Entwisle, D. R., & Hayduk, L. A. (1981). Academic expectations and the school attainment of young children. *Sociology of Education, 54,* 34–50.

Epstein, C. F. (1981). *Women in law.* New York: Basic Books.

Feldman, S. S., Biringen, F. C., & Nash, S. C. (1981). Fluctuations of sex-related self-attributions as a function of stage of family life cycle. *Developmental Psychology, 17,* 24–35.

Fischer, J. L., & Fischer, A. (1973). The New Englanders of Orchardtown, U.S.A. In B. B. Whiting (Ed.), *Six cultures: Studies of child rearing.* New York: Wiley.

Flavell, J. H. (1970). Cognitive changes in adulthood. In L. R. Goulet & P. B. Baltes (Eds.), *Life-span developmental psychology: Theory and research.* New York: Academic Press.

Flavell, J. H. (1977). *Cognitive development.* Englewood Cliffs, NJ: Prentice-Hall.

Flavell, J., & Ross, L. (Eds.), (1981). *Social cognitive development.* Cambridge: Cambridge University Press.

Forgas, J. P. (1982). What is social about social cognition? In J. P. Forgas (Ed.), *Social cognition.* London: Academic Press.

Frankel, D. G., & Roer-Bornstein, D. (1982). Traditional and modern contributions to changing infant-rearing ideologies of two ethnic communities. *Monographs of Society for Research in Child Development, 47,* No. 196.

Freeberg, N. E., & Payne, D. T. (1967). Parental influence on cognitive development in early childhood: a review. *Child Development, 38,* 65–87.

Ghuman, P. (1975). *The cultural context of thinking.* Windsor-Berks: National Foundation for Educational Research.

Glick, J. (in press). Discussant's comments. In E. Neimark & R. de Lisi (Eds.), *Competence and performance.* Hillsdale, NJ: Lawrence Erlbaum Associates.

Goodnow, J. J. (1976). The nature of intelligent behavior: Questions raised by cross-cultural studies. In L. Resnick (Ed.), *The nature of intelligence.* New York: Lawrence Erlbaum Associates.

Goodnow, J. J. (1980). Everyday concepts of intelligence and its development. In N. Warren (Ed.), *Studies in cross-cultural psychology* (Vol. 2). London: Pergamon.

Goodnow, J. J. (1982). Everyday ideas about cognitive development. In J. Forgas (Ed.), *Social cognition.* London: Academic Press.

Goodnow, J. J. (1984). Parents' ideas about parenting and development: A review of issues and recent work. In M. Lamb, A. Brown, & B. Rogoff (Eds.), *Advances in developmental psychology* (Vol. 3). Hillsdale, NJ: Lawrence Erlbaum Associates.

Goodnow, J. J. (1985). Change and variation in parents' ideas about development and parenting. In l. E. Sigel (Ed.), *Parental belief systems.* Hillsdale, NJ: Lawrence Erlbaum Associates.

Goodnow, J. J., Cashmore, J., Cotton, S., & Knight, R. (1981, April). *Mothers' developmental timetables and associated ideas.* Paper presented at the meeting of the Society for Research in Child Development, Boston.

Goodnow, J. J., Cashmore, J., Cotton, S., & Knight, R. (1984). Mothers' developmental timetables in two cultural groups. *International Journal of Psychology, 19,* 193–205.

Grusec, J., & Dix, T. H. (1982, April). *The socialization of altruism.* Paper presented at SRCD Study Group on Altruism and Aggression, Washington, DC.

Gutmann, D. (1973). Parenthood: Key to the comparative psychology of the life cycle. In N. Datan & L. Ginsberg (Eds.), *Life-span developmental psychology.* New York: Academic Press.

Hamilton, A. (1982). *Nature and nurture: Aboriginal child-rearing in North Central Arnhem Land.* Canberra: Australian Institute of Aboriginal Studies.

Hess, R. D. (in press). Approaches to the measurement and interpretation of parent-child interaction. In R. W. Henderson (Ed.), *Parent-child interaction: Learning and adjustment in children.* New York: Academic Press.

Hess, R., Kashigawi, K., Azuma, H., Price, G. G., & Dickson, W. (1980). Maternal expectations for early mastery of developmental tasks and cognitive and social competence of preschool children in Japan and the United States. *International Journal of Psychology, 15,* 259–272.

Hess, R. D., Price, G. G., Dickson, W. P., & Conroy, M. (1982). Different roles for mothers and teachers: Contrasting styles of child care. In S. Kilmer (Ed.), *Advances in early education and day care* (Vol. 2). Greenwich, CT: Johnson.

Irvine, R. L. (1982). Commentary. *Monographs of Society for Research in Child Development, 47,* No. 196 (pp. 52–53).

Jones, E. E., & Davis, K. E. (1965). From acts to dispositions: The attribution process in person perception. In L. Berkowitz (Ed.), *Advances in experimental social psychology* (Vol. 2). New York: Academic Press.

Kelley, H. H. (1972). Causal schemata and the attribution process. In E. E. Jones et al. (Eds.), *Attribution: Perceiving the causes of behavior.* Morristown, NJ: General Learning Press.

Kelly, G. A. (1955). *The psychology of personal constructs* (Vols. 1 & 2). New York: Norton.

Kessen, W. (1979). The American child and other inventions. *American Psychologist, 34,* 815–820.

Knight, R. (1981). Parents' beliefs about cognitive development: The role of experience. In A. R. Nesdale, C. Pratt, R. Grieve, J. Field, D. Illingworth, & J. Hogben (Eds.), *Advances in child development and research: Theory and research.* Perth: University of Western Australia Press.

Knight, R. (1983). *Parents' ideas about childhood and parenting: A constructivist approach.* Unpublished doctoral thesis, Macquarie University.

Kohn, M. L. (1963). Social class and parent-child relationships. *American Sociological Review, 68,* 471–480.

Labouvie-Vief, G. (1982). Dynamic development and mature autonomy. *Human Development, 25,* 161–191.

Loevinger, J. (1959). Patterns of parenthood as theories of learning. *Journal of Abnormal and Social Psychology, 59,* 148–150.

Lomax, E. M. R., Kagan, J., & Rosenkrantz, B. G. (1978). *Science and patterns of child care.* San Francisco: Freeman.

McGillicuddy-de Lisi, A. V. (1982). Parental beliefs about developmental processes. *Human Development, 25,* 192–200.

McGillicuddy-de Lisi, A. V., Sigel, I. E., & Johnson, J. E. (1979). Family as a system of mutual influence: Parental beliefs, distancing behaviors, and children's representational thinking. In M. Lewis & L. A. Rosenblum (Eds.), *The child and its family.* New York: Plenum.

Minturn, L., & Lambert, W. (1964). *Mothers in six cultures.* New York: Wiley.

Mortimer, J. T., & Simmons, R. G. (1978). Adult socialization. *Annual Review of Sociology, 4,* 421–454.

Much, N. C., & Shweder, R. A. (1978). Speaking of rules: The analysis of culture in breach. In W. Damon (Ed.), *New directions for child development: Moral development*. San Francisco: Jossey-Bass.

Neugarten, B. L., & Hagestad, G. C. (1975). Age and the life course. In R. H. Binstock & E. Shanas (Eds.), *Handbook of ageing and the social sciences*. New York: Van Nostrand.

Newson, J., & Newson, E. (1976). *Seven years old in the home environment*. Harmondsworth: Penguin.

Ninio, A. (1979). The naive theory of the infant and other maternal attitudes in two subgroups in Israel. *Child Development, 50*, 976–980.

Nucci, L. P. (1981). Conceptions of personal issues: A domain distinct from moral or societal concepts. *Child Development, 52*, 114–121.

Parke, R. D. (1978). Parent-infant interaction: Progress, paradigms, and problems. In G. P. Sackett (Ed.), *Observing behavior* (Vol. 1). Baltimore: University Park Press.

Parsons, J. E., Adler, T. F., & Kaczala, C. M. (1982). Socialization of achievement attitudes and beliefs: Parental influences. *Child Development, 53*, 310–321.

Pharis, M. E., & Manosevitz, M. (1980). Parental models: A means for evaluating different prenatal contexts. In D. B. Sawin, R. C. Hawkins, L. O. Walker, & J. H. Penticuff (Eds.), *Exceptional infant* (Vol. 4). New York: Brunner-Mazel.

Piaget, J. (1972). Intellectual evolution from adolescence to adulthood. *Human Development, 15*, 1–12.

Pinchbeck, I. N., & Hewitt, M. (1969). *Children in English society* (Vol. 1). London: Routledge & Kegan Paul.

Pinchbeck, I. N., & Hewitt, M. (1973). *Children in English society* (Vol. 2). London: Routledge & Kegan Paul.

Poole, M. (in press). Perspectives of Australian adolescents. In C. Bagley & G. K. Verma (Eds.), *Personality cognition and values: Cross-cultural perspectives of childhood and adolescence*. Calgary: University of Calgary Press.

Radin, N. (1972). Three degrees of maternal involvement in a preschool program: Impact on mothers and children. *Child Development, 43*, 1358–1364.

Reiner, A. (1983). *Yinbilliko: History of an alternative school*. Unpublished doctoral thesis, Macquarie Univeristy.

Roberts, G. C., Block, J. H., & Block, J. (1981, April). *Continuity and change in parents' childrearing practices*. Paper presented at the biennial Meeting of the Society for Research in Child Development, Boston.

Rosenkrantz, B. G. (1978). Reflections on 19th century conceptions of childhood. In E. M. R. Lomax, J. Kagan, & B. G. Rosenkrantz (Eds.), *Science and patterns of child care*. San Francisco: Freeman.

Russell, A., & Russell, G. (1982). Mother, father, and child beliefs about child development. Journal of Psychology, 110, 297–306.

Russell, G. (1979, August). *Comparisons between mothers and fathers: Some problems of method and some preliminary findings*. Paper presented to a symposium on Some Influences on Changing Family Relationships, Australian Psychological Society Annual Conference, Hobart.

Russell, G. (1982a). Highly participant Australian fathers: Some preliminary findings. *Merrill-Palmer Quarterly, 28*, 137–156.

Russell, G. (1982b). Shared care-giving families: An Australian study. In M. Lamb (Ed.), *Nontraditional families: Parenting and child development*. Hillsdale, NJ: Lawrence Erlbaum Associates.

Russell, G. (1983, August). *A cognitive mediational approach to observing and understanding social interactions*. Paper presented to a symposium on Observational Methodology in the Study of Social Interaction: Implications of Theory, International Society for the Study of Behavioural Development, Munich.

Russell, G., & Radin, N. (1982). Increased paternal participation: The fathers' perspective. In M. E. Lamb & A. Sagi (Eds.), *Social policies and legal issues pertaining to fatherhood.* Hillsdale, NJ: Lawrence Erlbaum Associates.

Sameroff, A. J. (1975). Transactional models of early social relations. *Human Development, 18,* 65–79.

Sameroff, A. J., & Feil, L. A. (1985). Parental concepts of development. In I. E. Sigel (Ed.), *Parental belief systems.* Hillsdale, NJ: Lawrence Erlbaum Associates.

Schaefer, E. S., & Edgerton, M. (1985). Parent and child correlates of parental modernity. In I. E. Sigel (Ed.), *Parental belief systems.* Hillsdale, NJ: Lawrence Erlbaum Associates.

Schaie, K. W. (1973). Methodological problems in research on adulthood and aging. In J. R. Nesselroade & H. W. Reese (Eds.), *Life-span developmental psychology: Methodological issues.* New York: Academic Press.

Schieffelin, B. B. (1979). Getting it together: An ethnographic approach to the study of the development of communicative competence. In E. Ochs & B. B. Schieffelin (Eds.), *Developmental Pragmatics.* New York: Academic Press.

Sheridan, A. (1980). *Michel Foucault: The will to truth.* London: Tavistock.

Shweder, R. A. (1981, May). *Anthropology's romantic rebellion against the enlightenment; or, there's more to thinking than reason and evidence.* Paper presented at the Social Science Research Council Conference on Conceptions of culture and its acquisition.

Shweder, R. A. (1982). Beyond self-constructed knowledge: The study of culture and morality. *Merrill-Palmer Quarterly, 28,* 41–69.

Sigel, I. E. (1982). The relationship between parental distancing strategies and the child's cognitive behavior. In L. M. Laosa & I. E. Sigel (Eds.), *Families as learning environments for children.* New York: Plenum.

Sigel, I. E. (1985). *Parental belief systems.* Hillsdale, NJ: Lawrence Erlbaum Associates.

Sigel, I. E., McGillicuddy-de Lisi, A. V., & Johnson, J. E. (1980). *Parental distancing, beliefs, and children's representational competence within the family context.* Research Report, Educational Testing Service.

Spinetta, J. J., & Rigler, D. (1972). The child-abusing parent: A psychological review. *Psychological Bulletin, 77,* 296–304.

Stolz, L. M. (1967). *Influences on parent behavior.* Stanford: Stanford University Press.

Troll, L., & Bengston, V. (1979). Generations in the family. In W. R. Burr, R. Hill, F. I. Nye, & I. L. Reiss (Eds.), *Contemporary theories about the family* (Vol. 1). New York: Free Press.

Turiel, E. (1978). Social regulations and domains of social concepts. In W. Damon (Ed.), *New directions for child development: Social cognition.* San Francisco: Jossey-Bass.

Tyler, L. E. (1978). *Individuality: Human possibilities and personal choice in the psychological development of men and women.* San Francisco: Jossey-Bass.

Whiting, B. B. (Ed.) (1963). *Mothers in six cultures.* New York: Wiley.

Whiting, B. B., & Marshall, N. (1976). *Child training practices and social change.* Unpublished manuscript, Harvard University.

Youniss, J. (1981). Moral development through a theory of social construction: An analysis. *Merrill-Palmer Quarterly, 27,* 385–403.

Youniss, J. (1982). Why persons communicate on moral matters: A response to Shweder. *Merrill-Palmer Quarterly, 28,* 71–77.

12

Comments on Goodnow, Knight, and Cashmore: A Family Perspective on Cognition and Change

David H. Olson
University of Minnesota

In this paper I first summarize some of the most salient points raised by Goodnow, Knight, and Cashmore (this volume), and comment on their suggestions. I them provide a more family based perspective on the concept of change which they used as a central theme. In addition, I propose some alternative theoretical and methodological approaches that could be considered if the concept of change was investigated at the family level rather than the individual level.

Goodnow and colleagues started with the assumption that change regarding parents' ideas about the nature of children and parenting would occur, that the change would be in a positive direction, and that change could be based on information gained in the process of parenting. After a well done review and critique, they concluded that change was not easy to define or locate, that it was not based on information but on the cultural context and functionality of those ideas. They also identified specific parenting areas that were more open to change than others.

After completing this review, they expressed concern regarding the lack of continuity between the research with adults and that with children and also the lack of continuity between the research on social cognition and socialization. They provide some useful suggestions regarding how to bridge these gaps by focusing the research on the quality of thought, categories of behavior, developmental scripts, and relationship across the generations. While all of these areas can provide useful domains for bridging, I would like to focus on the latter point, cross generational assessment. This I will do within the broader context of describing the value of a family orientation to understanding the concept of change.

Building upon their critique, I believe that much could be gained by dealing with change within the family context. This paradigm shift from the individual to the family level has considerable implications for the type of questions asked, the number of ages of the family members involved in the study, and the type of analysis that is required. I believe that the shift would generate new insights and issues that have not been raised by those who have studied cognitive development from an individual perspective.

Utilizing a family perspective raises a number of conceptual and methodological issues that will expand the current directions in the field of cognition and change. Conceptually, most of the current work on cognition and change has been at the individual level, sometimes dealing with adults and other times with children. Seldom has attention been given to the level of agreement between these two generations (Bengston & Troll, 1978). While generational comparisons are one step in the direction of becoming more family focused, the important issue is to emphasize the agreement between family members *within* the family and not to remain at the group level (i.e., all adults versus all children).

In considering the concept of *causality* and *change,* the family system perspective requires a paradigm shift from the individual perspective. Whereas family theorists have emphasized a system orientation based on the assumption of circular causality, theory and research in the child development field still primarily emphasize the linear causality model. More specifically, child development research has often focused on the parent's impact on the child, and in recent studies the child's impact on the parents has been considered. Both of these approaches still rely on a linear cause-effect model that assumes the causality is only one way. In contrast, the family system perspective assumes that causality is circular and that parent and child behaviors continually affect each other.

This paradigm shift from the individual to the family level and from a linear to a circular causality level has profound implications for the methodological approaches used in the studies of cognition and change. In terms of subjects, it means that parents (mothers and fathers) and children (sometimes several of them) would be included in the same study. This type of family involvement would enable investigators to explore the levels of agreement regarding the change between family members and across families.

Some of our recent family research using several family members demonstrates the increasing levels of complexity and insights that can be gained from such an approach (Olson, McCubbin, Barnes, Larsen, Muxen, & Wilson 1983). In a national survey of over 1,000 "normal" families across the life cycle, husbands and wives participated and one adolescent was included from families at the adolescent stage. One clear and consistent finding was the lack of agreement between a husband and wife and between the parents and their adolescent. The average correlation across a variety of scales assessing marital and family dynamics was .40 for husbands and wives and .30 for parents and adolescents. Squaring these correlations indicates that the level of agreement between family members only accounts for about 10% to 16% of the variance. This finding demonstrates the lack of agreement between family members, and in terms of research methodology it reinforces the importance of including more than one family member in any study investigating individual and family change.

While in general there was a lack of agreement among family members, there were some families whose members agreed often and other families whose members rarely agreed with one another (Olson et al., 1983). This finding opened up another level of family analysis. Comparing families that were congruent in their perceptions across several family members were compared with those that were highly incongruent. One analysis revealed that families that were highly incongruent on several measures also had a very high probability of having high levels of family stress, while highly congruent families usually had very low levels of family stress. This finding can be understood using the circular causality idea. The cycle could begin with the high levels of incongruence among family members increasing stress by minimizing understanding among family members and this increased stress could lead to greater levels of incongruence, thereby keeping the cycle moving.

One value in using parents and adolescents in the same study is that it becomes possible to discover bridges between studies of parents and children. One example is the study by Judith Cashmore (1982) in which she compared parents and children's perceptions about qualities that are important for the children. She found that the best predictor of the adolescents' positions was their perception of the parents' descriptions. Russell and Russell (1982) also demonstrated the value of involving both husbands and wives in the same study. Russell (1982) found that fathers' perception of caregiving became more similar to the mothers' after fathers had actually taken on a larger share of the caregiving tasks. Change in perceptions and greater levels of congruence occurs, therefore, when fathers become more involved in the same tasks (Russell & Radin, 1982).

Theoretical models of the family might also help shed new light on the topic of cognition and change. David Reiss (1981) has developed a typology of families that focuses on the family's cognitive style. He maintains that a family's style greatly influences how family members perceive their own world and how each member functions individually and within the family unit. The three major dimensions that he considers are family coordination, family configuration, and family closure. *Coordination* focuses on whether the family works as a group or functions more individually. *Configuration* assesses whether they are open to change based on ideas from inside or outside the family. *Closure* is a measure of how long they remain open and willing to work on some issue together as a unit. He has conducted extensive and intensive studies and has demonstrated the power of these family cognitive styles in understanding individual and family behavior.

Another theoretical model of the family focuses on family functioning with particular attention to the idea of change. Olson et al. (1983) have developed and tested the Circumplex Model of Marital and Family Systems in order to more adequately describe individual and family behaviors. The two central dimensions of the model are *family change* (levels of adaptability) and *family cohesion* (level of togetherness). On the change dimension, it ranges from very high levels (chaotic) to very low levels (rigid) with two mid-range levels (structured and flexible). Research and clinical assessment using the model to date have indicated that it is difficult to alter the level of change in a family unit. This finding supports the evidence cited by Goodnow et al. (this volume) and Roberts, Block, and Block (1981) that there is considerable stability in parental ideas and behaviors, which provides greater continuity than change.

The Circumplex Model also proposes that families that vary along the change dimension not only differ in their openness to new ideas but have different ideas about the best approaches to child rearing and socialization. One potentially fruitful line of research might be to assess parents' and children's ideas about parenting and compare these family assessments with their type of family system. This typological approach might lead to useful insights regarding the underlying dynamics of change within both individuals and families.

In closing, I have tried to build upon the comments by Goodnow et al. who suggested that more work needs to be done to link research with child and adults and to broaden the areas traditionally considered in studies on cognitive development. I am suggesting that the family perspective and methodology might be of value in expanding the theoretical arena and in bridging the gap between studies of child and parent behavior. In addition, the family system perspective would shift the question of causality regarding change from a linear cause-effect model to a circular causality approach that necessitates involving more than one person. This shift would provide both conceptual and methodological advances in the child development field. In regard to the concept of change, the inter-relationship between individual and family change might also help to clarify some of the important questions that have alluded past investigators.

REFERENCES

Bengston, V. L., & Troll, L. (1978). Youth and their parents: Feedback and intergenerational influence in socialization. In R. M. Lerner & G. B. Spanier (Eds.), *Child influences on marital and family interaction: A life-span perspective.* New York: Academic Press.

Cashmore, J. (1982). *Factors in agreement between parents and children on values and sources of skill.* Unpublished Ph.D. thesis, Macquarie University.

Olson, D. H., McCubbin, H. I. (1983). *Families: What makes them work.* Beverly Hills, CA: Sage.

Reiss, D. (1981). *The family's construction of reality.* Cambridge, MA: Harvard University.

Roberts, G. C., Block, J. H., & Block, J. (1981, April). *Continuity and change in parents' childrearing practices.* Paper presented at the biennial Meeting of the Society for Research in Child Development, Boston.

Russell, A., & Russell, G. (1982). Mother, father, and child beliefs about child development. *Journal of Psychology, 110,* 297–306.

Russell, G. (1982). Highly participant Australian fathers: Some preliminary findings. *Merrill-Palmer Quarterly, 28,* 137–156.

Russell, G., & Radin, N. (1982). Increased paternal participation: The fathers' perspective. In M. E. Lamb & A. Sagi (Eds.), *Fatherhood and family policy.* Hillsdale, NJ: Lawrence Erlbaum Associates.

Author Index

Subject Index